Requirements Writing for System Engineering

George Koelsch

Apress®

Requirements Writing for System Engineering

George Koelsch
Herndon, Virginia, USA

ISBN-13 (pbk): 978-1-4842-2098-6 ISBN-13 (electronic): 978-1-4842-2099-3
DOI 10.1007/978-1-4842-2099-3

Library of Congress Control Number: 2016956399

Distributed to the book trade worldwide by Springer Science+Business Media New York, 233 Spring Street, 6th Floor, New York, NY 10013. Phone 1-800-SPRINGER, fax (201) 348-4505, e-mail `orders-ny@springer-sbm.com`, or visit `www.springer.com`. Apress Media, LLC is a California LLC and the sole member (owner) is Springer Science + Business Media Finance Inc (SSBM Finance Inc). SSBM Finance Inc is a **Delaware** corporation.

For information on translations, please e-mail `rights@apress.com`, or visit `www.apress.com`.

Apress and friends of ED books may be purchased in bulk for academic, corporate, or promotional use. eBook versions and licenses are also available for most titles. For more information, reference our Special Bulk Sales–eBook Licensing web page at `www.apress.com/bulk-sales`.

Any source code or other supplementary materials referenced by the author in this text are available to readers at `www.apress.com`. For detailed information about how to locate your book's source code, go to `www.apress.com/source-code/`. Readers can also access source code at SpringerLink in the Supplementary Material section for each chapter.

Printed on acid-free paper

This is dedicated to the people who work to protect others around the world, men and women, military and civilian, especially those I served with in Afghanistan (yes, you too, Blue Devil).

Contents at a Glance

Contents

About the Author

George Koelsch is a system engineer who resides in Northern Virginia within the DC metro area. He started writing requirements 40 years ago while in the U.S. Army and has continued that work for the last 30 years as a contractor for the federal government. With a five-year stint as an industrial engineer at Michelin Tire Corporation, he learned to become an efficiency expert, which he then applied to system engineering to tailor the lifecycle development process before his contemporaries in the DC area were. In his spare time, he authored ten nonfiction articles on computers, coin collecting, stamp collecting, and high-energy physics. He decided to combine his two passions, system engineering and writing recently.

Acknowledgments

Over my career spanning four decades, I have worked with hundreds of people, many who helped mentor me in this field of system engineering, with a strong focus on requirements engineering, even before we called it that. To name all those people would produce too numerous a list, even if I could remember all their names, which unfortunately I cannot. Many of them when they read this book will recognize their contribution, and I hope that is sufficient, for that is all I can provide at this point.

That said, there is one individual who I would like to recognize for his contribution. I had been planning to write this book for some time; I was just not certain when I would begin. Over the last decade or so, I have been mentoring others in the fine art of requirements engineering. I had noted that the requirements books I had, as well as others I had read, did not measure up to my standard of what I thought a requirements book should be. I mentioned it to one particular co-worker who promptly said that I should write that book. That person is Adam Heath. It clicked. That was the time to start writing. So I did. Not only was he the spark for this project, but because of his background in book publishing, especially IT, his guidance has proved invaluable. He guided me through the query letter, book proposal, and refinement of the book itself. Adam, I cannot give you enough kudos.

Jonathan Gennick, the assistant editorial director at Apress, initially discovered me on behalf of one of the best IT publishing firms in the world, Apress, and worked with me to get the manuscript into the book it is. Jill Balzano, the project manager at Apress, worked with me throughout the entire day-to-day process from the initial upload until the book appeared in my hand. She never tired of the endless questions I had, answered them gladly, and kept everything moving along smoothly. The one person who made this text a much better book by his development editor tutelage is Chris Nelson. He taught me so much about writing a technical book that I cannot begin to mention. If you find this an excellent book, it is because of Chris. On the other hand, if there is any deficiency, it falls to me. To all the other people at Apress who I may not even be aware of, thank you so much. Each of you contributed to this book.

And, to all the other unnamed people out there, thank you.

PART I

The Foundation of Requirements

CHAPTER 1

The Importance of Requirements

Writing requirements is the most crucial aspect of systems engineering (SE). In this book, you will learn the best way to accomplish this. You will explore the requirements world, you will use the best tools, and you will learn to employ these tools. This book is intended for those of you who consider yourselves as beginners or maybe advancing to an intermediate level. You will acquire a good foundation that you can use throughout your career. Even if you never plan to write a requirement, use case, or user story yourself, you will learn what a good requirements engineer will do for you. Think about it. As a project manager, you need to know the capability of everyone on your team. Requirements are the most important part, as you will soon learn. Get it wrong, and you will have problems—significant problems. You will be exposed to the most likely problems and how to prevent them.

You may have read some survey of development methodologies before reading this book (or taking a system development course). If you haven't, it might be useful, but it certainly is not required. The traditional method used in lifecycle development is the waterfall method. The waterfall method consists of several major functional areas, where you perform one after completing the previous functional area.

Electronic supplementary material The online version of this chapter (doi:10.1007/978-1-4842-2099-3_1) contains supplementary material, which is available to authorized users.

G. Koelsch, *Requirements Writing for System Engineering*,
DOI 10.1007/978-1-4842-2099-3_1

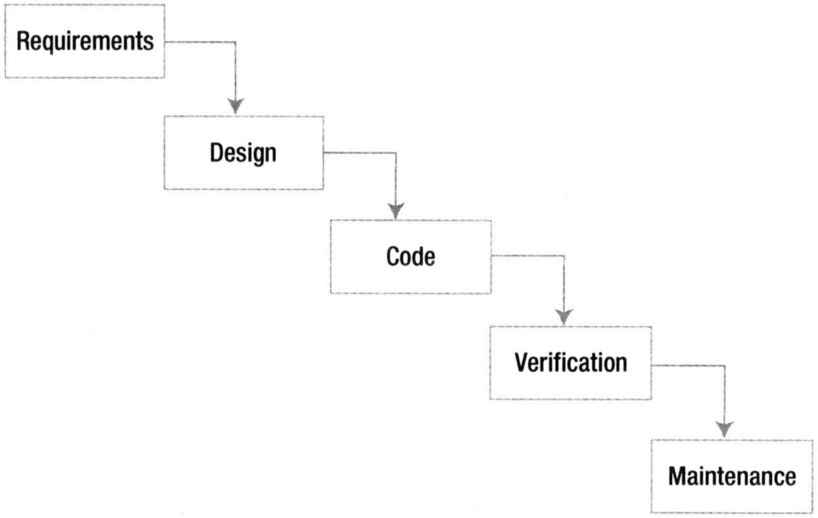

Figure 1-1. *Waterfall methodology*

Notice that the requirements function occurs first, appropriately, given its importance in development. Much of this book examines requirements—covered in much more detail later or this would be a very small volume indeed.

You may now begin your exploration of the advances in requirements engineering.

Requirements have moved along with the advances in systems engineering over the last several decades, as engineers tried to improve the process of SE as technology and demands of the marketplace influenced it, especially in software development (but not totally divorced from hardware). The waterfall methodology moved first to the V-method and then Spiral; then Rapid Application Development (RAD) and also eXtreme Programming (XP) came into vogue; and finally the last land to explore is agile, the latest and arguably the best methodology yet. Again, you will learn more on these various methods later in the book.

■ **Note** You will see the use of acronyms and abbreviations in this book. If you are new to the systems engineering environment, this use is indicative of the industry, so please get used to it. Chapter 3 will spend more time on this topic, where the "Language and Jargon" section expands on this usage.

Not only will you learn about requirements for software development, but also you will use these same skills for hardware development. As you will see in this book, the distinction within a project becomes blurred, as many projects have both a software segment and a hardware segment.

In this book, you will spend time reading about why you write requirements, how best to collect and document them, and how to maintain them. Basically, this does not change appreciably with the previously mentioned methodologies. This skill may go out of fashion. That said, the emphasis of agile has added user stories to the requirements function, which you will spend some time on, but you will also examine how requirements and user stories can and will complement each other.

There may be some proponents within the SE community who advocate that requirements are no longer necessary. Just as other people stand behind their beliefs, this book will defend the position presented here, which is that currently requirements are still necessary. Does that mean the approach presented here fits every situation you will encounter in your career? No, but what this book will also present are the conditions under which requirements work best. That way, you, as the requirements engineer, can determine the best way to control the requirements for your project. To quote Indiana Jones' father: "I want to teach you self-reliance."

The importance of requirements to a project will be discussed in this chapter. First, you need some introductory topics to help you with the focus of this book and its chapters, along with some conventions used throughout the book. Basically, you need a foundation before you build a house. The same applies to any endeavor—like learning about requirements.

Requirements Conventions Used in the Book

You will see references to BOSS. This is a system name used throughout the book to help write sample requirements, where BOSS means *big organization's suite of services*—just a name to use that shortens to BOSS for convenience. It will look like this:

> 1-1 The BOSS Access Control Function shall allow an authorized user to access the system.

Notice a number appears in front of the statement, the format used consistently throughout the book. First, you always need to identify a requirement uniquely. For this book, the number format starts with the chapter number, a hyphen, and then the sequential number for each requirement in the chapter. Second, this allows referencing requirements earlier in the book during discussions throughout this book. You will also see some requirements that have another number beside the *n-m* format. These numbers are being used to illustrate some aspect of the project and will more likely represent what you might consider in a requirements set, especially if done in a hard-copy document.

In some cases, you will see DRAFT in front of the requirement's *shall* statement. It will look like this:

> 1-2 DRAFT—The BOSS Access Control Function shall allow users to access anything on the system.

That means it may or may not be a good requirement. Thus, if you work in the future, you may not want to consider it as a good example, without reading the text surrounding it.

There will be additional situations where requirements will have a parent and child relationship. The first requirement has PARENT after the requirements number, indicating it is the parent. The subsequent requirements with CHILDREN after the number are subordinate to the parent requirement. They will look like this:

> 1-3 PARENT—The BOSS Audit Function shall allow system administrators to generate an audit report.
>
> 1-4 CHILD—The BOSS Audit Report shall include all login attempts, all failed login attempts, and who attempted the login.
>
> 1-5 CHILD—The BOSS Audit Report shall include who added, changed, or deleted database records.

In some situations (e.g., a format required by an organization for its hard-copy requirements document), these may be numbered 1-3, 1-3.1, or 1-3.2 to show the parent-child relationship. The use of the words PARENT and CHILD are just an aid to learning in this text. They are not recommended on the job, unless you find there is benefit for doing it that numbering alone does not alert people to it. It is your call.

You may also see the following:

> 1-6 (1-1) The BOSS Access Control Function shall allow an authorized user to access the system.

Why are there two numbers here to reference a requirement? This means that the next sequential number, 1-6, happens to be a repeat of one earlier in the book (in this case requirement 1-1). In many cases in this book, there is a need to refer to requirements from a previous chapter, so it might look like this:

> 12-73 (5-27) The BOSS shall...

Projects Used in This Book

Throughout this book, two projects will be examined to emphasize elements of importance to you. Not every example will use these two projects, but the vast majority of them will. Some examples may not fit the following two projects, but they will be invoked whenever it is most appropriate.

This book, as is used in the SE industry, follows the convention related to abbreviations and acronyms. In the previous sentence, you have seen the abbreviation SE for systems engineering. The convention dictates the first time an abbreviation or an acronym is used, you must spell it out and show its abbreviation or acronym in parentheses after it—like *systems engineering (SE)* in the first paragraph of this chapter. Then the next time you use *systems engineering*, you only need to write SE. This is a shorthand method that is used extensively in the industry, and you need to become proficient in it.

FBI Record Management Project

The first project mentioned earlier is the Federal Bureau of Investigation (FBI) Records Management System for the primary software-based project in this book. The federal government has to follow the dictates of the National Archives and Records Administration (NARA), which spells out the rules for how long temporary records are maintained. You will see various requirements dealing with the FBI's records management that expand on this project.

Remember, in most software-based projects, there may be some hardware aspects related to this system. That said, the primary hardware-based project in this book comes next.

Radiation Dosimetry Project

The second project will be a radiation dosimetry project for the United States Army. The purpose of dosimetry is to measure the radiation a person is exposed to, either in a laboratory, in a nuclear power plant, or in a nuclear battle field. The primary emphasis here is to examine radiation exposures to U.S. Army soldiers in a nuclear battlefield. There are five basic devices that make up the entirety of the system. They are the following:

- Individual radiation dosimeter
- Unit radiation dosimeter
- Dosimeter archive laptop
- Radiation dose rate meter
- Radiation dose rate mapping laptop

The **Individual Radiation Dosimeter** will be a small, portable device that will capture what one person, a soldier, is exposed to while in a nuclear environment. This device will be like a small watch that the person wears all the time and that stays with them regardless of what unit they are assigned to during their career.

The **Unit Radiation Dosimeter** is the device that will read the individual soldiers' Individual Radiation Dosimeters to collect all the readings. This can then be used to determine the effectiveness of the unit based on how much radiation they have been exposed to collectively.

The **Dosimeter Archive Laptop** collects all the information from the various Unit Radiation Dosimeters and consolidates them for archive/backup purposes as well as allowing higher-level roll-up of information reporting.

The **Radiation Dose Rate Meter** collects all the radiation information from various vehicles in a unit. Unlike an Individual Radiation Dosimeter, which collects what radiation that soldier experiences, whether or not shielded in a vehicle or shelter, the Radiation Dose Rate Meter collects the raw, unshielded radiation exposure. This can be the raw data to collect the dangerous areas for military operations. This is a snapshot in time, where the dosimeter captures the total exposure.

The **Radiation Dose Rate Mapping Laptop** collects all the information from the various Radiation Dose Rate Meters, plots the radiation data onto a map, and displays the designated radiation contours as an overlay. This allows commanders to modify their military operations based on the radiation remaining in their areas of operations.

Basic Definitions

Before going further, you need to understand some language that will be used extensively throughout this book. There are many more definitions throughout this book, but these are the foundations for your understanding.

Definitions of Requirements-Related Terms

Here are some foundational terms. First, let's start with what requirements are.

> **The definition of a *requirement*:**
>
> Define a need, desire, or want to be satisfied by a product or service.

That sounds reasonable. You will find *service* is used extensively to talk about service-oriented architecture (SOA), but again, you'll learn more about that later in the book. Think of a service as a function within a software application, (e.g., cut, copy, and paste in a word processer) and you have the idea. A product would be like a mouse, a printer, a scanner, or even your cell phone. Obviously, any of these products would take more than one requirement to define it fully. There is not a situation where only one requirement would ever define a product or service.

> **The definition of a *system*:**
>
> Meriam-Webster Online defines it as a group of related parts that move or work together.

Now think of this definition with respect to the samples used previously. You see that it applies to not only the mouse, printer, scanner, and cell phone but also to the cut, copy, and paste functions in a word processer. A system applies to both software and hardware. In fact, most systems these days combine both software and hardware.

> **The definition of an *application*:**
>
> Meriam-Webster Online defines it as a program (as a word processor or a spreadsheet) that performs one of the major tasks for which a computer is used.

An application is a collection of one or more functions, ranging from something as sophisticated as software running a nuclear power plant to something as small as a cell phone app, like the game Angry Birds.

> **The definition of a *stakeholder*:**
>
> Meriam-Webster Online defines it as one that has a stake in an enterprise.

You will spend a significant amount of time learning about stakeholders, especially in Chapter 9, as they are the people who will help define the requirements for the system. Keep in mind, though, one stakeholder rarely represents all the users of the system. For example, the people who enter health information in a Medicare system may not represent the people responsible for fraud detection, and neither stakeholders will understand system monitoring and steps necessary to keep the wide area network (WAN) working.

What role defines someone who works with requirements? That someone is called a *requirements engineer* (RE). Again, how do you define that role?

> **The definition of a *requirements engineer*:**
>
> Someone who collects, coordinates, advocates, and manages requirements.

Tip Did you notice that there now are two different definitions for RE, requirements engineering first and now requirements engineer? This can and will happen on your project, as it will happen again in this book. You will have to learn to handle this. Usually, you can see from the context what meaning makes sense. If not, ask to find out what meaning is correct.

While the requirements definition is quite self-evident, the terms used in the definition of the requirements engineer may not be well understood in this context. That means you are reading the proper book. By the time you are finished reading this complete text, not only will you understand all the functions an RE does, but also you will be able to perform those functions. Each of these terms will be examined in detail throughout the book, so do not worry. In addition, the reason the role of RE was mentioned versus the RE is because the role covers one engineer or a team of engineers. You will work both ways, as a one-person team and as one person on a team, and you may even lead a team of engineers doing nothing but requirements engineering. The size of the project drives the role of the RE.

How Long Does It Take Requirements Engineers to...

No, this is not a joke about REs. Are you kidding? The most important engineers on the project are the REs (and do not let anyone else tell you differently). However, that is a slight digression.

But seriously, folks.... You might logically ask how many engineers does each project need? The correct answer is that it depends. As you move through the various systems development methodologies throughout this book, you will see how it differs. For example, in the traditional waterfall method mentioned earlier, you would start with a significant team and spend nothing but months and even some cases years defining requirements.

■ **Real-World Note** Yes, I have done RE for three years on a ten-year project. Whereas with the agile methodology (more on that later), I have supported two dozen or more implementation team members by myself. Of course, that system was already deployed, with significant policy changes that kept me busy. It might not always have been that size, as that project had about 4 to 5 percent of the team as REs while I was there.

Does the size of projects affect what REs do? Yes, as the project size grows, one RE becomes insufficient, and you will need more. Your first reaction might be to say the following:

> When the project grows beyond one person, the answer depends on too many factors to discuss here or to give concrete guidance. Part of it depends on experience, and in fact, many times you do not know until you see it growing beyond the size of your team. This will be examined more later in the book.

However, the industry has some data on this. Capers Jones performed an industry survey in 2000, which he documented in the book *Software Assessments, Benchmarks, and Best Practices* (Addison-Wesley Professional, 2000). Jones discusses "very large projects of 10,000 function points in size (approximately one million lines of code)." Loosely, think of function points as a feature, say on a menu, just to give a reference. Specifically, Jones looked at the following types of projects:

- Management information systems
- Systems software
- Commercial products
- Military software
- Outsourced projects

On the low end, the percentage of "total effort on requirements development" for management information systems was 3.7 percent. The others ranged from 7 to 10 percent of total effort. The time involved in developing requirements was significant, ranging from 4.4 months for management information systems to 22.7 months for commercial products. Jones' book is an excellent resource if you want to dig more deeply into this (and other) topics. However, this shows roughly how much time requirements definition can take.

The first question that should pop into your head is, "How successful were these projects?" Alas, the author did not provide that data. The averages are for all teams regardless of how successful each project was. This is how you have to analyze data to understand truly what it means. At least there is an estimate for how much time a project should invest. As you will see with some of the defects that requirements generate, spending more time on requirements definition is better—provided you do not get trapped in analysis paralysis. What is that? Excellent question. Paralysis occurs when you spent so much time getting everything precisely right that you lose sight of what you're trying to collect. If you question every point of all stakeholders, then you take too much of their valuable time and they become reluctant to talk with you. (Remember, they have a day job to do—more about this in Chapter 9.) You will spend more time on how to enhance requirements definition when you get to the user story material in Chapters 12 and 13.

What Makes a Good RE?

This section will focus on two major areas, good communication skills and the attributes a good RE should have. We will examine each in detail with the various items a good RE should have. Not having one or more of these is not going to doom your chances to be a good RE. You have to exploit the strengths you have. Experience working requirements for years will more than compensate for a lacking in a particular attribute.

Personality Traits

Now you will examine the traits a good requirements engineer should have. Keep in mind, none of these is an absolute. It's more like the Pirates' Code, kind of like guidelines (although do not ask Captain Jack Sparrow's father). The point is, you need to have some aspects of these to be reasonably successful.

Patience

This process can take some time, as you saw earlier. Not every stakeholder or every user will know all aspects of a process. Sometimes it will take various techniques to tease their real needs from them. You will learn more about these in Chapter 9 to help with that. Other times, the participant may not be the best fit. You will search for better ones or spend more time with some you already have. In fact, asking people for suggestions can work. Showing you value their opinion goes a long way in establishing a rapport with people. Remember, nothing is more satisfying when a stakeholder recommends you to do requirements work for another person's project because, as they say, "He (or she) does excellent requirements work. Use him (or her) for your project." (I speak to that first hand, as it happened to me.)

Another aspect of patience deals with the time it takes to collect all the information needed. For example, you will run meetings that can run into hours. After an hour or two of meetings where you exchange information, you may feel mentally drained. It is hard work doing this. Obviously, this kind of work is not physical in a manual labor sense, but it can be taxing. When you have to focus hard listening very intently, you will lose energy. Think of those two three- or four-hour exams you may have had; you probably felt it then.

■ **Real-World Note** My record here in the United States is a solid two weeks in the same meeting. Yes, about 80 hours. In addition, my all-time record is overseas where I was essentially in the same meeting for three weeks. Think of how draining those meetings can be.

Meetings this long are exceptions. It was not that I sat in the same room, with the same people, for two or three weeks straight. In the two-week one, I was involved exchanging information only for my block for a day and a half. In the three-week meeting, it was actually several different meetings, with different groups of people. Also, I did not run the entire three weeks of meeting. The first day was a kickoff meeting where both the American and foreign representatives spoke. Then there was one meeting that talked about the interfaces between the respective systems. One of the developers ran that meeting. I also had one of my requirements engineers lead one day of meetings where I sat and advised as the purpose was to train this engineer to do customization of the system whereas she had become proficient in collecting requirements for the standard system up to that point. This gave me relief from having to ask questions, take notes, ask for clarifications, summarize what was said, and so on, for the entire 15 days.

Unlike the previous Real-World Note, usually you measure meetings in hours, not days. You need to know that it can happen. Having a team where you can take turns gathering the requirements certainly helps, but you do not always have that opportunity.

The exception for me occurred on many of my overseas trips. I was the only one collecting requirements. Granted, I was a senior engineer at that point. Nevertheless, you do not always control the number of people performing requirements analysis.

Again, you will improve with practice and experience. Just like World of Warcraft, you gain experience points as you play the game longer.

For one of my projects' meetings with stakeholders, I took an engineer to teach her how to collect customization requirements to our standard project. During the meeting, I could tell she was frustrated with how long it was taking to get what she needed. Part of the challenge was that we were overseas, and the language barrier contributed. After that meeting, I gently pointed out how challenging the process was and explained how getting the requirements on a particular schedule may not be practical in every case.

Clarity of Thought

This is one of the most important aspects of an RE. You always have to think and analyze what you hear. Understanding everything the stakeholders say is essential. This is so you can capture the "what" of their business process. In fact, you might want to consider writing what is called the Business Process Description (BPD) document. In this, you listen to what the stakeholders say and write it all down. However, you write the major and minor steps of what they do, not how they do it. Their steps could be done by hand, written on paper, or on a computer system, whatever they do, just not precisely how. Is this an exact science? No. Is this something you have to provide to people? No. You do it for your use. That said, sometimes you may want to check it with the stakeholders to ensure the steps are correct. Also, some organizations may create this document formally. If so, follow the required process.

Are you the person who has to capture it all? Not if you don't have to. This does not mean you should not have all the information, far from it. Instead, do not reinvent the wheel. Find out whether the stakeholders have something already that describes this. For example, do they have some documentation for a new person coming into their organization? It is usually good to start from this document. Naturally, you will have a lot of "how" they do it. However, you will have to think how that translates to "what." Sometimes they just have a document they have used to brief upper management. Do some digging and you will be surprised how much may be available.

User manuals may give some clues, but remember its primary focus is to describe how a system works, so you will have all the "how" and you will have to think about the "what."

■ **Tip** Many user manuals may just list a description of everything that is in the system without showing how a person will use it, like having a workflow or a scenario. The latter is important, whereas the former may not be.

Here is an example from a personal project I am working on:
Transfer
This is how you take candidate coins into your collection:

1. Androida will say, "Please select which denomination you want to transfer coins." She points to a pop-up menu that lists each denomination that includes coins you own. Click which of the denominations you want.
2. After you click, Androida will say, "Please click which specific coins by years and their associated mintmarks you want to transfer from Circulation List to Own List. Then click the Ready to Transfer button on the bottom." She points to all the coins in the denomination you own. Check the boxes of the one or more coins you wish to transfer. Then click the Ready to Transfer button.
3. After the transfer occurs, the denomination list reappears. You can continue to select coins to transfer until you click the Done with Transfer button at the bottom of the list. Then you return to the pull-down menu.
4. Hitting the Esc key clears the submenu.

Notice all the implementation here that says thing like "click" this or "select" that. This is not a user requirement. The essence of what the user really needs is more like the following statement that you could use to write requirements from:

> The user had indicated all they wanted was a way to select some coins they had and put them into a coin collection. She did not specify all these steps—just the one function of moving some candidate coins into this designation of a coin collection.

Test procedures may also have some useful information. Again, these are specific steps without the reason why it is done. Keep in mind, however, they are testing some wrong conditions on purpose to check range limits and other error conditions. One advantage is that test procedures should test all possible paths that a user may skip over, maybe because they do not remember something that rarely happens.

There is one additional aspect to clarity of thought, as you learn some of the limitations of requirements definition. Once you learn these limitations later in this book, you need to understand why something is a limitation. The reason is that when a new approach is available to fix the limitation, you will need to discern whether this improvement truly eliminates or at least reduces the problem. You will have to compare to the current limitation and see whether their fix is better or not by analyzing the before and after requirements.

Flexibility

No, this does not refer to being a gymnast but being flexible in your attitude. You must be adaptable to the situation. This is complemented by thinking, in that you have to understand the situation so that you can change when the situation demands it.

■ **Real-World Note** On a recent project, I had begun capturing the requirements the traditional way. In six to eight months, I had managed to capture the requirements for only the search function of the system. We had about a dozen major functional areas like this. The program manager was extremely frustrated by the lack of cooperation from the stakeholders, which was epitomized when she had said, "It's going to take us five years at this rate!" Thus, we needed a new approach. We decided to capture user stories (see part IV) with the stakeholders, but only capture *shall* statement requirements for the development and test teams. In the same amount of time as it had taken to capture requirements for search, we captured all the user stories for items that did not work well and areas that could be our ideal approach for all the remaining functional areas. In the next six to eight month, we performed gap analysis to cover the user stories for everything that was missing and then completed the requirements definition, with tracing between the user stories and requirements. By analyzing what was not working and thinking about alternate approaches, we came up with a better way. This worked because the customer was flexible.

Extrovertism

Extroverts are more comfortable working with people, and in fact, they can be energized by talking and working with people. Introverts are less inclined to be so energized. In some cases, exposure to people can be draining.

I know an Olympic gymnast who found meeting a dozen people in a social setting draining. Yet, performing in front of 30,000 people at the Olympics did not phase her. She blocked out the audience and focused on her small little world where she was queen. This approach worked for her as she has five Olympic medals.

Much of your work will occur in meetings. Sometimes they are just one-on-one; other times they have a dozen or more participants. If you are maintaining requirements for an existing project, you might not have a great deal of people to deal with. Alternatively, you will have worked with the people for a long time and feel comfortable with them.

Yes, extrovertism is not a requirement of all REs, but it certainly helps. If you are more introverted, working with people you know and are already comfortable with helps. Ask those you have a rapport with to assist in working with people or at least gather advice on dealing with people to help raise your confidence in dealing with certain people. It may be as simple as having more than one person from your team be involved to share exposure.

Confidence

Confidence flows both ways. You need to have it. So believe in yourself. Also, people will need to have confidence in you. Once you have experience, you will gain that confidence, both in yourself and others in you as you gain a reputation.

How do you gain that reputation? You need to be prepared, by covering the right subjects, by not wasting time by digressing, and by listening. As will be talked about in Chapter 9, asking clarification questions to help understand the subject discussed and summarizing what you have heard helps them gain confidence in you.

This isn't always about you coming across as knowing everything. If you give the impression that you know something and you do not, people will lose confidence in you quickly.

It also includes helping the stakeholders feel confident about themselves.

■ **Real-World Note** Once when I was overseas, one of the stakeholders mentioned how they did something in their manual process that we were going to automate for them. I told them how that was an improvement over how we did it. I went on to add that we had included improvements that other countries had provided, because we American do not have a lock on being the most intelligent in the world. Many people have excellent ideas. I explained that the development team had already incorporated some, and they were planning others. What this did was establish a rapport between our two countries.

In this example, I demonstrated that I had confidence in those I was working with, both their country and others my team had dealt with. They know what they do and why. I trusted their understanding and knowledge.

Confidence does not equate to arrogance. When someone comes across as a know-it-all, people are less likely to have confidence in that person, from my experience. How you word a response can help establish confidence or not. For example, saying, "Let me check for understand," helps to establish confidence rather than saying, "Yeah, I got that!" as you wave your hand to dismiss the stakeholder's point.

Negative Traits

Of course, there certainly are more traits, but you need to avoid the negative ones. For example, impatience will inhibit your abilities. Naturally, being short-tempered will be disastrous.

Thus, even temperedness and calmness are desirable qualities for you to embrace.

Ego can certainly get in the way, so check it at the door. These are not *your* requirements; you are just the vehicle by which they are captured. The stakeholders and users really own them. When someone suggests a change to something you have captured, remember that they are clarifying what *they* need, and they are working hard to ensure proper communications. If you attempt to own the requirements, you will be a reason some of the things that can go wrong will, as you will see next.

Remember in the "Patience" section, where I talked about the engineer who was frustrated about not maintaining her perceived schedule? I could see on her face that she was impatient. Knowing her, she was a short way from losing her temper, which would achieve nothing. Sometimes, fixing it may be a matter of taking a break. If need be, defer to another meeting so you can talk with some other people to get their assistance in clearing up any impediments to success. Ask people more seasoned what you should do. Do whatever you can to defuse a situation.

One minor point to be aware of is that you may not get to see the results of your work. You rarely will work on a project from initiation to the end.

■ **Real-World Note** At least that has been my experience. Maybe it is a manifestation of working on government projects where people move around a lot. I probably spent an average two years on a project, sometimes as long as four, but not often. Sometimes it was even shorter, but that was usually for other reasons, such as projects being canceled or delayed for things totally unrelated to anything I could control.

Maybe in the commercial arena, you may stay longer. That said, if people find you are a good requirements engineer, you will be in demand. When the next new and high-priority item comes along, they will want you. Thus, you may not see a project to completion. Alternatively, as in other cases, you are brought in to fix something that someone else did, and they did not do it so well. Again, this has happened. Don't let your ego keep you on a project longer than you should. Anyone (well, almost everyone) can maintain a well-established program. However, not everyone can start a project and turn it into a well-run program. Strive to be that person that people want. It probably won't be your very first project. Yet, it will come with time. In addition, this book should help you get there. This way you will not be one of those REs that cause requirements problems.

Good Communications Skills

We will examine the following aspect of good communication skills:

- The ability to respond to people's needs
- The ability to translate ideas
- A capacity for moderating different views or differences of opinion
- Persuasiveness

Of course, you will need to be able to write good requirements, user stories, use cases, and every other piece of documentation needed to capture requirements. This book will go a long way to help you get there for requirements specifics. However, if your grasp of English (or whatever language is appropriate for your project) is not so good, then maybe you need to rethink doing requirements engineering. This is not to say you need to create literary masterpieces, but you need to be able to write an understandable sentence. You will need to present your information to others so they understand it. For example, you may need to present requirements at a requirements review, so you will need to get up in front of people to explain not only your process but also your results. In addition, you must populate your requirements document or requirements database with everything you have created. You must write them well enough to be comprehensible. If your grasp of language is not up to the standards needed for the project, then take whatever steps necessary to ensure you can listen and write to the appropriate level.

Throughout my career, communication has been the source of the most problems. Some people have said that is not true because technology is the main challenge. However, I have seen communication problems repeatedly affect projects involving different types of technology and many different people on various teams. Communication failure is the common thread. Communication issues can be the fault of the RE, other people may be the cause, or both. Establishing a common language, as you will see in Chapter 3, will help immensely. One other part of the problem is that some people do not listen well. Back to the original point, some of those people felt that technology fixes all problems, so they stop listening to what other, more experienced people had seen. Listening is one significant aspect of communications.

Responsiveness

Because you must understand the full needs of the stakeholders, you have to put yourself in their shoes, so to speak. You need to understand how issues affect them and capture those needs. Some stakeholders may not get much visibility; for example, the people who administer the system may not have representatives in stakeholder meetings. Nevertheless, they have needs. What kinds of information and capabilities do they have? If you cannot find a good representative, you need to capture their needs somehow. How about the people who monitor the system, get the audit logs, track the system resource usage, and so on? They have needs as well. If you are in an information technology shop, you should have people like this around you. Talk with them. Or database administrators. Remember, if you talk to them about their needs, you will ingratiate yourself with them. (Well, most of them. Occasionally, you will meet the crusty old curmudgeon, but they are the exception rather than the rule.)

Translator

You are a translator of what the users and stakeholders say they need into words that the information technology (IT) department in your organization (or whatever it is called) needs. Basically, you are writing a contract between the two. Think of yourself as a lawyer for the two parties involved, without having to go through law school. Oh, and what you will write will be much more readable and understandable than the "conspiracy of obfuscation" that real lawyers perform.

■ **Note** Yes, I have opinions, and I will express them here. Most of the time I will be demonstrating the passion for requirements, but sometimes I use it to reinforce a point, like now.

Now, examine an example of translation (and you will see more examples in the next chapter and in Chapter 9). A stakeholder says, "When this specific error happens <insert their error here>, I need a red flashing button up in the upper-right corner of the screen." As you will see in the next chapter, they are telling you how to implement what they think they need. What they really mean is, "When an error condition happens, I need a message of what is wrong and how to proceed." This is not only getting rid of the implementation (the how) but also making it in what they need and, in this particular case, making it general enough to address all error conditions. This is a good point to generalize for groups of errors whenever you can. For example, if you have operating system (OS) errors, you might need a different requirement. Again, you'll learn more about that later in the book.

Communications goes two ways. Just as important as speaking and writing is listening. Some may argue that listening is the more important aspect of communications. Listening is at least equal in importance. When you are collecting requirements, you must listen intently. By that, you have to understand everything the person says but also the implications of what they say. For example, someone may say they need to export query results to a spreadsheet. Naturally, you will capture the statement, but then you need to ask the one question you will ask more than any other during your career—why? Why do you need to do that? It turns out that the user says they need the spreadsheet because the current query results tool does not provide the ability to manipulate the query results in the query tool (yes, this is an actual instance). They wanted to be able to move columns around and expand or contract the column sizes—maybe because the column does not display fully. Here are additional requirements that they may not have identified. That is why questions like, "What does not work for you?" or "What can be improved in, say, search?" are very useful questions.

Moderator

There are two aspects to this attribute. First, you must be able to run meetings, whether one-on-one meetings or groups of people. As an RE, you will have many of these. This is where you collect many requirements. They can be informal or formal. A workshop may be more structured than a face-to-face meeting, where that latter meeting may be just question and answer. With time, if you are not as comfortable with being a moderator at first, you will get very good at it with experience.

Second, you need to be able to moderate disagreements between people. Not that you are going to get into major controversies that splash across the headlines, but you will encounter people whose opinions or understanding do not match. It is your job to moderate those discussions. Sometimes it is nothing more than not speaking the same "language," but you'll learn more about that in the discussion about language and jargon in Chapter 3. Other times, the needs are very different, and you'll need to work with people to get to the heart of the matter. Maybe upper management needs to resolve it, so you must aid that process. In other cases, you may have someone who tries to dominate the conversation, not letting others speak. You will need to ensure everyone gets a chance, maybe going around the table, calling on each person so no one is left out, and not allowing the "dominator" to grab the floor much of the time.

Persuasiveness

This is a corollary to moderator. You will need to be the proponent for the requirements. You will need to sell what you have captured, whether on paper, in a database, or during a presentation. In addition, you will need to be able to convince people in positions of authority when they initially may not initially accept them. For example, it may require them to make some minor modification to their current system to save a significant amount of time when they convert to a new system. How do you do that? The best way is to show what is in it for them. If, in the long run, it is better for them, they generally will accept it.

Summary

You have learned about many good personal traits and some to avoid along with needing excellent communications skills to make you a good requirements engineer. Naturally, you will get better as you gain experience. Nevertheless, you should have some insight into what it takes to become a better RE as of a result of this discussion.

Of course, just because you are reading this book does not mean you will absolutely become a requirements engineer. Instead, you may be reading this so you know what an RE will do on a team you work on, or maybe you are managing the requirements team. Regardless, you need to know what REs can and should be able to do.

With that segue...

Challenges for Writing Effective Requirements

There are risks to writing requirements that can severely impact the system being developed or even while it is in operation. You will learn about these potential problem areas and general solutions that will then be expanded upon during the course of this book, with the intent of overcoming these challenges.

Insufficient Requirements

Insufficient requirements means that you are missing some or even all of the requirements. If you are missing requirements, when the system is deployed, the users or a subset of users will not have the functions you have.

Before analyzing this topic, a differentiation must be made from the agile methodology where you do just-in-time requirements. With agile, you must have all the requirements you need, when you need them. Insufficient requirements means that all the requirements needed are not provided when they are needed. You will learn more about agile in Part IV.

■ **Real-World Note** When I was teaching myself to use a new programming language, I wrote my first real program to manage my book collection. Yes, I could have found a program to do that, but this was a learning technique. After I had defined all my needs, I built a database with a user interface to perform CRUD. That is the standard IT term to represent Change, Read, Update, Delete. These were all the functions I needed. I had defined all the fields that I wanted maintained for my collection. Then I showed it to my wife who said it was missing the International Standard Book Number (ISBN). Now this number is used track the published versions of books around the world. If others would use these programs, that is a valid requirement. However, my wife said she wanted it, so I accepted that as a valid requirement (even though I believed she would never use it). I put that under the "Marriage Maintenance" section of requirements. Trust me, if you are married, you will understand. However, even I am not perfect when it comes to crafting requirements.

Insufficient requirements means there are gaps in the full description of the system. For example, maybe you forgot to include auditing of the user access function. If this is captured later and the function is added, without capturing the data associated with the people prior to that time, you will not have full auditing of the system.

Approaches to mitigate this problem are the following:

1. You should come up with preliminary requirement areas.
2. You should research if working in a new area.
3. You should go through the full process for gathering requirements covered in the rest of the book.

Insufficient requirements are more likely because #3 isn't done well than #1 or #2. As a result, you will spend extensive time learning how to perform good requirements gathering.

One way to look at insufficient or wrong requirements is to look at the cost to fix a problem with a requirement.

The Davis book states that fixing requirements left until after deployment is 100 to 200 times more than fixing the requirements during requirements definition phase. Thus, it is imperative to get requirements correct. Bear in mind, people will review (validate) the requirements so that you have the ability to correct them early. There are other techniques you will see throughout the book that will help to improve your requirements. The point is that you should get each requirement correct from the beginning to significantly reduce the cost of error fixing.

There is a variation on an insufficient set of requirements—*no requirements*. There is a joke where a programmer says to the requirements engineer, "I don't need any requirements; just let me code." To which the response should be, "Code what?" How would the coder know what to code? They coded what they thought the stakeholders needed. How do you think that went? You are correct if you said not well.

■ **Tip** Programmers do not think like users. This is not meant in a disparaging way. It is true that a good coder must think in computer language terms with a very special logic to be successful. Most users of systems are good at what they do, but they are not programmers. Thus, REs become the translator between users and coders.

Clearly, having no requirements is a recipe for disaster. No one—users, programmers, designers, testers, or even managers—know what to expect. Thus, any development effort must have some requirements.

Scope

Understanding the scope of a project is critical to establishing requirements for it. In some cases, it may be simple and clearly defined. However, in other cases, a project's boundaries can be vague or poorly defined, and this is one of the biggest sources of problems for writing effective requirements.

■ **Real-World Note** In my first foray into commercial software, I wrote a card game to run on PCs. You played against the computer only. You did not play with other players or over the internet. Simple and well-defined boundaries. My next effort that I am still working on is a game that is multiplayer and playable over the Internet. Here, the beginning and ending points are less well-defined.

Think of a personnel system that defines everything about a new employee when hired for the company. You define all their information about the person: name, address, phone numbers, and e-mail addresses. Does it include salary? Maybe. Maybe not, as that may fall under the payroll system. Does it include next of kin? Maybe that falls under the Benefits system as that deals with beneficiaries. Alternatively, maybe it falls under the Security group, which needs a list of the person's family because the person needs to checked out.

Any time there is a "maybe" answer, the boundary between systems, between services, between functions, or between applications must be defined. To reiterate, in most cases, that is not something you can do yourself. You must work with others to come to a common agreement. If it is between functions within your project, it is relatively easy since it is someone you probably work with regularly, and you have a project manager who can help make any decisions. If, however, your project interfaces with another organization or major project that you have no real connection with, the management chain up to the common manager may come into play. These negotiations become more complex, as budgetary constraints, schedules, and other factors complicate the process.

Note When having to work across organizational boundaries or with those working on other projects, competing egos can be another factor. This is why a good RE must have some of the attributes described earlier and be able to facilitate communication and cooperation.

The point is, define the boundaries of your scope precisely. This definition is necessary for establishing clear project requirements and thus helps ensure that resources are distributed efficiently. You need the definition to know what you need to be working on to begin with. It will also prevent two (or more) people or projects duplicating work or, worse, working in opposite directions.

Requirements Creep

Requirements creep, also called *scope creep,* means that the requirements change significantly from when they are initially defined until the system is completed.

We all have heard about an aircraft, weapons system, building, or other project that was planned to cost $X million but ended up costing twice that amount or more by the time it was finally completed. A significant factor in many of these cases is requirements creep (or scope creep). This requirements creep occurs in hardware, software, or both. Defining requirements expecting that nothing will change with time is unreasonable. Nothing stays the same. Later, some people realize they need those inevitable requirements. Then, they say, "While we are here, we need to add...."

To combat this scope creep, the agile methodology was developed based on the Toyota production system founded between 1948 and 1975. This lean approach to requirements is to craft them just before they are needed (using the analogy of "just-in-time" production).

In this approach, you define functional needs near the beginning of the project. Then designers and stakeholders prioritized what functions they want (and can do) when. Then you craft requirements as they are needed.

Volatility

Volatility is different from scope creep (i.e., added requirements). Volatility means that already existing requirements change; requirements have not been added. For example, the original requirement for availability says this:

> 1-6 The BOSS system shall be available 99% of the time.

Then someone realizes that this system will become a probe that will travel to Pluto. Oops, that availability is not sufficient so they change it to the following:

> 1-7 The BOSS system shall be available 99.999% of the time.

Trust me, this later requirement will cost a lot more than the original estimate. You will see this more in Chapter 9.

Stove-Piped Requirements

Stove-piped requirements mean this project is done in a vacuum. I don't mean in a physical vacuum like outer space, but the team works in a vacuum compared to the rest of the organization. This is more likely to happen in large organizations where it may be difficult to communicate every project throughout the organization. Or think of the Department of Defense, where security issues or classified projects limit the access to information; it can be even harder for people to know what everyone else is doing. Thus, the possibility could exist that duplication of effort occurs. Note that *siloed* projects mean the same thing as stove-piped.

Think of every project designing its own security access portion of the application. The user is required to enter a user ID and a password. The security team has deemed that the person can try three times, and if they fail, then they are locked out. How much time and cost are associated with defining the requirements, developing the code, testing it, and implementing it for each project? Rather, one approach should be developed and tested and then used by all of them.

This is something you may not run into on your first effort. In fact, you may never encounter it. Why? Because many, if not most, organizations have fixed this issue.

Recently, the federal government continued to shrink IT budgets. One of the benefits is that they were forced to see the light for standardizing approaches for their IT projects. By that, they had to not only share code, by reusing services that had been already developed and worked well, but also share things like requirements, architecture, coding standards, and so on.

Why do things more than once, when one time will do? You would think that people would have done this decades ago. However, there are factors that have worked against it. Because of environments that fostered restricted communications such as security access, people did not necessarily know what people in adjacent offices and organizations were doing. Only when they had to be creative did they begin the steps toward standards and sharing. That's not to say it was easy.

I attempted to reuse the solutions for addressing existing similar needs by finding requirements on a large document retrieval project that was already in production. I had little success. In part, I found the reason was that while the organization was using a service-oriented architecture (SOA), there were no real requirements defined for it. At first I assumed that I could not access the requirements for the document retrieval system. Once I did find the requirements, I found they had documented very few of the requirements, especially for the SOA portion of the system. I was the one who created these requirements, and then my project shared them with others, so other projects did not have to re-invent the wheel.

The preceding example illustrates the kinds of clues to look for. If you are going to write requirements for common items, like a report generator or access control or searching capabilities, you might want to ask around to see what other people have done.

PROJECT-SPECIFIC REQUIREMENTS VS. COMMON ONES

There is a difference between requirements specific to your project and what should be common requirements. Here are some examples:

- 1-8 The BOSS search functions shall provide Boolean operators: AND, OR, and NOT.
- 1-9 The BOSS search functions shall default the search results to the following fields:
- Spacecraft type
- Spacecraft dimensions
- Spacecraft weight
- Spacecraft storage capacity

Clearly, the first requirement (1-8) is a standard type requirement that should apply to any project that has a search capability. Yet the second one (1-9) would only apply to a program that applies to spacecraft specifically.

How do you overcome not being able to find out what other projects are doing? Very carefully. This is not something you can do yourself, in most cases. Work with your supervisor, say the requirements lead, or if this is you, work with your program/project manager. Without their buy-in, it will prove daunting because as a team you must go to the other projects and convince them to share their requirements. If the other team is not on board with the approach, you will not get their requirements, and there will be no way to share requirements between the teams.

Assuming you get cooperation, you need to compare your needs. Find the common ground. Then articulate your particular differences. Those are the ones you need to define. You will see more detail later how best to accomplish that.

Users Are Not Sure What They Need

The challenge here is the users you are talking with are not certain what they need. Sometimes they have not been thoroughly informed why they are participating in your effort. Other times, they are totally unfamiliar with how new systems or improved replacement systems are developed. While they do not need to understand all the details of how a system is conceived until it is delivered to them, they will at least need to know what the requirements process should be.

You will definitely learn much more about this when you get to Chapter 9. That said, if your users/stakeholders do not know what they need, that is going to put you at risk. If they do not know, who will? You will learn more about how to find the right people to interview, techniques like structured questions, group interviews, brainstorming, and so on.

Therefore, you need to find the right people, which may not always be easy or even possible. In that case, you need to help the users find out what they need. Earlier in the chapter, you read about how you need to be a translator from what they say they need to what they really need. You also need to guide them to help them to find what they need.

Back when I was a graduate student, running labs to supplement the lectures, the students would come to me asking questions how to find an answer. To ensure that they would understand how to find answers in the future, what I generally did was ask a series of guided questions that led them to find the answer themselves. I could generally tell when they figured it out, as their face would light up, so to speak, when they discovered it. They felt engaged because they had done it.

You can do the same also. If you said, "I understand their process is X, Y, and Z. Is that right?" They would have an answer. Maybe yes, maybe no, but it would not be enlightening for them and would provide little value added to you. Instead, follow the approach provided here and guide them with questions that start at the general level and work down more detailed, engaging them in the process. Again, this will be emphasized later.

User Needs Not Satisfied

All your work has been implemented, and it's the big day of the delivery of the system, and the first team of users sits down at their computer and use it. Then the open revolt happens. They do not like it and demand that the old system be returned to them.

Think this will not happen? Trust me, I have heard of it happening more than once. Fortunately, it had not happened on one of my projects.

If the outcome of a project is that users' needs are not satisfied, it means you have missed requirements or that you wrote them insufficiently to focus on the real need. If you leave requirements out, you missed some aspects that the users need. This will cause people to reject the system, or at best, they may be slow to embrace the system. This could be as bad as work stoppage or people being reluctant to use the new system. There are ways to mitigate this. For example, have the users review your requirements work. It may not need to be the detailed requirements, but it should the business process description that helped generate the requirements, or better yet, the user stories. As you will see later, you write user stories in terms of what a user understands, rather than as requirement "shall statements."

Missing the focus is slightly different. For example, you write a series of requirements describing the system monitor functions for the system. However, when you deliver it, they say, "Wait a minute, I do not know who changed what records are saved in the system. That's what I need to know." What you had heard and described in requirements and what the developers coded was "tracking how many records were added." In reality, the users were trying to determine when storage needed to be added over time. That is not what you heard. So you completely missed the mark.

A way to help prevent this is to rephrase what the user stated in different words. What this does is force you to think about what the user said, convert it to terms you understand, and validate their need. The users will be glad to correct you if you miss your mark. Moreover, do not take offense, as you are trying to capture what they want.

Multiple Interpretations Cause Disagreements

Every statement you write should have only one meaning, or interpretation. If there is the possibility of multiple interpretations, then there is likely to be disagreements among the people who interpret those statements.

If the language used in the requirements is incorrect or not understood by everyone, then someone may not interpret it (and design it) the way the stakeholders and ultimate users may want. You will find out more about this in Chapter 3. You will learn the importance of word *interpretation.*

For example, there was a project with two different groups involved in the development effort. Those people who had a history of developing large systems within the organization used the word *recall* to mean removing a bad record from the database. However, the people who would use the new system used *recall* to mean calling for a group of hard-copy documents from an archive to be given to someone. Neither definition was incorrect. However, because of people's background, they meant different things and initially caused confusion.

Other times you use a word, but just not precisely enough. For example, look at the following requirement:

> 1-10 DRAFT The BOSS record function shall capture the time that the record is added to the database.

That looks OK on the surface. However, *time* can be interpreted multiple ways. For example, most people might figure that is just the local time that the transaction took place. OK, if that is what is meant. What if this is a system that is for a nationwide company that has offices in four time zones? Then which is it? You must specify one time so the system compares like times. Now, assume this need exists for a bank system in one time zone, so local time is satisfactory. Well, is it, say, Central Standard Time or Central Daylight Time or both? If the latter, when does it change over?

A requirement engineer must be very precise.

Are the Requirements Verifiable?

If you cannot verify that a need has been met, what good is that need? How will you know when it is done? The point is that you must have a means of verifying or validating the accuracy and efficacy of the requirements that you write. There can be various ways of doing this, such as having the test team validate them or, as discussed in preceding sections, having users verify that the requirements actually describe what is needed.

You must be able to envision some verification method for the requirement. There is more later about the various forms besides actually testing it. Suffice to say, you or someone else on your team should be able to say, "Yes, I can verify this." Having your test team validate your requirements is an excellent technique. Moreover, as you gain experience, you will continue to improve in your own ability to check your work.

However, examine the following example:

> 1-11 DRAFT The BOSS user interface shall be so easy to use that my great-great grandfather will be able to use it.

For the time being, ignore whether this is a worthwhile goal. Look at the criteria you need to test—my great-great grandfather.

When I was young, I met two great-grandfathers, and one lived until I was a late teen. However, I never met one of my great-great grandfathers because he had died before I was born.

Therefore, that brings up a real issue for verifying the statement. You cannot verify it. Yes, this is a ludicrous example, but it does make a point. You cannot validate some statements. The following is another example:

> 1-12 DRAFT The BOSS software shall operate on the surface of Jupiter.

Since humans currently have no hardware that can operate on Jupiter, there is no way to test it. This is a little more representative, but not a great deal, but at least you are getting the idea of the kind of issue identified here.

Wasted Time and Resources Building the Wrong Functions

Sometimes a system is built, and the first reaction from users is, "Where is the search function? That's what I need the most." This is not limited to search but any number of functions the users want but did not get.

This problem could indicate some requirements are missing. On the other hand, too much emphasis was placed on items that do not have the same importance. The implied importance of each requirement is that they carry the same weights unless you specify otherwise. By that, if you have 100 requirements for the system administrator and only 10 for the other 80 percent of the users, you will spend about 89 percent of your time working the requirements for only 20 percent of the users. If the system is not primarily focused on system administration functions, they you may have captured too many requirements for system administration rather than the rest of the function. You must assign priorities to fix this issue. You must really examine the importance of each requirement. Then if most of your high-priority areas do not have many requirements, you may need to spend more time defining those areas. Another way is to look at each function and see how important it is. How many requirements define it? The more time you have spent defining this function may dictate the number of requirements associated with the function. However, something that is very complex will take more time to define, potentially skewing its importance. You will see more focus on this as you examine requirements throughout the rest of this book.

There are shortcuts, as will be talked about in user interface design, architecture, and so on, where the use of standards can significantly change the importance.

Regarding the missing requirements, the elicitation phase presentation will help to prevent this.

There is also a potential source caused by the developers who include functions that users did not ask for. They may think it is a neat improvement. Alternatively, it is something they have wanted to do for a long time. There are some elegant items coders like to add, which cost time and money at the expense of important functions. This is why developers need to have their proposed changes approved, regardless if it is waterfall, agile, or any other development methodology. Developers are not the only ones who have things added. Some managers, whether part of the development team or managers in charge of users, can decide they want functions added at the expense of the functions users need. Another technique you will hear more about later may help reduce this by getting people to state how often a particular function is used. Granted, legal or policy reasons may demand it. However, if such justifications do not exist, that is an indication that a function is not necessary.

As you can see, controlling this is important. Also, the distinction between this problem and scope or requirements creep can be blurred. The important point is to understand the challenge to overcome it.

Summary

You have been introduced to the most common and most important challenges in writing effective requirements, insufficient requirements, scope, requirements creep, volatility, stove-piped (siloed) requirements, users who are not sure what they need, user needs are not satisfied, multiple interpretations causing disagreements, whether the requirements are verifiable, and wasted time and resources building the wrong functions. The goal is to teach you how to mitigate these problems. You have seen some general solutions to these challenges. The rest of the book will dive into the details of how to eliminate each of these or significantly mitigate the impact of the challenges. In addition, in the last chapter, these problems will be examined against what was presented to see whether the addressed techniques helped to prevent them.

An early study cited in B.W. Boehm's *Software Engineering Economics* found that "approximately 60 percent of errors occur during the requirements definition." Yes, this is an older study, yet there doesn't appear to be more recent studies or evidence to suggest that this has changed. The point is, the problems listed in this chapter do occur. This book will present ways to help prevent them. Keep in mind, if there are missing requirements or misinterpreted requirements, they may not manifest themselves until much later in the project's lifecycle, possibly when it gets deployed. That is problematic as it can cost much more to fix them then. You need to vigilant to help prevent this.

Now, you will see what good requirements can accomplish.

Will this book teach you to manage all aspects of RE such that you can immediately become a manager of a team? This book can give some guidance. There are many other good sources that can help with that. This book will give you the foundation for your first job as an RE; it's basically an excellent introduction to crafting good requirements. The most important element to help with higher responsibility is experience doing the job. You learn by doing.

That said, in the right person's hands and in a startup project where almost everyone is new, you might be able to use this text as a guide, but that is the exception rather than the rule. You will see throughout this book, there are rules and there are guidelines, and many times the distinctions are blurred. Remember, earlier in this chapter I stated that you need to think. Well, you are going to learn how to do that when going through the requirements process. It is left to you to implement it—to gain your needed experience.

References

Boehm, B.W. *Software Engineering Economics.* Englewood Cliffs, NJ: Prentice-Hall, 1981.

Davis, Alan M. *Software requirements: Objects, Functions, and States.* Prentice-Hall, Inc. Upper Saddle River, NJ, 1993, p25-26.

Jones, Capers. *Software Assessments, Benchmarks, and Best Practices.* Addison-Wesley Professional, 2000.

Exercises

We are going to do something out of the ordinary here. Rather than ask for specific questions and answers for this chapter, we will do something differently. You will do the two exercises for this chapter, based on the limited information you have from Chapter 1 (and if you have any experience as a requirements engineer). Then, put your responses aside, as you will look at it again at the end of Chapter 15 to see if you have the same answers. There is no right or wrong answer; just see whether your understanding changes with time.

Exercise 1

Examine the problems that can happen as described in the "Challenges for Writing Effective Requirements" section in this chapter and rank which ones you think are the most critical to fix and why.

Exercise 2

Examine the problems that can happen as described in the "Challenges for Writing Effective Requirements" section in this chapter and rank which ones you think occur most frequently and why.

CHAPTER 2

What Makes a Good Requirement?

Now that you understand why you need requirements and what happens if you do them improperly, you must begin in earnest to learn what makes a good requirement. First you must understand the fundamentals of a good requirement, including the proper form of a requirement and how to handle negatives within a requirement statement. The bulk of this chapter will address the attributes that make a good requirement. Then I will finish with how to deal with common errors in requirement statements.

Understanding Requirements

In Chapter 1, you saw some examples of requirements. A requirement was defined as a need, desire, or want to be satisfied by a product or service. Now in this chapter, you will examine the important elements of a requirement.

Wikipedia defines a requirement as "a singular documented physical and functional need that a particular design, product, or process must be able to perform." (Wikipedia's reputation may not be as strong as some other sources, but sometimes its definitions are very accurate.) Wikipedia also adds that it is a statement that identifies a necessary attribute, capability, characteristic, or quality of a system for it to have value and utility to a customer, organization, internal user, or other stakeholder.

Note In Chapter 13, you will see a definition that is similar, reinforcing the similarity between requirement statements and user stories.

The Form of a Requirement

Now, let's examine some of the key aspects of a requirement. It is a **singular** statement. One requirement will address a physical and functional need that the product must perform. Focus on that one statement. That is important. There will be only one need per statement. Of course, there is the **need** as well—a necessary attribute, capability,

G. Koelsch, *Requirements Writing for System Engineering*,
DOI 10.1007/978-1-4842-2099-3_2

characteristic, or quality of a system. This is something you get from the stakeholder, whoever it may be. The third part is the **product, process, function, service, app** (we will default to the word *function* as a lowest common denominator in this book from now on).

■ **Note** Obviously one requirement cannot do everything related to a need all in one statement. Multiple requirements are necessary to ensure all aspects of that capability are addressed.

Each singular (singular described part earlier) requirement must consist of these following three elements:

- Function (function described part earlier)
- Verb
- Need (value to the customer, whoever that customer is, which varies greatly)

Now, deconstruct one of the requirement samples used in Chapter 1:

> 2-1 (1-1) The BOSS Access Control Function shall allow an authorized user to access the system.

This requirement breaks down accordingly:

> The BOSS Access Control Function = Function
>
> shall allow = Verb
>
> an authorized user to access the system = Need

The verb is absolutely critical. In all your work, the requirement statement must have the word *shall* as part of the verb to indicate that is it a required statement (aka requirement). Without it, it is not required.

There are different schools of thought on the use of *shall, should, will, must,* and *may*. The convention in this book, however, is that every requirement statement must have one and only one *shall* in it. That makes it a requirement. The other four words in the previous paragraph do not make it a requirement. They are called *qualifiers*. Statements with those as verbs are like the adjectives of a normal sentence; they are nice to have but not necessary.

■ **Note** If your organization uses a variation on that, adapt accordingly.

IEEE also uses the *shall* approach. Similarly, the federal government, including the Department of Defense (DoD), typically uses *shall*. In their book *Software Requirements, Third Edition*, Karl Wiegers and Joy Beatty advocate *shall* because

> *We have seen the verb 'will' to be used statements of facts, 'should' to be a goal that needs to be achieved, 'must' to be a performance statement.*

Furthermore, Requirement Experts Website, on October 2012, stated, "Shall is used to indicate a requirement that is contractually binding, meaning it must be implemented, and its implementation verified." It also states, "Will is used to indicate a statement of fact." In addition, it defines *should* as, "Should is used to indicate a goal which must be addressed by the design team but is not formally verified." I agree with these definitions completely. Other sources reinforce them. Most projects use the same definition. *May* carries no force at all, and *must* really is not well defined.

Thus, use *shall* in every requirement (as shown in this book) unless you are on a project that uses a different approach to which you need to adapt.

Dealing with Negatives in Requirements

There are some rules that people will tell you about writing requirements. One rule, which does not fit well as part of the attributes, is that you should never write a negative requirement. Part of the reason some people use as justification is that you cannot state everything a system should not do, as the entire universe is infinite.

Now, look at an example:

> 2-2 DRAFT The BOSS Sampling function shall not use more than ten percent of the raw data in a sample.

Usually, there is a better way to say a negative. For example, you could state the previous requirement as follows:

> 2-3 The BOSS Sampling function shall limit sampling of the raw data to more than ten percent of the total.

There are other words you can use instead of *no, never, not,* or *none* such as *prohibit, limit* (as earlier), or some other construct.

Does that mean you would never use a negative? Purists would say so.

■ **Real-World Note** As you will see in this text, I am not purist. I have spent too many years in the real world writing requirements. I have found the rule is more like the Pirate Code in the first two *Pirates of the Caribbean* movies: it is more of a guideline than a rigid rule.

Sometimes there is just no other way to write something other than with a negative.

OK, so what is an example?

It is hard to find good example, but having said that, here are some examples:

> 2-4 The system shall not override user selected contrast and color selections as prescribed in Section 508. (United States Government. "Resources for understanding and implementing Section 508." Feb. 2015, `www.section508.gov/`)

> 2-5 The system shall not disrupt or disable activated operating system accessibility features.

> 2-6 If the search is too complex, the system shall not crash while executing a search.
>
> 2-7 The system report generator shall not require a per seat license fee for every user.

Now, you will examine the many elements that are necessary to make a good requirement. This is different from the different types of requirements, such as security requirement or business rules to name a couple, but are the attributes that basically every requirement statement should have regardless of the type of requirement.

Attributes of a Good Requirement

The attributes of a good requirement are the following:

- Accurate, or correct*
- Atomic
- Complete*
- Concise
- Consistent*
- Does not conflict with other requirements
- Does not duplicate with other requirements
- Independent
- Prioritized*
- Realistic
- Traceable*
- Traced to a source
- Unambiguous*
- Understandable by stakeholders
- Unique
- Verifiable*

Some books you will read will show more and show less. Nothing is gospel here. These are teaching elements. The Institute of Electrical and Electronics Engineers (IEEE) standard 830-1998, titled *Recommended Practice for Software Requirements Specifications*, recommends the attributes marked with an asterisk (*) in the previous list.

■ **Note** Modifiable is included in the IEEE list, whereas this deals with the ability to modify requirements, and this deals more with the document as a whole rather than an individual statement. They are correct, but you will examine the list of attributes as being associated with an individual statement.

This shows that no one really agrees on exactly how many attributes comprise a good requirement.

■ **Real-World Note** Some books I have seen include thirteen attributes or ten or the same eight as IEEE depending on their focus. However, from a teaching standpoint, I tend toward a more comprehensive approach so that you consider as many aspects as practical. With time, this will become second nature for you.

At this point, all these various attributes may not be obvious, yet as you read further in this book, you will see the benefit of having a wider list of attributes than a smaller list. Gap analysis is one area that benefits from this expanded list. However, you will see more about that much later in this text.

When you are first starting out, you will want to review your requirements and check them against the list of attributes. Eventually, you will not need to think about it as it will become instinctual.

That said, you will examine each one of these attributes in the following sections of this chapter. You will see references to them throughout this book, as they are the foundation of everything you will do hereafter.

Some of these attributes you will see again, when you get to user stories later in the book, as well you should. Good requirements and good user stories should have attributes in common.

Here is the mnemonic to help you remember them:

```
  C        C  I
CRUD      CAPUT
  D        V
```

This mnemonic is CUD CRUD and CAV, IT CAPUT. Clearly, it is not the best one ever invented, but hey, it is a method for you to try to remember them. It is not as elegant as ROYGBIV for the colors of the rainbow, or HOMES for the names of the Great Lakes. However, if this helps you remember the attributes, then this is a successful mnemonic. (If you want to be immortalized, you come up with a better one, send it in, and you can receive credit in the next version of this book. You will achieve your 15 minutes of fame.)

There is no significance to the order these attribute are listed in or to the order that they are examined. Each attribute has its own significance that you should understand within that context. Without further ado, onto these attributes.

Now you will examine each attribute individually.

Accurate

An accurate requirement is defined as a precise statement of the system's capability, its inputs, its outputs, its interfaces, and how it interacts with its environment.

When crafting a requirement, the potential exists for not being precise or accurate. One obvious mistake would be if a user says they need the results of queries within five seconds of initiating a query and you wrote the requirement as follows:

> 2-8 DRAFT The BOSS query function shall begin displaying the results of a query within 10 seconds of initiating a query.

You can see this statement did not accurately capture what was requested (ten seconds versus the needed five seconds). A simple misstatement of a metric is rarely the issue when not accurately capturing the need. More likely, it is an inaccurate translation of the need. For example, the user says they need the display of all the cards dealt out within six seconds.

What was captured was the following:

> 2-9 DRAFT The BOSS Solitaire Dealing function shall begin displaying the first card within six seconds of activating the Dealing option.

What the user actually wanted was the following:

> 2-10 The BOSS Solitaire Dealing function shall finish displaying the last card within six seconds of activating the Dealing option.

This is a simple example, but you get the idea. The first requirement deals with the start of the function, whereas what the user wanted, and the correct requirement, was the display of the final dealt card.

Chapter 9 will spend some time on how to tease out what the users really need. Chapter 1 stated how you are a translator. Getting what the users' needs are accurately is a challenge. It takes practice.

Atomic

You need to define each requirement at the atomic level.

No, you are not going to get into nuclear physics; this refers to decomposing the requirement down to its lowest, logical level. Not only is it important to show what should be done (e.g., not have multiple requirements in one statement), but also you will see the explanation why. For a given system, you might see the statement that said this:

> 2-11 DRAFT The BOSS Access Control function shall provide a display and print capability of the access control list.

For example's sake, say for this system, there are ten such functions, and they all need the same print and display capability. Testing begins. Then you learn that the print capability does not work. That means all ten requirements fail, or 100 percent. However, when you break the statements into ten print and ten display requirements, only 50 percent of the requirements fail. You now know accurately what failed. Take the previous requirement and break it down as follows:

> 2-12 The BOSS Access Control function shall provide a display capability of the access control list.

> 2-13 The BOSS Access Control function shall provide a print capability of the access control list.

There is another reason why you should split the requirement into two statements. Following this example, say that the development manager has one person working the display functions and one person working the print functions. This way you have provided each with their respective ten requirements, rather than having to share the responsibility. You have allocated the requirements uniquely, as you should.

You should look for connecting words like *and, or, nor, yet* and *but* to remove by splitting requirements to individual requirements. You will learn about cases where you cannot split requirements in Chapter 6. Even in these, you can eliminate the conjunctions (those connecting words from grammar. Yes, the reason you went into engineering was to get away from English. Alas, you failed!).

Parent-Child Requirements

Another variation exists in decomposing requirements to the atomic level. This is the situation where you have a parent requirement that has requirements subordinate to that requirement, or child requirements. Here is an example of a parent requirement (the second requirements number after the 2-14 is the requirements number in this system's set of requirements, which is included to show how a parent-child requirement should be numbered to show the relationship):

> 2-14 3.1.1 PARENT The BOSS Authentication function shall require all users to authenticate themselves before they can use the system.

Because you need to explain what this means, you need to provide more information to completely describe authentication. Thus, you should add the following:

> 2-15 3.1.1.1 CHILD The BOSS Authentication function shall require all users to enter a valid username.

> 2-16 3.1.1.2 CHILD The BOSS Authentication function shall require all users to enter a valid password.

> 2-17 3.1.1.3 CHILD The BOSS Authentication function shall require all users to enter a valid system domain name.

> 2-18 3.1.1.4 CHILD The BOSS Authentication function shall require all users to enter a valid username, password, and system domain name in three tries or they are locked out of the system.

> 2-19 3.1.1.5 CHILD The BOSS Authentication function shall lock out users for one hour or when reset by a system administrator.

■ **Note** This last requirement is not a compound requirement that needs to be broken apart. Yes, it has an *or* in it, but in this case, either condition can be met to allow the user to try to authenticate again. Breaking them apart really would not capture the conditional aspect of this requirement.

Now, move onto the children of the original requirement. Each requirement stands on its own, as it should. The only real difference is that they are related to the first requirement, 3.1.1. You should also reflect this with the numbering scheme. Instead of numbering the second through sixth statements 3.1.2 through 3.1.6, you should use 3.1.1.1 through 3.1.1.5 reflecting that they are subordinate to 3.1.1. You will examine more about this in the "Traced to a Source" section later in this chapter.

Complete

This is an interesting and difficult attribute to capture, so you will spend some time on it. This is a value that addresses both the individual requirement and the entire set of requirements.

Completeness of an Individual Requirement

At the requirement level, is all the information necessary to define the function, the verb that describes what action it should do, and the result of that action that completes the description of the need?

Examine this example:

> 2-20 DRAFT The BOSS Access Control function shall provide a display.

What should the system display? Yes, it's a simple example, but it illustrates the missing data. Sometimes, as the last set of requirements where you looked at parent-child requirements, you should provide the complete set of data by providing additional requirements related to the particular topic. That gets into looking at the system description as a whole, which you will come back to shortly.

In the meantime, focus on individual requirements for now. You have a challenge to read each requirement you craft to determine whether it is complete. Look at the following requirement:

> 2-21 DRAFT The BOSS individual radiation dosimeter shall capture exposure of 1000 rem.

You are not expected to be radiation experts; just accept that the statement has legitimate expressions of radiation exposure. (FYI, this radiation exposure is very significant, in fact, as it is likely to be lethal.) Nevertheless, you need to answer the question, is this complete? The answer is no. Why? This one statement by itself means there are many more requirements necessary to show all the values that need to be captured. The user said they needed an individual radiation dosimeter that captured up to 1000 rem. Thus, you might need to write the following 999 requirements:

> 2-22 DRAFT The BOSS individual radiation dosimeter shall capture exposure of 999 rem.

> 2-23 DRAFT The BOSS individual radiation dosimeter shall capture exposure of 998 rem.

> 2-24 DRAFT The BOSS individual radiation dosimeter shall capture exposure of 997 rem.

And down to the following:

> 2-25 DRAFT The BOSS individual radiation dosimeter shall capture exposure of 1 rem.

Clearly, this is not practical. While complete, do you really want to write it that way? Of course not. You could write it as follows:

> 2-26 The BOSS individual radiation dosimeter shall capture exposures of a maximum of 1000 rem.

If so, then you need to write a requirement for the minimum value.

> 2-27 The BOSS individual radiation dosimeter shall capture exposures of a minimum of 1 rem.

Of course, you could write it as one requirement as follows:

> 2-28 The BOSS individual radiation dosimeter shall capture exposures in a range of 1 to 1000 rem.

That looks complete, correct? Well, yes and no. What is missing? What increments must the exposures be captured in? Well, you ask when the stakeholder, they say it in individual rem values.

> 2-29 The BOSS individual radiation dosimeter shall capture exposures in increments of 1 rem.

Wait, you can write all that in one requirement as follows:

> 2-30 DRAFT The BOSS individual radiation dosimeter shall capture exposures in a range of 1 to 1000 rem in increments of 1 rem.

So, should you capture it this way? The requirement is complete. Yes, but you should not combine them because this is not atomic as was discussed in the previous section. The reason is the range of values is one requirement, and the increment is another. In addition, these two values would require testing them in different manners. While you have not learned about verification yet, it helps to think about all attributes whenever you can.

Now, move on to another aspect of individual requirements. There are situations where you may have an incomplete requirement temporarily. In the previous case, the user said they wanted the individual radiation dosimeter from one rem to some higher number that he did not know and would have to check with someone else to get the upper limit. You should capture the requirement so it is not lost or forgotten about, as follows:

> 2-31 The BOSS individual radiation dosimeter shall capture exposures in a range of 1 to (TBD) rem.

What is TBD? It stands for To Be Determined. In this case, some other expert is going to determine the upper maximum. The original stakeholder knew that 450 rem was a value of interest to people in the military battlefield, but the stakeholder did not know if that was correct so he or she deferred the decision.

If you have a TBD, that means the requirement is not complete. So, why do you even address it here? Because it comes up—a lot. In fact, back in the ancient days when REs did requirements documents on paper (yes, even before word processing), you had TBD sections with a work-off plan for all of them. A work-off plan is a listing of each TBD and how it will be eliminated, as well as when each will be completed if possible. Some books will recommend you do this. In fact, they would assign unique numbers to each TBD to aid in tracking. If you have more than a handful, this might be a wise approach to take. Once you get the information, place it in the requirement and, *voila*, it is complete.

There is a variation on the TBD called the TBR, which stands for To Be Reviewed. In the case of a TBD, the stakeholder did not know the value of interest; the stakeholder did not provide any value. What if this same stakeholder had guessed 800 rem but said the stakeholder was uncertain if that was correct and needed confirmation. In this case, the requirement would look like this:

> 2-32 The BOSS individual radiation dosimeter shall capture exposures in a range of 1 to 800 (TBR) rem.

Notice that this includes the suggested value, as it at least gives some indication of a reasonable limit. Again, once you confirm the upper limit, remove the TBR, completing the requirement. These TBRs can be included in the TBD/TBR work-off plan.

Completeness of a Group of Requirements

How do you determine when you have completely described the system of interest? Look at Figure 2-1. The rectangle is the universe of everything outside the project of interest. The circle inside that rectangle is the project of interest.

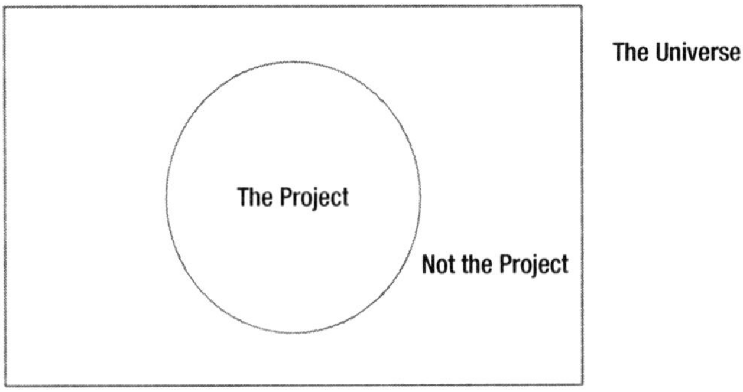

Figure 2-1. *The project inside everything it interacts with*

The key is the boundary, the edge of the circle. Remember in Chapter 1, you read about the scope of the project, "...that means that the boundary between systems/services/functions/applications must be defined." When you have described everything inside the edge of the circle and on the edge, you are complete.

Sounds simple, right? Yes, it sounds simple, but it is not in practice. You need to define every action, every need, all performance needs, design constraints, architectural constraints, policy constraints, environmental constraints, and all external system interfaces with all inputs and outputs.

If you have a self-contained system with no external interfaces, say a game like Microsoft Solitaire, you have it much easier. In many, if not most, cases, you will have other systems/apps to exchange data, which means you have a much broader stakeholder base. There is one additional complication in defining your requirements. If you require external interfaces to make changes, you may have resistance because of budgetary, political, or even egotistical reasons. This complicates your efforts significantly. Ideally, the first time you do this, you will have a mentor because this is the most challenging aspect of capturing requirements. During the discussion about collection of requirements, you will learn about this more.

Meanwhile, back at the project requirements focus, there are items to consider. Make certain you define any graphics well such as figures, tables, and diagrams labeled with all units provided and any other pertinent information provided. In fact, speaking of units, you always need to include them in requirements regardless if they are associated with graphics. A glossary is useful. You will hear more about this in Chapter 3.

Chapter 1 briefly touched on gap analysis. The focus of that emphasis is to capture the completeness of the requirements set. As mentioned, you will learn more about how to do this in Chapter 9 on collection requirements. Suffice to say, what you need to do is find all the missing capabilities. You have to ask yourself, as well as others, what things should this system do that have not been discussed? Sometimes, this takes a bit of creativity. Actually, this can make it fun as you can ask some questions you might not normally ask. For example, should you drop your smartphone onto concrete from 3 feet up?

The answer is that the phone company and their manufacturers would say no. Why? They want it not to be survivable to what users might consider reasonable. For the record, when the U.S. Army was developing radiation detection equipment, their sophisticated electronic equipment did have such a requirement. Why? Because soldiers might use these pieces of hardware in the field, in potential combat situations, and the devices might see some rough treatment. Think of the hardware bounced around in a vehicle as it jostles over rough terrain. It needs to be tough. Do you think laptops that can take that kind of treatment? No. If you think they can, Google *hardened laptops*.

Therefore, as a phone user, you want the following requirement:

> 2-33 The cell phone shall perform all its functions after being dropped onto concrete from a height of three feet.

The next time you want to replace your phone, ask what models have been tested to survive being dropped. You might be surprised—and not necessarily pleasantly.

Next, continue investigating requirements that you should specify for all conditions that can occur. Do cell phones need to survive an electromagnetic pulse (EMP) from a nuclear weapon detonation? What is the likelihood that the cell towers would survive unless they were nuclear hardened? Probably not. Even if they were then, would there be a power infrastructure to support the towers? Not likely. Thus, you cannot expect our phones to survive if the infrastructure around them would not. Thus, EMP survivability for our cell phones is not a reasonable requirement. This is an extreme example, but when looking for "all conditions," this gets to be interesting. You have to do what some people call "thinking around corners" so you consider items that normally do not occur. However, are conditions that your system, whether hardware or software, will operate? Think of the conditions a satellite has to operate in. They are much harsher than on Earth.

Examining or considering unusual conditions is interesting.

■ **Real-World Note** I will digress just a bit to describe what someone did when performing my job before I became the test manager. This individual did the Butt Test. Now this is not something you will find on the Internet (I checked). What this person did when a new piece of code came in was to turn on the system, put the keyboard on the chair, and promptly plop down on it. Hence, the name Butt Test. Needless to say, I did not carry on this (insert your adjective here) test when I took over. The idea, I suppose, was to see what happened when a lot of different keystrokes happened at the same time. I do not know what any of the test results were nor, frankly, do I care. The reason is that I had no requirement to test this. Nor have I ever seen any other project with such a requirement either.

One aspect to think about in completeness is the data elements in the system. Find out what the users need, not what the designers and coders need to manage the data. That is for them to specify. When you collect these values, not only what are their formats, ranges of values, or other conditions, but why should it be part of the system, and how will they use it. Why collect someone's Social Security number when all you are doing is delivering the Sunday newspaper to him or her? Do you think this does not happen? Oh, it does. You must understand how stakeholders might use the value.

Do not fall into the trap that you see the previous set of requirements list a bunch of values so you assume you need all these values.

■ **Real-World Note** I spent five years as an industrial engineer, basically an efficiency expert. Our instructors taught us to question every fact we collected and to get each answer from at least two different sources. I am not advocating that you need to perform this type of validation, but the principle is important.

Make certain you understand why each value is important to the users.

For example, say you have a requirement in the older set of requirements like the following:

> 2-34 DRAFT The system shall maintain an index key field for the person data.

Upon investigating, you find, in the old system, the system populated person data in three separate tables and the software needed a way to link the tables together. However, you cannot assume the same implementation in this new system (in fact, you learn later, they do it with one table, so there is no need for this field). This is not a valid requirement.

You need to consider error conditions under completeness. What kinds of errors do you want to prevent? In the past, users have asked for error checking of query statements, as they want proper formatting invoked before initiating the query. This saves the user from having to correct something before they wait for the system to reject it, sometimes taking a significant amount of time. In addition, users have asked for the capability for the system not to crash when a complex search was run (it happened, in fact with quite regularity).

There are a couple of minor items to consider. Like when you populate the requirements in a document, you should number all the pages. You will learn more about documents in a later chapter. Also, all requirements need to be uniquely identified. You will see more about this in a later section of this chapter.

You should specify all applicable requirements to achieve completeness. This is the toughest attribute to check. Just before you finish requirements definition, the one thing a requirements engineer dreads is for a user to say, "I forgot that I need...." This text will do all it can to help prevent this by preparing you satisfactorily.

Concise

What you want is requirements that are short and sweet. You have learned about not having compound sentences, which fits nicely into the concise attribute. The shorter the statement, the likely the easier it is to read. This means you are using shorter, more precise words and more active verbs.

Now, look at two options.

Here is option 1:

> 2-35 DRAFT The BOSS system software shall maintain a unique sequence of numbers for each record associated with the person data so someone can retrieve the record based on these numbers.

Here is option 2:

> 2-36 DRAFT The BOSS code shall assign unique numbers for each person record.

Clearly, the second option is better. First, the statement uses 11 words versus 29 words, and it employs more concrete words like *code* versus *system software*. Second, notice the statement dropped the phrase dealing with retrieval using the record numbers as that really is another requirement.

Another aspect of concise writing is the clarity that a good requirement should bring. A requirement should be understandable by a nontechnical person.

If a non-IT person saw the following requirement:

> 2-37 DRAFT The BOSS SOA implementation shall follow OOP practices on all objects.

this person would clearly not know what that meant. Try to target every requirement for that type of person. That is not always practical. However, if a particular stakeholder asks for a need that you translate into one or more requirements, that person should be able to understand it. When administrative or systems people have requirements, these are IT people and they better understand technology statements, even if non-IT people do not. Thus, sometimes you will have to write to the audience. Maybe you do not even present the administrative or systems requirements to the standard stakeholders. That approach has worked well in the past. You are not withholding information; you just focus on those requirements and needs that affect these typical users. (OOP means object-oriented programming.)

Consistent

Consistent requirements complement each other. Here you will focus on consistent usage. For example, you must use consistent terms. Many of you may have heard of the Mars probe that was lost when the vendor who built it used English measurements when metric measurements were called for. Therefore, if a command was sent that said go X distance in kilometers, when it measured it in miles, the craft would have gone 60.2 percent farther. So, use consistent measurements in you requirements.

That also means within a particular grouping of requirements, use the same measurement. Here's an example:

> 2-38 DRAFT The BOSS query function shall return the results of a simple query against one table within two seconds.
>
> 2-39 DRAFT The BOSS query function shall return the results of a complex query against ten tables within three minutes.

Instead, they should read as follows:

> 2-40 DRAFT The BOSS query function shall return the results of a simple query against one table within two seconds.
>
> 2-41 DRAFT The BOSS query function shall return the results of a complex query against ten tables within **180 seconds**.

One reason is that someone reading the requirements may miss the difference of the unit of measure in the second requirements. This helps to prevent it.

In addition, how you refer to selection capability is important.

> 2-42 DRAFT The BOSS print choices shall be offered from a picklist.
>
> 2-43 DRAFT The BOSS print choices shall be available from a pull-down menu

---

■ **Warning** Usually the two requirements are not written one right after the other. What happens when there are a few dozen or a few hundred requirements in between them (or if it was more than a thousand?). It is difficult to spot when you read through them. A way to check is to have a mechanism that you can filter on topics, and see this limited list on one screen. For example, when you view a topic in Microsoft Excel, you see the information much closer together, and it is easier to spot. Another technique is for you to set them aside and read them some days later, and you might pick up inconsistencies. Alternatively, having others review your requirements can help. It could be something simple in an airport system where one requirement says *outbound* and another time *return*.

This book touches on jargon, or the use of terminology in the next chapter, but you must use terms consistently throughout the document. Do not say *query* sometimes and *search* another, unless they have different meanings. Be careful here as some people may use the terms differently. Most people use *search* to be just that. However, one group of people use *search* when they want to *research*. However, when they are looking for something specific, then it is *query*, not *search*—even though they use the same search tool. Go figure.

Here is another example:

> 2-44 DRAFT 3.1.69 The BOSS system shall accept dates in the mm/dd/yyyy format.
>
> 2-45 DRAFT 4.3.2.13 The BOSS Data Entry function shall allow entry of dates in the format:
>
> - dd/mm/yyyy
> - mm/dd/yyyy
> - yyyy/mm/dd

Clearly, the second requirement allows three different formats, whereas the first one accepts only one. Wait, you say, the requirements cover different areas within the system. One is at the system level, while the other covers only the data entry function. Good point, however, the lower one conflicts with the top level. If you write the statements the following way, you could accept it.

2-46 3.1.69 The BOSS function shall allow entry of dates in the format:

- dd/mm/yyyy
- mm/dd/yyyy
- yyyy/mm/dd

2-47 4.3.2.13 The BOSS Data Entry system shall be accept dates in the mm/dd/yyyy format.

Here the more restrictive is acceptable at the function level, whereas the system level is more general. That said, be certain that you confirm that the function level truly accepts only the single format and just is not a mistake.

Does Not Conflict with Other Requirements

Now, you need to understand about inconsistency between requirements. Look at a set of reliability requirements for a hardware system.

2-48 DRAFT Each BOSS subsystem shall have a reliability of 0.990.

2-49 DRAFT The BOSS system shall have a reliability of 0.950.

On the surface that looks reasonable. However, there is some missing information that masks an inconsistency. What is important to this inconsistency is the number of subsystems that are in series. In this example, you use the following formula, since all the subsystems have the same reliability:
R(system) = R(subsystem)^N(number of subsystems in series)

■ **Note** We will spend more time on reliability so you will understand this better in Chapter 5.

Equation 1: R(system) = 0.990^10, which yields a value of 0.904

Clearly, you cannot achieve the specified system reliability. You have several options. Option 1 is you should consider changing the number of the subsystems. If you have five subsystems and calculate .990^5, you get a number of 0.951, which meets the second requirement. However, the designers say that is not possible.

The second option is to ask the stakeholders if they would settle for 90 percent reliability. They say no. Thus, the third option is to change the reliability of the subsystems. By changing the reliability requirement to 0.995, then you get a value of 0.951. In this case, the users accept the change in the requirement (who wouldn't when they provide a better value?) and the designers say it is practical, so you agree on the following requirements for ten subsystems:

2-50 Each BOSS subsystem shall have a reliability of 0.995.

2-51 The BOSS system shall have a reliability of 0.950.

Not always is the inconsistency so number intensive. It may be more like the following:

> 2-52 DRAFT The BOSS ranking subsystem shall be high, medium and low options.
>
> 2-53 DRAFT The BOSS priority function shall allow critical, high, medium and low options

Are *ranking* and *priority* the same? Yes, in this case. Are *subsystem* and *function* the same? Yes, in this case. Are *high, medium,* and *low* and *critical, high, medium,* and *low* the same? Yes, in this case. Although these requirements happen to be consistent at one level, you can see that the terminology is not, which shows that you can have more than one inconsistency.

Now, examine another pair of requirements:

> 2-54 DRAFT The BOSS New Phone App shall ensure I can use the phone based on a biometric.
>
> 2-55 DRAFT The BOSS New Phone App shall be delivered to existing phones.

Assume from a design standpoint that the capturing of a biometric cannot be accomplished without some hardware change to a phone. Then, there is no way that existing phones that do not have that hardware can accomplish the first requirement. If it can be done with software, than these two are not in conflict.

Sometimes the conflict may not be so obvious. Take the case of the following:

> 2-56 DRAFT The BOSS New Phone App shall provide state-of-the-art machine learning capabilities.
>
> 2-57 DRAFT The BOSS New Phone App shall be delivered within three months to existing phones.

Here the problem is that machine learning as described here would not fit into, say, a 16GB smartphone. Thus, it will not occur within three months. Unless you know a bit more about the system in question and its memory, you might not catch this inconsistency. If uncertain, ask experts.

Does Not Duplicate Other Requirements

This inconsistency is a bit more straightforward than the last ones. Basically, the same statement is made in two different places. Given that you have hundreds of requirements (or thousands), this can happen. You may have heard the same requirement from two different sources, and you did not remember capturing it before. Or, and this is very likely, as on a bigger project there will be more than one requirements engineer, two (or more) people will capture the same requirements. It may be as simple as this:

> 2-58 DRAFT 3.1.5.5 The BOSS priority function shall allow critical, high, medium, and low options.
>
> 2-59 DRAFT 4.7.8.2.1The BOSS priority function shall allow critical, high, medium, and low options.

Did you notice how far apart the requirements numbers are? That can explain part of the problem.

DUPLICATE REQUIREMENTS

And yes, even I have done it. Of course, my "excuse" to the reviewer who caught it was, "I had to put something in for you to catch so that you would feel validated in finding something."

You can consider that "excuse" as public domain and use it to your advantage. However, maybe not in the first couple of years. It does not work when that is one of hundreds of comments.

Other times, slight inconsistencies can mask the duplication, as shown here:

> 2-60 DRAFT 3.12.5 The BOSS print choices shall be offered from a picklist.

> 2-61 DRAFT 4.1.1.18 The BOSS print choices shall be offered to the user.

You might have to spend some time looking through your requirements to catch these kinds of duplicates. This should become a step in your checklist of the steps you should take during the review of your complete set of requirements. How you organize your requirements is important. That may help capture these kinds of errors when they are close together.

Independent

By this attribute, there are two potential meanings for it. First, a requirement should be able to stand on its own. Second, a requirement should be independent of a particular implementation.

Stand on Its Own

To understand the requirement, there should be no need to know any other requirement.

> 2-62 The BOSS Authentication Function shall require the user to enter a username, password and domain name.

This requirement has all three parts: the function, the verb and the action. Now, examine an alternate statement.

> 2-63 DRAFT It shall require the user to enter a username, password and domain name in that order.

What is *it* in this requirement? The author probably assumed it was "The BOSS Authentication Function," but he/she should state it so, to ensure a requirement statement can stand alone. Instead, you should write it as follows:

> 2-64 The BOSS Authentication Function shall require the user to enter a username, password and domain name in that order.

■ **Real-World Note** This does happen; even I have done it when I was crafting a lot of requirements from notes or even business process descriptions. You are frantically cutting and pasting and words are flying around in your text, and you miss it (pun fully intended). I remember the days when I actually did physically cut and paste. Yes, I am a crusty old curmudgeon.

That is why you should always go back and read what you have written. Look for any such pronouns such as *it, they, them, some, all, a few,* and *several.* This list is not exhaustive, but you get the idea.

Implementation Independent

This potential violation is more likely, yet as a concept it can be more difficult to find. A requirement should not contain any unnecessary design and implementation information. You will come back to the word *unnecessary.* Why do you not want to specify a design? First, you are a requirements engineer. Odds are you are not a design engineer or system architect. Even if you have some training and experience as such, it is *not* your role to specify design. Why is that?

REs are to specify "what" you want the project to do, not "how." You must leave the designing and architecting to those responsible for the architecture and design. In addition, you do not want to limit their design by locking them into a particular approach. They are paid the big bucks to do that, just like you are paid big bucks to be an expert at defining requirements. Therefore, you will let them do their job. Now, examine this next statement:

> 2-65 DRAFT The BOSS Personnel Data Capture function shall store the personnel data in a text file.

Is this correct? No. Wait a minute, shouldn't you specify that you want to store the data? Yes, and you should. The problem is with saying "...in a text file." That is design, and that is the designer's and/or architect's decision. The requirement should read as follows:

> 2-66 The BOSS Personnel Data Capture function shall store the personnel data.

Here is another one:

> 2-67 DRAFT The BOSS Personnel Radiation Dosimeter shall be protected in a metal case to prevent damage by the soldier wearing it while going through normal activities in the field.

Is this correct? On the surface, it might appear to be. However, maybe a metal case might interfere with the passage of the particles that are meant to be detected. Again, you have restricted the designers. Therefore, you should write it as follows:

> 2-68 The BOSS Personnel Radiation Dosimeter shall be protected to prevent damage by the soldier wearing it while going through normal activities in the field.

The metal case was taken out. Here is another example to consider:

> 2-69 DRAFT The BOSS shall be developed using Java.

Ha, you say, this clearly is implementation specific. Yes, on first blush, you are correct.

When reviewing the requirements on a new project, I found just such a requirement. I asked the program manager if this was implementation specific. The PM told me that our project was an umbrella program that other applications would be including under our umbrella. The customer we were developing it for wanted a common development environment. Thus, this was a valid requirement.

A clarification is in order. Some requirements theorists say that this is a constraint, not a requirement. They mandate all constraints belong in a special section. With the advent of requirements databases, a special section (as in a document) is not as easy to do. You can organize requirements into sections somewhat by arranging them with specific unique identifiers. The point is that this is a valid need so you call it a requirement. For some projects that want constraints handled separately, you can have a special constraint field in your database and mark this following requirement as a YES:

> 2-70 The BOSS shall be developed using Java.

■ **Real-World Note** I have one more point to make about this requirement. I have used it as a question in requirements interviews. I state the requirement and ask the interviewee if it is valid. Most say no, that it is implementation. Only one in the dozens I interviewed answered it correctly as Maybe. Then I went on to explain why correctly, as a possible constraint. Therefore, if you ever encounter this question, you now have the right answer.

Naturally, as a beginning RE, you may not know where the boundary is between what is design and what is a requirement. This will come with practice. It also helps to read other requirement sets.

■ **Warning** People write requests for change (RFCs) as a mechanism for modifying existing projects. In these documents or forms (whatever manner these RFCs come in), usually there is a "Requirement" section. The potential problem is that anyone can write these requests, not just REs: users, designers, testers, or even managers. Most of these people do not have expertise with writing requirements, let alone crafting good requirements. If users write these, remember that they are not requirements engineers and write what they want the system to be. Usually they say something like, "I want a pull-down to list all my choices" and so on. Know who is writing these statements. Unless you know that an RE wrote them, do not consider them gospel.

Prioritized

Priority is the importance of a requirement or a group of requirements.

Assigning a priority means assigning a relative importance like high, medium, and low. This reflects what you need to do with requirements. This helps alleviate the problem mentioned in Chapter 1 where a list of requirements with no other information gives the impression that they all have the same importance. They do not. Nor should you list requirements without some qualification to the importance. You should start assigning one of four priorities to each requirement. (You can use three, five, or whatever number works best for your project.)

There is a distinction between priority and rank. Priority is the level of importance. In this book, ranking is numbering within a priority. In other words, in what order should the critical priorities be worked off? Rank 1 should definitely come before rank 10.

The recommended four priorities are Critical, High, Medium, and Low. Other than the "critical to life" needs, those items that are necessary for the project or the rest of the functions to work all are critical. For example, in the radiation dosimetry project, collecting the radiation exposure is critical, or none of the follow-on functions will work. You should apply the same approach to a software application. Without collecting and/or ingesting data into the application, none of the manipulations of that data will work. Those are the critical functions.

■ **Note** In Chapter 5, the text will use Critical and High functions in one of the definitions there, so having defined priorities proves useful there to help identify those functions.

Many High functions are the mission-essential functions that manipulate the data that the critical functions have provided. This would be analyzing the radiation exposure or querying the database. The Medium functions would be less important, say reports of data for management. The Low functions are the remaining items.

One word of caution when you get to Low functions. If stakeholders find functions that no one seems to understand, that begs the question why anyone wants them. Here you may be getting to functions that really do not add value. This is one of the reasons that requirements engineers need to review the functions that developers want to create, so they do not provide things that stakeholders and users do not need. Trust me, they like to do neat things and think they know what users want. Do not let them, at least without checks and balances. Run it past the users if you are uncertain.

Who makes the decision on these priorities? While you as a requirements engineer can propose these values, the responsibility rests with the stakeholders. Even if you propose the priorities, the stakeholders must review them. If you have thousands or even several hundred, you might group the requirements together so the stakeholders have fewer decisions to make.

Here is one set of example requirements with the priority provided after the statement:

> 2-71 The BOSS Unit Radiation Dosimeter shall collect the radiation exposure during the unit's mission. Critical
>
> 2-72 The BOSS Unit Radiation Dosimeter shall display the real-time radiation exposure during the unit's mission when activated by a user. High
>
> 2-73 The BOSS Unit Radiation Dosimeter shall generate a display of the radiation exposure values over the unit's entire mission. Medium
>
> 2-74 The BOSS Unit Radiation Dosimeter shall generate a graphic display of the radiation exposure values over the unit's entire mission. Low

Here is another set of example requirements with the priority provided after the statement:

> 2-75 The BOSS Casualty Data Collection function shall allow an authorized user to enter each unit's daily casualties. Critical
>
> 2-76 The BOSS Casualty Query Collection function shall allow an authorized user to query each unit's daily casualties. High
>
> 2-77 The BOSS Casualty Report Collection function shall allow an authorized user to generate a report of all units' daily casualties. Medium
>
> 2-78 The BOSS Casualty Query Collection function shall allow an authorized user to generate a report of one unit's daily casualties over a month. Low

The IEEE standard 830-1998 says that requirements should be ranked for importance and/or stability to indicate either the importance or the stability of that particular requirement. First, you addressed the stability of a requirement when you learned about TDBs and TBRs in the "Complete" section. You should accept that some requirements are more important than others. IEEE defines stability with how likely it is to change.

■ **Real-World Note** Honestly, as I think back over my career, I never have really estimated that. Alternatively, for that matter, I am not certain how useful this aspect of the attribute would be. Part of this may relate to the age of this standard—1998, almost two decades old. The environment is much more dynamic now than it was in 1998.

In addition, you will see more later in this chapter and the book how requirements change over time and how to address that. Thus, you should not worry about this aspect, unless you encounter a project where the management uses it and insists upon it. Then follow their well-defined approach (assuming it exists). Beyond that, read the IEEE standard and other sources to learn more about it.

IEEE breaks requirements into four ranks: essential, desirable, conditional, and optional. Essential means absolutely needed, without which the system cannot function. Think of life-critical aspects of an application. The next highest level is desirable but not life-threatening or disastrous to the application. Conditional requirements would enhance the product but would not affect the application if they were not included.

Finally, optional requirements may or may not be worthwhile.

Why would you capture something that is optional? This gives the designers some flexibility. These elements would be included in the design after the coders implemented all the rest of requirements and resources still exist to finish these needs. Alternatively, sometimes when designers are working on higher-priority items, they can include these optional items with very little impact to their effort. You, as a user, get more bang for your buck.

Does that mean you should not identify essential, desirable, conditional, and optional? No, if you need to capture this information, do so. Whatever is necessary to manage your requirements, that is for you to do. You want to clarify the language used related to your project.

Wait, you said priority, not rank. IEEE said rank. Here you get into a language issue. In this text, ranking means assigning a rank number within a priority to each requirement.

While IEEE used rank, this text recommends performing ranking within priorities, so you want to consider that distinction. In fact, when you get to Chapter 13 later in the book, again you will see prioritizing (with the four values) and then ranking numerically within each priority. This helps with the backlog management.

Alan Davis in his book *Software Requirements: Objects, Functions, and States* uses annotated as the attribute instead of the IEEE rank attribute. This is used to clarify terminology again.

Realistic

Is each requirement realistic, possible, feasible, or doable (other words for this attribute) in the timeframe the program wants it? Here's example:

> 2-79 DRAFT The BOSS Venus Probe shall be able to hover at any altitude using anti-gravity pulse generators.

First, ignore the possibility that this is implementation specific. Assume it is an architectural constraint.

■ **Note** It does not take a rocket scientist to know this is not realistic since we currently have no anti-gravity capability. Nor are we likely to have it any time soon. (I hope I am proven wrong. That said, I would much rather be pleasantly surprised rather than negatively so because we counted on such a breakthrough.)

However, if you had said the following:

> 2-80 The BOSS Venus Probe shall be able to descend slowly in the Venusian atmosphere by using a parachute.

this is much more feasible as the atmosphere is much denser than Earth's atmosphere, making a parachute practical. In fact, the Soviet Union and United States both have used parachutes in the past.

What about the following?

> 2-81 DRAFT The BOSS Earth Internal Probe shall be capable to image the fluid interior of the Earth using positrons.

Current physics understanding and engineering capabilities says that this is not possible. First, there are not very many positive-charged electrons available. Second, this is not the right particle to use for this type of imaging (maybe neutrinos, but that is not state-of-the-art yet). Third, being an anti-particle, it would destroy itself when it hits its particle pair. So, no, this is not feasible.

> 2-82 The BOSS Submarine Probe shall be capable to image underwater vehicles using sonar.

Watch any submarine movie, and it will validate this requirement.

What about software? How do you apply this rule? Look at the following statement:

> 2-83 DRAFT The BOSS Chess Software shall be capable of beating a Chess Grandmaster.

Is this feasible? If you have read about Gary Kasparov's two matches with the IBM computer Deep Blue, then you know that this is feasible, as the computer won the second match 3½ to 2½. (FYI, Gary won the first encounter 4 to 2.) Therefore, yes, it is feasible. What about the following?

> 2-84 DRAFT The BOSS Physician Diagnosis Software shall completely duplicate all the diagnostic functions of a physician.

While machine learning is making tremendous strides in decision-making algorithms, it does not appear to be so yet. These types of applications are providing assistances to doctors, but only that—assistance. Remember that with the advances made in this field, the previous statement may date this book. For everyone's sake, we as a people should hope so.

How do you determine whether something is feasible? That is the rub. If you do not have a good understanding of the technology, it will be a challenge. You can do research, say on the Internet, to find out capabilities and limitations of technology. You can talk with experts around you. You will find that developers, designers, and architects can be valuable resources. If they are not overwhelmed with work, you will be surprised how open they will be to share their knowledge.

Know that not every requirement will need to be scrutinized so. As you go through this book, you will recognize many if not most requirements are doable, because you have seen them done. Think about every application you have ever used, every device, or app on your phone and you will realize that you have a more extensive field of experience to draw from. In most cases, it is just common sense. If you use science-fiction books as textbooks, then you might miss the mark.

Here is an actual example. The stakeholder said that he wanted a biometric used to check every person who used the system. Unfortunately, this was not a situation where people would use a biometric to authorize people to use a system, a one-to-one match for each person. One-to-one matching would be using a retinal scan to allow you to enter a restricted area. The stakeholder wanted to compare the biometric against the complete set of people in their system, a many-to-many comparison. A many-to- many comparison would be at the airport where the TSA at U.S. airports are checking all people's pictures (many) against their list of people on the "no-fly list," also many. For this stakeholders request, he only had a server with networked workstations; he did not have that capability built into the system to do a many-to-many comparison.

Given what I described in the previous paragraph, what I did was capture the requirement. I told the stakeholder that what he had said was a valid need and a realistic requirement. I did indicate that the capability was not yet built into the system we were working on, so it would not be part of the first delivery. I did explain that doing a significant search against a large biometric database was intensive and may not run on our current hardware configuration. He accepted my explanation. A couple of years later, we had begun building the biometric capability into the system so that the requirement was feasible. How did I know this? I had been with the project for more than a year or so at that point, and I had a good idea of our current capabilities, as well as what we had planned for the next few years. Therefore, I could speak with some assurance that the requirement in question was doable. So—feasible.

Thus, making the determination, while challenging sometimes, it can be done. Trust your judgment, and validate when you are unsure.

Traceable

The IEEE standard 830-1998 defines the traceable attribute as traceability to an origin and to future development or enhancement documentation. If you look at their document, they do not differentiate between traceable and traced. This book, as do other texts (*Software Requirements* by Davis, and others), does make this distinction. Here, traced means pointing a requirement to a source, which will be covered in the next section. The first section will talk about traceability to subsequent documents here.

Traceability

Traceability will show what design specifications are written that address the requirement. Odds are, they will be one or more design specifications. In addition, the testers will write their test plans and procedures. Every requirement must have at least one design specification and at least one test procedure. If they do not, you have a problem, as you will be unable to verify that all the needs are met. Table 2-1 shows examples.

Table 2-1. *Traceability for the BOSS System's Authentication Requirements to Other Documents*

Number	Requirement	Design Spec	Test Procedure
3.1.1.1	The BOSS Authentication function shall require all users to enter a valid username.	2.1.1a, 2.1.2, 2.2.2c	TP-3.1
3.1.1.2	The BOSS Authentication function shall require all users to enter a valid password.	2.1.1b, 2.1.3,	TP-3.1
3.1.1.3	The BOSS Authentication function shall require all users to enter a valid system domain name	2.1.1c, 2.2.2a, 2.2.2b	TP-3.1
3.1.1.4	The BOSS Authentication function shall require all users to enter a valid username, password and system domain name in three tries or they are locked out of the system.	2.1.1d	TP-3.1

Table 2-2 shows another example, separate from the BOSS system.

Table 2-2. *Traceability for a Cell Phone System to Other Documents, Separate from the BOSS System*

Number	Requirement	Design Spec	Test Procedure
4.7.2.1	The cell phone shall perform all its functions after being dropped onto concrete from a height of three feet.	4.7.2.1.1, 4.7.2.1.2, 4.7.2.1.3	PD-7.9

This is one of the easier aspects to do, just tedious. Some of the work you will do is not the most exciting part of the job. It is important that you do it nevertheless. You will also need to do it jointly with other members of the team. Sometimes, you will find you will force them to do their job when they did not realize they had to. That is satisfying when you actually influence the design and/or testing.

Traced to a Source

As mentioned in the preceding section, this deals with tracing your requirement back to a source. This may be nothing more than listing the meeting where a group of stakeholders met to define their needs.

Do you need to specify exactly who said it? Usually not. A description of the type of user, if you know, can be helpful. Do you need to know the name of the person, when they may not be there three years later when you follow up? No. However, if you know it was a lawyer in the legal department, or the HR rep, that will be useful if you need to follow up later.

Sometimes policy documents dictate a requirement. If so, state the policy, even to the paragraph number if you can.

What if you have a team of engineers collecting information from various sources (usually because the project is too big for one person)? You may need to validate other people's requirements. This is always a good idea. It helps you learn as well as the person being reviewed.

In addition, you may discover someone who is not following the guidance provided here.

■ **Real-World Note** I had an engineer who wrote a requirement that stipulated that our existing system needed to be rewritten as a Microsoft Access database. Here comes the most important question you can ask (which we will spend more time in Chapter 9)—why? Her rationale was that the stakeholder had asked for it. I must point out that we already had delivered the system to several other clients, which were several large WANs with an Oracle database. I asked why this particular customer wanted it that way. She said that their current system was written in Access and they would not have to do any transition recoding. So, with this smaller customer, for one WAN we would change the entire implementation (and the reduced capability of Microsoft Access versus Oracle)? I do not think so.

Thus, the source of a requirement is important. In addition, as discussed earlier, not just because it was that way in the old system either. Validate those requirements. How should you track the source? You should do so like in the previous section, as another field in your database.

See some examples in Table 2-3.

Table 2-3. *Traceability for the BOSS System's Authentication Function*

Number	Requirement	Source
3.1.1.1	The BOSS Authentication function shall require all users to enter a valid username.	BOSS Security Manager
3.1.1.2	The BOSS Authentication function shall require all users to enter a valid password.	BOSS Security Manager
3.1.1.3	The BOSS Authentication function shall require all users to enter a valid system domain name	BOSS Security Manager
3.1.1.4	The BOSS Authentication function shall require all users to enter a valid username, password and system domain name in three tries or they are locked out of the system.	Network Administrator at administration meeting, June 4, 2014.

Again, Table 2-4 shows an example separate from the BOSS system.

Table 2-4. *Traceability for a Cell Phone System Separate from the BOSS System*

Number	Requirement	Source
4.7.2.1	The cell phone shall perform all its functions after being dropped onto concrete from a height of 3 feet.	Every person who has dropped a cell phone!

Unambiguous

This attribute, dear reader, is the most difficult one of the 16. You will spend more time trying to get it correct, and in spite of this, you will have continual challenges with it. Even after doing this for more than 30 years, I still have to work hard at this. It has gotten better, but it never goes away.

Ambiguity in General

Let's look at ambiguity in general and why it can challenge you. Unambiguous means that a knowledgeable person interprets each requirement statement only one way. In this case, a knowledgeable person is someone who is a stakeholder or user of the system or will be involved in the project in some way, so they will have knowledge of the system. An English literature major being exposed to Einstein's theory of relativity will likely not be a knowledgeable person on that subject.

Honestly, this particular attribute will cause you more issues in your career than any others, possibly combined. Why? First, English, despite all those (usually in the humanities) who will tell you that it is precise, it is not. Have you ever had an argument with someone when upon further examination (usually after heads have cooled off) that you learned that what each of you said was correct, just that you did not agree on the meaning? That is why this text contains a chapter devoted to language and how to mitigate its flaws. Look at a dictionary. How many words on a page have only one meaning? That right there is part of the problem—the complexity yet beauty of the language.

■ **Real-World Note** I was at a conference once where I was talking with someone from Australia, and he said, "You Americans use the word *oversight* wrong." He emphasized the second syllable to mean a mistake by missing something. The context used in the previous presentation was *oversight* with emphasis on the first syllable to mean someone watching over something. Both definitions are correct, but context was so important.

How do you fix this?

There are those who advocate the use of something more precise like mathematics or models developed for the software and hardware development environment. You will see more why this may not be as effective as these IT theorists advocate in the next section on getting the stakeholders' buy-in.

Note Given that models have limitations for requirement uses, you will see a survey of some of these tools for you to get at least an understanding of them and can consider them when appropriate.

Thus, you will continue to examine using words as precisely as you can. The first thing you can do is find any words that can have multiple meanings. When you find them, put them in the glossary to define which one you are using. Now you cannot have hundreds or thousands of glossary terms. One way to cut this down is to use a specific phrase rather than two or three individual terms to reduce the number of entries in the glossary.

Realize that the stakeholders can review the requirements to help ensure that statements are unambiguous. Remember that they have particular institutional knowledge that the developers, who many times are in a different office, may not have. Thus, there may be a different understanding of the words.

One of my last projects had a group of developers who had no knowledge of what the stakeholders did. I had worked on defining the requirements for two years before the developers began looking at the requirements and found it almost incomprehensible because they did not understand what the users did. It was a difficult learning curve for them. We gave them training and had our subject-matter experts (SMEs) talk things over with them to clarify what their business process was. It wasn't because the requirements were wrong or that the developers were dumb; it was like trying to read a foreign language without the translating dictionary. Ideally this is the worst case; it was for my career.

One point new ambiguity occurred was during the transition from a document-based set of requirements to a database set of requirements. That spawned an additional problem that had not existed before. The document used acronyms and abbreviations—well, the best way to describe it was an epidemic. The military and most of the rest of the federal government uses, and will always use, that shorthand. It is the language of a project and an organization. I will talk learn about it in Chapter 3. However, they have been used in this text. The policy was that the first time you used an acronym, you spelled out its meaning the first time and then put the acronym in parentheses. After that, in the document you just used the acronym. This saved time and space.

In documents, that was no problem as people read them sequentially. However, with the advent of the database, that was not always the case. A developer would not necessarily look at the complete set of requirements, and if he/she did not see that SME was spelled out two paragraphs before (like here), then he/she might have missed the meaning.

How do you overcome this? Spell out the acronym the first time you use it in a requirement, and if used again, then use the acronym. While that flies in the face of the conciseness that acronyms buy for us, it overcomes the potential ambiguity issue.

You can fall into other traps. For example, look at the following:

> 2-85 DRAFT The BOSS Personnel Data Entry Function shall allow the entry of a name that is up to thirty characters long.

Is that valid? For two reasons, no. First, is that the first name, the last name, or the whole name? What if it is a Russian name, including the patronymic (middle name)? Will 30 characters be enough? In addition, it is best to break the name into parts, like first name, middle name, and last name. Wait a minute. What if it is someone hails from Latin American or the Middle East where there could be four parts to a name? You have to look at the range of names you could have.

Second, what do you mean by up to 30 characters? Do you allow exactly 30 characters? If so, say "up to and including 30 characters." If it is more than 30, are those beyond 30 discarded? Does the user get an error message? You need to clarify this.

Look at the following requirement for another example of a different kind of ambiguity:

> 2-86 DRAFT The BOSS Personnel Data Entry Function shall only allow the user to display one record.

Does this mean that only one record is displayed? If that was the intent, it does not say that. It means the display is the only option available to the user, no add, no update, no delete, no print, nothing but displaying the record. This shows that misplacing one word can give the wrong requirement. Reword it as follows:

> 2-87 The BOSS Personnel Data Entry Function shall allow the user to display only one record at a time.

If the intention was to restrict the actions of the users, reword it more clearly.

> 2-88 The BOSS Personnel Data Entry Function shall allow Read-Only user to only display records.

Subjective Terminology

Subjective terms also can be difficult. Here is a requirement that was actually written by someone (granted in the late 1980s but written nevertheless):

> 2-89 DRAFT The BOSS shall be user-friendly.

You can run into a lot of subjective words that everyone will have at least one different interpretation. The previous alleged requirement falls into that trap. One way to determine whether something is subjective is to try to define a way to test it. If you cannot, then it is subjective. Alternatively, if you could think of more than one way to interpret what it is, it is ambiguous. This alleged requirement begs the question, what is user-friendly? Each person you talk to would define it differently. They envision the user interface differently. The solution is to write a requirement like the following:

> 2-90 The BOSS shall follow our Organizational User Interface Standard.

Of course, that standard has to exist already. You will spend a little more time on user interfaces in Chapter 10.

There is a plethora of words that fall into the subjective (hence ambiguous) trap. This includes any word that ends in *ly*, such as the following:

- Accurately
- Adequately

- Effectively
- Efficiently
- Expandability
- Quickly
- Robustly
- Safely
- Timely

Even taking the root word, like *accurate*, does not eradicate the issue. Each work requires a specific statement that defines what *accurate* means. Here's an example:

> 2-91 The BOSS radiation dose rate meter shall capture exposures with a minimum accuracy of 0.1 rem per second.

Is this easy to do for every one of these potential words? No. It is necessary, however, to ensure the statements are unambiguous.

Other sources will tell you to fix problems with unspecific words like acronyms, and/or, TBDs, etc., and so on. Earlier in this section, you saw how to fix acronyms and how to fix TBDs discussed the Complete attribute. Now, for the phrase *and/or* that has been used this in this book, even this chapter. For example, earlier, this chapter said the following, "That is design and that is the designer's and/or architect's decision." Look at the last six words.

"...the designer's and/or architect's decision."

It could mean the following:

"...the designer's and architect's decision."

Alternatively, it could mean the following:

"...the designer's or architect's decision."

However, the convention in this book is that it means both statements are potential true. Therefore, if it shows up in a requirement, both ways have to work. Most projects have used this definition. So, when you are on a new project, find out if this is the case. If there is no preference, add it as a project convention.

Etc. and *so on* used in a requirement means there is missing information. If you do not have all the options, actions, data elements, or choices, use TBD and follow the guidance from the Complete attribute.

Troublesome Parts of Speech

You can run into vague words (in addition to adverbs, those *ly* words) like the following (this list is not exhaustive):

- Complete
- Derive
- Exhaustive

- Maintain
- Manage
- Handle
- Support

You will need to spell out what the word means, such as "maintain means add, change, delete, read, and print."

You have to avoid indefinite pronouns. Here are some examples:

- Almost
- Any
- Anybody
- Anything
- Few
- Just about
- Many
- Most
- Much
- Several
- Some
- Somebody
- Someone

Consider the following candidate requirement:

> 2-92 DRAFT The BOSS radiation dose rate meter shall capture as much radiation exposures as the user experiences during a mission.

What does *as much* mean? What number should be considered, 1 rem/second, 5, 22, or 2897? You must be specific. You have already said the minimum of 0.1 rem/second. You should specify the upper limit.

> 2-93 The BOSS radiation dose rate meter shall capture exposures with a maximum accuracy of 100.0 rem per second.

This is good because now you have given the full range, the upper and lower values. You may be tempted to use modifying phrases:

- *as* or *if* in front of:
  - Appropriate
  - Needed

    - Necessary
    - Required

- Shall be considered

What do any of those phrases mean? It means the list is either incomplete or you are not certain if all the items in the list apply. Be specific, or add a TBD or TBR to the requirement and then work off that TBD or TBR.

Passive Voice

Last but not least, you need to consider passive voice. With passive voice, the subject of the sentence receives the action of the verb rather than performing it. Here's an example:

> 2-93 DRAFT The Social Security number shall be entered by the user.

Alternatively, here's one even less specific:

> 2-94 DRAFT The Social Security number shall be entered.

The first statement demonstrates an example of passive voice. Using the active voice, it will read as follows:

> 2-95 The user shall enter Social Security number.

The big difference is the change from *shall be entered* to *shall enter*, which is more active with the verb *be* removed and more concise, as it has one less word and four fewer letters. In fact, the sentence went from ten words to seven. This gets the requirement even more concise, the fourth attribute for a good requirement.

In the second example, who should enter this code? Should the system use machine learning because it should know all the Social Security numbers (SSNs) for every user? That might work if it is internal to a company. In fact, that would be a very good requirement. Alternatively, should the user enter it? The statement is unclear. Make it clear by specifying who enters it.

▒ **Note** I have to admit that I fail to write in the active voice in every *shall* statement. In fact, if you look through this chapter, you may find some examples. In those cases, I was attempting to make a teaching point, or the requirement structure may dictate passive verbs.

An organization's style may drive you to passive statements sometimes, so watch for it.

■ **Real-World Note** I will finish up with a situation that happened to show an odd example of how active verbs were involved with me. Some years ago, I wrote a transition plan for a new application that we were preparing to replace a legacy system. As part of that effort, I drafted the plan and then sent the document out within my organization for review. Another person had a comment on the document where she said, "It needs more active verbs." Not only was I a little surprised by this, because the style of the organization was to not attribute who would do something, therefore forcing passive voice more than I liked to do. That said, she even had a list of active verbs she recommended that she passed to me—in the meeting, in front of everyone. I had one of my buddies come up to me later and said, "I could not believe you did not go off on her." I did not, as you cannot. If you do, it only gets you a reputation that you may not want to have. However, I did a little investigation. I looked at her list, and I had included all of her verbs except one, procure. In addition, it made sense that I would not use that one since by the transition to production phase, everything had long since been procured. I then looked through the first three of my seven sections (it was a long document and I did not need to be exhaustive) to find the active verbs I had used that she had not considered. My list was comparable to hers. Therefore, I wrote her an email with my findings. I explained about her list and gave her my list. My point with this anecdote is that active verbs versus passive verbs is a question of magnitude. A purist will say that you should have no passive verbs. However, when you have the other attributes to follow, passive verbs sometimes work better.

Understandable by Stakeholders

While the previous attribute is the hardest to achieve, this attribute "understandable by the stakeholder" is the absolute most critical of all the attributes. If the stakeholders do not understand what you have written, you will never move to the next phase, because the stakeholders will not accept the system—ever. Interestingly enough, trying to get the requirement "unambiguous" and "understandable by the stakeholder" may sometimes be mutually exclusive. English, despite what people will tell you, is not a precise language. Mathematics is a precise language. Why do you think all the scientists of the world (and probably universe) use it instead of any other language? Alas, you cannot write requirements in mathematics. (Hm, unless some smart person discovers a way to do so...but that is a digression.) That is why some people advocate using modeling and/or Extensible Markup Language (XML) or Unified Modeling Language (UML) to get more precision.

However, gentle reader, your stakeholders are not mathematicians, may not be able to follow various models, or read XML or UML (more about this in Chapter 12) because these techniques are rigorous and most of your stakeholders are not prepared for such rigor. Does that mean you have the wrong stakeholders? Absolutely not. They are where they are for a reason. They are the users of the system; they are the resident experts at using the applications to do their jobs well, which they do; and they are the managers of those people. If they were IT people, they would be in the IT department.

So, what is a requirement engineer to do?

Write, early and often. And listen. Listen intently. You have to listen to what people say when you interview them, when you sit in meetings with them, and when you read their e-mails and documents complaining about their problems. You have to read how they say things. See what is missing. By that, what terms are they not using? That will help you understand the technology terms that they do not know. Sometimes, you have no recourse but to teach them the new way. However, keep that to an absolute minimum when you are writing your requirements.

The Collection phase in Chapter 9 will examine this in detail; you will learn to listen carefully, and by getting the users engaged in the process, you will establish a rapport. Do not destroy that rapport by writing requirements that they do not understand. Once you lose them, it is very difficult to get them back.

■ **Real-World Note** Some years ago, I was meeting with the stakeholders, the people who would be actually using the system, not the managers who these people would report to who had a passing interest in the application. We had been discussing various requirements. One of the stakeholders gave a very emphatic requirement that they wanted us to meet. I had a junior requirements engineer with me who started to say that an International Organization for Standardization (ISO) standard made the requirement invalid. I put my hand on his arm to stop him talking before he completed his statement. I said, "This is your system, so we will do what you want. This standard does not apply to your situation." That stakeholder had his hand up with his finger pointed at me, as if to argue vehemently why we must do it. He stopped his finger in mid-jab, and said, "Oh." It was obvious, he expected an argument, and he did not receive it. There was a brief pause, and then we continued in a most congenial environment. I had listened very carefully to their real need and did not let some perceived standard stand in the way of capturing what they wanted. In this case, it dealt with some disputed territory that the standard violated their sovereignty. I established a rapport with them. I never had an issue working with these people thereafter.

Since you will write your requirements in English (or whatever language you use), you will need to be grammatically correct. Honestly, if you have difficulty even writing one sentence, you may want to rethink this as a career path. Alternatively, if you think you are OK since you will manage the whole team and will not need to write requirements, you are sadly mistaken. You will be writing a lot of other things instead, like reports up the management chain and people evaluations, both subordinates as well as your own. In business, you need to be able to communicate, both verbally and written. If you have a challenge, fix it. Take classes and practice.

Part of the challenge to making this attribute work is that for you to succeed here, you may have to compromise some of the others, succinctness for example (aka conciseness). You may need to spell it in a bit more detail to convince the stakeholder what you mean. As stated at the beginning of this section, it is critical that you convince the stakeholders, so do whatever is necessary to achieve that, even if you must compromise on conciseness or other attributes. Thus, succeeding with this attribute will go a long way in mitigating the requirements problems. That is the payback for making requirements that the stakeholders understand and therefore accept them as their own.

Unique

Unique refers to not only that the requirement statement itself is unique from every other statement but also that reference to each statement is unique. If you have met the "do not duplicate" attribute, you will have unique requirement statements.

Thus, this is probably the easiest requirement attribute to achieve—providing a unique identifier. This allows you ease of finding and referencing a requirement.

You have seen several examples throughout this chapter, references like a number such as 4.3.1.7 or an alphanumeric such as QUE-103. This text does not recommend one approach over the other. That said, you will need to check your requirements tool as it may dictate what you can and cannot have. (Don't you hate dictatorial software?) There is one potential trap regarding numbers.

Something as simple as numbering requirements has risks? Yes, and here it is. Some people assign a group of numbers by functional areas before they start crafting their requirements. It might look like QUE-101 to QUE-200 for query requirements and RPT-1301 to RPT-1400. (We do not recommend this approach.) However, if you must, say because it is already instituted, here is the trap. What happens when you have 253 query requirements? You have not allowed sufficient space. So if you must do this, allow more numbers than you ever anticipate. Then multiply that number by at least 2 to ensure you cover all contingencies.

Wait, you might say, this text has not provided any examples of requirements written uniquely. Given how the text presented them, yes it has. Look at the requirements attribute, traced to a source, and you will see four examples that are uniquely written with unique identification.

As I said, this is an easy attribute. The best attribute was saved for last, one that is not as easy.

Verifiable

You must ensure that the developers accomplished what the users need. The key word here is verifiable. Many people will use the term *testable*. They are incorrect. Testing is only one aspect of verification, which can be accomplished by the following means:

- Testing
- Demonstration
- Inspection
- Simulation
- Analysis

You can remember this with mnemonic STAID. (No, this has nothing to do with the word *staid* or its meaning of sedate. Nor does it have anything to do with the character of a requirements engineer. It is important to put that to rest very quickly.)

Now, on to the discussion about each one of these types of verification. Wait, why do REs need to go into the specifics of the types of verification? For a couple of reasons. First, on many projects, you will need to propose a candidate verification method for each requirement. You are not going to define how to verify it; just choose a method. Naturally, you should work jointly with the test lead. Alternatively, at worst, after you have proposed a draft, have the test lead review your proposals.

Second and more importantly, you need to know these types of verification so that you can make a reasonable assessment regarding the verifiability of your requirements. You need to look at a definition of each one of the following:

- *Test*: A measurement to prove or show, usually with precision measurements or instrumentation, that the project/product complies with requirements.
- *Analysis*: A quantitative evaluation of a complete system and/or subsystems by review/analysis of collected data.
- *Demonstration*: To prove or show, usually without measurement or instrumentation, that the project/product complies with the requirements by observation of results.
- *Inspection*: To examine visually or use simple physical measurement techniques to verify conformance to specified requirements.
- *Simulation*: Executing a model over time to simulate a portion of the system.

Now, here is an example of each type of verification.

Testing

This is by far and away the most common form of verification.

Here is a sample:

> 2-96 The BOSS Query Function shall generate results within 2 seconds of entry of the query 80% of the time.
>
> 2-97 The BOSS Query Function shall generate results within 30 seconds of entry of the query 100% of the time.

The previous definition said that *test* is a measurement to prove or show, usually with precision measurements or instrumentation, that the project/product complies with requirements. Clearly, the example is measurable to determine whether the requirement is met. Notice this example gave a value less than 100 percent of the time; you need to give some upper limits. Obviously, with an example for 99.99 percent of the time, it begs the question what happens that last 0.01 percent of the time. If you never specify anything, then a developer might think he has an infinite time to complete that last percent. Never give them an out.

■ **Real-World Note** I had a developer tell me that because the requirements document did not explicitly state that February 32 was invalid, he did not need to validate dates. He was categorically wrong as an older version of the requirements document did have it listed, but it shows you how silly some people can be. The person was being absolutely serious. You cannot make this stuff up.

Inspection

The previous definition said that an inspection examines visually or uses simple physical measurement techniques to verify conformance to specified requirements. Now, look at the following example:

> 2-98 The BOSS Query Function shall generate its queries using a SQL server.

■ **Note** SQL = Structured Query Language.

Accept that this is a valid requirement (some may argue that point, but there are instances that it applies—for organizational or architectural reasons). In this case, you need a way to see the query statements generated by BOSS, and by looking at it (examining) you can determine whether they are SQL statements or not.

The inspection may be as simple as looking at just one element to pass the requirement. For example, in the following requirements

> 2-99 The BOSS Central Code module shall have the name of the vendor who wrote it.

all you have to do is look at the code for that single module and see whether the vendor's name exists. If so, the requirement passed.

Now back to the earlier SQL statement requirement, which may take a great deal of inspection to ensure the full spectrum of SQL statements is addressed. This could take dozens or more inspections, depending how they are generated.

Another example that is more frequent with hardware development is shown here:

> 2-100 The BOSS computing device shall have a Universal Serial Bus (USB) port for connecting external devices.

All you have to do is look at the outside of the device to see whether a USB port exists. Naturally you will have to verify that it operates, but that would be additional requirements.

Demonstration

A demonstration proves or shows, usually without measurement or instrumentation, that the project/product complies with requirements by observation of results.

As a follow-on to the last requirement in the previous section, examine the following requirement:

> 2-101 The BOSS computing device USB port shall allow the connection of a USB drive and recognize the files therein.

In this case, you connect the USB drive into the BOSS USB port, and if the BOSS displayed the files, you have demonstrated this requirement.

Simulation

The previous definition said that a simulation is executing a model over time to simulate a portion of the system. NASA uses this technique quite often to duplicate environments that do not exist on Earth or are hard to duplicate. Take a look at the following requirement:

> 2-102 The BOSS Venus Probe shall survive 250 mph winds.

Earth does not have speeds that fast here naturally (thankfully). Therefore, a wind tunnel of significant speed would need to be built to test this requirement to simulate the winds. That does not mean you have simulated absolutely every detail, but as closely as practical. Of course, anyone who knows anything about Venus knows it has very high temperatures and crushing pressures to consider as well, but you were just examining one requirement.

For software, consider the following requirements:

> 2-103 The BOSS Query Function shall handle an average of 50 users at a time with no degradation to query response times.

> 2-104 The BOSS Query Function shall a peak load of 200 users for an hour with only twenty percent addition to the query response times during that hour.

You may be unable to get 50 users to test this, let alone have 200 people trying to test this. The best bet is to have a simulation package that duplicates the actions of a user to put the appropriate levels of stress to the system.

Analysis

Analysis is defined as a quantitative evaluation of a complete system and/or subsystems by review/analysis of collected data. You will verify the following requirement by analysis:

> 2-105 The BOSS game device shall have a mean time before failure of 200 hours. (It costs $10, so don't expect it to last forever!)

Here you would have collected all the run times of the ten devices you ran for two weeks straight without turning them off. Tabulate all the time they ran before they failed. Total the number and divide by ten. If the result is greater than 200 hours, the requirement passes.

Remember that you may have requirements where you stress the system by turning it on and off every ten minutes for the entire two weeks to see what that does to the time to failure. (Who and how they test that for two weeks 24 hours a day is for the test team to address, and they would suffer through the sore fingers.) You get the idea for analysis.

Code reviews are a form of analysis where other people on the team, or senior programmers, look at a developer's code to see potential errors. For example, if coding standards exist, the code is analyzed against that standard. Standards help not only to eliminate bugs, but in the long run to ensure maintenance. Keep in mind that people do not stay on a project forever, so someone else may have to maintain it. Coding standards help with that transition.

Wrap-Up of Verifiable

A requirement is verifiable if there exists a cost-effective process with which a person or machine can check that the software product meets the requirement. Think back to that Venusian probe. If you had a test budget of $100,000 for the entire probe, odds are you could not verify the wind speeds, let alone the temperature and pressure requirements. In fact, you probably could not afford to build it, if that is the size of your test budget, but that is another matter.

Finally, nonverifiable requirements include phrases like *works well, good, user-friendly* (see the earlier example with this as an alleged requirement), and *usually happen*. These words cannot be verified because it is impossible to define the terms *good, user friendly, well,* and *usually*.

If a method cannot be devised to determine whether the software meets a particular requirement, then that requirement is not verifiable and either you should remove it or, most likely, you should revise it.

One More Attribute: Modifiable

You have examined 16 attributes for individual requirements. Granted, some have applicability to all or part of the entire group, like traceability. You might consider at least one more that you might hear about—modifiable.

■ **Note** You may read about others in some sources, but they are most likely just different terminology for ones addressed here. Alternatively, you can consider them so minor as to not spend time here. You are trained well enough to determine whether their suggestion has merit.

The 830-1998 standard includes this one. It applies modifiability to both the individual requirement and the entire group of them. Every requirement is modifiable by very definition, so there is no reason to focus any time on it.

Modifiability with regard to a document or a group of requirements deals with how modifiable that document or database is. Organization is important, and breaking groups of requirements that have functional similarity is important. This supports a document's table of content, index, and cross-references to other documents. Document organization will be examined in Chapter 7.

Capability Within a Requirement

Examine one more aspect within a *shall* statement. You will have seen the phrase "the capability to" in some of the requirements already shown as examples in this book. This is not an attribute of a requirement but a convention many if not most REs use. This phrase, "the capability to," has a very specific meaning. It means allowing the user the option to do something. Here's an example:

> 2-106 The BOSS Access Control function shall provide a capability to assign an access control list to search results.

This means the user has the option to assign an ACL to search results. However, the user does not need to do it for every search result. Look at the following statement:

> 2-107 DRAFT The BOSS Access Control function shall automatically provide a capability to assign an access control list to search results.

Does this make sense? Do *automatically* and *provide the option* go together? No, the system does not make choices every time. Yes, there could be rules where decisions are made, but those are specific rules, and the system is not really deciding but just following rules.

Usually the phrase *the capability to* is written as *provide the user the capability to.* There are developers who do not understand this. Therefore, it is your job as the RE to educate them. Sometimes this is easier than others.

■ **Real-World Note** I had one program where they had been using the phrase for more than ten years for providing any capability of the system, not as an option. I realized it was not worth the effort to try to reeducate an entire team. Besides there were more than 1,000 requirements and it was not worth the time and effort to fix it for little value added, since the system was being replaced and these developers would not be part of the new system.

Types of Errors That Can Occur with Requirements

Capers Jones, on Dr. Dobb's web site (see the "Reference" section), said there are three chronic problems with requirements.

- Many requirements are dangerous or toxic and should be eliminated.
- Some clients insist on stuffing extra, superfluous features into software.
- Requirements are never complete and grow at rates greater than 1 percent per calendar month.

Dangerous or Toxic Requirements

First, you should learn what one of these kinds of requirements is. These are requirement defects that testing may not detect. One of the most prominent examples of a toxic requirement was the Y2K bug. Requirements for years had been written to capture dates including years. However, no one ever specified the format of the year. That was left to programmers who for decades, because of space considerations in storage (when it was very expensive), wrote the year as the last two digits. Instead of 1929, it was stored as 29. In the 1960s, when a program was written, no one worried about the year 2000 as it was so far away. However, after the year 2000, if the year was 29, would it be 2029 or 1929?

How do you prevent these? As was said, testing may not catch it as tests were written based on the assumption of the year as two digits. So, using formal reviews of requirements helps to eliminate them. Why? You draw from other people's experience to recognize good requirements versus these toxic or dangerous ones.

Extra, Superfluous Requirements

This was talked about this earlier in the "Prioritized Attribute" section of this chapter. When all stakeholders prioritize and rank requirements, this helps to identify these. Even if people do not say, "I see no need for this," others will push it so far down the priority list that it is not likely to ever be worked on.

■ **Real-World Note** Some years ago, I was holding a meeting where we were ranking changes requested from the users. One of the newer people said, "If my change is considered a Low priority, even with a High ranking, with emphasis on working off all the High and Medium priorities, my change is likely to never be worked on." Absolutely correct. That was when I knew the whole group of stakeholders really understood.

Incomplete Requirements

Studies have shown that requirements grow from 1 to 4 percent per month. This is where one of the major drawbacks came with the traditional waterfall method. The project would spend the beginning period of the project defining requirements and freeze them for the rest of the development.

In the Jones article mentioned earlier, he states that 15 percent is a good annual growth rate. Taking that as a conservative representation of reality, in six years, you will have doubled your number of requirements. If your program took that long, think how out of touch with the needs of the users you will be.

How do you fix that? Various methods evolved from the waterfall development methodology to ultimately (now, at least) achieving the agile approach where requirements are defined in detail just before the work is done. This helps with capturing the reality at that point. Then changes are considered as they are known. It may not be perfect, but it works considerably better than the waterfall approach. This will be discussed much more in Chapter 13.

Others

Several problems were discussed in the attribute sections, such as missing or wrong requirements, or ambiguity. In other readings, you may encounter discussions of *misplaced requirements*. This means a requirement is placed in the wrong section in the document. In Chapter 11, you will learn about management of requirements in a database. How is something misplaced in a database? By misplaced requirements, if you group like requirements (e.g., search, reporting, access) into functional areas and user access requirements are in the search section, that is what is meant by misplaced.

However, what if you have a requirement like the following?

> 2-108 The BOSS Access Control function shall provide a capability to assign an access control list to search results.

You would think this belongs to the Access Control section. However, it also talks about search. Should it go there instead? On the other hand, should it be in both? You would argue that it may not be a big deal since a good database has searching and filtering that will allow you to find these when you need it. Never should it be in both, since that means you have duplicate requirements. Remember that.

References

IEEE-SA Standards Board. "IEEE Std 830-1998, IEEE Recommended Practice for Software Requirements Specifications." Sponsor: Software Engineering Standards Committee of the IEEE Computer Society, Approved 25 June 1998, p4, 6-7, 8.

Wikipedia. "Requirement." Feb. 2015. `http://en.wikipedia.org/wiki/Requirement`

Wiegers, Karl, and Joy Beatty. Software Requirements, Third Edition, Microsoft Press, 2013.

Davis, Alan M. *Software requirements: Objects, Functions, and States*. Prentice-Hall, Inc. Upper Saddle River, NJ, 1993, p191 to 193

United States Government. "Resources for understanding and implementing Section 508." Feb. 2015, `www.section508.gov/`

Lou Wheatcraft. October 9, 2012. "Using the correct terms—Shall Will Should." Requirement Experts. Feb. 2015, `www.reqexperts.com/blog/2012/10/using-the-correct-terms-shall-will-should`

Jones, Capers. "Chronic requirements problems." November 26, 2012. The World of Software Development. Dr Dobb's. Feb. 2015, `www.drdobbs.com/architecture-and-design/chronic-requirements-problems/240012797`

Exercises

Exercise 1

Examine the 16 attributes of a requirement and rank the order that you should accomplish them and why. Ties are acceptable. Maybe a flow chart or swim lanes might help depict it.

Exercise 2

For half of the 16 attributes, write an example hardware requirement for each one, ones that are different from those already provided in the book. Which half? Good question, and we don't care. You can do the first eight, the odd numbers, the even number, or only the prime numbers. It is your choice.

Exercise 3

For the other half of the 16 attributes that you did not use in Exercise 2, write an example software requirement for each.

Exercise 4

Try to rewrite these requirements eliminating the negative from the statement:

a. The system shall not override use selected contrast and color selections as prescribed in Section 508.

b. The system shall not disrupt or disable activated operating system accessibility features.

c. The system shall not use color coding as the only means of conveying information, indicating an action, prompting a response, or distinguishing a visual element.

d. The system's software shall not use flashing or blinking text, objects, or other elements having a flash or blink frequency greater than 2Hz or lower than 55 Hz.

e. If the search is too complex, the system shall not crash while executing a search.

f. When the system identifies spelling errors, the system shall not auto-correct without user acceptance.

g. The system report generator shall not require a per seat license fee for every user.

Exercise 5

Write requirements to define what the customer wanted in Figure 2-2.

CHAPTER 3

Specialized Language

Every organization, even down to the project level, has its unique way of communicating. Is it to be exclusionary? No. Well, at least that is the case the vast majority of the time. As an RE, you will have to be precise with your use of language. As it turns out, most people have developed special words, phrases, terms, acronyms, abbreviations, and meanings as a way to do that with their respective organizations, even down to the project level. In addition, they try to do this the most economical way possible in their communications. While a requirement or user story is a contract between the user and the developer, it is *not* written in legalese. You do not need to be a lawyer to write requirements. In fact, most lawyers could not do requirements work, as they are not trained to think like an engineer.

That said, you have to recognize that when you start on a project, you need to learn what means what. You need to communicate the way the people do in your organization and the respective project.

The Use of Language

As a requirements engineer, you need to be very precise. Mathematics is very precise. An equation has only one meaning. Unfortunately, words and language are not so precise. Words have different meanings. How people use words is influenced by factors such as who they are, such as HR versus engineers, and how their cultures vary. By cultures, I am not just talking about cultures in different countries or even regions within a country; even companies have different cultures. For example, Google has an "innovate" culture, whereas an organization like the U.S. Army, with its strict discipline, clearly has a different one. Even departments within an organization can develop different cultures. A programmer by their need to create software focuses their culture to support that work, being very detailed and sometimes very structured. However, human resources, which deals with people on a daily basis, can have a much more flexible approach in part because no person is identical and how to interact with them is much more of an art form. These cultural differences can influence the language these diverse people use.

That means you have to know what the meanings of words signify to the affected parties. Just because they say the same thing does not equate to the same meaning. Look at a dictionary, and see how many words have different interpretations. Are they wrong? No, it is just that where they come from influences what they mean.

G. Koelsch, *Requirements Writing for System Engineering*,
DOI 10.1007/978-1-4842-2099-3_3

For example, on a project to develop a records management application, the records managers used the term *recall*. To them this means recalling a hard-copy document from the physical archive where it was stored. Meanwhile, to the developers, who think database-centric, *recall* means deleting a record in the database that was incorrect.

Is either definition incorrect? No. However, unless you know these two definitions existed and they are shared with both parties, you can see that communications will quickly become difficult.

How do you fix this? First, you have to listen actively. By that, I mean intently. If the sentences surrounding specific words seem not to match up, then ask questions about the meanings. Also, read documentation about how people do their business. You will get context for words and help to understand their usage. It is not always easy, but with time, you will get used to it.

■ **Real-World Note** I actually have done rocket science before. As such, I participated in a meeting where people argued for an hour what a month was. Sounds silly—a month is a month. Right? Well, in this case, three different groups were arguing. One used a calendar month, another used a lunar month, and the third used a sidereal month. Therefore, it turns out they were all correct. Alas, being junior at the time, I did not really understand the issue. The real issue was that each person had their own system coded with their definition. The three groups needed to interface with each other. I did not identify the real problem at the time. It was that group A wanted to keep their definition and make everyone else write the code to convert their value to their. Group B wanted the same for their definition, as did Group C. What was the correct solution? Each group should calculate the cost associated with that group for all three definitions. Then the costs from each group would be totaled for each definition to determine the total cost that is the least, and that was what should be done.

The lesson here is that language is important. However, not every issue is the fault of communication or language, but there are hidden issues and hidden agendas. Not always are words the real problem. The example in the Real-World Note demonstrates the phrase "reading between the lines" since the people were using word precisely, yet their real message was misdirection. In this case, one side will want the other two to take the cost. Remember, resources are a significant influence. (Sometimes it is the most easily understood metric, so people default to it.) Empire building is also important to some. However, that is a topic for another book. Trying to understand these hidden meanings can be difficult. The example happened earlier in my career, and I did not recognize the real issue because I had not really experienced enough to recognize it. By alerting you to it, you may be able to "read between the lines" sooner. Experience will definitely help with this. You could argue that I have not helped you if experience is the only solution. On the contrary, telling you to be aware of it will help you by knowing that this can happen. I wished someone had alerted me to the likelihood of it back when this happened. That said, it is possible that even my more seasoned colleagues may not have recognized it. Thus, they may learn something from this discussion.

Lexicon on a project is the words and phrases unique to that environment, and they are very important. The challenge for you as an RE is to understand that phrases have specific meanings. For example, look at these two definitions:

SRD: System Requirements Document

SRS: System Requirements Specifications

Sometimes SRD and SRS mean the same thing on one project, yet on another project, the SRD relates to the requirements definition phase, where the SRS relates to the design phase. Neither is wrong; it just depends on terminology of project or the particular organization. Because of the importance to each project, you must ask what goes into each document.

Defining Specialized Terms

Words have different meanings, and you need to find those words that have different meanings as they relate to the project, which can be more specific to the project. You should identify these specific terms, capture them, be able to use them appropriately, and even in some cases educate others who are using them inappropriately.

For example, *recall* was a jargon word for the database experts. In the software industry, there are many words that take on specific means, like *bit* has a very specific meaning for IT, whereas for the non-IT savvy public it just means something very small. The previous section dealt with the clash of jargons. The discussion here talks about the learning you will have to do to become proficient in the project and organizational jargon.

How do you do this? Pretty much the same way presented in the "The Use of Language" section in this chapter. Also, read whatever documentation you can find. There is online help for existing systems that can provide help. Look for any business process documents, concept of operations, or any other document that might help to explain what the project and organization does. Most importantly, pay particular attention to the glossary section. That will go a long way to help you learn the meaning of jargon for a particular project and/or organization. For example, in the discussion about *recall*, you would provide the two different meanings. It is a good idea to identify what organization or group of people use the particular meaning. This way, when you meet with these people, you will likely remember their particular definition.

It does not hurt to create your own glossary document that is a compilation of all the terms you run across in your research. It may not hurt to include the source of the meaning (document, organization, etc.) as you may learn different projects or offices have different meanings for the same terms. Now you have a cross-reference. Creating this document early in the program helps you learn and later you have it for reference. When other new people come on board, you now have something to offer to them to help them up the learning curve. Also, you should consider terms that apply to requirements in general. Finally, you need a list specific for your set of requirements. If you write a requirements document, you will include it in the document. Or, if you have a database for your requirements, you should include them there also.

These definitions help when you work with people. When the terms are used, you can confirm the meaning. Not only does this ensure everyone understands, especially you, but this may help identify when people are using different meanings. This helps to mitigate confusion. This helps to eliminate ambiguity, as we talked about in Chapter 2.

The last, tried and true method is just the elapse of time. You will get exposed to everything important over time. As time advances, the number of jargon words will diminish. A subset of jargon (and not necessarily a small subset) is abbreviations and acronyms, which will be presented in the next section.

Acronyms and Abbreviations

Every project and every organization has its own list of abbreviations and acronyms. On your first day on a new program, you will be exposed to all these terms that people use. For example, if someone said "The RAM requirements generated most of the DRs on the STB." What they said was "The reliability, availability, maintainability requirements generated most of the deficiency reports on the system test bed." Chances are that you will not know all those meanings. This is the shorthand the team uses to help with communications. It gets so ingrained that, after a period of time, not everyone remembers the precise definition, just what it represents.

How do you overcome your gap in understanding? You have to learn these acronyms. All of them? Well, not always, but you do need the ones you use 90 percent of the time. It just takes time where you hear them a lot, ask people what they mean, read documents and check which ones they use, and start using the acronyms yourself to get comfortable with them.

■ **Real-World Note** I have a technique I developed and use for every project. When I first show up, I capture every abbreviation I hear and ask what they are. I then create a text file with them listed in alphabetical order. This does two things. One, I have a handy reference that I can use for reference during the learning curve as I come up to speed on the project. Over time, as new people come onto the project, I become very popular as I have a tool that I give to people to help them with their learning curve. Second, by virtue of keying in the acronym or abbreviation, it helps to reinforce in my mind what it means.

In the old days when REs wrote requirement documents (before spreadsheets and databases), the first time they used an abbreviation and acronym, they spelled it out and showed its abbreviation or acronym in parentheses after it [e.g., United States of America (USA)], and thereafter in the document, they used only the abbreviation or acronym.

■ **Note** This text follows this practice of writing out the meaning and following it by the acronym or abbreviation. In addition, the practice includes adding a summary of all acronyms and abbreviations at the end of the document. See Appendix A for the list in this book.

When REs moved off the documents to, say, a database, they needed to modify this approach. You now follow that rule within the requirements or user stories only. By that, look at the following example:

> 3-1 3.2.1 The Audit Reporting Service (ARS) shall only allow the ARS admin role to access the ARS to prevent unauthorized users from seeing the report.
>
> 3-2 3.2.2 The Audit Reporting Service (ARS) report shall consist of...

Notice requirement 3-2 spelled out the same abbreviation in requirement 3.2.2. Why? Excellent question. Since they are right next to each other, and if the requirements were printed out, it would be redundant. Did you say you are supposed to minimize redundancy? Absolutely. However, with the advent of databases, you might query and/or print out only a group of requirements. What happens if 3.2.2 is separated from 3.2.1, which introduced the abbreviation, and it was spelled it out there only? Then the reader would not know precisely what it means, possibly causing confusion. In addition, one developer might do the development of the authorization section, whereas a different developer does the reports. If you spell the acronym out in both, now you can separate the requirements.

How many should you expect? The realistic answer is that it depends. What is the breadth of the project and the organization? Sometimes it has been only a few hundred. Look at how many exist in this book in Appendix A as an example. Long-lived projects that have wide usage and an organization that is widespread could have orders of magnitudes more. Yes, more than one order of magnitude.

Early in my career, someone suggested if it had been a long time (the definition of *long* was subjective) since someone had seen an acronym, it should be redefined. In fact, some authors use the guidance to spell them out on the first use in each chapter unless the book is specifically a linear tutorial. Readers of technical books in particular are highly nonlinear in the way they use the material, so it behooves them to follow this guidance.

■ **Real-World Note** I worked for a DoD organization some years ago. I was in the process of managing two different source documents that each had more than 400 pages each, with more than 40 abbreviations and acronyms on each page. If I had access to an intern or summer-only person who needed something to keep them busy, I might have been able to combine the two and reconcile the duplicates. I did not, so I had more than 32,000 abbreviations and acronyms in those documents. Now the two documents included most of the abbreviations and acronyms used throughout DoD, and this would not be typical of what you will experience. It does give you an idea of the upper limit. A couple of thousand is not unusual.

Learn to use the ones you encounter routinely, and just have the list ready for the infrequent times you need it. You can call up this acronym list as one of the first files each day to use for reference. It should be one of your everyday tools. This is not limited to just requirements engineers but anyone on a program. This is also a tool that can be used to help communication across groups and ensure everyone reading the requirements is on the same page.

■ **Note** You may have noticed that many times I just said "acronyms" rather than "acronyms and abbreviations." To be precise, an acronym is the first letter of a phrase that is capitalized and it can be pronounced, like RAM used earlier. LASER is another one that means Light Amplification by Stimulated Emission of Radiation. An abbreviation is the first letter of a phrase that is capitalized, but it cannot be pronounced. In the earlier phrase in the first paragraph of this section, DR and SBT fit the abbreviation definition. You just say the letters DR and SBT rather than trying to force a pronunciation. What has become standard in the IT industry is to just say "acronyms" to include acronyms and abbreviations.

Summary

In this chapter, you learned about precision in language. Many projects and organizations have special meanings for words that may not be consistent with how you have used it in the past, so you will have to recognize these meanings. Acronyms are shorthand used by many, such that it almost appears to be a foreign language the first time you read or hear it. You will need to learn these frequently used ones, and have a list for the less frequently ones. Basically, you will learn the specialized language for wherever you work.

Exercises

Exercise 1

List three examples of terms or phrases that you can think of that can have different meanings that might be important to a project (not ones already presented in this chapter).

Exercise 2

List how many different acronyms have been presented up to this point in this book.

PART II

Types of Requirements

CHAPTER 4

Functional Requirements

Now that you understand the attributes of a good requirement, you will consider the different types of requirements. Why do you care about the different types of requirements? "Shouldn't I just start collecting and writing them?" Interesting question. How will you know where to start? More importantly, how will you know when to stop? What are the different types or categories of requirements that will help you know when you have captured all you need?

There are two major types that will be discussed, functional and nonfunctional requirements. In this chapter, we will take a general look at requirements but then focus on the functional types. In Chapter 5, we'll examine the nonfunctional types.

Understanding Types of Requirements

As noted, there are functional and nonfunctional types of requirements. There are other types subordinate to them, which you will see in this and the next chapter. When you look at other sources that discuss requirements, you will see almost as many variations in what they describe as the different types as there are different sources. The intention here is not to be the definitive definition but to capture as complete a list of the different types of requirements you need to capture so you have as comprehensive a set as practical. Remember one of those sources of errors that was mentioned earlier that said "not capturing all the requirements?" That is why you are examining these types so you mitigate the risk of missing requirements.

So, how do we define the two main types of requirements?

> *A functional requirement describes what functions a system (i.e., hardware and software) should perform.*
>
> *A nonfunctional requirement describes how the system should behave and defines what constraints are placed upon the system's behavior.*

You may not fully understand the differences quite yet. In the subsequent sections, you will examine a list of the different kinds of requirements that fall into each category to get a better understanding. The quick and easy way is that anything that does not fall into

G. Koelsch, *Requirements Writing for System Engineering*,
DOI 10.1007/978-1-4842-2099-3_4

the function requirements does fall into the nonfunctional requirements. Some sources will use the term *behavioral* requirements instead of functional and use *nonbehavioral* requirements instead of nonfunctional. They mean precisely the same thing.

Naturally, this text will reinforce the requirements with examples, many of which you saw in Chapter 2.

At some point in your career, you may be exposed to some types not considered in this book. For example, if you are involved with a satellite development program or a DoD program for the nuclear battlefield, you may have something called *survivability*. This means surviving in a hostile environment, like the vacuum of space with the hot and cold extremes, or surviving blast, thermal, and radiation exposures of a nuclear detonation. You will have to determine which category these requirements fall into. For the example of survivability, I would put it in the nonfunctional requirements.

There are potentially many different stakeholders who have an interest in getting these nonfunctional and functional requirements correct. This is because for many large systems the people buying the system are completely different from those who are going to use it (customers and users). There may be one significant factor that you cannot control: cost. The reality of financial constraints may limit some of the requirements you write. That is a trade-off analysis you will not spend time on in this text.

Now let's look at the various types of functional requirements and then turn to the nonfunctional types in the next chapter.

Types of Functional Requirements

Functional requirements define *what the system should do*. You will look at examples of the various functional types in this chapter. Remember that you have seen many examples when you examined the attributes of a good requirement, so a number of these will look familiar. The following list outlines the types of functional requirements we'll be looking at in this chapter:

- Business rules
- Transaction corrections, adjustments, and cancellations
- Administrative functions
- Authentication
- Authorization levels
- Audit tracking
- External interfaces
- Certification requirements
- Searching/reporting requirements
- Historical data
- Archiving
- Compliance, legal, or regulatory requirements

- Structural
- Algorithms
- Database
- Power
- Network
- Infrastructure
- Backup and recovery

As you look at the list of the types of functional requirements, you might think that some are unique to software or hardware. This can be the case. However, in most cases, these types can apply to both. In each subsection, you will examine at least one example to represent both the hardware and software needs to demonstrate that it applies to both. You will see a requirement highlighted if one type is unique to one or the other. In addition, the same approach applies to the nonfunctional requirement types.

Business Rules

Business rule requirements will generally be the larger section since many requirements can fall into this. What do you need your system to do? What are the features you need to have it do for you?

For example, in the Radiation collection example, you could start with this:

> 4-1 The BOSS Unit Radiation Dosimeter shall collect radiation exposure from nuclear fallout in a nuclear battlefield for the individual who is wearing the dosimeter.

You need to define all the features and activities for the various functions within the system. This chapter will address all these functional requirement types. In Chapter 7, you will learn how to organize documents (if you need to make a hard copy of your files or database). In Chapter 11, you will learn how to organize the requirements in the requirements database, although using the structure you learn about in this chapter is one approach. Remember, there is no one correct way to organize it. It is whatever works for you and your organization. You'll learn more about that later.

For a software example, you can have the following:

> 4-2 The BOSS Payroll Function shall capture all payroll activities for the BOSS Company.

Realize that this is just one of many such requirements you will need to list to completely define your system. Obviously, this is a high-level requirement that needs subordinate requirements. For example, you might have the following:

> 4-3 The BOSS Payroll Function shall capture all people who will have payroll activities within the BOSS Company.

Based on the discussion earlier, 4-2 is a parent requirement, and 4-3 is a child requirement. That relationship was not obvious until you crafted requirement 4-3.

What kinds of features do you need to capture? The simple answer is everything. While the answer is simple, actually doing so is more challenging. Naturally, you will analyze this in more detail in Chapter 9. However, you will need to define all the kind of information that needs to be created, read, updated, and deleted (also known as CRUD—and no, it is not cruddy!), searched, reported on, and any other operations that need to be performed on it.

For hardware systems (with embedded software or not), you need to define everything it must do. Think of a car. At a very high level, you need to move from point A to point B. Then you get down to details such as moving forward in more than one gear ratio and going in reverse, steering the vehicle, looking in multiple directions, and so on.

Think of your phone. You need to be able to communicate with another person. So, you need to be able to connect with other phones (which implies some phone standards, but more on that later). You need to be able to receive calls. You want to have preloaded contacts that are easier to select from rather than remembering the phone numbers from memory. (Unlike the pre-digital age, you had to remember them.) Now, you want the ability to take pictures, see video, and so on. You need to break all these functions down into groups and then define all the requirements.

Transactions

This topic will cover several aspects of transactions. Not only will you examine entry of a transaction, but changing, deleting, deactivating/cancelling, and error checking and handling. I broke this into three sections, transaction entry, transaction change, and transaction errors, so you can see how to handle each.

Transaction Entry

Now the first logical step to build up information is to add data. You should start with entering one record. Here is an example:

> 4-4 The BOSS Payroll Transaction function shall allow the designated user to bulk enter Personnel records into the system.

■ **Note** You need to define a person record in other requirements.

You could also enter multiple records.

> 4-5 DRAFT The BOSS Payroll Transaction function shall allow the designated user to bulk load Person records into the system.

You will need to define what bulk means, or you would not be certain what should be accomplished here.

> 4-6 The BOSS Payroll Transaction function shall allow the designated user to import multiple Person records into the system.

Transaction Change

As was said earlier, if you can enter something, you can craft a requirement for update or change an individual transaction.

> 4-7 The BOSS Payroll Transaction function shall allow the designated user to modify a Person record in the system.

For your specific project, you will have to see whether the same will apply for multiple transactions.

Now you must examine delete, cancel, and deactivate. Should all records be deleted? In most cases, no. Usually once you create a record, you will be doing other things to it. Take the example where a company hires you, and they create your person record in the payroll system. You work for five years, and you get a paycheck, so that person record in the payroll system has five years of salary information. Should that be deleted? No. There are legal reasons why that information should not be deleted. In this case, once you leave, they will deactivate your person record.

> 4-8 The BOSS Payroll Transaction function shall allow the designated user to deactivate a Person record in the system.

Does that mean a record should never be deleted? There are special circumstances, like when a record is entered with the data so incorrect (especially in an import that went wrong) that someone should be able to delete it, but on a very restricted basis.

> 4-9 The BOSS Payroll Transaction function shall allow the system administrator to delete a Person record in the system when the record was entered in error.

When you are initially populating a database and certain functions are not working quite correctly, you may need to delete a record. When training takes place on a database, you also may need to remove certain records. Again, this must be done on a very limited basis. Alternatively, maybe you will write requirements specifically for a training database. Should you document a development database? Or are you specifying training, testing, and development environments? That's something for you to consider.

Transaction Errors

Now look at errors. Maybe information was somehow entered incorrectly and needs to be fixed. In some cases, this can be done even before the transaction is stored.

Think of error conditions that occur.

> 4-10 The BOSS Payroll Transaction function shall check that the person identifier already exists in the system.

If the person is not in the system, what happens? The user should receive an error message. You may have seen such messages from some applications or maybe even operating system errors such as this:

> Error code 201

As a user, that tells you absolutely nothing. You have no idea what went wrong, and you certainly do not know how to fix it. You need a good explanation of what is incorrect and then how to repair it.

> 4-11 The BOSS Error Checking Function shall identify in clear text that an error has occurred with suggestions how to repair the condition but at least how to continue.

Whenever possible, you do not want an error message display that provides no way to continue. If you had a need to check that the area code of your one company building, you would want it to check the area code portion of the phone number and when 999 is entered, but 703 is a valid code, rather than just rejecting 999 as invalid. This is one area where you may spend a bit more time, giving more details. Look at all kinds of errors that might occur and have the error message give as much information as possible to the user. However, you have a good start.

Administrative Functions

Administrative functional requirements describe the functions that a system administrator (SA) performs on your system. Think of this as the person who can do virtually anything that most users cannot. These are the functions that maintain the system as a whole. The requirement should take the following form:

> 4-12 The BOSS System Administrator shall be able to (describe specific function).

First, make certain that there are at least two system administrators. The expression you may hear is, "What if he/she is hit by a bus?" First, you want to know where there are these crazed bus drivers so you can avoid them. Second, you should never be single-threaded no matter what management says. Have a requirement like this:

> 4-13 The BOSS System Administration function shall ensure at least two System Administrator accounts exist in the system.

What functions should they have? In some cases, data management in general is highly restricted, and the SA will perform all data-related functions, such as adding, changing, and deleting data. In other cases, there may be only a subset of data that is restricted to the SA. For example, give people accounts to the system as follows:

> 4-14 The BOSS System Administrator shall be able to add user accounts.

> 4-15 The BOSS System Administrator shall be able to change user accounts.

> 4-16 The BOSS System Administrator shall be able to deactivate user accounts.

> 4-17 The BOSS System Administrator shall be able to reactivate user accounts.

> 4-18 The BOSS System Administrator shall be able to delete user accounts.

You need to understand the difference between *deactivate* and *delete*. Deletion of accounts is a very rare case, say when a user erred when creating an account. Deactivate is when a person will no longer need access, although it could be reactivated again when the need arises—say a person has taken an extended leave of absence or gone to another part of the company, such as overseas.

SAs need the capability to manage system preferences and system values, back up and restore data, and generate and maintain system reports. Some system reports fall into the system monitoring reports that tell the SAs what the working condition is of the system, helping them to keep it running smoothly and efficiently.

If there are specific security levels within the system, the SAs usually maintain that. In some instances, there may be a security officer (SO) responsible for this function, but in others, the SA function performs it. Here the SA or SO assigns the different categories of access of the data or portions of the data. For example, if you have an HR system, most employees of the organization would have read access only. The HR personnel would have Add, Change, and Delete access. The SA or SO will create and maintain these levels.

SAs spend a significant amount of time monitoring the system; hence, most SAs are network or hardware types of individuals, where the maintenance of the accounts and other data manipulation is almost a secondary duty for them. However, your mileage may vary.

Authentication

Authentication is a mechanism to validate that the person or system is authorized to interact with the system. This is a mechanism put in place to verify the person/system is who they say they are. Think about paying for something online. When you pay via a credit card, you have to put in that three- or four-digit number on your card as a mechanism to prove you have the card. (Of course, that is not foolproof, such as when someone has your physical card.) There are devices to access computer systems to prove who you are. Think of biometrics where they read your fingerprint or perform a retinal scan as a way to ensure you are who you are.

Thus, the stakeholders will decide whether authentication is necessary for your system. It will aid in access control. The level of authentication then is important. For example, you could specify varying levels, like so:

> 4-19 The BOSS HR Regulation Function shall require fingerprint authentication to perform all tasks other than reading.
>
> 4-20 The BOSS HR Payroll function shall require retinal scan authentication to perform all tasks other than reading.

One area that is growing in use for authentication is biometrics. Therefore, it is important for you as an RE to know something about biometrics when you need to specify this type of authentication. First, the two requirements are one-for-one comparison. The system is only verifying you are who you say you are. This is not using, say, facial recognition at the airport to look for people on the no-fly list, where you are looking at all people and comparing them to a list of, say, thousands of people, a many-to-many comparison, which is much more difficult to accomplish than one-to-one comparison. One caveat with the many-to-many comparison usually applies only to identification. Since biometrics is being discussed here, the many-to-many comparison was included for completeness.

Additionally, and you can verify this by doing some research, biometric techniques have varying levels of confidence. Actually, facial recognition is one of the least effective (at the time of this writing, but it is improving) because of the few discrimination features and how faces vary day to day, with, say, facial hair or length of hair; the angles of the imaging versus the standard that it is compared to; and many other factors. Fingerprints are the most pervasive biometrics as they have been collected by far the longest, by decades. Retinal scans are the best at this point. (Obviously, DNA is the absolute best, but that is very difficult to use for a comparison needed in a matter of seconds or minutes—at least based on current technology.) However, each biometric has limitations for use.

Retinal scans would be difficult in airports. Think of the delays that would add to going through security. In addition, the public may be reluctant to expose themselves to it. Therefore, you must consider these factors. Do you need biometrics? If so, is it one-to-one, one-to-many, or many-to-many? What biometric should you use? If not biometrics, say you are in a trusted environment, what do you add to your system to authenticate the person or system? You need to look at the potential for harm if the system is compromised and the likelihood of it this compromise occurring. Here's an example:

> 4-21 The Nuclear, Chemical and Biological (NBC) Officer shall be able to authenticate access to the BOSS Unit Radiation Dosimeter by entering his/her service number.

While this information needs a level of control, it is not catastrophic if others knew the information, which is the reason for the lesser level of authentication. The payroll system in the first two requirements in this section is more of a risk than the HR regulations, which is the reason for the higher level of protection.

Authorization Levels

Earlier in the "Administrative Functions" section, you briefly saw varying access levels of the data mentioned. Therefore, for the access, the HR data would look something like this:

> 4-22 The BOSS HR regulations shall be able to read by all company employees.
>
> 4-23 The BOSS HR employee only shall be able to add HR regulations.
>
> 4-24 The BOSS HR employee only shall be able to change HR regulations.
>
> 4-25 The BOSS HR employee only shall be able to delete HR regulations.

You will have to determine whether deactivate and reactivate is necessary for each function where deletions are possible.

You should examine all types of data that reside in your system and determine who can CRUD (change, read, update, or delete)—HR regulations, personnel information, payroll data (while it might be nice, should everyone have change privileges to their salary?), vendor data, billing, and so on.

This is not limited to only database or software systems. Think of the BOSS radiation system. You may want to have only the NBC officer in the unit read the values of the BOSS individual dosimeters so they may be able to determine the likely effectiveness of units after exposure to a nuclear battlefield. Alternatively, you only allow military medical personnel to read the values of a given soldier to determine what treatments a given person may need. For this example, assume it is both. Therefore, you would have something like this:

> 4-26 The NBC Officer shall be able to run the BOSS Unit Radiation Dosimeter to collect the individual radiation exposures of a designated unit.
>
> 4-27 The Medical Doctor shall be able to run the BOSS Unit Radiation Dosimeter to collect individual radiation exposure of a given person to assist with radiation treatment.

Audit Tracking

Audit tracking here does not refer to an Internal Revenue Service (IRS) audit, although there is a similarity. This process tracks important data and what happens to that data. For example, you want an audit of all transactions that the SA does. Given that is the most powerful person on your system, you want to know the history of changes made. Therefore, you want statements like the following:

> 4-28 The BOSS Audit Function shall capture all adds, changes, deletions, deactivations, and reactivations made by all system administrators.
>
> 4-29 The BOSS Audit Function shall provide a report that capture all adds, changes, deletions, deactivations, and reactivations made by all system administrators.
>
> 4-30 The BOSS Audit Function shall provide a report that capture all adds, changes, deletions, deactivations, and reactivations made by a specified system administrators.
>
> 4-31 The BOSS Audit Function shall provide a report that capture all adds, changes, deletions, deactivations, and reactivations over a given time frame.
>
> 4-32 The BOSS Audit Function shall provide a report that capture all adds, changes, deletions, deactivations, and reactivations for specified data records.

Remember that there are a lot more variations that you may think of or need, depending on the analysis. Realize that these audits may help if you have an SA that causes a problem, but that is the rare case (assuming your organization has good policies and pay in place). More likely, if an issue happens with some data, the auditing will help track down the reason so that the problem can be fixed or at least prevented in the future.

You will also want to do auditing for access to the system. Therefore, you will need the following auditing requirements:

> 4-33 The BOSS Audit Function shall capture all adds, changes, deletions, deactivations, and reactivations to access made by all security officers.

> 4-34 The BOSS Audit Function shall provide a report that capture all adds, changes, deletions, deactivations, and reactivations made by all security officers.

There are more potential requirements depending on your needs. In addition, here are some requirements for the Unit Radiation Dosimeter:

> 4-35 The BOSS Unit Radiation Dosimeter Audit Function shall provide a report that capture all adds, changes, deactivations, reactivations, and deletions of access to the BOSS Unit Radiation Dosimeter.

> 4-36 The BOSS Unit Radiation Dosimeter Audit Function shall provide a report that capture all adds, changes, deletions, deactivations, and reactivations for specified data records.

Do you need auditing of everything that exists in your system? Well, it depends. On what? It depends on the importance of the data therein. You can see the importance of the data that an SA or SO does, so it obviously needs to be audited. Now think of the online game World of Warcraft. Do you think everything that happens on that is audited? With millions of users and all the activity they do, it is not likely. Therefore, it comes down to how important it is to track changes to the data. If it does not change frequently, such as HR regulations, then you probably want it; in fact, it is most likely required.

On a more business-related note, do you need to audit all reads of the system? Chances are you do not. That said, there may be specific types of data for which you may need to do so. For example, you may want to track all queries of the roles and responsibilities assigned to users. If managers and SAs are reading this information, that is probably OK, and even a person checking their own data is also permissible. However, wouldn't you like to know if one employee is searching all his/her co-workers' data? This may be an intrusion of some kind.

In addition, are there laws or policies that require it? That is a decision for you to make, but not in a vacuum, as there are specialized stakeholders who will help you decide this.

External Interfaces

When you examine external interfaces, you are evaluating a system, program, or application that is not part of the system, program, or application you are defining. For example, if you are defining the personnel system for your organization and the organization already has the access control application implemented organization-wide, the access control application is external to the personnel system. In this case, you should capture the following requirement:

> 4-37 The BOSS Personnel System shall provide all access functionality by interfacing with the BOSS Access Control Application.

This is only identifying what interface the personnel system must have. You must specify much more information to define exactly what all the elements are and in what formats. You will see this level of detail in Chapter 7.

You need to apply the same approach to hardware as well. For example, an aircraft needs to interface with air traffic control, so you need to define that. In this case, the air traffic control specification is defined first, and then all aircraft need to follow that interface. Otherwise, if the aircraft defined a different one each time, what kind of mess would you have in the air? Think of one place where you see this implemented—especially if you have traveled to other states and countries and had different rental cars. The dashboards for cars are inconsistently implemented, such that the controls, like wiper blade activation, are often not where you expect them to be. Thus, for the radiation detection system, you will define the following interface:

> 4-38 The BOSS Individual Radiation Dosimeter shall interface with the BOSS Unit Radiation Dosimeter using a USB connection.

■ **Note** Here you have specified what particular connection the system must use. It could be Bluetooth or other standard ones available.

Whenever practical (and that is the important aspect), use something that is commercially available to allow flexibility to use standard equipment. Again, you must specify much more information to define exactly what all the elements are and in what formats. As before, you will see this level of detail in the Chapter 7.

Certification Requirements

Are there certifications that your organization or government requires for work done on your system?

■ **Real-World Note** For example, I have worked on systems where a security certification is necessary or systems cannot go into production.

Therefore, you may need a requirement such as the following:

> 4-39 The BOSS shall meet the Security Certification specified by (enter the appropriate organization here, say ABC Company Security Office).

This may spawn additional requirements that are specified in the security certification process, so you need to do some examination of it.

This also may apply to hardware, both computers, as well as the BOSS Dosimetry project:

> 4-40 The BOSS Unit Radiation Dosimeter Calibration Source shall meet the Nuclear Regulatory Commission Radiation Certification.

Note Don't take this reference to the NRC radiation certification as gospel; this is just fiction made up for this text. You need to know the correct certification to meet. This is just illustrative.

You get the idea. This can be an empty section or very small, depending.

Searching and Reporting Requirements

For many computer systems, this can be a large portion of the requirements as you specify what search and reporting requirements you need. This is also important for any embedded systems where data is resident inside the system that various users need to retrieve. This section of requirements will tell you how the users can retrieve the data.

Many of the systems in the past dealt solely with Boolean searches. If you do not understand what this means, you will need to learn it ASAP. Therefore, this will likely be your first requirement:

> 4-41 The BOSS Search Function shall execute user specified queries using the following Boolean operators:

1. AND
2. OR
3. NOT
4. AND NOT
5. OR NOT
6. ()
7. NEAR—Term A and Term B are within N number of words

With the advent of more sophisticated search capabilities and the fact that many users are not trained Boolean users, other more robust techniques exist that may help users find what they need; for example, concept search exploits related terms without the user having to enter them specifically. For example, a user is interested in bombs. However, using Boolean-only operators, the user would need to have something like this:

> Find Bombs OR Explosives OR IED OR Weapons of Mass Destruction

You can see how quickly it gets complicated and still may miss something if they forget a particular word or phrase. (FYI, IED stands for Improvised Explosive Device.)

Thus, you probably want to have something like the following:

> 4-42 The BOSS Search Function shall execute user specified queries using the Concept Search capabilities to find terms that are related to terms entered by the user.

Examine an example for a medieval history class you might take. You need to find out about the Vikings. You would search on Vikings but not the Minnesota Vikings, so you might also omit football or NFL. However, did you consider Norse or Scandinavia or Scandinavian?

Writing good queries is an art form (just like writing good requirements). That said, requirements engineers need to provide the tools that could aid the user in finding the most correct information without overloading them with false hits. Another area that is growing in state-of-the-art querying is the use of machine learning. You will not see a big dissertation on this here as you can research it yourself if you do not understand it; however, it provides the capability to find subjects that may be close to what you are looking for, but you might not necessarily make a connection. There are many implementations of machine learning such as Latent Semantic Indexing (LSI), Entity Extraction, Natural Language Processing (NLP), and many more. You may need to add requirements for machine learning.

> 4-43 The BOSS Search Function shall exploit machine-learning techniques to find data that are related to terms entered by the user.

Again, this may be a high-level requirement that you need to decompose, but this is the start point.

Of course, you need to specify what data a user can query. In most cases, users can see everything within a database. Other times, you will restrict what they want. You will learn more about that in the "Security" section in Chapter 5. However, the user may want to restrict what data elements they want returned. If you have 45 data elements in your vendor data but you want only the company name, address, phone and fax numbers, and points of contact, you should allow users to define that.

> 4-44 The BOSS Search Function shall allow users to specify the data elements returned in their query results.

> 4-45 The BOSS Search Function shall allow users to specify the order data elements returned in their query results.

> 4-46 The BOSS Search Function shall allow users to specify the format of the data elements returned in their query results.

This allows users to control how the data looks to them. Of course, there are many more query/search requirements. That said, once you define good search requirements, you should be able to reuse these core requirements the rest of your career. This gets into the requirements reuse previously mentioned.

Will there be search requirements unique to systems? Absolutely, just as there are data elements unique to a particular program or system, the manipulation of some of these elements will be different. Reuse what you can. In fact, ask around. Someone else in the company or organization may have done your work for you. Use it if you can find it. (Sometimes it is hard to locate, but the reward is good once you find it. Think of it as a requirements treasure hunt—finding the gold at the end of the rainbow.)

Now, what is the boundary between search and reporting? Well, gentle reader, this distinction is very distinctly blurred. A search result presented on your screen is in its essence, a report, usually just provided to the requester. Some define a report as something more formal and possibly more detailed. The report may be automatically generated by the system, on a specific schedule, and even distributed to various consumers of the data. Of course, the traditional report is printed out, though now reports are often distributed electronically in PDF or other forms. Printing becomes a personal preference.

The point is that the need will exist to create a hard copy in some instances. Of course, you could always save the report to a file also.

Here comes the quandary. Do you provide only the report generator and let users define all their reports, or do you have some canned reports that the development team creates and maintains? Realistically, you will generally see a mixture. How many of the canned reports are created by development is the main variable.

You will need to have some of both, then. Therefore, you will start with the following:

> 4-47 The BOSS shall provide a report generating capability.

Again, this is a high-level requirement that you need to decompose, but this is the start point. Now you need to list all the functions you want the report generator to provide. As with the general search requirements, once you have described report generator requirements, that should be the last time you have to define them, reusing them thereafter. In addition, as stated, reuse if someone else has done the work. Why reinvent the wheel when someone did it for you?

If you strike out finding a prebuilt set, what should you do? Actually, this is quite easy. Do some research of what capabilities report generators do, convert them to requirements, and you are done. You should look at more than one report generator, as some may be more specialized than others. Some may focus more on graphical representations versus textual capabilities. How many different graphical representations do you want? How much flexibility in column and row specifications do you need?

Many times, you create several dozen user stories (more about these in Chapters 12 and 13) and more than 100 requirements. All of these requirements should be of the following format:

> 4-48 The BOSS report generating capability shall provide (enter the need here).

Do not forget to provide the ability to create report templates that users can reuse and modify to suit their needs or to copy existing reports and modify appropriately.

Next, have a section for the canned reports. Here, you will have the following form:

> 4-49 The BOSS Report Function capability shall generate a (Report Name) Report which included the following data values scheduled every (enter the time period here, e.g., daily, weekly, monthly, quarterly, annually, every third Wednesday).
>
> 1. Value A with Format NNNN
> 2. Value C with Format AAAAAA
> 3. Value D with Format NNAAA
> 4. Value Q with Format AAAAAAAAAAAAAAAAAAAAAAA

Is the canned report automatically generated, only manually activated, or both automatically and on occasion activated by a user? You have to specify it. Think about paper orientation, page size, and so on. What formats are reports saved to? Can they be exported to other applications, say Microsoft Excel or Microsoft Word or some other application your organization uses?

One word of caution with these two areas, search and reporting—cost. Given the number of capabilities in the market place, one likely solution is for the organization to buy a commercial, off-the-shelf package to do it. That is good. Why reinvent something someone else has already done? However, given the size of some organizations, you may want to place some constraints in the requirements set. For instance, you may want a requirement that says the following:

> 4-50 The BOSS Report Function capability shall not require a per-seat fee.

This is so that if you have an organization that has 5,000 people and a $10 per-seat license per year, you have a $50,000 bill just for your users every year. Some people may say this is out of scope for requirements, but REs should be responsible for the entire project, not just technical requirements. You will have to judge how much impact you can have. Ask for it, and the powers that be will take appropriate steps.

Compliance, Legal, or Regulatory Requirements

These are laws, regulations from government, compliance statements from organizations, and even internal policies and regulations that a given part of the organization or their particular systems must follow. In records management within the federal government, for example, there are mandated requirements all federal agencies must follow. State governments have them as well.

> 4-51 The BOSS website shall have every non-text item on a page is to have a text description to be fully compliant with Section 508 of the US Rehabilitation Act.

> 4-52 The FBI BOSS Records Management function shall retain a record of every hardcopy document in the permanent archive for the life of the Republic.

You will have to follow whatever legal, regulatory, or policy needs specified for your organization or type of project. It varies depending on what business you are in or project you are working on. Your stakeholders will know this, in many cases your senior stakeholders.

There may be other elements that you must comply with. For example, your company may have particular human resource compliance policies such as the following:

> 4-53 The BOSS Human Resource (HR) Policies shall only be modifiable by HR administrators.

> 4-54 The BOSS Human Resource (HR) Policies shall only allow a person's Social Security Number to be used for HR purposes when the person gives permission to do so.

Legal regulations apply to various mandated laws such as Health Insurance Portability and Accountability Act (HIPAA) of 1996 levies rules about the release of your personal medical information.

> 4-55 The BOSS Human Resource (HR) Medical Policies shall be in compliance with HIPAA regulations.

This previous statement may need to be broken into more detailed requirements based on what data you collect and need to disseminate. This shows the high-level requirement you need to decompose, but this is your start point.

These types of requirements may not come from your typical system users but more specialized stakeholders, so you will need to do digging. You will see more about this when in the elicitation phase.

Historical Data

If you have a dynamic database, say all the purchases and sales by your large tire-producing company, you will have growth of data. Given that your data will grow, you need to define storage and retention requirements to accommodate this growth of data. Therefore, you can have requirements like the following:

> 4-56 The BOSS Tire Purchasing and Sales function shall generate 3 Gigabytes of data per year for five years.

You base this on a calculation of 1,000,000 purchases and sales per year and 2,000 bytes per transaction or 2 gigabytes. Then 50 percent was added to accommodate for unexpected surges.

You should also have a statement that defines the length of time given data should be available to be easily recalled by the users.

> 4-57 The BOSS Tire Purchasing and Sales data shall be available online for five years.

Is it a coincidence that this statement has the same length of time? Probably not. What drives this time period? How often do people need to access the data, whether for query or reporting? If it is less than once a year, clearly do not keep it online. However, if it is dozens of times by several departments, then keep it. Of course, the cost of storage may affect this decision when development comes along, so be prepared to justify why you gave the time period.

For the radiation dosimetry project, you could have this as well:

> 4-58 The BOSS Unit Radiation Dosimeter shall be able to maintain data for 1,000 transactions.

What happens after 1,000 transactions? Good question. That leads to the subject of the next section, archiving.

Archiving

At some point, the data within your system may grow beyond the storage capacity. In the case of the radiation dosimetry project's 1,000 transaction limit, the project has the capability to archive the data to a hardened laptop for long-term storage. Thus, you will have requirements like this:

> 4-59 The BOSS Unit Radiation Dosimeter shall have the ability to download up to 1,000 transactions to the BOSS Dosimetry Archive Laptop.
>
> 4-60 The BOSS Dosimetry Archive function shall be able to maintain data for 5,000,000 transactions for fifty years.

Why so long? Think of the medical reasons associated with a soldier applying for benefits with the Veterans Administration after the war; the government must maintain the data for as long as the person was alive. Maybe 50 years is too short. Think of an 18-year-old soldier who lives to 90 years old. Don't forget the following requirement:

> 4-61 The BOSS Dosimetry Archive Laptop shall allow the ability to recall archived transaction data.

Trust me, the ability to recall it is very important or why bother to archive it?

You need to apply the same process to the database storage of a computer system. Think of an FBI records management system. Assume that 10 gigabytes of electronic information is generated per year. Then you should have requirements as follows:

> 4-62 The FBI BOSS Records Management data shall be archived after five years online.
>
> 4-63 The FBI BOSS Records Management Archived data shall allow the ability to recall archived transaction data to the online system.

How long should the data be archived? The compliance, legal, or regulatory requirements section earlier would be the likely source that would specify such needs. For the U.S. government, permanent records are for the life of the Republic. Therefore, you might have the following:

> 4-64 DRAFT The FBI BOSS Records Management Archived data shall be maintained for the life of the Republic.

Hm, is that really practical? Are you going to be around to ensure this happens? You know you will not—life expectancy is not that long. So, how do you handle this? From past experience, very large systems may last 5 to 15 years, so the life of the Republic clearly is not met. One way is the following:

> 4-65 The FBI BOSS Records Management Archived data shall be maintained for the life of the FBI BOSS Records Management System.

> 4-66 When the FBI BOSS Records Management System is being replaced, the FBI BOSS Records Management Archived data shall be migrated to the replacement archive system so the data can be maintained for the life of the Republic.

Elegant, no? Important, clearly. How do you verify that? Hm, good question. That one cannot be implemented until the next system comes along, but the requirements should be carried forward, and then it can be verified by the next development effort.

Structural

This section primarily applies to hardware systems. You are looking for those items that address how hardy the part needs to be. For example, if you are building a bridge, how much of a load must the bridge be able to support? Here's an example for a bridge across a small ravine that spans about 100 feet:

> 4-67 The BOSS Lost Creek Bridge shall support two lanes of traffic of 300 tons.

■ **Real-Word Note** I am not specifying a legitimate requirement here. I am using this for illustrative purposes only. When you are capturing this type of requirement, you need to be an expert, or more often you will receive such specifications from engineers or other expert sources.

You will need to consider many factors, such as wind shear, and all other such needs. You must define any force applied to your system. Will it be exposed to lightning, rain, snow, hail, salt, seawater, freezing, heat? Will the system be moving? If so, drag will be a factor. Will oxidation be a factor? The DoD has extensive documentation to help with these kinds of factors. You need to define all these environment stresses to the hardware that will affect the structural integrity.

■ **Real-World Note** I am not a structural engineer, so I cannot begin to define all these requirements. That is true for most REs, so you will need assistance in this. I have written many requirements for areas I was not an expert by getting help from those who are.

There could be structure in software, such as architectural structure for a database, which is specified by architects. Users specify the data that resides within that structure but not the structure itself. Chapter 7 details the user data needs you need to define in the database section. Sometimes, you may have specific structural requirements as standards your organization needs to follow. That is about all you would do for requirements. Design specifications are another matter. Then the designers would get specific about what they have chosen. The architect may have identified that the BOSS Architectural standard must be followed. The designer provides a statement that "the BOSS HR system will use the ORACLE database, which meets the BOSS architectural standard."

Notice that this type of requirement is hardware specific.

Algorithms

Algorithms capture any formulas or specific manipulations of data elements that need to occur. It could be something as simple as calculating how much postage to put on a first-class envelope based on the weight as follows:

> 4-68 The BOSS Cost of First Class Letter Postage data element shall be determined with the following look-up table:

Weight	Cost
1 ounce	$0.49
2 ounce	$0.70
3 ounce	$0.91
3.5 ounce	$1.12

Alternatively, it could be something more like Einstein's famous equation $E = MC^2$, as follows:

> 4-69 The BOSS conversion of mass to energy data element shall be determined by multiplying the change in mass by the speed of light times the speed of light, using the metric units.

The requirements are as unique to the needs of your system. For example, in the radiological collector, the energy is collected by the energy of the particles and photons incident on the collectors, and a conversion to the REM equivalency must be specified. You will not do that here as that is beyond the scope of this text, but you understand the need for it. If you are in a situation where such a technical capability is needed, find the resident expert that can explain to you what requirement needs to be captured.

Note REM stands for Roentgen Equivalent in Man. This is a unit of radiation exposure. You are not expected to understand exactly what it means, just that it is a unit to consider in the radiation dosimetry project.

Depending on the kind of project you are working on, you may not have any algorithms, especially sophisticated mathematical formulas.

Notice that this type of requirement is software specific. Yes, hardware may have algorithms embedded in them, but they reside in the software.

Database

Here you are going to learn what data elements and formats you should use when defining data to store in the proposed system. You will spend a significant amount of time learning how to do this in Chapter 7. However, you will need to define all the elements that users need. For example, in the record management example:

> 4-70 The FBI BOSS Records Management shall store the record title/subject in a text field of up to 80 characters.

For the hardware example, you would do the same:

> 4-71 The BOSS Individual Radiation Dosimeter shall store exposures in a range of 1 to 800 Rem.

> 4-72 The BOSS Individual Radiation Dosimeter shall store exposures in the following format, NNN where N is numeric only.

■ **Note** You will not specify all the elements that might eventually exist in the database itself. The programmers and designers will need additional items, such as indexes, key fields, etc., that a user does not need. You should define only the data elements the users need.

Notice that this type of requirement is software specific. The dosimetry requirements are for the software embedded in the system.

Again, reference Chapter 7 for the detailed examination.

Power

This is very straightforward. What power do you need for your system? For the dosimetry project, you might have the following:

> 4-74 The BOSS Individual Radiation Dosimeter shall require 5 volts direct voltage.

Will this require the individual radiation dosimeter to have an adapter to recharge it? If so, you may not need to replace batteries. The soldier will be walking around away from equipment. Thus, the combat situation might mean that the device cannot connect to a charger easily. However, the Unit Radiation Dosimeter might need all of the following:

> 4-75 The BOSS Unit Radiation Dosimeter shall use an internal 12 direct current source of power.

> 4-76 The BOSS Unit Radiation Dosimeter shall use an external 110 to 120 alternating current source of power with 60 Hz.

> 4-77 The BOSS Unit Radiation Dosimeter shall use an external 220 to 240 alternating current source of power with 50 Hz.

Why do you need U.S. and non-U.S. specifications? Because this system can be deployed anywhere in the world.

Do you need to specify this for the computer system, say the records management system? If the application will be placed into an existing network, no. If, however, you are going to specify the hardware for your system, then you do need to. Here's an example:

> 4-78 The FBI BOSS Records Management shall use an external 110 to 120 alternating current source of power with 60 Hz.

This system will not be deployed anywhere except in the United States; hence, the U.S. power grid is sufficient.

Notice that this type of requirement is hardware specific.

Network

As part of your requirements, you will define any network that is needed for your project. Will you need it for the dosimetry project? The individual dosimeters are read by the Unit Radiation Dosimeter, through a direct connection, so no. The Unit Radiation Dosimeter is a stand-alone device, so no network is involved. The backup is an external hard drive, and even the connection to the archive is by Wi-Fi, so technically you have no network. However, you should ask yourself these questions for each project.

The records management project is another matter. You will have a network for it. Of course, if the FBI center you go into has a network that the application will reside on, you just need to specify that. However, if one does not exist, you will need to specify what your network should consist of.

> 4-79 The FBI BOSS Records Management shall need a server for application and data records of the system.

You will need more information about the server. However, you will derive some of the specifications from the storage that the system needs, how much memory, and so on. So, let the developers and designers come up with it. What will the user need to connect to the server?

> 4-80 The FBI BOSS Records Management shall need 240 individual devices to connect to the server to access the application and data records of the system.

Elsewhere you will learn about any growth, but you should have a good estimate of the number of users when you write this requirement. What kind of network must it be? If it is known, capture it. Any other data should be specified also, from the needs standpoint, not the implementation. Is this a LAN, just a local network, in say one building, or is it a WAN, a wide area network, say in multiple states, or an entire city? All these needs affect the network requirements.

Notice that this type of requirement is hardware specific.

Infrastructure

Let me differentiate between structural requirements and infrastructure requirements. Structural requirements deal with the item itself. This includes what kinds of things it is made of and how it might be built to withstand its operational environment. Infrastructure consists of the things around the item so that it can do what it needs to do. The easiest example is to think of yourself as a "system." When you go to work, what things are at your place of employment so you can do your job? Those things are the infrastructure.

If you were going to build a call center, what kind of support would you need? If the building existed, that is one item out of the way. You would need something like the following:

> 4-81 The FBI BOSS Records Management Call Center shall need an external 110 to 120 alternating current source of power with 60 Hz.

What phone connectivity will you need? Will you need Wi-Fi? Internet connectivity? If so, what throughput will you need? If you do need to construct the building, what specifications will you need? Here the experts will be necessary.

For the dosimetry project, will you need infrastructure? Since this is a system deployed in the field, the system probably will not require infrastructure, except for possibly the archive system. Where will it reside? How will the system transmit the archived data to it? Does power, security Internet, possibly Wi-Fi, and so on? Probably not? If so, you will need the following:

> 4-82 The BOSS Dosimetry Archive Laptop shall need a Wi-Fi source at the Brigade headquarters (HQ) element to receive archive transmissions from the field BOSS Unit Radiation Dosimeters.

Notice that this type of requirement is hardware specific.

Backup and Recovery

You will want to have a backup and recovery function within your system. Otherwise, what happens if your system crashes and wipes out all your data? Therefore, you might have something like the following:

> 4-83 The FBI BOSS Records Management shall have a complete system and data backup once a week.

Obviously, losing a week's worth of data in unsatisfactory, so you should have maybe a daily incremental backup, where that service captures the difference from the previous day. However, is even losing one day's worth of data acceptable? Most likely not. Therefore, you may want to capture backups of transactions as they occur.

> 4-84 The FBI BOSS Records Management shall capture an incremental backup of each transaction as they occur.

You will need to specify where the backup is. Will you have one onsite? If so, what happens if a hurricane, earthquake, terrorist bombing, tsunami, tornado, or flood hits? You should have a backup site in a completely different site as well.

For the recovery aspect, you should specify how quickly you should be up and running. Here's an example:

> 4-85 The FBI BOSS Records Management shall be able to recover from the operational system within four hours from the local backup.

This may be unacceptable for many mission-critical situations, where it may be in seconds. It depends on your needs. It may be longer if you have to do it from the remote site. There it may be dependent on getting users to the remote site. It might be a day.

Would you need the same backup for the dosimetry system? An individual dosimeter may not be catastrophic, as there are other people in the same unit. The Unit Radiation Dosimeter might want a hard drive backup and a restore feature.

> 4-86 The BOSS Unit Radiation Dosimeter shall capture an incremental backup of daily transactions.

> 4-87 The BOSS Unit Radiation Dosimeter shall be able to recover from the operational system within four days from the local backup.

Why so many days? Good question. If the laptop is inoperable and cannot be repaired, it needs to be replaced. How quickly can one be acquired? Second, is it critical that the information be readily available compared to other operational status? Probably not, so the four days may be acceptable.

Summary

This chapter covered a lot of functional requirements. In the next chapter, you will learn about nonfunctional requirements.

There are potentially many different stakeholders who have an interest in getting these nonfunctional and functional requirements correct. This is because for many large systems the people buying the system are completely different from those who are going to use it (customers and users). There may be one significant factor that you cannot control—cost. The realism of financial constraints may limit some of the requirements you write. That is a trade-off analysis you will not spend time on in this text.

Exercises

Exercise 1

At the Three Mile Island Nuclear Power Plant, their control room had alarms and flashing lights to alert operators of emergency situations. One factor that inhibited responses was the constant sounding of the alarms and the flashing of the lights. Should sounding alarms and flashing lights be used in the future? If so, why and how? If not, why not?

Exercise 2

Define the requirements for a phone to only call and receive phone calls, with no other features.

CHAPTER 5

Nonfunctional Requirements

This chapter defines the nonfunctional requirements. For example, with the advent of cybersecurity in the last several years, security is a very important section of any system. This chapter will cover reliability, availability, maintainability, extensibility (scalability), and security. Security is not technically spelled with "ility," yet it is lumped in here. It is justified if the term became *securibility*, to coin a term. However, in interest of shorter and more understandable works, the text will use *security*, and you know it belongs in this chapter.

The government makes up a lot of words that are longer than they need to be, like "it has utility" rather than "use" or "prioritization" rather than "assign priority," and the list goes on. You might keep to the KISS principle. This was something from the Army: Keep It Simple, Stupid. This is not to say you are stupid; it was targeted for those who made things a lot more complex than they needed to be so they could sound impressive.

The Types of Nonfunctional Requirements

Some sources may call these behavioral requirements, but they are everything that does not fall into the functional requirements. Nonfunctional requirements define how the system should do it. Nonfunctional requirements do not specify implementation. Look at the following list of types, and you will see what is covered.

- Architectural
- Capacity, current, and forecast
- Documentation
- Efficiency
- Effectiveness
- Environmental
- Fault tolerance
- Privacy
- Performance

G. Koelsch, *Requirements Writing for System Engineering*,
DOI 10.1007/978-1-4842-2099-3_5

- Resilience
- Robustness
- Accessibility
- Availability
- Data integrity
- Extensibility
- Interoperability
- Manageability
- Maintainability
- Portability
- Quality
- Reliability
- Recoverability
- Scalability
- Security
- Serviceability
- Stability
- Supportability
- Testability
- Usability

Starting with the previous elements from the Stack Overflow web site ("What is functional and non-functional requirement." *Stack Overflow*. Feb. 2015. `http://stackoverflow.com/questions/16475979/what-is-functional-and-nonfunctional-requirement`), most other sources use many of this list, but others are appropriate.

Architectural

Your organization may mandate some architecture standards that your system must follow. Here's an example:

> 5-1 The FBI BOSS Records Management shall be designed with a Service Oriented Architecture (SOA).

As you learned in Chapter 2, requirement 5-1 could be an implementation if taken on its face value. However, given that an architectural study by the organization in question decided this was the best architecture approach for the system being considered, you will have to capture it. Alternatively, you might have something like the following (or both):

> 5-2 The FBI BOSS Records Management shall follow Representational State Transfer (REST).

REST is an architectural style of the World Wide Web. Are there architectural requirements for hardware? Of course, there can be, so it depends on your organization and what you are trying to build. Here's an example:

> 5-3 The DoD BOSS Records Management Computer system shall follow Common Operating Platform Environments (COPEs) Architecture.

Even small items like the dosimetry system may have architectural requirements that may need to be applied. You will have to investigate your organization.

Capacity

In this section, you will examine the storage capacity you need for your system. In the FBI record system, you need to investigate how much capacity you need for these records. Are these just text documents? If the answer is no (which is very likely), then what resolution of images do you need to store? Will there be color images? Will you have video? Black and white or color? What about sound files? How many of these types of records will you need to store, and how many years' worth? Once you know all the answers to this type of information, you can come up with a requirement like the following:

> 5-4 The FBI BOSS Records Management shall have a capacity of 12 Terabytes of data.

You should also write requirements to answer the questions in the previous paragraph. This will define how many text documents of what size you will have, how many other file types will you have, how many years of data, and how long before it goes to archive, if at all. You will address storage growth in the next chapter in the scalability section.

What about hardware that is not a computer system? Will you need some storage capacity for the individual dosimeter? Here's an example:

> 5-5 The BOSS Individual Radiation Dosimeter shall store 1000 bytes of data.

> 5-6 The BOSS Unit Radiation Dosimeter shall store 1,000,000 bytes of data.

The previous example does not have the ability to expand these two different dosimeters. However, they could be updated in the future. That is not always the case for every system. Consider a deep-space probe where there is no way to upgrade the capacity of the system. There may be more efficient coding, but the hardware itself will not change.

You have to ask the same kinds of questions as you did for the computer system earlier. There could be some alphanumeric data. Chances are, however, these probes travel the solar system to gather images among other types of data. Is color important for images (probably)? If so, what resolution do you need? How many do you want to store at a time before you transmit back? There are factors to consider in answering this last question. What is the transmission rate of the probe? If you can only transmit 1 kilobit per second of data, it makes no sense of store terabytes of data to transmit every hour. Therefore, you might come up with a requirement like this:

> 5-7 The BOSS Oort Cloud Space Probe shall store 1 gigabyte of data.

Then you will need to answer all the questions in the previous paragraph in requirements as well.

Constraints

There can be many constraints to your system that you need to address. These statements are restrictions on what you can do. Some you will learn about separately, like environmental or privacy constraints. Others might be architectural constraints, which you examined earlier.

For example, the individual dosimeter cannot be a large and cumbersome device that the individual soldier must wear. It might be similar to a wristwatch, such as the following:

> 5-8 The BOSS Individual Radiation Dosimeter shall weigh no more than 4 ounces.

For the records management project, you might have the following:

> 5-9 The FBI BOSS Records Management shall require all records to be in one of the following formats only:

- DOC,
- DOCX,
- XLS,
- XLSX,
- PPT,
- PPTX,
- JPG, or
- TIFF.

Notice that some constraints may be harder than others, such as a device that has to be moved from a naval ship to a Zodiac inflatable, by a 120-pound sailor. Thus, you have a carrying constraint and the specification of the minimum size of the person involved. You will see other types of constraints in this chapter like peak load, availability, capacity, daily and hourly loads, life spans, and size limitations. No doubt, you will encounter others in your career. Capture them, but highlight them as constraints.

Documentation

Documentation is the documents that already exist related to a project. Documentation is different from a document that captures all your requirements. Are there specific requirements for documentation that is part of the system? Here's an example for the dosimetry project:

> 5-10 The BOSS Unit Radiation Dosimeter shall have a hardcopy user guide that explains all the functions of the BOSS Unit Radiation Dosimeter.

For the records management project, you should consider a similar requirement:

> 5-11 The FBI BOSS Records Management System shall have an online user guide that explains all the functions of the BOSS Records Management System.

Your organization may require documents, say, a system administrator's manual or a frequently asked question guide for a help desk that supports a system. You will need to find all these needs during the elicitation phase.

Efficiency

According to Merriam-Webster's Collegiate Dictionary, *efficiency* is

> *the ability to do something or produce something without wasting materials, time, or energy*[1]

For hardware, this could be energy efficiency, say the efficiency that solar power is converted to energy used by a consumer, either a person or hardware. For computer systems, it can be the efficiency of certain functions and resources. Take a formatting of the hard drive on your laptop. If a particular operating system consumed 75 percent of the disc capacity, would that be considered very efficient? Probably not.

Therefore, you may want the following requirement:

> 5-12 The FBI BOSS Records Management System Operating System shall make 99.5% of the data hard drive available for storage.

For the dosimetry project, you can have this:

> 5-13 The BOSS Individual Radiation Dosimeter shall alert the user when the battery drops below 90% power so that the batteries can be changed.

---

[1]By permission. From *Merriam-Webster's Collegiate® Dictionary*, 11th Edition ©2016 by Merriam-Webster, Inc. (www.merriam-webster.com/)

At first blush, you might consider 90 percent to be a very high threshold. However, knowing how logistics system operate, usually slowly, and especially during a combat situation, the replacement parts for low-priority items may be long. There are factors like that you may need to consider.

Effectiveness

You need to define how good certain functions are within your system.

For the dosimetry project, you might have this:

> 5-14 The BOSS Individual Radiation Dosimeter shall capture 99% of the radiation the individual soldier is exposed to.

For the records management project, you might have the following:

> 5-15 The FBI BOSS Records Management System Operating System shall ingest 100% of records submitted.

One hundred percent may seem impossible, but from a legal perspective, it is a necessity. In addition, you will have statements elsewhere that address the fixing of records that are submitted but do not meet the proper format or fail ingestion into the database for some other reason.

Fault Tolerance

What happens when a portion of the system, but not the entire system, fails? Think of a flat tire on your car. You can still drive, even though it is in a degraded mode. You will need to consider whether such conditions will happen with your system and specify how effectively it can operate. For example, if a jet fighter has lost one engine of two, would the pilot be able to land?

You will have determined what fault tolerance is required for your project. For the records management project, you should have a similar requirement:

> 5-16 The FBI BOSS Records Management System shall have all functions implemented as services within a service oriented architecture to allow the system to operate in the event of one or more services failing.

For the example of the fighter, you would have the following requirement:

> 5-17 The XF-36 jet fighter shall be able to land with only one of its two engines operating.

You will need to determine fault tolerances needed for your project. Your organization may have guidelines on this, so research it.

Privacy

There are several situations where you need to consider privacy issues. People are rightfully concerned about their personal information. This is a critical business consideration given consumer concerns about their person information. Also, in the medical field, HIPAA receives a significant emphasis. The Health Insurance Portability and Accountability Act of 1996 defines what the medical field must follow to protect an individual's privacy relating to his or her medical information. Therefore, in the dosimetry project, you might have the following requirement:

> 5-18 The BOSS Unit Radiation Dosimeter shall store ensure individual radiation dosages are protected in accordance with HIPAA compliance.

In addition, even for the records management, the system must protect privacy. Here's an example:

> 5-19 The FBI BOSS Records Management shall have protect the privacy of individuals identified in a record in accordance with Federal Government Privacy policies.

Check the application of privacy rules for your project and capture them appropriately.

Quality

For our purposes, *quality* is a degree of goodnesss. There are two levels of quality you want to consider. First, if you take all these nonfunctional requirements together, it should define quality for the system. That means you then look at goodness at the individual requirement level, which we will do now.

Now examine the records management project. For argument's sake, assume not all their documents have been converted to digital format yet. Therefore, they are working on documents that are 25 to 30 years old. Now you need to address the goodness of the documents to be converted. Back in that era, people were still using an antique called a *typewriter*. In addition, not all the paper was as good—think multiple-page forms. Also, documents were copied multiple times. The quality of documents to be scanned can degrade with age and the fragileness of the paper. Since you are going to scan this, you need to come up with a quality of the scan.

> 5-20 The FBI BOSS Records Management scanning shall capture 75% of the characters per page to be considered a quality scan.

Now the default scan will be 300 dots per inch (DPI). If the scan does not meet the 75 percent, the process will be repeated at the 600 DPI, 1200 DPI, and finally 2400 DPI. If the 75 percent cannot be achieved at 2400 DPI, the quality achieved there will be the default.

Are there quality requirements that would apply to hardware type systems? Yes. You will examine a simple example for the radiation dosimetry project.

> 5-21 DRAFT The BOSS Unit Radiation Dosimeter shall capture gamma ray exposure between 200KeV and 1.00 MeV with a 99% accuracy.

By the way, this requirement is not correct, so don't reuse it (but it verifies the importance of experts). (KeV = Kilo-electron Volts and MeV = Mega-electron Volts.)

Resilience

Resiliency requirements define what must be preserved when an outage of the system occurs. Here's an example for the records management system:

> 5-22 The FBI BOSS Records Management shall maintain all records during an outage until such time as the system is restored.

For the dosimetry project, consider the following:

> 5-23 The BOSS Individual Radiation Dosimeter shall maintain the individual exposure record during the loss of battery power until such time as the power is restored to the system.

For both projects, there of course will be other needs, and you will need to define them all.

Robustness

Robustness means that the system does not crash easily and is able to withstand changes that might weaken it.

■ **Real-World Note** I worked on a system where a very complex query that spanned multiple tables would cause the user's connection to it to fail. That is unacceptable. This is somewhat related to fault tolerance.

Therefore, you might have a requirement like this:

> 5-24 The FBI BOSS Records Management Search Function shall not cause the system to fail.

In the radiation dosimetry project, you could have the following:

> 5-25 If the energy exposure exceeds 1.00 MeV, the BOSS Unit Radiation Dosimeter shall ignore the energy rather than overload the sensor.

As usual, you will need assistance in capturing such expertise-loaded subject areas.

Environmental

What are the external environments that your system will need to operate in? Will this be a 24-hour, seven-day-a-week computer system? Will this be the same environment your dosimetry project must operate in? You will need to address temperature ranges, rain, wind, snow, humidity, and any other such factors. Will a sensitive probe need to be dropped or banged about (think of a watch on a soldier in a combat zone)? Therefore, you can have examples like the following:

> 5-26 The BOSS Unit Radiation Dosimeter shall be exposed to temperatures ranging from -40 to 140 degrees Fahrenheit.

Remember, these devices must operate anywhere in the world.

For the records management project, you should have the following:

> 5-27 The FBI BOSS Records Management shall operate from 6 a.m. to 11 p.m. daily Monday through Friday.

If it is a job done during the day, why would you not just base it on 8 to 5 in Washington, D.C.? If you have lived in that area, you will know people will come to work early to avoid the horrendous traffic. Plus, the FBI is in all four time zones. What about Hawaii and Alaska? Is 11 p.m. sufficient? Maybe not. For this exercise, you assumed records management took place in the continental United States. You will need to confirm that is correct.

Data Integrity

Data integrity refers to maintaining and assuring the accuracy and consistency of data over its entire lifecycle. This could be the corruption or loss of data because of a hardware failure, such as a spot on a hard drive that goes bad. Alternatively, data integrity is corrupted when a record cannot be found because the pointer within a database loses its link.

> 5-28 To prevent malicious corruption of the BOSS Unit Radiation Dosimeter, the system shall retain its data for 90 days after a designated user authorizes deletion of a record on the Unit Dosimeter.

For the records management project:

> 5-29 The FBI BOSS Records Management System shall maintain data integrity by keeping backups of all updates to the database for every record transaction.

Standards

There may be many and varied standards that are regulated on your project or even that your organization levies on you because of company policy. There could be programming standards for your developers. HR has standards of conduct for employees and ethical standards. The DoD has a whole series called military standards, or MIL-STD for short. The EPA has environmental standards. There are company architectural standards; even

Microsoft has standards for its software development. Those are only a few. You learned about one kind of standard in the previous chapter that might apply to your project, such as the following:

> 5-30 The BOSS shall follow this company's Organizational User Interface Standard.

The DoD has many standards for its hardware development such as DoD Manual 4120.24-M, Defense Standardization Program (DSP) Policy and Procedures. This can drive you to requirements such as the following:

> 5-31 (5-26) The BOSS Unit Radiation Dosimeter shall be exposed to temperatures ranging from -40 to 140 degrees Fahrenheit.

You will need to find all standards that will apply. They should not be difficult to find as people will let you know what they must follow.

Performance

Chapter 4 began with arguably the biggest and most important group of requirements (business rules), and this topic probably has the second biggest and most important group of requirements: performance.

Merriam-Webster's Collegiate Dictionary defines *performance* this way:

> 1 *a: the execution of an action*
>
> *b: something accomplished: deed, feat*
>
> 2 *the fulfillment of a claim, promise, or request: implementation*
>
> 3 *the manner in which a mechanism performs, e.g., engine performance*[2]

How something performs, whether it is hardware or software, is what is important to us. System performance affects almost every section in this chapter and the preceding one. In fact, reliability, availability, and maintainability requirements are almost exclusively performance requirements, as you will soon see. In this section, you will learn about how many, how often, frequency, confidence levels, and so on—anything you can quantify. Other than maybe a definition of something, there is a number associated with a performance requirement.

Where do you put these requirements? While you could place performance requirements in their own section, it may work best to do this with the particular function you are talking about. That helps to reinforce the point that most every function should have performance requirements, or you should at least spend some time thinking about if performance requirements are necessary for that function.

---

[2]By permission. From *Merriam-Webster's Collegiate® Dictionary*, 11th Edition ©2016 by Merriam-Webster, Inc. (`www.merriam-webster.com/`)

I want to look at the following:

- Performance response time
- Workload performance
- Platform performance

These are good types of performance values, but only as a start. You have seen many values in this chapter that define performance values such as the number of users, response times, throughput, concurrency, resources, and many of the nonfunctional requirements like scalability that you have already examined in this chapter.

Check out that web site as some explanations of details related to various performance values. It gives guidance of user reactions to how quickly they receive feedback.

Now, examine example performance values.

Performance Response Time

How quickly do you want your request to be completed, whatever it is? Think of the records management project. You have received a request to find a particular set of documents from 1998. How fast should you get your results?

> 5-32 The FBI BOSS Records Management Search Function shall return the results within 4 seconds, 80% of the time.

The value "80% of the time" is important. It is the confidence level of your requirement. The results should meet four seconds in four out of five queries. Does that sound slow when you compare it to Google? However, think of a database that may have millions or tens of millions of records that could be megabytes of data each. That is a very good result.

What about the other 20 percent of queries? Excellent question. You need to address them in some way. You can increase the confidence level and the response time appropriately. Here's an example:

> 5-33 The FBI BOSS Records Management Search Function shall return the results within 10 seconds, 90% of the time.

And here's another:

> 5-34 The FBI BOSS Records Management Search Function shall return the results within one minute, 99% of the time.

There is more than one way to address the last one percent. One way is parallel to the requirements you already have, like so:

> 5-35 The FBI BOSS Records Management Search Function shall return the results within ten minute, 100% of the time.

Or like this:

> 5-36 The FBI BOSS Records Management Search Function shall return all query results in less than ten minutes.

Workload Performance

Another factor you need to consider is the workload on the system. Another name for this you may see in some text is concurrency. How many users will there be for your system? That is a capacity value (see the "Capacity" section in this chapter). You might have the following:

> 5-37 The FBI BOSS Records Management Search Function shall have 500 users.

However, those are not concurrent users. If you spread that over 24 hours a day, if it was a 24/7 system, you would have about 21 per hour. Is this system likely to be used that way? Probably not. Maybe about 10 hours a day, from the East Coast to the West Coast, so that would be 13 hours a day, or about 40 an hour.

> 5-38 The FBI BOSS Records Management Search Function shall have 40 average concurrent users.

However, assume in this case that you have learned that about 40 percent of the people use it in the first two hours of work and 300 users are in the Eastern Time zone, 50 users in each of the Central and Mountain Time zone, and 100 in the Western Time zone. You are left with a 120-user peak in the first two hours.

> 5-39 The FBI BOSS Records Management Search Function shall have 120 peak concurrent users.

Does the same apply for searches? If there are that many people querying the database, does it affect the response time? That is a question you need to address. Maybe if each person is doing only one search in those two hours, that is 120 searches in two hours, or an average of one a minute, so in that case, if that is representative, you may not need to address your search response time.

However, if each of the 120 users in the peak two hours is doing ten search each, they may not be evenly spaced apart, so you may need to specify something like the following:

> 5-40 The FBI BOSS Records Management Search Function shall return the results within 10 seconds, 80% of the time during the peak two hours of the day.

Or, you might have to say it this way:

> 5-41 The FBI BOSS Records Management Search Function shall return the results within 10 seconds, 80% of the time when there are 100 searches initiated within 10 minutes.

You may need to address each confidence level during the peak times. This is an important aspect for any performance requirement. Not only should you address normal activities, but also you need to address peak loads.

Here you have a relatively low workload for the example system. Think of Google or Amazon; they would have a much higher set of numbers, probably the high end of the spectrum of the number of users, frequency of queries, and so on. You may have situations that are in the thousands or even tens of thousands of users like a Google, Amazon, or eBay. In those cases, you will have to craft the same type of requirements, but the values will be significantly different. Analysis and discussion with the experts may be required to address these situations.

Platform Performance

Here you will learn about items like computers, printers, scanner, servers, type of network, operating system, and any other peripherals you could consider for a computer system. Naturally, performance applies to other hardware as well. For example, you should have the following:

> 5-42 The BOSS Individual Radiation Dosimeter shall capture exposure to radiation within one second of exposure.

Some responses are not driven by the user needing something within a certain time but driven by other needs like the previous requirement where exposure needs to be collected quickly in the event of other radiation exposure.

You need to consider transfer rates. Therefore, you might have the following:

> 5-43 The BOSS Unit Radiation Dosimeter shall capture the readings from the BOSS Individual Radiation Dosimeter within two seconds once the Individual Dosimeter is locked into the reader.

You will need to do the same for all the items within the computer system. Here's an example:

> 5-44 The BOSS Network Printer shall print at least one hundred pages a minute.

Here's another example:

> 5-45 The BOSS Network Scanner shall scan at least twenty pages a minute at 2400 dots per inch.

You will need to examine every possible performance value to determine what needs a requirement. The guiding rule should be, if you find a number associated with a piece of hardware, consider a requirement for it.

You may become involved with a piece of hardware that you do not have a strong background with. For example, many of you may not have had significant experience with radiation detection. As you have seen from the analysis so far and with more to come, the challenges will be subdivided sufficiently enough that many aspects are understandable after the analysis here that then you can work with the experts to harness their knowledge to translate the needs into good requirements.

Performance Profiles

Sometimes you may need to consider performance profiles that are different from one another. For example, you are looking at a local area network (LAN) for sales offices in company dispersed around the country. Some offices are larger than others. After some research, you find that your company has offices with the following sizes:

- Small offices range from 3 to 6 people.
- Medium offices range from 10 to 26 people.
- Large offices range from 30 to 56 people.

Note You will need to add these definitions to your glossary.

You will need to provide performance requirements that may vary based on this. Here are some examples:

> 5-46 The BOSS Network Sales Server for a Small Sales Office shall store 10 megabytes of sales records.
>
> 5-47 The BOSS Network Sales Server for a Medium Sales Office shall store 40 megabytes of sales records.
>
> 5-48 The BOSS Network Sales Server for a Large Sales Office shall store 100 megabytes of sales records.

There may be many values that you have to consider differently depending on different profiles. Why? First, you would not want to spend the money and resources for a large office when you are installing a small office. You need to focus the performance to suit the needs.

Throughput

Merriam-Webster's Collegiate Dictionary defines *throughput* like this:

> *the amount of material, data, etc., that enters and goes through something (such as a machine or system)*[3]

Now examine an example for the dosimetry project. In the archive section, you might consider the following requirement:

> 5-49 DRAFT The BOSS Unit Radiation Dosimeter shall have the ability to download up to 1000 transactions to the BOSS Dosimetry Archive Laptop.

This specifies how many transactions, but there is no time element. Therefore, you should have something like this:

> 5-50 The BOSS Unit Radiation Dosimeter shall have the ability to download up to 1000 transactions to the BOSS Dosimetry Archive Laptop in 5 minutes.

Given that you know each record can be 1,000 bytes of data, that gives you 1 megabyte of data in 60 seconds, or 166,667 bytes per second throughput requirement. That is quite doable by most systems.

[3]By permission. From *Merriam-Webster's Collegiate® Dictionary*, 11th Edition ©2016 by Merriam-Webster, Inc. (`www.merriam-webster.com/`)

What about the records management project? Do the same kind of analysis. Consider the backup capability. You know you should have 10 gigabytes of data each year. Now assume that will be the maximum you need to back up. You have determined you should perform a complete backup each week. Does that mean you have an entire week to accomplish this? Maybe, if it ran in the background yet it did not affect the operation of the system. That is probably not the case. Could you be updating the database while a backup is running? Operationally, that is not a good practice. So, what time do you have to do it?

The same process is applied to the database storage of a computer system. Think of an FBI records management system. Assume that 10 gigabytes of electronic information is generated per year. Now assume that the backup can run overnight. Then since you have the system operational from 6 a.m. Eastern time to 11 p.m., that means you have 7 hours to do the transfer. Then you would have a requirement as follows:

> 5-51 The BOSS Weekly Backup shall be completed between 6 a.m. to 11 p.m. on Thursday night, with a throughput of 400 kilobytes/second.

Then during your analysis, one manager says that the backup can happen on the weekends. That yields an additional 48 hours. What does that do to the calculation?

> 5-52 The BOSS Weekly Backup shall be completed between 11 p.m. starting on Friday night and 6 a.m. on Monday, with a throughput of 51 kilobytes/second.

That is a significant improvement, if that is needed. That gives you the idea of what performance is like.

Reliability, Availability, and Maintainability (RAM)

This is probably the one area within this book that will exploit mathematics to any significant degree. Network throughput calculations are probably the only other mathematical area, and that is relatively simple compared to RAM.

Reliability, availability, and maintainability are values that are related to each other, which is why they are usually studied as a group. *Reliability* is how reliable the system. Reliability is how reliable the system is. *Availability* is how available the system is. *Maintainability* is how maintainable the system is. To understand them better, there are specific terms and associated values associated with those terms. We will spend some time gaining an understanding of them.

Definitions

You are going to see many new terms and concepts for RAM. You need these terms to lay the foundation for RAM calculations.

Mean Time to Repair (MTTR)

This describes the average time to repair a failure. If a card dies in your network server or in a desktop, it could be very quick. Say 15 or 30 minutes. However, what if the entire server fails? Do you wait for someone to repair it, when it could be several hours or more than one working day to fix it? Probably not. If it is just the matter of having a hot spare that switches automatically, you do not even lose any time. Now what if the spare is not connected and all it requires is connecting the system and it is functional? Then maybe it takes 30 to 60 minutes to fix it. However, what if all you have is a machine without fully configured operating system for your use and without the applications installed on your machine? That will be a significant wait time, at least hours and probably days. Moreover, what if the people who fix it are not even part of your department? Then you have put in a repair request, and you have to wait for them to show up before any work begins.

That brings up a very important question relating to MTTR. Does this include wait time? If the answer is yes, then you are covered. If, in your organization, the answer is No, then you need to include wait time. That definition comes next.

Wait Time

Wait time is the time from the onset of the failure until the work begins on the failure.

Some people like to keep the wait time separate to track it. In many cases where a different organization is responsible for the service of hardware and software, the wait times create significant impacts on an organization. My experience shows most federal organizations I have worked with separate the hardware maintenance and software maintenance so that tracking wait time for that maintenance is very important. This is not a criticism of how this is done, just that some organizations can use wait time. In addition, it is not clear that they track how much time they lose in critical functions. This is something to be aware of in your organization. What good is it to have a small MTTR if no one looks at how much time is lost to wait time?

Mean Time Between Failures (MTBF)

This is the average operational time between failures. If you have three system failures every 30,000 hours, then your MTBF is 10,000 hours. That is straightforward enough. Of course, achieving it is another matter, not to mention verifying that kind of requirement. That is not the responsibility of this text—another course or volume will discuss that. What you need to define is what the value should be. In this era with so much computing power and equipment, this value should be quite high.

As you can see, these MTTR, wait times, and MTBF values seem to be related, which they are. You will continue to look at them and how they interrelate.

Availability

Availability defines how much of the time the system is operational. More precisely, availability is the percentage of time that the system is up and running. The two most important types of availability are operational availability and inherent availability.

Operational availability includes the time to repair a fault, the time spent waiting to repair the fault, and the time between faults. The formula for it is as follows:

Operational Availability = MTBF / (MTTR + Wait Time + MTBF) * 100% **EQUATION 1**

■ **Note** The more general definition for operational availability is uptime divided by the sum of the uptime and downtime. This includes the MTTR and logistics downtime or wait time. In addition, periodic maintenance would come into the calculation, as well as any unscheduled maintenance. For the examples here, we will not look at the maintenance downtime.

Inherent availability includes the time to repair a fault and the time between faults. Since Wait Time is not included, the formula for inherent availability becomes the following:

Inherent Availability = MTBF / (MTTR + MTBF) * 100% **EQUATION 2**

Let's look at some examples. You must use wait times as that reflects where problems can be hidden if not shown.

Plugging these values:

MTBF = 1000 hours

MTTR = 10 hours

Wait Time = 100 hours

into this equation 1:

Operational Availability = MTBF / (MTTR + Wait Time + MTBF) * 100%

yields the following:

Operational Availability = 1000 / (10 + 100 + 1000) * 100% = 90.09%

The CEO sees this wait time of 100 hours and says that number is totally unacceptable. He tells his maintenance manager that number must be reduced to 10 hours. What does that do to the availability?

Now plug these values:

MTBF = 1000 hours

MTTR = 10 hours

Wait Time = 10 hours

into equation 1:

Operational Availability = MTBF / (MTTR + Wait Time + MTBF) * 100%

which yields the following:

Operational Availability = 1000 / (10 + 10 + 1000) * 100% = 98.04%

As you can see, that made a significant improvement in the availability. Why was inherent availability never calculated? It was included as you will see some discussion elsewhere that uses it. However, it is my opinion that inherent availability does not reflect the reality of a system because it ignores the time spent waiting for something to be repaired. Look at the examples you have seen, and as an exercise for yourself, what would be the availability without wait time? You will see it is higher than when wait time is included. When wait time went from 10 hours to 100 hours, the operational availability dropped significantly. However, it does not reflect the real work. That is why we do not use it here.

Wait, you say, shouldn't maintenance be included in this calculation? Good catch. In this case, no maintenance downtime is assumed.

You have to include the time that the system is not in service for maintenance in the total time calculation.

Maintainability

The Department of Defense defines maintainability as a measure of the ease and rapidity with which a system or equipment can be restored to operational status following a failure. Now we will analyze the primary calculated values within maintainability.

Mean Time to Maintain (MTTM)

This describes the average time the system is down for maintenance.

Mean Time Between Maintenance (MTBM)

This is the average operational time between maintenance.

MTBM defines how much of the time the system is operational. More precisely, availability is the percentage of time that the system is up and running. The formula for it is as follows:

Maintainability = MTBM / (MTTM + Wait Time + MTBM) * 100% **EQUATION 3**

When wait time is included in the MTTR, this formula becomes the following:

Maintainability = MTBM / (MTTM + MTBM) * 100% **EQUATION 4**

Again, let's consider some examples.

Plugging the following values:

MTBM = 1000 hours

MTTM = 10 hours

Wait Time = 10 hours

into equation 3:

Maintainability = MTBM / (MTTM + Wait Time + MTBM) * 100%

yields the following result:

Maintainability = 1000 / (10 + 10 + 1000) * 100% = 98.04 %

So, how do you include maintenance with inherent availability (which is called operational availability)?

You must average the two values. If they both are 99 percent, it averages to 99 percent.

Now, look at some more examples.

In this first example, plug the following values:

MTTM = 10 hours

MTBM = 1000 hours

into equation 4:

Maintainability = 1000 / (10 + 1000) * 100% = 99.0099%

And, plug the following values:

MTTR = 1 hour

MTBF = 1000 hours

into equation 1:

Inherent Availability = 1000 / (1 + 1000) * 100% = 99.9001%

In this second example, plug the following values:

MTTM = 10 hours

MTBM = 5000 hours

into equation 4:

Maintainability = 5000 / (10 + 5000) * 100% = 99.8004%

And, plug the following values:

MTTR = 1 hour

MTBF = 1000 hours

into equation 1:

Inherent Availability = 1000 / (1 + 1000) * 100% = 99.9001%

In this third example, plug the following values:

MTTM = 10 hours

MTBM = 1000 hours

into equation 4:

Maintainability = 1000 / (10 + 1000) * 100% = 99.0099%

And, plug the following values:

MTTR = 1 hour

MTBF = 5000 hours

into equation 1:

Inherent Availability = 5000 / (1 + 5000) * 100% = 99.9800%

In this fourth example, plug the following values:

MTTM = 10 hours

MTBM = 5000 hours

into equation 4:

Maintainability = 5000 / (10 + 5000) * 100% = 99.8004%

And, plug the following values:

MTTR = 1 hour

MTBF = 5000 hours

into equation 1:

Inherent Availability = 5000 / (1 + 5000) * 100% = 99.9800%

Reliability

Basically, reliability of the system, component, or whatever the item is means it does not fail. To be more explicit, for hardware, reliability is the probability a component fails, whereas for software, reliability is the probability software will produce an incorrect output or not provide a result at all.

For the purposes here, you will only define reliability for the entire system and major functional areas (services and/or subsystems). For a system's requirements, breaking down the hardware or functionality further is beyond the scope of this text and should be done more by a reliability engineer in conjunction with a requirements engineer.

The reliability, R, function over time, t, is defined in the following equation where the value lambda, λ, is the failure rate, which is defined as 1/MTBF:

$$R(t) = e^{-\lambda t}$$ **EQUATION 5**

When you have two items in series (say the computer and the operating system), the reliability for both is as follows:

R (system) = R (computer) * R (OS) **EQUATION 6**

Then this series continues for the application on the top so it would be as follows:

R (system) = R (computer) * R (OS) * R (app) **EQUATION 7**

If you have both R(computer) and R(OS) = 0.90, substituting these values into equation 6, you get .9 * 0.9 or 0.81. If R(App) = 0.90, with R(computer) and R(OS) = 0.90, and you substitute that into equation 7, you have 0.9 * 0.9 * 0.9 = 0.729.

If you had ten services in one suite of services, it would be as follows:

R (total) = R1 * R2 * R3 * R4 * R5 * R6 * R7 * R8 * R9 * R10 **EQUATION 8**

If R1 through R10 all equaled 0.9, then substituting that into equation 8 would yield 0.348678. This would not be a very reliable system.

However, when things run in parallel, how does the formula work?

$$R_{total}(t) = 1 - [1 - R_1(t)]\,[1 - R_2(t)]$$

$$= R_1(t) + R_2(t) - R_1(t)\,R_2(t)$$ **EQUATION 9**

So if you have both R1 and R2 = 0.90, substituting these values into equation 9, you get the following:

$$R_{total} = 0.90 + 0.90 - 0.81 = 0.99$$

Now you see the benefit of putting items in parallel.

And if a third one with R = 0.9 is added to equation 9, you get the following:

$$R_{total} = 0.990 + 0.900 - 0.891 = 0.999$$

This clearly demonstrates why items, whether they are hardware or software, should work in parallel whenever practical.

This is as much as you will see here about reliability. Usually, you will define availability and maintainability for systems. Only if you get very specific hardware would you get into very sophisticated reliability calculations.

At most, for your purposes here, you would write the following:

5-53 The BOSS shall have an overall reliability of 0.999.

This would allow the designers to identify the proper configuration to meet that. If you need more detail, you now have the tools to do some breakdown for subsystems and services.

Failure Definition

The requirements must provide a clear definition of a project failure. At a minimum, if the hardware that software resides on fails, that is a system failure.

Therefore, a requirement would look like this:

5-54 The BOSS system shall be available 99.99% of the time.

5-55 A failure of the BOSS system shall occur when any of the following critical functions are not working:

- Security access to the system
- Searching the mission database
- Adding records to the mission database
- Updating records within the mission database
- Deleting records from the mission database

Notice that this did not list reporting or auditing. Remember there can be more functions depending on your system. In addition, stakeholders, not designers, define these critical functions. Also, special users like administrators do need representation in this special case but have only limited items that they can demand be included.

What is crucial to this requirement is that the unavailability is independent of the cause. Users are not properly reflected in availability. Please keep this approach included in all projects you work on. Do not let developers and designers whine that it is too hard. In addition, some say that you cannot define availability on software.

■ **Real-World Note** I did bring an innovation, even early in my career. Up to that point in time for this organization, computer system operational availability was defined only by determining whether the mainframe was up. This type of definition may have had a much broader definition, but I did not research it at that time. If other hardware or even software would not operate, that was not considered. Therefore, if the mainframe was operating, but your terminal, the operating system, the line connecting you to the mainframe, or the application was not working, that made no difference. The system was still considered "operationally available." From a user standpoint, clearly it is not. I defined operational availability by users being able to perform mission-critical functions. If any of the mission-critical functions could not be accomplished for any reason, hardware, software, operating system, etc., the system was not available. Not only have I brought that definition to every project I have worked on, but also, when I returned 25 years later to that original organization, they were still using that definition. As for defining availability for software, I could define it and I did. Believe me, it was embraced by the stakeholders, which was why 25 years later, it is still being used.

■ **Tip** The study of RAM is the topic of many books, and you could spend entire courses in this effort. In fact, the U.S. Army course was 120 hours long. There are very detailed and very complex theories presented at symposia. What is interesting is that the value of these very sophisticated approaches compared to more simple theories (e.g., the normal distribution of failure, where electronic failures are random) may be very insignificant. In fact, rarely do you see validation of the initial assumptions to justify why the new theory is significantly better. This is not to say they are not better, but someone needs to validate why the more complex theory is better than tried-and-true, more simple approaches. If the difference is only 1 or 2 percent, go with the simple theory.

Security

One of Merriam-Webster's Collegiate Dictionary definitions for *security* is

> measures taken to guard against espionage or sabotage,
> crime, attack, or escape[4]

Wait a minute, you say, "Why do I need security since this will be a stand-alone system? I will not connect it to the Internet or any other servers." First, you still will need to control who can access the system. Will you allow the office cleaners to access your billing system that specifies what you charge people? Will every employee have access to all functions in the payroll system (e.g., allow them to see everyone's salary)? No. Second, you will need to decide whether data will be imported to this stand-alone system. If so, then you will need additional requirements to ensure security is maintained. Third, if you project will be connected to other systems, then further protections are needed, especially if it will connect outside the organization to include the Internet.

Realize in your work as an RE, you will generally be collecting the requirements as specified by the stakeholders. That said, there is some value added that you can provide to these same stakeholders. Every person will not know everything that is needed to collect the requirements for the entire system. You will work with as broad a spectrum of stakeholders as you can to ensure everything is covered. In Chapter 10, you will learn about doing gap analysis to find those areas that may not have been covered at all or covered sufficiently. By having a list of candidate topics like these, you may help ensure that the stakeholders do cover all their requirements.

[4]By permission. From *Merriam-Webster's Collegiate® Dictionary*, 11th Edition ©2016 by Merriam-Webster, Inc. (`www.merriam-webster.com/`)

These three aspects will be examined in the following sections. In addition, I had added a fourth section in security called *reuse*. Why reusing requirements is not the sole area where you will likely reuse requirements, in my experience, it is the one area where previous security requirements can be reused the most. So, it is introduced here. Just realize that any requirement or groups of requirements can be reused.

Access Control

Here you specify how people get access to the system. Usually you have some sort of unique user identification (e.g., user ID) and password. If there is more than one area within the system, or system of systems, where there are different groups within system, you may need to select from those areas.

You should consider some requirements like these:

> 5-56 The BOSS system shall maintain unique user identification for every person who will use the system.
>
> 5-57 The BOSS system shall maintain a password for every unique user identification on the system.

■ **Note** You will need to decide whether the users themselves create their own password, whether the system creates them, or whether a system administrator creates them. Usually, this is defined by the organizational policy.

You will need more:

> 5-58 The BOSS system shall allow a user three attempts to enter their user ID and password (and select the domain, where appropriate) before that session is ended.

You will need to know what your organization's policy is regarding how a failed login attempt is handled.

> 5-59 When the user has failed to enter their user ID and password correctly, the BOSS system shall allow the user three attempts to log in after one hour.

Or it might be as follows:

> 5-60 When the user has failed to enter their user ID and password correctly, the BOSS system shall only allow the user three attempts to log in again after a system administrator has authorized it.

Once a person has access to the system, you will need to define the roles and responsibilities that various users can have on your system. Some of what is discussed here will be standards, but there will be additional roles depending on the nature of the system. For example, an HR system will have significantly different roles than will a hospital system or an online auction system. Nevertheless, you should consider some of these:

> 5-61 The BOSS system shall allow roles that allow people to read the database.
>
> 5-62 The BOSS system shall allow roles that allow people to add to the database.
>
> 5-63 The BOSS system shall allow roles that allow people to change the database.
>
> 5-64 The BOSS system shall allow roles that allow people to delete from the database.
>
> 5-65 The BOSS system shall allow for system administrator roles.

Keep in mind, that one user can have multiple roles.

> 5-66 The BOSS system shall allow users to have multiple roles.
>
> 5-67 The BOSS system shall allow for system administrator roles.
>
> 5-68 The BOSS system shall allow for system monitoring roles.
>
> 5-69 The BOSS system shall allow for system auditing roles.

■ **Note** You will need to define what functions are associated with system administrator, auditor, and monitoring roles.

This clearly is not a comprehensive list, but it will get you started.

Import From and Export to Outside the System

As mentioned earlier, you have to protect information coming to your application. You will address the formatting of the data in the interface in Chapter 8.

> 5-70 The BOSS shall ensure all data to be imported into the system has no viruses.

Will users of other system that exchange data with your system be able to access your data? In most cases, you would think not, but if you don't specify so, you run the risk of someone controlling your data without you controlling what they can access.

> 5-71 The BOSS shall ensure all users external to the system do not have access to the BOSS data.

Clearly, there are more aspects to consider, but they depend significantly on whether you have systems connected to your system. Now what about exporting data? You will specify what applications you will export to and what formats are supported.

5-72 The BOSS shall provide users with the capability to export data to Microsoft Excel in .xlsx format.

5-73 The BOSS shall provide users with the capability to export data to Microsoft Excel in .csv format.

5-74 The BOSS shall provide users with the capability to export data to Microsoft Word in .csv format.

5-75 The BOSS shall provide users with the capability to export data to Microsoft Word in .docx format.

When defining formats, you need to decide whether you will provide backward compatibility, like .xls for Excel and .doc for Word, as well as other typical formats for these types of applications.

You must address if there is data within your system that cannot be exported or if it must be controlled in some manner. Why would you need to do that? There are various reasons, such as was mentioned, say payroll information or even proprietary information. Therefore, you might have requirements such as these:

5-76 The BOSS shall prohibit payroll data from being exported from the System.

5-77 The BOSS shall prohibit company proprietary information from being exported from the System.

Naturally, you will need to have identified what constitutes this kind of information, with requirement like the following somewhere in your list:

5-78 The BOSS shall identify all payroll data within the System.

5-79 The BOSS shall identify all company proprietary information within the System.

You may have a restriction that no data may be exported, so you have the following:

5-80 The BOSS shall prohibit any data from being exported from the System.

Once you understand the flow of data to and from your system and any associated restrictions, you will be able to apply import and export security requirements.

Connections to Outside the System

You will learn about interfaces with other systems elsewhere. This subsection addresses protection of the data. First, you must address the authorization of users to move data to and from your systems, as in these examples, including the appropriate data format:

5-81 The BOSS shall provide users with the capability to export data to ANY System in .csv format.

5-82 The BOSS shall provide users with the capability to import data from ANY System in .csv format.

Next, you should address the authorization system to move data automatically to and from your systems, as in these examples:

> 5-83 The BOSS shall provide ANY System to import data in .csv format.

> 5-84 The BOSS shall provide ANY System to export data in .csv format.

If you have specified a format different from any industry-standard formats, you will need to use that either in addition to the industry-standard formats or in lieu of those formats.

> 5-85 The BOSS shall provide ANY System to import data in the format specified in ANY System Interface Format.

> 5-86 The BOSS shall provide ANY System to export data in the format specified in ANY System Interface Format.

This brings up another point that people say is a limitation of good requirements engineering—requirements referencing other requirements or other documents. Purists say that you should never reference requirements or other documents. Our approach is this rule is like the Pirate's Code mentioned previously. By that, you will run into situations where following rules so absolutely makes it such that you have to work inordinately hard to work around them. Otherwise, you might have to duplicate the interface specification again, and that adds nothing to the requirements.

There is another rule that requirement purists insist on—you should never write a requirement with a negative in it. For example, consider the following requirement:

> 5-87 The BOSS shall prohibit payroll data from being exported from the System.

That was instead of writing it as follows:

> 5-88 The BOSS shall not allow payroll data from being exported from the System.

Clearly, the first way is better. That said, there might be instances where it is nearly impossible to write any other way. For example, if you had a system that needed to have a specific query like this:

> 5-89 The system shall query for books about Vikings but not the Minnesota Vikings football team.

Chances are you would not write something that specific. This was an example of a "negative" in a requirement statement.

If you are going to connect to the Internet, you are going to need additional protection, such as firewalls. Here you will need to talk with an engineer who specializes in this. Here is a start:

> 5-90 The BOSS shall have a firewall to protect itself from Internet intrusion.

> 5-91 The BOSS shall have virus protection.

> 5-92 The BOSS shall prevent keystroke capture.
>
> 5-93 The BOSS shall protect against denial of service (DOS).

Reuse

Once you have defined certain security requirements, particularly access control, you should be able to reuse them throughout your career. Perform requirements reuse whenever you can.

■ **Real-World Note** One day, I associated almost 700 requirements to one project. That sounds quite impressive, until you realize that I was reusing 700 requirements I had written before. It still is not as easy as just copying 700 statements. I had to search more than 1,000 statements and decide for each one if it belonged to the new project. I did reject more than 300 statements and had to modify dozens to make it appropriate to the new project.

This reuse is an exercise to consider for every project. People have been doing code reuse for decades. However, my experience in some federal government organization shows not enough have been doing it for requirements; although this could be happening anywhere in the industry, I cannot speak to it first-hand.

Reuse can come in two variants: completely copying existing requirements and copying some existing requirements but modifying the statements to reflect the new system.

Here is an example of copying.

The previous system is called PSS.

> 5-94 The PSS system shall require a customer to enter his name as a first name and last name.
>
> 5-95 The PSS system shall require a customer to enter an email address.

For our reuse, we will use our system BOSS.

> 5-96 The BOSS system shall require a customer to enter his name as a first name and last name.
>
> 5-97 The BOSS system shall require a customer to enter an email address.

Notice that only the names of the system changed, nothing else. The PSS could be a current system or even a predecessor to BOSS. If the requirement has not changed, there is no reason to modify the text.

Now, examine an example where the text of the requirement will be modified somewhat. This could be caused by changes to the environment or the requirement does not fit the original exactly.

Again, the previous system is called PSS.

> 5-98 The PSS system shall require a customer's company name.

> 5-99 The PSS system shall require a customer's company address.

For our reuse, the new system is BOSS. The difference for this new system is that the companies in question are online, so some modification to the requirements is in order.

> 5-100 The PSS system shall require a customer's company **online name (e.g., OnLineCompany.com)**.

> 5-101 The PSS system shall require a customer's company **URL (e.g., `http://onlinecompany.com/sites`)**.

These are just simple examples; you will likely have many more that you would reuse, as in the previous Real-World Note, where 700 were reused.

Real-World Note Part of the challenge I have encountered results from working in a classified environment. For reasons of security, people did not talk between different projects. One example of this problem was discovered in the first Gulf War, where people within the government were not sharing information that should have been shared, because security did not allow them to share within the U.S. government. Because people were accustomed to working in what was unaffectionately called a *stove-piped* environment, people did not share code and certainly not requirements, and in some cases the data itself. This was a tough culture to change as it had gone on for many decades. However, you should see less resistance to it now as you move into the workforce.

Cybersecurity is a growing field. Unless you have a degree in this or extensive experience in that field, you will need to work with an expert to get this defined properly.

Tip There are very consistent areas that you should consider for reuse. The hardware configuration probably will not change much in your organization, along with related functional areas such as systems administration, auditing, printing, and monitoring. Of course, searching, system access and related roles and responsibilities, and report generation will have many of the same requirements for every application. What will be different is the data that is accessed. There will be others, but the number of reused requirements will be less and subject to your organizational needs.

Scalability

This "ility" refers to a system's ability to scale up (or down) either to additional capabilities or to allow for growth. Some organizations may call it *extensibility*, but it is essentially the same thing. For this text, we will use *scalability*.

■ **Tip** As you learned in Chapter 3, however, different organizations may use them slightly differently, and this will not be elucidated here. You must read the concepts in this and the next section and use them as you need in accordance with your organizational direction.

Now, examine some of these capabilities you want to address here.

You want to be able to scale up the system as more data is added. Say you anticipate your healthcare benefit application will grow 20 percent a year. You need to capture that growth once you have estimated the size of the original database.

For example, the requirements could be as follows:

> 5-102 The BOSS system shall be able to store 6 terabytes of data when deployed.

> 5-103 The BOSS system data shall be able to grow by 24% per year.

In addition, as new features are added to a system of services, you need to add a feature/function/service without having to completely redo the entire suite of services or a significant portion of them. Of course, this is supposed to be the benefit of SOA, but that does not mean you have a true SOA implementation, if at all.

Refer to a statement like the following:

> 5-104 DRAFT The BOSS system shall be extensible/scalable.

The previous statement is not a good one, based on what you learned in Chapter 2. So, how should you do it?

> 5-105 The BOSS system data shall be able to add five services per year without impacting the system performance requirements.

As you can see, this statement captures a quantifiable value for the number of services added while ensuring that performance. That may require the designers to add hardware to support the new capabilities, but they know what the need is.

You might need to address throughput scalability. Do a little research on the Affordable Care Act standup of their web site in 2013. It had real throughput scalability issue, which created quite a brouhaha. It causes one to wonder just what requirements they had for the Alternative Care Act (ACA), aka the Obamacare system. That is another area you might want to consider writing requirements for if you will have significant throughput fluctuations in your system. Look at an actual example when the U.S. government stood up their ACA. They had determined an average number of enrollees per unit of time.

How do you address that?

> 5-106 The BOSS system data shall permit 30,000 people to enroll onto the system per day.

However, what is likely to happen both early when the system goes operational and near the end of the enrollment period? That is when a significant number of people are likely to use the system. As history showed, there were significant issues with the system being unable to handle the demands. Therefore, the normal value shown previously would be insufficient to address the needs.

How would be fix it? You should add a requirement like the following:

> 5-107 The BOSS system data shall permit a peak of 300,000 people to enroll onto the system per day.

This is an important aspect to any performance requirement. Not only should you address normal activities, but also you need to address peak loads, especially in the extensible/scalable aspect.

Some sources say you might examine platform considerations, contractual considerations, software, and response time. The first one will examined last. You saw response time in detail in the "Performance" section of Chapter 4. Scalability requirements are a natural extension of those requirements, like when you look at performance for simple queries versus performance at peak times. Contractual considerations are something that clearly are not part of the requirement phase, more the design and development phase, and sometimes the operations and maintenance phase. This brings you to the platform and software considerations. Again, they belong in the design phase, rather than the requirements phase. In the traditional waterfall method, these factors were captured in the design specifications presented at the end of the design phase. The main reason for not specifying the topics in requirements is because these topics are implementation, which you know requirements engineers are not supposed to define.

You could consider the following scalability topics:

- How to accommodate increasing numbers of users.
- The number of SQL statements that can run and provide results simultaneously (assuming SQL will be the query statement of choice in your database—a big "if").
- How to accommodate increasing numbers of transactions per second.
- Not only should you address the total number of users, but also you need to address total number of concurrent users.

Think back to the peak user requirement you saw:

> 5-108 The BOSS system data shall permit a peak of 300,000 people to enroll onto the system per day.

That works out to an average usage of 2,083 people per minute. Think about it, if this was enrollment for the ACA website, would everyone take a turn throughout the day? With Americans only having four different time zones in the continental United States, that is highly unlikely. You are more likely to see it in an eight-hour time period, spread over the four time zones. So, how can you accommodate that? Consider something like the following requirements:

> 5-109 The BOSS system data shall permit a peak of 30,000 people to enroll onto the system in one hour.

That works out to 8.33 people per second—on average. Again, you have to consider peak numbers and figure people will be on the system for say 5, 10, or even 20 minutes per person. You must write a requirement that takes into account that the peak time on for people is roughly 10 minutes. That drives up to a number of concurrent users like this:

> 5-110 The BOSS system data shall permit 10,000 concurrent people to enroll onto the system in one hour.

■ **Note** Concurrent users are people on the system at the same time.

There are some things many people have not always thought about when scaling their systems—pull-down or pop-up menus. Assume you are writing an airline system and you want to add or delete specific flight numbers. You want this to be done quickly and with the least effort.

Traditionally, software had that information hard-coded into the system. That meant that to get the change, the code needed to be rewritten, tested, and then deployed. That process could take up to six months, depending on how quickly the turnaround time was. For this type of system, that is totally unacceptable. How do you fix it? Make it so the items on such lists are in files that can be easily rewritten and then just called by the application, without putting the list internal to the code. The update to the list is made and then sent to every customer location for replacement and can be available immediately.

Are you affecting the implementation? You could argue yes, but think of it more of an architectural constraint because of responsiveness to the customers' needs. The requirements to consider are as follows (notice the "negative" statement):

> 5-111 The BOSS system lists shall entered in files external to the code so updates do not require a recompilation of the code.

You may need more requirements than this, but you will know your environment better than most.

Real-World Note You need to learn about the system as much as you can. With that information, you will prevent potential misunderstanding about the system. I had a situation similar to creating lists where the discussion dealt with modification to a pull-down list. I had visited a stakeholder and they complained about old values in the list no longer being valid, and they wanted them removed from the list. I explained this to the developer, and he went ballistic on me, saying that doing that would screw up the referential integrity of the database and he would not do it. I calmly pointed out that I said that the customer did not want to see the values. I had said nothing about deleting the values from the database. To which the developer said, "Oh."

So, you need to learn enough about the system (at least once it is deployed) so you can look out for the customer and work with the developers, designer, architects, testers, and even those who deploy it so you can aid the customers.

To generate growth over time whether for extensibility, scalability, or even just performance, some knowledge about the past is useful. If you have an older system that is fairly stable, you can get some good projections, with one proviso. If you are just improving on an old system but adding significantly new capabilities or new data sources, this projection may not be so stable.

Assume you were digitizing all your old hard-copy records; you probably have a good idea how much you have to digitize and how much that is likely to grow. For example, the federal government when they were given an Executive Order that says all digital records must be included by 2019. That means all existing digital records need to be included. You may not have a grasp of how much your organization has in e-mail, hard drive files, and databases. There could be significant growth there. Factors like this will significantly affect your growth that would not be represented by adding, say, 50 percent to existing hard-copy records. It could be a factor of three, four, or even ten times more.

In addition, newer systems may not have good historical information to help with estimating growth. Here, being conservative to keep costs down will have severe adverse impacts very quickly. It is better to estimate higher numbers rather than be too low. A word to the wise: This also explains the push by organizations to embrace the cloud architecture to help mitigate scalability. However, that discussion is beyond this text. Besides, it is implementation (unless mandated by architecture).

Usability

As defined by Merriam-Webster's Collegiate Dictionary, *usability* is

> *convenient and practicable for use*[5]

---

[5]By permission. From *Merriam-Webster's Collegiate® Dictionary*, 11th Edition ©2016 by Merriam-Webster, Inc. (`www.merriam-webster.com/`)

Usability is how effectively users can learn and use a system. While many people think this applies only to computer software, think of your phone. That is a complete system with both hardware and software. Alternatively, think of your car. That needs to be easy to use.

Note If you have ever test-driven many different makes of cars, say, at CarMax, or traveled often where you have lots of rental cars, you will understand that while the operation of the vehicle is consistent, the user interface, where everything in the interior is and how it works, varies drastically, which reinforces the point for standardization. That is another topic to discuss elsewhere.

How do you define user interface requirements for software and hardware? In part, a user interface is an implementation. Remember, what is good is clearly subjective, and requirements cannot capture subjectivity.

Then how can you capture user interface needs? One approach, and many projects take this, is to define user interface standards. This approach can take the subjectivity out of the requirements.

Another approach that is used extensively is prototyping. Again, you will learn more about this approach in Chapter 9. Basically, developers try approaches, run them by stakeholders, get feedback, and keep cycling through this process to get a valid approach that is acceptable to users.

Because of the importance of usability, you will spend a good deal of time on it. Thus, this topic will be captured in the Chapter 10 on user interfaces, given its importance.

Accessibility

Accessibility is the degree to which a product, device, service, or environment is available to as many people as possible. This usually focuses on people with disabilities or special needs and their right of access, enabling the use of assistive technology.

Do not confuse accessibility with usability, which is the extent to which a product or service achieves specified effectiveness, efficiency, and satisfaction goals. A significant source of accessibility comes from the U.S. government in the form of Section 508 of the U.S. Rehabilitation Act, which U.S. federal agencies must comply with in order to make their web sites accessible to the general public as well as government workers. Check out the U.S. General Services Administration web site, which has online training courses for free to learn about these rules.

What requirements should you capture for this subject? Obviously, you could say the following:

> 5-112 DRAFT—PARENT The BOSS shall be fully compliant with Section 508 of the US Rehabilitation Act.

As you have seen before, this does not address every aspect of it. You should go through Section 508 to address children requirements that are needed to be addressed for your situation.

Note There are exemptions to 508 compliancy, such a military intelligence gathering systems in a combat zone and other special cases. Read about these and see if your situation applies. Look at `www.section508.gov/`.

What are some candidate children requirements?

> 5-113 CHILD The BOSS shall provide a text equivalent for every non-text element (e.g., icon selection).
>
> 5-114 CHILD The BOSS shall provide a text equivalent for image linkages.
>
> 5-115 CHILD When electronic forms are designed to be completed online, the BOSS form shall allow people using assistive technology to access the information, field elements, and functionality required for completion and submission of the form, including all directions and cues.

Clearly, this list is not complete; just a few examples were illustrated. However, you get the idea.

Interoperability

Merriam-Webster's Collegiate Dictionary defines *interoperability* as the

> *ability of a system (as a weapons system) to work with or use the parts or equipment of another system*[6]

For software, interoperability describes the ability of different programs to exchange data via a common set of exchange formats so that they can read and write to the same file formats. The lack of interoperability can happen when people do not follow standards.

In software without standard data exchange formats, even within one application, the interface between modules of code becomes very complex. You can see how the need to have an interface with every other module grows quickly to be unmanageable. Hence, the industry developed SOA where there was an enterprise service bus (ESB), the foundation/framework that all services (think a phone app) interact with, where the ESB provides the communications among the services. Then the services have one standard interface that they all must use. This is not intended to be a tutorial on SOA but introduces the concept so that you understand the concept and how you can write requirements should you need to define SOA and help craft interoperability requirements.

---

[6]By permission. From *Merriam-Webster's Collegiate® Dictionary*, 11th Edition ©2016 by Merriam-Webster, Inc. (`www.merriam-webster.com/`)

How do you write requirements for this? You might try something like this initially:

> 5-116 DRAFT—The BOSS shall be interoperable.

However, when you think back to the attributes of a good requirement, more than one attribute is not met. It clearly is not atomic, written to its lowest level. Additionally, this is subjective. Is it verifiable? Clearly, you need to be more specific. How about the following?

> 5-117 DRAFT—The BOSS shall follow the service-oriented architecture.

That is better, but again this clearly is not decomposed to the lowest level. What should you be defining? In this case, look at a write-up on SOA to see what capabilities it needs and capture those. For example, you could write the following:

> 5-118 The BOSS shall have a communications layer with only one interface for all services must follow.

> 5-119 The BOSS shall require all services to communicate only to the communications layer, not with other services.

Notice that this statement did not specify an ESB, JBoss, JEMS, and so on, but only using generic terms like *services* to keep from forcing an implementation onto the designers. That said, if your management or office architect has mandated that SOA will be followed, you can start with the SOA requirement written as draft earlier. That would be the parent requirement, say requirement 1.1, with all the SOA detailed requirements written as children to that 1.1 (e.g., 1.1.1, 1.1.2, ... 1.1.N, where N is some number). That way, the testing would be done at the 1.1.N level, not at the 1.1 level, so you still have good requirement attributes.

Portability

Portability is the ability to run on numerous different computing platforms. You should address the following questions, at a minimum:

- Can you application run on different operating systems?
- Can you migrate the data to other systems?
- Will your web applications work on different browsers?
- Can the application run on different platforms without significant rework?

Look at requirements to consider as a start for the first three at least.
Different Operating Systems

> 5-120 The BOSS shall work on Windows 8.

> 5-121 The BOSS shall work on Mac OS X.

> 5-122 The BOSS shall work on Unix version 7.

5-123 The BOSS shall work on Linux version 3.13.

5-124 The BOSS shall work on Android OS 4.4.

5-125 The BOSS shall work on Unix.

Different Systems

5-126 The BOSS shall work on personal computers.

5-127 The BOSS shall work on Android phones.

5-128 The BOSS shall work on Xbox 360.

Different Browsers

5-129 The BOSS shall work on Internet Explorer 11.

5-130 The BOSS shall work on Firefox 29.

Remember to specify what, not how—that's what the developers get paid the big bucks for. (Of course, given the RE's significant value to the project, —REs should get bigger bucks. First, REs impact more defect reduction, and there are fewer REs than coders.)

Stability

In the medical field, this would relate to how long a drug would maintain its effectiveness. This would apply to any substance whose properties change with time. Clearly, the medical field is the primary area where this occurs.

5-131 The BOSS high blood pressure drug shall retain its potency of 95% for 12 months.

Does this apply to hardware components? That depends on if there are elements within the system that change with time. If, say, a battery is included, you might need to specify the life of the battery as it ages.

5-132 The BOSS Unit Radiation Dosimeter battery shall provide 5 volts DC for three years without replacement.

What about software? Can you think of any component of a software system that is volatile with time? None come to mind. (If you can, write to me.) The only stability relationship to software deals with how stable requirements in total are with respect to the original system. This would deal more with how well you maintain the requirements scope creep of a project, to help ensure its success, and not specific to particular group of requirements. In addition, the same would apply to any system, hardware and software. You have heard of cost overruns of military systems. That usually is significant changes in requirements with time.

Supportability

Supportability refers to "the inherent characteristics of design and installation that enable the effective and efficient maintenance and support of the system throughout the life cycle," from class lecture at San Jose State University.

These are the requirements to make the deployment and maintenance as efficient as practical. For example, consider the following for the hardware project:

> 5-133 The BOSS Unit Radiation Dosimeter shall require no maintenance by the individual who wears its.

For software, it could involve requirements like the following:

> 5-134 The BOSS services shall be replaceable individual units that can be plugged into the infrastructure with requiring no affect to other services in the system.

There are more opportunities for additional supportability requirements, of course, so it may take some digging on your part to find them. You will see more about this subject in Chapter 8.

Testability

Initially, you might think that this is not something you would specify in the requirements, that this is captured in either contract documentation or test planning documentation. What about having certain testability built in to the hardware and software?

In the hardware example, look at the testability requirement:

> 5-135 The BOSS Unit Radiation Dosimeter shall require quarterly comparison of individual dosimeters against the BOSS Radiation Calibration Source.

There can be more examples of diagnostics in hardware systems. Think of a military aircraft that needs diagnostics run against various systems without requiring the aircraft to be taken down for maintenance.

In, the software example, think of diagnostic requirements:

> 5-136 The FBI BOSS Records Management Scanning function shall contain sample records to be used for scanning calibration.

As always, there are many more examples that you will want to consider for these types of requirements. A significant driver is the likelihood of change over time or the difficulty of making updates to the system. Think of software controlling a nuclear power plant or hardware on a deep-space probe. Testability is how easily something can be tested.

Recoverability

This means the ability to recover from some event, say, the crash of a system. How quickly do you return to full operations? Here's an example:

> 5-137 In the event that the FBI BOSS Records Management system crashes, the system shall be returned to full operations in 48 hours from the beginning of the crash.

Of course, there can be varying grades of recovery. Here's an example:

> 5-138 In the event that the FBI BOSS Records Management system crashes, the six critical functions shall be returned to operations in 4 hours from the beginning of the crash.

You will need to define what your critical functions are. Naturally, six may not be your number. This was just for the example. Notice that the requirement specified when the clock started—from the beginning of the crash. You could use start with the time the crash was detected or when the crash completed. Remember, some crashes may be gradual. This is why you should use the start of the crash.

The criticality of the system will drive how quickly you will want the system restored. In some extreme cases, you want it within, say, five seconds, in life-critical systems. This will drive design decisions such as the backup capability of the system and where all backups are stored with respect to the operational system. You may have an immediate backup co-located for quick switchover and maybe a second backup at another facility in the event of a natural disaster that destroys or eliminates the operational location for some significant time.

Would you use this requirement for hardware? Of course, not only do applications crash, but so do computer systems. If a lightning strike fries your server's hard drive, you need a way to recover. In fact, look at the two requirements in this section. Nowhere does it say hardware or software. Therefore, these requirements apply to both.

Serviceability

Serviceability means how easy it is to perform service when it is required. Here's an example:

> 5-139 The BOSS Unit Radiation Dosimeter battery shall be replaced with removal of the battery storage cover in five second and the battery replacement in three second.

For software, it could be the following:

> 5-140 The BOSS pick list values shall be replaced by copying a new XML file to the deployed software system without requiring recompiling any code.

Manageability

Manageability is defined as the ability to manage the system to ensure the continued health of a system.

The distinction between manageability and maintainability may not seem like much, but the nuance is important. Earlier in this chapter, you saw very detailed maintainability requirements, but here are some additional examples of maintainability requirements:

> 5-141 The BOSS Unit Radiation Reader shall have hardware functions as standalone cards that can be removed and reinstalled as plug and play components.
>
> 5-142 The BOSS Unit Radiation Reader shall have software functions as standalone services that can be removed and reinstalled as plug and play software components without affecting the rest of the software.

Now, look at some manageability requirements.

> 5-143 The BOSS Unit Radiation Reader shall have the ability to expand Random Access Memory chips on the standalone memory cards that can be removed and reinstalled as plug and play components.
>
> 5-144 The BOSS Unit Radiation Reader shall have software pick lists stored as files in order to add, change, or delete values without having to recompile the code and instead just replace the file.

The best distinction is to equate maintainability with the current system and to equate manageability with the future system. In addition, *future* does not mean years or decades from now; it could be weeks or days. Nevertheless, it helps to deal with the timing of changes. Having looked at other definitions, the boundary between the two is blurry. Regardless, this distinction you may or may not need to make. Nevertheless, if you combine the two, consider both the current and future aspects and you will not go wrong.

Summary

This chapter covered the more numerous nonfunctional requirements. Because of the more specialized nature of them, you will find that most stakeholders will be less knowledgeable about these types of requirements than the functional ones discussed in Chapter 4. In Chapter 9 you will learn some techniques for how to collect nonfunctional requirements. This chapter gets you started by identifying the types of requirements you will need to define.

References

"What is functional and non-functional requirement." *Stack Overflow*. Feb. 2015. `http://stackoverflow.com/questions/16475979/what-is-functional-and-non-functional-requirement`

United States Government. *Resources for understanding and implementing Section 508*. Feb. 2015, `www.section508.gov/`

Zargar, Ali. "Supportability." Tech 101 class lecture from Department of Aviation and technology at San Jose State University. Feb. 2015. `www.engr.sjsu.edu/azargar/Tech-101/TECH%20101-Supportability.ppt`

"*Merriam-Webster's Collegiate® Dictionary*, 11th Edition ©2016 by Merriam-Webster, Inc. (`www.merriam-webster.com/`)

Office of the Under Secretary of Defense (Acquisition, Technology, and Logistics). *DoD 4120.24-M Defense Standardization Program (DSP) Policies and Procedures*. March 2000.

"How to write Performance Requirements with Example." 2012. 1202PERFORMANCE, Performance by Design, Feb. 2015. `www.1202performance.com/atricles/how-to-write-performance-requirements-with-example/`

Exercises

Exercise 1

Define survivability with respect to the Hubble replacement. Determine whether this is functional or nonfunctional. Explain why.

Exercise 2

Define survivability with respect to the M-1 main battle tank replacement. Determine whether this is functional or nonfunctional. Explain why.

Exercise 3

Define cybersecurity for the Department of Defense's Internet. Determine whether this is functional or nonfunctional. Explain why.

Exercise 4

At the Three Mile Island Nuclear Power Plant, their control room had alarms and flashing lights to alert operators of emergency situations. One factor that inhibited responses was the constant sounding of the alarms and the flashing of the lights. Should sounding alarms and flashing lights be used in the future? If so, why and how? If not, why not?

Exercise 5

Define the requirements for a phone to only call and receive phone calls, with no other features.

Exercise 6

Define the requirements for deep-space probe in the "Capacity" section in this chapter and show that the numbers work for transmission rate and capacity.

Exercise 7

In the "Quality" section, you examined the following scan scenario.

> 5-140 (5-20) The FBI BOSS Records Management scanning shall capture 75% of the characters per page to be considered a quality scan.

Now the default scan will be 300 DPI. If the scan does not meet the 75 percent, the process will be repeated at the 600 DPI, 1200 DPI, and finally 2400 DPI. If the 75 percent cannot be achieved at 2400 DPI, the quality achieved there will be the default.

Write the remaining requirements to address the last three sentences.

Exercise 8

This is a RAM exercise.

R1 to R6 all have reliabilities of 0.9. For the following configuration, what is the reliability for the following combination?

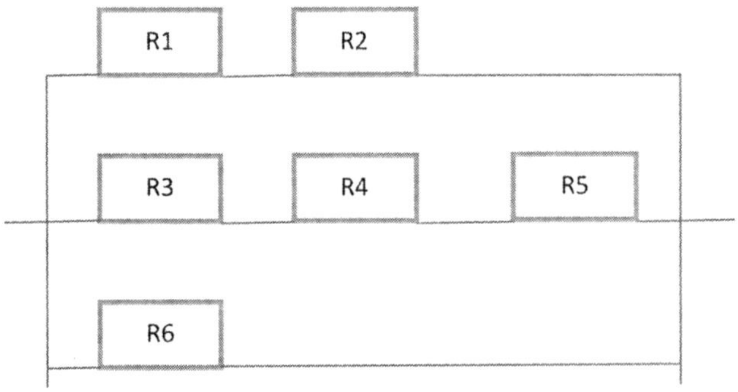

Exercise 9

Write the access requirements for the BOSS system that is stand-alone but with import of data.

Exercise 10

What areas on your cell phone's specific phone services would need scalability?

Exercise 11

Write sample requirements to address portability so that the application can run on different platforms without significant rework.

CHAPTER 6

Lists of Items and the Order of Steps and Data Elements

Chapter 2 stated you define your requirement down to the atomic level. So, does that mean you have only one value in each *shall* statement? The answer is no. As with most things in life, and requirements definition, it depends. Examining the following examples will help you determine when a list within a requirement will work, versus just a list of requirements. Experience working requirements will help you judge as you see what works one way versus the other. Another situation where lists of items occur is in the specifications of messages, which you will examine here. Then we look at lists of requirements that have a sequence or order associated with them. Finally, you will examine the order of data elements.

Now, let's explore these various types of lists in this chapter.

Lists of Items in Requirements

The point of this section is to distinguish when to use lists of items and when to separate things into different requirements. If you remember in the discussion on the atomic attribute for a requirement, one rule said that you need to have only one statement per *shall* statement. "Have only one value" was never explicitly stated. Now, examine an example where you want to collect information on a person where the data you are interested in is as follows:

- First name
- Middle name
- Last name
- Street address with apartment number
- City
- State
- Home phone
- Cell phone

G. Koelsch, *Requirements Writing for System Engineering*,
DOI 10.1007/978-1-4842-2099-3_6

You want requirements to capture these values for the Person Collection Function. You could write each as a separate requirement, where you will have the following:

> 6-1 DRAFT The BOSS Person Collection Function shall collect First Name.
>
> 6-2 DRAFT The BOSS Person Collection Function shall collect Middle Name.
>
> 6-3 DRAFT The BOSS Person Collection Function shall collect Last Name.
>
> 6-4 DRAFT The BOSS Person Collection Function shall collect Street Address with apartment number.
>
> 6-5 DRAFT The BOSS Person Collection Function shall collect City.
>
> 6-6 DRAFT The BOSS Person Collection Function shall collect State.
>
> 6-7 DRAFT The BOSS Person Collection Function shall collect Home phone.
>
> 6-8 DRAFT The BOSS Person Collection Function shall collect Cell phone.

There is one drawback to this approach. Given that all these values should be collected at the same time, with them listed separately, you could lose this connection. Therefore, you should consider the following approach:

> 6-9 The BOSS Person Collection Function shall collect the following data:
>
> a. First Name
>
> b. Middle Name
>
> c. Last Name
>
> d. Street Address with apartment number
>
> e. City
>
> f. State
>
> g. Home phone
>
> h. Cell Phone

Does this fly in the face of the edict to identify requirements as atomic? Yes...maybe. Remember the reasons to capture requirements at the atomic level? First, capture the requirements down to the lowest possible level. What is the lowest level here? Is it the data value level, or is it the collection of data level—the data values grouped together? It is at the collection of data level. If you still are uncertain, then look at the other area you should consider. Would these values be worked on by different people, for coding and/or testing? Given that someone would probably code these on one screen or tab, they would be worked as a unit. In addition, a tester would test all the data as one test.

However, you argue, if the phone number fields do not work, then you have the quandary of only part of the screen/tab and the associated requirement does not work. You are absolutely correct. Phone numbers would likely be coded and tested by the same person. Therefore, these values need to be worked on together. That need overrides the atomic principle for requirements. If one of two phone numbers works, it is only partially satisfied. Thus, you do not follow the atomic principle in this case.

Is there ever a case where you should separate the requirement? Well, in Chapter 2 you saw the example of the "print and display" type of requirements. In that case, initially all the requirements were written as "The system shall print and display…." You need to separate all the requirements into one statement for "print" and another requirement for "display." That still holds true. Therefore, what you have now are two ends of the spectrum. You definitely separate functions that are different, whereas you keep them together when they are small groups of data values that belong together. So, somewhere in between those two endpoints, you have to make a judgment call.

What factors should you look for that will help discriminate when to do one approach versus the other? This is a judgment call based on what we have discussed.

Now, look at another situation. The system needs to allow all users various accesses to the data within the system. Users will be able to read the data, add data, change existing data, and delete the data. Which of the two approaches make sense here?

Here is option 1:

> 6-10 DRAFT The BOSS Access Control Function shall allow a user to have an access to the data consisting of the following:
>
> - Read
> - Add
> - Edit
> - Delete

Here is option 2:

> 6-11 DRAFT The BOSS Access Control Function shall allow a user to have read data access.
>
> 6-12 DRAFT The BOSS Access Control Function shall allow a user to add data access.
>
> 6-13 DRAFT The BOSS Access Control Function shall allow a user to have edit data access.
>
> 6-14 DRAFT The BOSS Access Control Function shall allow a user to have delete data access.

One additional point is important here: a user could be assigned more than one access function. This points to a distinction: of the options are not mutually exclusive, that is another reason to combine them. For example, users who have access to add, edit, or delete data also should have access to read the data. So, someone may have read and add access; or read, add, and edit access; or access to all four functions. Thus, in this case, option 1 is the correct answer.

Consider also that there could be a variation on the add access function. Some users in the organization can suggest that a new person be added to the picklist, and one or more other users are able to approve the addition. So, when someone joins the team, a person who has Suggest rights can propose the addition of the person. The "suggester" proposes the name in a blank field at the bottom of the picklist. The name does not show up for everyone on the picklist until an "approver" accepts the name. If the "approver" rejects it (say because the person is only an intern who will go away in two months), then the name is not added to the list. In this example, you would add the two options, Suggest and Approve, to the requirement as such:

> 6-15 DRAFT The BOSS Picklist Control Function shall allow a user to have an access to the data consisting of the following:
>
> - Read
> - Add
> - Edit
> - Delete
> - Suggest
> - Approve

In this situation, you might need additional requirements to explain what role the Suggest and Approve actions would be.

Back to the earlier discussion of when do you use a list of requirements versus one requirement. What happens if the number of data values grows significantly? Ask yourself if it is likely they would be done on one screen or tab; then that may help to write one requirement. However, what you learned earlier said that you are supposed to write the requirements in a manner that does not limit the design. You are absolutely correct. Then the answer becomes a judgment call. Would 12 values on one presentation (screen/tab/etc.) be OK? Probably. Again, it gets to the stakeholder needs. Do the values need to stay together? If so, then the answer probably is yes, do one requirement.

What if the number of data values is 25 or 67? Now you see it gets much harder. Twenty-five maybe, again, if they are significantly related to each other. However, you really need to analyze whether they cannot be grouped in some way. Think of a medical history form where it asks if you have had any of several dozen conditions or diseases. If there are two groupings of data values, then you should have two requirements. As for the 67 data values, you really need to analyze it carefully. If you were adding a new person to your engineering company, in your HR department you would have a Personnel Branch, Payroll Branch, Retirement Branch, and Disciplinary Action Branch. In the Engineering department you have Software Maintenance Branch, Software Maintenance Branch, Branch, Hardware Maintenance Branch, Software Development Branch, and Integration Branch. Even though there are nine branches, you still would likely break them apart by departments, with one requirement for each department, and then list the branches as elements within the department.

There may be situations where it is difficult to break a significant list of values into groups. Look at that situation in the next section.

Lists of Data Elements

You will look at a series of data elements in a message. Messages are a technique used between systems. In the particular example, these messages are between a mission-control system and a space probe. Messages are either commands to the spacecraft or data messages back from the probe portion of the spacecraft. This is actually a simple example because only image data is collected. In the real world, messages can be much more complicated with very intricate values passed between systems. What will be used for this example will be long but the same kind of data repeated. Real-world examples could have variable records that are dependent on the data collected. This example will have image data and its location, with many repeated pairs of this data. Messages that are thousands of bits of data are not unusual.

Now, consider a message you want to send to and receive from a deep-space probe being planned to explore the trans-Saturnian planets. You have to specify the message format you are going to use to transmit commands and receive their data. The message for the probe's collected data is going to be more than 2,000 characters long, with very specific formats and possibly many parts to it. No, this is not a real project, just one that was fabricated as an example. However, I have used very complex, long messages just like this. The reason for the length of a message is to capture a picture that has to specify either color or significant shades of gray and the location of each pixel.

Maybe before you examine the specifics of the topic of data elements, you need to have some background so you understand some of the points the stakeholders need to consider. In this case, the stakeholders are NASA. The first item to consider is how far away the probe will likely be.

Uranus (the closest approach the body will have to us) is 2.6 trillion kilometers.

Pluto (the farthest approach the body will have to us) is 4.2 trillion kilometers.

Given that the speed of light is 300,000 kilometers per second, it will take about 2.4 hours to send a message to Uranus at its closest and about 3.9 hours to send a message to Pluto at its farthest. Yes, that is hours, not seconds. Even going to the earth's moon has about a 1.3-second delay. Therefore, a major factor is not waiting for a response before continuing a message. Thus, the message has to be complete, with a significant ability to check that the values are sent and received.

This example will not consist of the entire system here but will show some representative examples of messages. For this example, the system will send two types of messages to the probe, when in reality, there could be dozens or even hundreds of messages. The mission-control system will send a request for system diagnostics. In the other pair of messages, the system will send a request for the spacecraft to send an individual image captured from the imaging system on board. Yes, also, there could be other detectors from parts of the electromagnetic spectrum, not to mention telling what the probe should be sensing. This gives you the magnitude of what space probes may consist of, yet you will examine only two aspects to keep the example relatively simple.

You are going to consider the data element technique for requirements, where you create one requirement for each data element. You must capture the following attributes for each data element (as is appropriate, as you may not use all):

a. Requirement number

b. Field number/designator

c. Field name

d. Description of the field

e. Length of the field

f. Format of the field

g. Units of the field

h. Any special Information related to the field (ranges, selectable items, etc.)

■ **Note** You may think of more for your unique situation, but you have a good foundation here.

What is a most important distinction from how you defined requirements for data elements before is the use of a requirement number for each one. The reason you do this is what was discussed at the end of the previous section; when you will have many values, you want each one tracked, especially given all the attributes you need to define for each data element. When the message is built and verified, each data element must be verified against each attribute of that data element. The discussion in the list of data elements was not that specific.

Now, examine the four messages.

Diagnostics Request

This will be a simple message. However, it introduces the format that you will see through the rest of this section because of the nature of the messages sent. Remember, everything will be eventually reduced to zeroes and ones, so most messages are numerical, as they are for this example in general. You will also examine how you can use this same approach for more sophisticated messaging techniques when you consider interfaces in a later chapter. Each field is a fixed length, whereas some messages are variable in length, just not for this example.

This message sends a diagnostic request to the spacecraft. Here is the requirement and the associated message:

> 6-16 The BOSS Probe Request Message shall contain the following:

7. Probe Diagnostics Request Message

Req. No.	Number	Name	Description	Length	Format	Units	Special Info
7.1	1	Activate	Command activation of the probe controller	3	NNN	N/A	007
7.2	2	CallDiag	Call diagnostics of specified subsystems	4	NNNN	N/A	0001 to 2401; 0001 is all subsystems
7.3	3	Sleep	Return command activation subsystem to sleep mode	3	NNN	N/A	999

Notice that Units does not apply here. In reality, the message would not repeat a blank field. This is just here to be illustrative. Field 1 will always be 007 since this tells the spacecraft this is a diagnostic message. Field 2 will specify which subsystem should be diagnosed, ranging from 1 to 2401. If 0001 is used, it requests diagnostics for all the subsystems on the spacecraft. Field 3, 999, means the message is done.

There may be some requirements that must be accomplished before messages can be passed that are unique to each system, applications, service, or device . You will capture them in the header section of the interface requirements and/or in the system's requirements, such as whether data is over synchronous or asynchronous transfer. Are the transfers at specified times? On the other hand, are they called on command? Are they two-way or just one-way? There are more possible considerations that will not be elaborated on here because the diverse nature of what you will encounter.

Diagnostics Response

This message captures the results of the diagnosis performed based on the diagnostic request message.

> 6-17 The BOSS Probe Response Message shall contain the following:

201. Probe Diagnostics Response Message (for only one specified subsystem)

Req. No.	Num-ber	Name	Description	Length	Format	Units	Special Info
201.1	1	Message type	Diagnostics response	4	NNNN	N/A	0070
201.2	2	DiagTyp	Is it all subsystems or just one specified (2 for this message)	1	N	N/A	1 = all, 2 = one subsystems
201.3	3	Diag-Status	Return code of the status of the subsystem	3	NNN	N/A	999
201.4	4	Called-Diag	Specified subsystem	4	NNNN	N/A	9999
201.5	5	Done	End of message	2	NN	N/A	99

Field 1 will always be 0070 since this tells the spacecraft this is a diagnostic response message. Field 2 will specify whether this is just one subsystem (value = 2) or all subsystems (value = 1). Field 3 will specify the subsystem diagnostic status. Field 4 will specify which subsystem should be diagnosed, ranging from 1 to 2401. If 0001 is used, it requests diagnostics for all the subsystems on the spacecraft. Field 5, 99, means the message is done.

This example did not show all the subsystems being diagnosed here. Fields 3 and 4 would be repeated as many times as there are subsystems (assume 1138); you would have fields 3 through 2278, with 2279 for the last value in the message. You can see why it would be too long for this text.

Image Request Message

This message sends an image request to the spacecraft. Here is the requirement and the associated message:

> 6-18 The BOSS Probe Image Request Message shall contain the following:

8. Probe Image Request Message

Req. No.	Number	Name	Description	Length	Format	Units	Special Info
8.1	1	Activate	Command activation of the probe controller calling for image	3	NNN	N/A	008
8.2	2	CallImage	Call the specified image	8	NNNNNNNN	N/A	
8.3	3	Sleep	Return Command activation subsystem to sleep mode	3	NNN		999

Image Response Message

This message sends an image response to the spacecraft. Here is the requirement and the associated message:

> 6-18 The BOSS Probe Image Response Message shall contain the following:

202. Probe Image Response Message

Req. No.	Num-ber	Name	Description	Length	Format	Units	Special Info
202.1	1	Activate	Command activation of the probe controller	4	NNNN	N/A	0080
202.2	2	Image-Sent	Specified image being sent	8	NNNNNNNN	N/A	0001 to 9999
202.3	3	Line 1 block 1	Defines the line number of image and block number	4	NNNN	N/A	0101
202.4	4	Image-Value	Compressed value of specified block	8	NNNNNNNN	N/A	
202.5	5	Line 1 block 2	Defines the line number of image and block number	4	NNNN	N/A	0101
202.6	6	Image-Value	Compressed value of specified block	8	NNNNNNNN	N/A	
202.7	7	Line 1 block 3	Defines the line number of image and block number	4	NNNN	N/A	0101
202.8	8	Image-Value	Compressed value of specified block	8	NNNNNNNN	N/A	
202.9	9	Line 1 block 4	Defines the line number of image and block number	4	NNNN	N/A	0101

(*continued*)

Req. No.	Num-ber	Name	Description	Length	Format	Units	Special Info
202.10	10	Image-Value	Compressed value of specified block	8	NNNNNNNN	N/A	
202.11	11	Line 2 block 1	Defines the line number of image and block number	4	NNNN	N/A	0101
202.12	12	Image-Value	Compressed value of specified block	8	NNNNNNNN	N/A	
202.13	13	Line 2 block 2	Defines the line number of image and block number	4	NNNN	N/A	0101
202.14	14	Image-Value	Compressed value of specified block	8	NNNNNNNN	N/A	
202.15	15	Line 2 block 3	Defines the line number of image and block number	4	NNNN	N/A	0101
202.16	16	Image-Value	Compressed value of specified block	8	NNNNNNNN	N/A	
202.17	17	Line 2 block 4	Defines the line number of image and block number	4	NNNN	N/A	0101
202.18	18	Image-Value	Compressed value of specified block	8	NNNNNNNN	N/A	

(*continued*)

Req. No.	Num-ber	Name	Description	Length	Format	Units	Special Info
202.19	19	Line 3 block 1	Defines the line number of image and block number	4	NNNN	N/A	0101
202.20	20	Image-Value	Compressed value of specified block	8	NNNNNNNN	N/A	
202.21	21	Line 3 block 2	Defines the line number of image and block number	4	NNNN	N/A	0101
202.22	22	Image-Value	Compressed value of specified block	8	NNNNNNNN	N/A	
202.23	23	Line 3 block 3	Defines the line number of image and block number	4	NNNN	N/A	0101
202.24	24	Image-Value	Compressed value of specified block	8	NNNNNNNN	N/A	
202.25	25	Line 3 block 4	Defines the line number of image and block number	4	NNNN	N/A	0101
202.26	26	Image-Value	Compressed value of specified block	8	NNNNNNNN	N/A	
202.27	27	Line 4 block 1	Defines the line number of image and block number	4	NNNN	N/A	0101

(*continued*)

Req. No.	Num-ber	Name	Description	Length	Format	Units	Special Info
202.28	28	Image-Value	Compressed value of specified block	8	NNNNNNNN	N/A	
202.29	29	Line 4 block 2	Defines the line number of image and block number	4	NNNN	N/A	0101
202.30	30	Image-Value	Compressed value of specified block	8	NNNNNNNN	N/A	
202.31	31	Line 4 block 3	Defines the line number of image and block number	4	NNNN	N/A	0101
202.32	32	Image-Value	Compressed value of specified block	8	NNNNNNNN	N/A	
202.33	33	Line 4 block 4	Defines the line number of image and block number	4	NNNN	N/A	0101
202.34	34	Image-Value	Compressed value of specified block	8	NNNNNNNN	N/A	
202.35	35	Sleep	Return command activation subsystem to sleep mode	3	NNN	N/A	999

Field 1 will always be 0080 since this tells the spacecraft this is an image message. Field 2 will specify which image this is, ranging from 1 to 999. The odd field numbers from 3 to 33 give the location of this particular pixel. The even field numbers from 4 to 34 give the color of this particular pixel. Field 35, 999, means the message is done.

Count the number of pixels, and you have only a 4-by-4 image. If you multiply that by the 999 different images, you have a bigger picture that is 15,984 pixels. Compare that to the megapixels that your phone has and you will see that is not very big. It may be the eight-character value has some compression. For messages of this kind, this would be implemented, but we will not go into that here.

What you have seen is what looks like a long message, yet the amount of data is not very big. Messages would likely be broken into smaller packets (aka messages) to ensure they are being transmitted correctly.

You might want to consider one additional field for the data element table—a Required field. By this, you should indicate whether a field must be provided or the record is not complete. Thus, the field value will be Y or N only—well, it may be conditional. Conditional means when you fill in one particular value, which means there are one or more additional fields to complete.

In an example of conditional entry is where a person is registering for something that requires an e-mail address. On the user screen you (as this person registering) see a field that captures how many e-mail addresses you want to be notified of blog updates. The acceptable values are 0 to 6. If you have a number other than 0, you have to be able to enter e-mail addresses. The "how many e-mail addresses" field is required, whereas the "e-mail addresses" field is conditional.

This example is of user interaction with an application. You will learn about this user interaction more in Chapter 10.

Order of Steps in Requirements

What is the difference between order of steps and lists of items? You saw the list of items in the previous section. However, order was not important to those items. Those requirements were just related to each other. You will encounter situations where certain steps must be accomplished in a specific order. The sequencing of requirements is addressed in this section.

The section titles were chosen carefully. For some lists, like those discussed in the preceding section, sequence is unimportant. However, for a list of steps, the sequence or order matters. That means you have particular actions that need to be ordered in a specific way. Order was not necessary in what you learned earlier in this chapter. Here they are.

Think of what you do when you sit down at your computer in the morning, with it turned off. There are certain steps you take. First, you turn it on. Wait, maybe you plug it in (you did not want it left on because the glow of indicator lights keep you awake at night). Then you turn it on. Wait for the desktop to come up. Call up your applications you want open.

What you do may be different, but you get the idea. If you had to capture requirements for this, you need to break it down initially like this.

■ **Note** We will spend some more time talking about this approach of specifying order when you get to use cases in a later chapter.

Now, consider a more realistic example. Here is the order that must be followed for an employee using a healthcare benefits system:

a. Add employee to benefits system

b. Employee enrolls into benefits system

c. Employee pays employee portion of benefits system

d. Enter employee transactions into benefits system

e. Benefits system pays employee for appropriate amount

f. Reports generated benefits system

You could draft the requirements as follows:

> 6-19 DRAFT The BOSS healthcare function shall allow an employee to be added to the benefits system.
>
> 6-20 DRAFT The BOSS healthcare function shall allow employees to enroll in the benefits system.
>
> 6-21 DRAFT The BOSS healthcare function shall allow employee to pay for the benefits.
>
> 6-22 DRAFT The BOSS healthcare function shall allow employee transactions to be entered into the benefits system.
>
> 6-23 DRAFT The BOSS healthcare function shall allow the benefits system to pay employees for the appropriate amount.
>
> 6-24 DRAFT The BOSS healthcare function shall allow reports to be generated from the benefits system

What is lost is that each requirement 6-19 through 6-24 must have the requirement previous to it done before it can be accomplished. You cannot enroll in benefits packages if you do not have access to the system.

How do you handle this in a requirement? You follow the process similar to in Chapter 4 where you write one requirement.

> 6-25 The BOSS healthcare function shall be executed in the following order:
>
> a. Add employee to benefits system
>
> b. Employee enrolls into benefits system
>
> c. Employee pays employee portion of benefits system
>
> d. Enter employee transactions into benefits system
>
> e. Benefits system pays employee for appropriate amount
>
> f. Reports generated from the benefits system

Notice that the requirement specifically states in the *shall* statement "executed in the following order" to indicate that order is important.

Please notice that this requirement is at a high level, and given the need for atomic requirements, this may not be at the correct level. That said, this requirement might still be necessary for a particular application to capture the order. There would be subsequent requirements for each of the six numbered items in requirement 6-25. It is likely, in fact, that each one of those six could have ordered steps within them. This means that there would be parent-child relationships between these requirements.

For example, let's take item 2 and decompose it further.

> 6-26 The BOSS Enroll Employee to Healthcare Benefits function shall be executed in the following order:
>
> 1. Select a Medical Plan
> 2. Select a Dental Plan
> 3. Select a Vision Plan
> 4. Select a Life Insurance Plan
> 5. Select a Short-Term Disability Plan
> 6. Select a Long-Term Disability Plan

You may ask why this is a required order? We needed an example, and in this case, the insurance provider required it this way.

■ **Note** Sometimes there are business processes or policies that mandate certain things that logically may not seem necessary. Given what is stated by managers well above your ability to change, you will need to follow those specific decisions.

Order of Data Elements in Requirements

Earlier in this chapter, we talked about the listing of data elements. Do you need to order data elements, just like you did when listing? Good question. The answer is no. Some people might argue that. For example, do you enter addresses like this?

- Apartment number
- Zip code
- Street number
- City
- Street number
- State

Of course not. Then, you, gentle reader, say that you should specify an order. However, theory says it is not required to be in a specific order. Of course, you should present the data to the user in the order of terms users are accustomed to seeing them. Then, the answer is that the order is specified in the user interface. That is for a later chapter.

Of course, it makes sense to define the fields in the database schema in that same order. Requirements theorists agree with that. So, then why not say the order of the fields should be specified in requirements? If you remember from requirements definition rules, you do not specify implementation. Specifying the order of data fields in a table or database is just that—design how, not what.

The key element that you need to answer is the question, "Is there something in the order of the fields that is absolutely important to what the user must do?"

■ **Tip** In my experience, I really cannot think of an example of order in data fields. Wait. What about that example from earlier in this chapter where you asked for how many e-mail addresses the user has? If you specified a number other than 0, a field must be populated. That is order. Good point. However, I would point out that by identifying the "e-mail addresses" field as conditional, you have already specified the order. Stating this conditional relationship of data fields, and then defining a specific order is redundant. If I uncover an example of the need for ordering data elements, I will put it in a revised version of this book. So, if you find such an example, please share it will me, and I may be able to give you your 15 minutes of fame by including you and your example in that revision.

Exercises

Exercise 1

Reorder the following steps in an appropriate order for building a two-story house with a full basement:

- Put on the roof.
- Lay the wires, plugs, etc., for the electric system.
- Add the ceiling for the first floor.
- Place the flooring for the first floor.
- Place the walls for the second floor.
- Place the walls for the basement.
- Paint all basement interior wood.
- Add the ceiling for the second floor.
- Place the walls for the first floor.
- Dig out the basement.
- Add the insulation to the attic.
- Add all the appliances.

- Place the dirt and fill around the basement foundation.
- Add the plumbing.
- Paint all second-floor interior wood.
- Place the concrete walls for the basement.
- Add the exterior walls for the first floor.
- Add the insulation to the second floor.
- Add the exterior walls for the second floor.
- Add the insulation to the first floor.
- Place the interior walls for the basement.
- Paint all exposed exterior wood.
- Paint all first-floor interior wood.
- Add doors and windows.

Exercise 2

Write the following as requirements:

> Think of what you do when you sit down at your computer for the time in the morning, with it turned off. For example, in my case, I...turn it on. Wait, maybe I plug it in (when I am traveling). Then I turn it on and wait for the desktop to come up. I call up my applications I want open. I do my e-mail app first to check e-mail and have available for research. Then I open the word processor so I can write my books. I call up the file manager so I can open various files that may not be in my recent list in the word processor.

CHAPTER 7

Data Interfaces and Documents

In this chapter, you are going to learn about data elements in the various systems you will explore in this chapter. In the first section, you will examine data elements within a requirement associated with an example system. This section will also introduce how these data elements can become part of what is called a *database*, basically defining all the different types of data that reside in the database that the developers will create. Second, you will consider the data elements to share between two systems, called an *interface*, usually specified in an interface control document (ICD). Then, you will learn about input and output data elements. Finally, you will study document formats for ICDs that were just introduced. While we are on the subject of interface documents, you will see that the documents include general requirements documents, which will be introduced. There are many different ways of putting them together, should you need to do so. Some organizations like the DoD and IEEE have specified some. Others exist, and you will see them so you can pick which to use, when you are required to do so.

Defining Requirement Data Elements

Now you will examine in detail how to define data you need to capture in the systems you are developing requirements for, as will be demonstrated in the following examples. In the first subsection, you will consider defining the elements within *shall* statements only. In the second subsection, you will discover some situations that need you to not only define the data elements but specify details about the data elements.

Defining Data Elements Within a Requirement

In this first example, you are going to define the Person record for the BOSS HR System. Assume that you are in the United States.

For the example, you should start with the following data:

- First name
- Middle name
- Last name

G. Koelsch, *Requirements Writing for System Engineering*,
DOI 10.1007/978-1-4842-2099-3_7

- Street number
- Street name
- Apartment number
- City
- State
- ZIP code
- Home phone
- Cell phone
- Office phone
- Office extension
- Home e-mail address
- Office e-mail address

One approach is to define each data element as one requirement like this:

> 7-1 The FBI BOSS HR Person record shall contain the Last Name of the person.
>
> 7-2 The FBI BOSS HR Person record shall contain the Street Number of the person.
>
> 7-3 The FBI BOSS HR Person record shall contain the Street Name of the person.

And so on through all the fields.

You also need the format for each field, so maybe you add the following requirements:

> 7-4 The FBI BOSS HR Person record Last Name field shall be alpha characters.
>
> 7-5 The FBI BOSS HR Person record Street Number field shall be numeric characters.
>
> 7-6 The FBI BOSS HR Person record Street Name field shall be alphanumeric characters.

Then complete this for all the fields. Wait, you ask, could we combine the two, such as the following?

> 7-7 The FBI BOSS HR Person record shall contain the Last Name of the person, in an alpha character format.
>
> 7-8 The FBI BOSS HR Person record shall contain the Street Number of the person, in a numeric character format.
>
> 7-9 The FBI BOSS HR Person record shall contain the Street Name of the person, in an alphanumeric character format.

Of course, we now seem to be combining two separate requirements into one. However, consider that this work will be done together. One developer would not put the name of the field in, with another person doing the format. So no, this is not violating requirement engineering principles.

In fact, there is more you need to define for your record. How big should each field be? You need to add that as well. Therefore, you should consider the following:

> 7-10 The FBI BOSS HR Person record shall contain the Last Name of the person, in an alpha character format, with the field size of 25 characters.
>
> 7-11 The FBI BOSS HR Person record shall contain the Street Number of the person, in a numeric character format, with the field size of 12 characters.
>
> 7-12 The FBI BOSS HR Person record shall contain the Street Name of the person, in an alphanumeric character format, with the

This captures the requirement but is getting a little cumbersome. Is there a better way to capture the data? Maybe an easier representation? Of course. That leads into the next section.

Defining Data Elements Within a Database

Before you learn how to capture elements within a database, you might need to know what a database is.

A database is nothing more than a collection of data elements. Depending on how a database is designed, it can consist of one or more tables. I am not going to give you a complete dissertation on database design, just enough to consider in your definition of the elements that you need to define as part of your requirements work.

Think of a table as a file but a bit more structured. The easiest representation is a spreadsheet, with columns and row. Each column is a different data element, and a row is a collection of all those different elements to create one record. You can think of a requirement with all its different data elements making up one table. The complete table can consist of one or more records. Do not worry about how many tables are in a database, as that is for the database design, which you know is the purview of the developers,

So, begin the requirement's data element definition. You can accomplish it in a table, where you specify the field name, the format, and then the field size.

■ **Note** In some documents you may even see the database field name that may be different from the field name that the user is familiar with (e.g., Last Name is LastName or last_name). In this situation, you should not care, as that is implementation.

Here is a proposed table for this project:

> 7-13 The FBI BOSS HR Person record shall contain the following data:

Field Name	Format	Size
First Name	Alpha	30
Middle Name	Alpha	30
Last Name	Alpha	30
Sex	Alpha (M/F/T)	1
Street Number	Numeric	15
Street Name	Alphanumeric	30
Apartment Number	Alphanumeric (e.g., 3B)	6
City	Alpha	30
State	Alpha	2
Zip Code	Numeric	10
Home Phone	Numeric	12
Cell Phone	Numeric	12
Office Phone	Numeric	12
Office Extension	Numeric	5
Home Email Address	Alphanumeric	45
Office Email Address	Alphanumeric	45

You may want to add a Comments field for information like in the Apartment Number format where you should explain why alphanumeric was important. Maybe you want special formats also, say for the phone where you list it with no dashes like 8005550000, or maybe you include it as 800-555-0000. Since space is not a premium, use what the users understand, with spaces or hyphens. Alternatively, do you want to break it into three separate parts of the field? This isn't recommended, as that is specifying implementation. Let the developers do their job, unless there is some business need that drives it.

Another candidate for a Comments field in this table would be a range of values. If ZIP codes do not use all hundred thousand values, you may want to highlight that here.

■ **Note** The following is not true, but just to show an example, if the ZIP code had started with 10000, the range might be 10000 to 99999.

You could enter that example of a clarification in a Comments field. If you have a data requirements table with many data ranges, add a separate column in the table. Besides having the record table make the requirements much easier to read, you can add columns (and rows if need be) much easier. You need to consider one point for traceability: maybe you need to number or identify each row of your table. When testing happens, if e-mail addresses fail because the "at" symbol (@) was not allowed, then you need the spell out the affected fields. If the rows were identified, you could just say that requirement 3.4.2.1 o) and p) failed. Therefore, that is one recommended change.

Another field to consider in the data table is a description. If you have values where the title or name of the field may not satisfactorily describe the field, then add a description field, also to give some explanatory text to provide more detail. For other tables, you may have default values, like for an office phone, where the main office has one phone number that everyone has, with just a different extension. The main office number is the default. Of course, you could have fields that are true/false, yes/no, and so on. There are other data types to consider, like the Boolean true/false, yes/no, memo fields that are long text strings, or BLOBs (Binary Large Objects—for graphics or mixture of text and graphics).

The following are some other topics to consider when writing requirements related to data. Keep in mind that these are all optional, depending on your situation:

- *Data retention*: Is there some reason to keep data for a certain period of time? Clearly, this has merit for the records management project. Earlier, you learned that permanent records must be retained for the life of the Republic. What about temporary records? The federal government has to follow the dictates of the National Archives and Records Administration (NARA), which spells out the rules for how long temporary records are maintained.

- *Data volumes*: This is something you can define in capacity, but it is provided here as a reminder.

- *Data currency*: How current does the date need to be? For example, do you need to keep expense reports available for employees to examine for 20 or 30 years? Probably not. Maybe one year or three or five at the most is sufficient to keep them online. They may be needed for historical or archival reasons, so they can be moved to a different system.

- *Data security*: Is there data that needs to be handled with a higher security level than everyone having access to it? For example, think back to an earlier chapter where you learned medical information has to follow HIPAA protection. For the HR project, you will need to add a privacy indicator to the field for HR personnel files, especially if the SSN is used. Payroll records will need some extra protection as well.

- *Data relationships*: Is there more than one value associated with another? In the previous example, you did that for phone numbers, but you identified them with different names. Think of awards received by an individual; they could be zero, one, or several. There is no consistent number. Maybe you should define one field that would hold all awards with the Person record having a field of up to 2,000 characters to describe them all.

When you have addressed all these items, you have done a good job of describing data in a computer database.

What about hardware, say, for the Dosimetry project you have been examining? Do you need data definition? Would you have data here? Absolutely. You might consider something like the following:

> 7-14 The BOSS Unit Radiation Dosimeter system shall contain the following data:

Field No.	Field Name	Format	Size
1.	First Name	Alpha	30
2.	Middle Name	Alpha	30
3.	Last Name	Alpha	30
4.	Sex	Alpha (M/F/T)	1
5.	Soldier ID (SSN)	NNN-NN-NNNN	11
6.	Soldier's Unit	Alphanumeric	100
7.	Start And Stop Date	MM/DD/YYYY to MM/DD/YYYY	24
8.	Exposure in REM	Numeric NNNN.N	6
9.	Comments	Alpha	100
10.	Cumulative Exposure in REM	Numeric NNNNN.N	7
11.	Date Issue to Soldier	MM/DD/YYYY	10

Notice there is an added field number so that you have traceability like the one discussed earlier; this way you achieve uniqueness for each field.

If you add a Comment field to this table, you might put the following in for the Unit field:

> Complete unit description from highest level e.g., CENTCOM (Central Command), to lowest unit level, platoon or detachment. May do a hierarchy but not all have the same number of levels, so just one string of characters.

There are some other considerations you might need to capture in these radiation requirements that are not addressed here. What happens when the soldier is transferred to another unit? The answer is beyond this chapter, but the radiation exposure reading should be taken for the individual soldier and a new record initiated when the soldier transfers to the new unit. In addition, what happens if the dosimeter is lost or broken? How will the data be reconstructed? These are other considerations that will not be explored here, but policies and procedures in the U.S. Army will help to define those candidate needs.

Interface Control Documents

As was said in the introduction to this chapter, now you will learn how to share data elements between two systems, in other words, how the two (or more) systems interface. The first step is to analyze the data itself that you need to capture for your requirement. Then, you will need to capture these data element requirements into documents, usually the ICD.

The "Connections to Outside the System" section in Chapter 5 introduced the following requirement:

> 7-15/5-85 The BOSS shall provide ANY System to import data in the format specified in ANY System Interface Format.

Now you will learn how to specify this system interface. You did part of this in the previous section of this chapter when you defined the data elements. However, you will have to expand it a bit more. Why? Well, you will have two systems that need to be connected. Not only will you have the data elements, but also both systems need to agree on all the values, their formats, their sizes, and any other restrictions on the data. You will find when you learn about elicitation that this is one of the most challenging efforts in requirements definition. Remember that argument about the definition talked about in Chapter 3? It was in this interface definition phase that this took place. This biggest issue deals not with agreeing on what the values should be but when someone has to spend money to change their data to meet a standard they do not follow, that's when they object most vehemently.

So, what kind of data should you capture when defining an interface? Start with the data elements described in the requirement in the previous section, though note that not all of the fields will apply to every interface.

- Field Name (user understanding of the name)
- Interface Field Name (what is the field name used by the two systems?)
- Field Description (detailed description of what goes into the field)
- Field Type
- Field Format
- Field Size
- Field Defaults
- Field Range
- Field Units
- Field Precision (what accuracy of the unit $0.01 for currency, for example)
- Priority
- Timing
- Frequency
- Volume
- Sequencing (is order of the transmission important?)
- Other Constraints (e.g., whether the data element may be updated and whether business rules apply)
- Security

- Control Factor (privacy, or another protection level that is not security)
- Source (some values go from one to the other, but not in both directions)
- Comments

Some of the fields are not part of every record, but may be associated with a collection of records. For example, security might be the same for a group of records sent. That would be part of the header element of the file transmission. You have to identify these types of fields and when they are used.

Is there a validation that the message was sent? Is the message sent in bulk (say once a day) or when a transaction happens?

Now, look at the HR Person record. You need some of the data to be transmitted to the HR payroll system. You might have something like the following:

> 7-16 The BOSS Payroll Function shall receive the following data from the BOSS Payroll Function:

Field Name	Format	Size	Description	Comments
First Name	Alpha	30	Employee's first name	
Middle Name	Alpha	30	Employee's middle name	
Last Name	Alpha	30	Employee's last name	
Sex	Alpha (M/F/T)	1	Sex of person	T = Transgender
Person Identifier	Numeric	15	BOSS employee number	System generated when employee starts with company

This is a simple interface, but it is a good starting point. In addition, the potential elements provided will help you start defining your projects.

Naturally, the same approach occurs for hardware. In the dosimetry program, there will be an interface between the individual and unit dosimeters. It could be defined as follows:

> 7-17 The BOSS Unit Radiation Dosimeter system shall contain the following data:

Field Name	Type	Format	Size
First Name	Alpha	Text string	30
Middle Name	Alpha	Text string	30
Last Name	Alpha	Text string	30
Sex	Alpha	Choice (M/F/T)	1
Soldier ID (SSN)	Numeric	NNN-NN-NNNN	11
Soldier's Unit	Alphanumeric	Alphanumeric string	100
Start And Stop Date	Date	MM/DD/YYYY to MM/DD/YYYY	24
Exposure in REM	Numeric	NNNN.N	6
Comments	Alpha	Text string	100
Cumulative Exposure in REM	Numeric	NNNNN.N	7
Date Issued to Soldier	Date	MM/DD/YYYY	10

Notice that you need to capture the precision in the Exposure in REM field. Since this is the only one such value in the entire list, you do not add a Precision column for every value. Instead, just capture a separate requirement. If you have multiple values in your situations, then you might want to add a Precision column. An additional change takes place after the transfer from the individual dosimeter to the unit dosimeter. The Exposure in REM field value is added to the Cumulative Exposure in REM field, and then the Exposure in REM field value becomes zero.

If your project will use something other than a standard interface (e.g., USB, Blu-ray), then you need to specify every element and whether there is a specific set of pins to connect the two devices. Shortly, you will see how to combine everything in an ICD.

Input/Outputs

Now you will learn about what things to consider for inputs into the system in question. Next you will examine what outputs the system will generate (e.g., provide data to users of the system).

Outputs

Why do you need to define this when you have already defined all the functional and nonfunctional requirements? Just like the ICDs and other kinds of requirements, there are special items to consider.

Think of this guideline: *define what results you need from the system.* Otherwise, why are you developing, building, or procuring the project in the first place? The results could be data, like the exposures a soldier receives in a nuclear battlefield (the Radiation Dosimetry System). The results could be capturing all the permanent records from the FBI (the FBI Records Management System) to comply with all the federal records policies and laws.

Naturally, this specification of output data is a bit more complicated than just this major objective. What UI is necessary (an output, and for accepting inputs from users)? What reports are needed? You learned about this in the "Searching & Reporting Requirements" section in Chapter 4. If you haven't defined data to report to users, whether in formatted reports or just displayed in certain screen shots, do so now. Here's an example:

> 7-18 The BOSS Unit Radiation Dosimeter system shall provide the following data when requested for an individual soldier:
>
> - First Name
> - Middle Name
> - Last Name
> - Sex
> - Soldier ID
> - Soldier's Unit
> - Start And Stop Date
> - Exposure in REM
> - Comments
> - Cumulative Exposure in REM
> - Date Issue to Soldier

For the HR project, you might have the following outputs:

> 7-19 The BOSS HR Personal Function shall provide an Organizational Person report for each person in a designated organization:
>
> - First Name
> - Middle Name
> - Last Name
> - Sex
> - Street Number
> - Street Name
> - Apartment Number
> - City

- State
- Zip Code
- Home Phone
- Cell Phone
- Office Phone
- Office Extension
- Home Email Address
- Office Email Address

Obviously, this is just one of a multitude of reports. Of course, as mentioned in Chapter 4, how many reports will the development team prepare that need to be defined as requirements? The rest will be developed by users, where they do their own defining of requirements that do not need to be shared.

Inputs

Given that you have the needed outputs, you can define what information to enter or input, by whatever means necessary, to support that output.

For the dosimetry project, you should consider the following:

> 7-20 The BOSS Unit Radiation Dosimeter system shall receive the following data:

- First Name
- Middle Name
- Last Name
- Sex
- Soldier ID
- Soldier's Unit
- Start And Stop Date
- Exposure in REM
- Comments
- Cumulative Exposure in REM
- Date Issue to Soldier

For the HR Personnel project:

> 7-21 The BOSS HR Personnel Function shall require the user to enter the following data elements:

- First Name
- Middle Name
- Last Name
- Sex
- Street Number
- Street Name
- Apartment Number
- City
- State
- Zip Code
- Home Phone
- Cell Phone
- Office Phone
- Office Extension
- Home Email Address
- Office Email Address

Transformations

Naturally, you need any transformations from the inputs to the outputs. Ideally you have captured that already, but this is a sanity check. For example, you might have a report of an entire unit's radiation exposure between given start and end dates, maybe with average, mean, mode, maximum, and minimum values. What data is transformed (changed) in the process? Certainly, you should not have the maximum and minimum values transformed. The biggest transform is the average, where the system needs to look at the historical data stored in the Unit system and calculate the exposure for every soldier in the unit during the time period in question. Then the total is determined and divided by the number of soldiers. The mean is determining the value where 50 percent of the values are below and 50 percent of the values are above.

Those are simple transformations. In some cases, the input value is changed to create an output value.

Consider that you have a report that is needed to identify the risk of cancer long-term based on exposure.

REM	Cancer Odds
< 0.05	0
0.05 to 0.5	1:4000
0.5 to 5	1:400
5 to 10	1:200
10 to 25	1:80
25 to 70	1:30

Now the system will need to transform the soldier's total exposure to a cancer odds value in the report.

For the HR personnel paycheck project, the system needs to calculate a paycheck. The salary/hourly rate is defined in the database. In addition, the database has the elections for benefits for that person. The system needs to determine the bi-weekly pay, minus all the deductions including benefits, payroll taxes, Social Security, Medicaid, and any other deductions from the pay to determine the paycheck (the output).

Interface Control Document Formats

Chapter 4 mentioned how to organize documents. In Chapter 11, you will consider how to organize the requirements in the requirements database. If you are going to put all the project's requirements into a requirements tool, why should you capture interface requirements into an ICD? Unlike project requirements, when two different systems connect to each other, the requirements must be agreed upon by both parties. Thus, an ICD is a document mechanism to represent the requirements that both have accepted. While you may put your interface requirements into your tool for you to manage them, they must be segregated in a way that reflects this shared ownership of the requirements. Now back to how you will organize interface requirements. Although using the structure talked about in Chapter 3 is one approach, there is no one correct way to organize it. It is whatever works for you and your organization.

Now move onto formats for document templates for ICDs. Why are you considering formats for ICDs? First, you need to see the various ways you can put these documents together, depending on the kind of interface you are defining. Some hardware interfaces are very specific and need a special way to represent them. Second, by seeing the different sections of the various documents, you may get some ideas of requirements you may need to collect for your specific interface. No book can prepare you for every contingency, but by exposing you to various approaches, it may spark ideas for you to consider.

It is helpful to look at some actual templates that show standards that organizations use. In this section, let's look at several from the federal government. Remember, this is to show examples of how you might organize data and what to capture. None of these approaches is specifically recommended, but they serve as useful references. All the material in the specific government document subsections is taken from the government sources (see the "References" section for complete citations) except for some explanatory or introductory text that I distinguish from the quoted material by setting it in italic type.

HUD Guidelines for the Data Requirements Document Checklist

This checklist is provided as part of the evaluation process for the Data Requirements Document. The checklist assists designated reviewers in determining whether specifications meet criteria established in HUD's System Development Methodology (SDM). The objective of the evaluation is to determine whether the document complies with HUD development methodology requirements.

Attached to this document is the DOCUMENT REVIEW CHECKLIST. Its purpose is to assure that documents achieve the highest standards relative to format, consistency, completeness, quality, and presentation.

Submissions must include the following three documents, and must be presented in the following order: (First) Document Review Checklist, (Second) the Data Requirements Document Checklist, and (Third) the Data Requirements Document.

Document authors are required to complete the two columns indicated as "AUTHOR X-REFERENCE Page #/Section #" and "AUTHOR COMMENTS" before the submission. Do NOT complete the last two columns marked as "COMPLY" and "REVIEWER COMMENTS" since these are for the designated reviewers.

Here is the requirement section and what goes into it. Besides addressing the requirement, they require author reference and author comments and Reviewer section with whether the requirement is complied with or not, and any reviewer comments.

REQUIREMENT	
1.0	**GENERAL INFORMATION**
1.1	**Purpose:** Describe the purpose of the Data Requirements Document.
1.2	**Scope:** Describe the scope of the Data Requirements Document as it relates to the project.
1.3	**System Overview:** Provide a brief system overview description as a point of reference for the remainder of the document, including responsible organization, system name or title, system code, system category, operational status, and system environment or special conditions.
1.4	**Project References:** Provide a list of the references that were used in preparation of this document.
1.5	**Acronyms and Abbreviations:** Provide a list of the acronyms and abbreviations used in this document and the meaning of each.
1.6	**Points of Contact:**
	1.6.1 **Information:** Provide a list of the points of organizational contact that may be needed by the document user for informational and troubleshooting purposes.
	1.6.2 **Coordination:** Provide a list of organizations that require coordination between the project and its specific support function (e.g., installation coordination, security, etc.). Include a schedule for coordination activities.

(*continued*)

REQUIREMENT

2.0 DATA DESCRIPTION

2.1 **Logical Database Design:** Describe and depict in a graphic representation the logical organization of the data and defined relationships, including business rules relevant to the data model or to specific data items.

2.2 **Data Characteristics and Categorization:** Discuss the data elements to be used by the system.

2.2.1 **Static Data:** List the static data elements used for either control or reference purposes, including data element name; synonymous name; type; definition; format; range of values or discrete values; unit of measurement; precision; data item names, abbreviations, and codes; and characteristics, such as accuracy, validity, timing, and capacity.

2.2.2 **Dynamic Input Data:** Include the following for each data element: data element name; synonymous name; type; definition; format; range of values or discrete values; unit of measurement; precision; data item names, abbreviations, and codes; and characteristics, such as accuracy, validity, timing, and capacity.

2.2.3 **Dynamic Output Data:** Include the following for each data element: data element name; synonymous name; type; definition; format; range of values or discrete values; calculation or algorithm used to derive data value; unit of measurement; precision; data item names, abbreviations, and codes; and characteristics, such as accuracy, validity, timing, and capacity.

2.2.4 **Internally Generated Data:** Include the following for each data element: data element name; synonymous name; type; definition; format; range of values or discrete values; calculation of algorithm used to derive data value; unit of measurement; precision; data item names, abbreviations, and codes; and characteristics, such as accuracy, validity, timing, and capacity.

2.3 **Data Constraints:** State the constraints on the data, indicating the limits of the data requirements with regard to further expansion or use, such as the maximum size and number of files, records, and data elements.

2.4 **Data Retention:** Describe the data retention requirements as follows: historic retention to include the collection of data to be retained and its format, storage medium, and time parameters; periodic report data (retention period after generation of reports and retention period of periodic reports after summary reports are generated); and Summary Reports data (retention period after generation).

2.5 **Impacts:** Describe the impact, if applicable, of the data requirements on equipment, software, user, and developer organizations.

2.5.1 **Equipment:** Describe the impact of the data requirements on equipment.

2.5.2 **Software:** Describe the impact of the data requirements on software.

2.5.3 **Organization:** Describe the impact of the data requirements on the user and developer organization.

2.6 **Data Storage:** Estimate the data storage and processing requirements in terms of size and number of records.

(*continued*)

REQUIREMENT

2.7 **Scales of Measurement:** Specify for numeric scales, units of measurements, increments, scale, zero-point, and range of values.

2.8 **Measurement Conversion Factors:** Specify the conversion factors of measured quantities that must go through analog or digital conversion processes.

2.9 **Frequency of Update and Processing:** State the expected frequency of data element change and the expected frequency of processing input data elements.

3.0 DATA HANDLING

3.1 **Source of Input:** Create a table identifying the source from which data elements will be entered, such as an organizational unit or operator.

3.3 **Medium and Device:**

3.2.1 **Input Medium and Device:** Describe, in detail, the format of data to be input to the proposed system.

3.2.2 **Output Medium and Device:** Identify the medium and hardware device intended for presenting output data to the recipient.

3.3 **Recipients:** Name the organization or system that will be receiving output data.

3.4 **Data Collection Procedures:** Describe procedures that will be used to collect data, including a detailed format for the input data.

3.5 **User Access:** Describe or depict the user or user types and their associated create, read, update, and delete permission.

3.6 **Error Handling:** Identify the process for handling inaccurate or incomplete data.

3.7 **Data Responsibilities:** Determine and describe the organization that will be responsible for managing the data.

3.8 **Security:** Describe the security classification for the data and the degree of security of the algorithms.

You can see from the emphasis on the information to be provided that this is focused more on software than hardware. Yes, hardware is addressed, but more elements focus on data specification. The next example will have a stronger hardware focus, as you would expect.

DoD

Next, you will consider what the Department of Defense requires for their documents. Notice that most of what you see in this section is hardware related.

The DoD uses the following document formats as a standards.

MIL-STD 962D (Military Standard)

These are extracts related to DoD interfaces. Notice how much more emphasis they have on hardware. Given that they develop weapons, aircraft, battleships, and submarines, to name a few, they need hardware focus. Yes, software elements are addressed also. Another alert is that the DoD is much more structured in their approach, as indicated by their reference to other documentation. While all this might make it more challenging to read, remember your focus is to see what data they want collected. What you read now is from their web site. The first three paragraphs are extracted from the foreword to the document. The DI-SDMP-81470 is their precise presentation of what you would read.

Foreword

5c. DoD interface standards should be developed to specify the physical, functional, or military operational environment interface characteristics of systems, subsystems, equipment, assemblies, components, items, or parts to permit interchangeability, interconnection, interoperability, compatibility, or communications. Non-Government standards should be used to the extent possible to specify interface requirements. DoD interface standards should only be developed to specify military-unique interface requirements. DoD interface standards may be cited as solicitation requirements without need for a waiver by the Milestone Decision Authority.

3.13 Interface standard. A standard that specifies the physical, functional, or military operational environment interface characteristics of systems, subsystems, equipment, assemblies, components, items, or parts to permit interchangeability, interconnection, interoperability, compatibility, or communications.

5.2.1 Interface standards. Interface standards shall specify the physical, functional, or military operational environment interface characteristics of systems, subsystems, equipment, assemblies, components, items, or parts to permit interchangeability, interconnection, interoperability, compatibility, or communications.

As you can see, these three paragraphs give the high-level scope of what should be included in the following document. The elements described are what you need to keep in mind for your use.

8.4.2.2 DI-SDMP-81470 Department of Defense (DoD) Interface Standard Documents

"Data Item Description" is a standard name used for these types of documents, and everything after it reinforces it. Keep in mind as you read it to concern yourself more about the items within the document, not so much the exact format (unless you are working on a DoD project, which will be discussed at the end).

DATA ITEM DESCRIPTION
Title: DEPARTMENT OF DEFENSE (DoD) INTERFACE STANDARD DOCUMENTS
Number: DI-SDMP-81470A Approval Date: 1 August 2003
AMSC Number: D7505 Limitation: N/A
DTIC Applicable: No GIDEP Applicable: No
Office of Primary Responsibility: OSD-SO
Applicable Forms: N/A

Use, Relationships: A DoD interface standard will be used to specify the physical or functional interface characteristics of systems, subsystems, equipment, assemblies, components, items or parts to permit interchangeability, interconnection, interoperability, compatibility, or communications.

This Data Item Description contains the content and format preparation instructions for DoD interface standards and their associated documents that are described in the following paragraphs of MIL-STD-962D. Only those documents listed below will be required when specified individually on contract.

a. DoD Interface Standard - Paragraphs 4.1 through 5.15.

b. DoD Interface Standard Revision - Paragraph 5.17.

c. DoD Interface Standard Change - Paragraphs 5.18 through 5.18.7.

d. DoD Interface Standard Inactive for New Design Notice - Paragraph 5.19.2.

e. DoD Interface Standard Cancellation Notice - Paragraph 5.19.3.

f. DoD Interface Standard Reinstatement Notice - Paragraph 5.19.4.

g. DoD Interface Standard Reactivation Notice - Paragraph 5.19.5.

h. DoD Interface Standard Administrative Notice - Paragraph 5.19.6.

This DID supersedes DI-SDMP-81470.
Requirements:

1. Reference documents. The applicable issue of the documents cited herein, including their approval dates and dates of any applicable notices and revisions, shall be as specified in the contract.

2. Format and content. Format and content for DoD Interface Standards shall be as follows:

    a. DoD Interface Standard. Format and content of DoD Interface Standards shall be in accordance with MIL-STD-962, paragraphs 4.1 through 5.15.

    b. DoD Interface Standard Revision. Format and content of DoD Interface Standard Revisions shall be in accordance with MIL-STD-962, paragraph 5.17.

    c. DoD Interface Standard Changes. Format and content of DoD Interface Standard Changes shall be in accordance with MIL-STD-962, paragraphs 5.18 through 5.18.7.

    d. DoD Interface Standard Inactive for New Design Notices. Format and content of DoD Interface Standard Inactive for New Design Notices shall be in accordance with MIL-STD-962, paragraph 5.19.2.

    e. DoD Interface Standard Cancellation Notices. Format and content of DoD Interface Standard Cancellation Notices shall be in accordance with MIL-STD-962, paragraph 5.19.3.

f. DoD Interface Standard Reinstatement Notices. Format and content of DoD Interface Standard Reinstatement Notices shall be in accordance with MIL-STD-962, paragraph 5.19.4.

g. DoD Interface Standard Reactivation Notices. Format and content of DoD Interface Standard Reactivation Notices shall be in accordance with MIL-STD-962, paragraph 5.19.5.

h. DoD Interface Standard Administrative Notices. Format and content of DoD Interface Standard Administrative Notices shall be in accordance with MIL-STD-962, paragraph 5.19.6.

3. END OF DI-SDMP-81470A.

The exact format may not help as much as the data elements that the DoD needs. If you work in this DoD environment, your best bet is to find an example of one such document, and then it might become a bit more understandable. Remember, from any of these examples, take what you need and use them. Again, the point was the focus on hardware here.

NASA Training Manual for Elements of Interface Definition and Control

This NASA example also has a strong hardware focus, and the text is more readable than the DoD example because there are not so many references to other documents. This document is more self-contained. Keep in mind that NASA has a strong space orientation, so some of their needs may not match your needs. Again, take what you need, but the explanations here are very good.

2.1 Purpose of Interface Control

An interface is that design feature of a piece of equipment that affects the design feature of another piece of equipment.The purpose of interface control is to define interface requirements so as to ensure compatibility between interrelated pieces of equipment and to provide an authoritative means of controlling the design of interfaces. Interface design is controlled by an

Interface Control Document (ICD).

These documents

1. Control the interface design of the equipment to prevent any changes to characteristics that would affect compatibility with other equipment
2. Define and illustrate physical and functional characteristics of a piece of equipment in sufficient detail to ensure compatibility of the interface, so that this compatibility can be determined from the information in the ICD alone
3. Identify missing interface data and control the submission of these data
4. Communicate coordinated design decisions and design changes to program participants
5. Identify the source of the interface component

ICDs by nature are requirements documents: they define design requirements and allow integration. They can cause designs to be the way they are. They record the agreed-to design solution to interface requirements and provide a control mechanism to ensure that the agreed-to designs are not changed by one participant without negotiated agreement of the other participant.

To be effective, ICDs should track a schedule path compatible with design maturation of a project (i.e., initial ICDs should be at the 80% level of detail at preliminary design review, should mature as the design matures, and should reach the 99% mark near the critical design review).

2.3.1 Electrical/Functional

Electrical/functional interfaces are used to define and control the interdependence of two or more pieces of equipment when the interdependence arises from the transmission of an electrical signal from one piece of equipment to another. All electrical and functional characteristics, parameters, and tolerances of one equipment design that affect another design are controlled by the electrical/functional ICD. The functional mechanizations of the source and receiver of the interface electrical signal are defined, as well as the transmission medium.

The interface definition includes the data and/or control functions and the way in which these functions are represented by electrical signals. Specific types of data to be defined are listed here:

1. Function name and symbol
2. Impedance characteristics
3. Shielding and grounding
4. Signal characteristics
5. Cable characteristics
6. Data definition
7. Data transmission format, coding, timing, and updating
8. Transfer characteristics
9. Circuit logic characteristics
10. Electromagnetic interference requirements
11. Data transmission losses
12. Circuit protective devices

Other data types may be needed. For example, an analog signal interface document would contain function name and symbol, cable characteristics, transfer characteristics, circuit protective devices, shielding, and grounding; whereas a digital data interface would contain function name and symbol, data format, coding, timing and updating, and data definition. Additional data types under the electrical/functional heading are:

1. Transmission and receipt of an electrical/electromagnetic signal
2. Use of an electrically conductive or electromagnetic medium

Appendix A shows recommended formats for electrical and functional interface control drawings.

2.3.2 Mechanical/Physical

Mechanical/physical interfaces are used to define and control the mechanical features, characteristics, dimensions, and tolerances of one equipment design that affect the design of another subsystem. They also define force transmission requirements where a static or dynamic force exists. The features of the equipment that influence or control force transmission are also defined in this ICD. Mechanical interfaces include those material properties of the equipment that can affect the functioning of mating equipment, such as thermal and galvanic characteristics. Specific types of data defined are:

1. Optical characteristics
2. Parallelism and straightness
3. Orientation requirements
4. Space or provisions required to obtain access for performing maintenance and removing or replacing items, including space for the person performing the function
5. Size, shape, mass, mass distribution, and center of gravity
6. Service ports
7. Indexing provisions
8. Concentricity
9. Surface finish
10. Hard points for handling
11. Sealing, pressurization, attachment, and locking provisions
12. Location and alignment requirements with respect to other equipment
13. Thermal conductivity and expansion characteristics
14. Mechanical characteristics (spring rate, elastic properties, creep, set, etc.)
15. Load-carrying capability
16. Galvanic and corrosive properties of interfacing materials

Other data types may be needed. For example, an ICD controlling a form-and-fit interface would generally contain such characteristics as size and shape of the item, location of attachment features, location of indexing provisions, and weight and center of gravity of the item. However, an ICD controlling a structural load interface would contain weight and center of gravity, load-carrying capability, and elastic properties of the material if applicable to the loading conditions. Not all ICDs controlling a form-and-fit interface would have to contain all types of data given in this example, but some form-and-fit interface definitions contain more than the 16 types of data listed. Indexing definitions may require angularity, waviness, and contour definitions and tolerances.

Additional data types under the mechanical/physical heading would be:

1. Dimensional relationships between mating equipment
2. Force transmission across an interface
3. Use of mechanically conductive media
4. Placing, retaining, positioning, or physically transporting a component by another component
5. Shock mitigation to protect another component

Appendix B (from ref. 5) shows a mechanical/physical drawing.

This extensive variety of possibilities and combinations prevents assigning a standard set of data types or level of detail to a form-and-fit interface. Each interface must be analyzed and the necessary controlling data identified before the proper level of interface definition and control can be achieved. This holds true for all examples given in this chapter.

2.3.3 Software

A software interface defines the actions required when interfacing components that result from an interchange of information. A software interface may exist where there is no direct electrical interface or mechanical interface between two elements. For example, whereas an electrical ICD might define the characteristics of a digital data bus and the protocols used to transmit data, a software interface would define the actions taken to process the data and return the results of the process. Software interfaces include operational sequences that involve multiple components, such as data-processing interactions between components, timing, priority interrupts, and watchdog timers. Controversy generally arises in determining whether these relationships are best documented in an electrical/functional ICD, a software ICD, or a performance requirements document. Generally, software interface definitions include:

1. Interface communication protocol
2. Digital signal characteristics
3. Data transmission format, coding, timing, and updating requirements
4. Data and data element definition
5. Message structure and flow
6. Operational sequence of events
7. Error detection and recovery procedures

Other data types may be needed.

2.3.4 Supplied Services

Supplied services are those support requirements that a piece of equipment needs to function. Supplied services are provided by an external separate source. This category of interface can be subdivided further into electrical power, communication, fluid, and environmental requirements. The types of data defined for these subcategories are:

1. Electrical power interface:
    a. Phase
    b. Frequency
    c. Voltage
    d. Continuity
    e. Interrupt time
    f. Load current
    g. Demand factors for significant variations during operations
    h. Power factor
    i. Regulation
    j. Ripple
    k. Harmonics
    l. Spikes or transients
    m. Ground isolation
    n. Switching, standby, and casualty provisions
2. Communication interface:
    a. Types of communication required between equipment
    b. Number of communication stations per communication circuit
    c. Location of communication stations
3. Fluid interface:
    a. Type of fluid required
        i. Gaseous
        ii. Liquid
    b. Fluid properties
        i. Pressure
        ii. Temperature
        iii. Flow rate
        iv. Purity

v. Duty cycle

vi. Thermal control required (e.g., fluid heat lost or gained)

4. Environmental characteristic interface:

   a. Ambient temperature

   b. Atmospheric pressure

   c. Humidity

   d. Gaseous composition required

   e. Allowable foreign particle contents

Other data types may be needed. Appendix D shows an example of a supplied services interface for air-conditioning and cooling water.

There is a lot more information in this manual, but this is just a representative example of items to consider in an ICD, if appropriate for your project. As was said earlier, NASA has a strong space focus and your project may not, so those elements do not apply. However, the good descriptions of what they want should help you better understand what is needed.

Centers for Medicare & Medicaid Services CMS eXpedited Life Cycle (XLC)

This document template is much more succinct than previous formats. It is presented to show the Open System Interconnection (OSI) application layer. When your project uses this, you might want to include this in your ICD specification.

1.1 PURPOSE OF INTERFACE CONTROL

Provide the purpose of the Interface Control document. For example: This Interface Control Document (ICD) documents and tracks the necessary information required to effectively define the <Project Name> system's interface as well as any rules for communicating with them in order to give the development team guidance on architecture of the system to be developed. The purpose of this ICD is to clearly communicate all possible inputs and outputs from the system for all potential actions whether they are internal to the system or transparent to system users. This Interface Control is created during the Planning and Design Phases of the project. Its intended audience is the project manager, project team, development team, and stakeholders interested in interfacing with the system. This ICD helps ensure compatibility between system segments and components.

This template requires the following information:

- Interface Type
- Interface From
- Interface To
- Description of Interface
- Other Information

For the following:

- OSI (Open System Interconnection) Application Layer
- OSI Presentation Layer
- OSI Session Layer
- OSI Transport Layer
- OSI Network Layer
- OSI Data Layer
- OSI Physical Layer

REQUIREMENTS DOCUMENTS

Since you are learning about interface control document formats, it is worthwhile to introduce the concept of requirements document formats. Requirements documents, referred to as *system requirements documents*, *system requirements specifications*, *functional requirements documents*, *project requirements documents*, *software requirements documents*, and many other variations on that theme, are also varied just like the ICDs. You will not see them defined in a chapter but in Appendix B. There are several reasons for this. One, those documents could use up an entire book with all the templates that exist. If some people think reading about requirements is dry, imagine how dry *that* book would be. Instead, you are rescued from that exposure, unless you really need it. The most compelling reason for putting the formats in Appendix B is that you may never write a complete requirements document. With the advent of so many projects developed using the agile methodology, you would not present all the requirements at once. You would just provide the ones needed for a particular sprint. Therefore, you would not need a complete requirements document. For that major reason, it is included only for reference when you need it. You may get some ideas for areas of requirements to ask about, but ideally that has covered it so far.

References

Housing and Urban Development (HUD) System Development Methodology (SDM). January 2009. Release 6.06, U.S. Department of Housing and Urban Development. Feb. 2015, `http://portal.hud.gov/hudportal/documents/huddoc?id=sdm.pdf`

DoD MIL-STD 962D. 1 August 2003. *Department of Defense Standard Practice: Defense Standards Format and Content.* Feb 2015, `http://everyspec.com/MIL-STD/MIL-STD-0900-1099/MIL_STD_962D_1179/`

Department of Defense. *DI-SDMP-81470 Department of Defense (DoD) Interface Standard Documents.* Data Item Description, 1 August 2003, p1 to 2.

Lalli, Vincent R., Kastner, Robert E. and Hartt, Henry N. *Training Manual for Elements of Interface Definition and Control, NASA Reference Publication 1370.* January 1997, p 3 to 6.

Centers for Medicare & Medicaid Services CMS eXpedited Life Cycle (XLC) Interface Control Document Template. Feb. 2015, `www.cms.gov/Research-Statistics-Data-and-Systems/CMS-Information-Technology/XLC/Artifacts.html`

Exercises

Exercise 1

If the HR record was for an international company, what variations in the names and addresses would you need to address? You might need to conduct research on the Web to find out. Are three names enough? Do all country use States and ZIP codes?

Exercise 2

In the HR record, are all the specifications discussed in the fields correct? For example, could the street address be numbers only? Check rural addresses in Wisconsin. Are there any other changes you should make in the data fields?

CHAPTER 8

Physical Requirements

If you are working on software, you might think that you do not need to worry about physical requirements. Nothing could be further from the truth. On many application projects, you will need to specify specific physical characteristics that the hardware will need to have. In addition, there are applications that are *turnkey systems*. A *turnkey system* is a complete system that provides not only software but also the hardware and everything in between. It could be a stand-alone system, a LAN, or even a WAN (a group of LANs connected together). When you have a turnkey system, you will need to define characteristics for the hardware.

What characteristics do you need to address? You will see that you have examined some aspects already, but you have never completely addressed all the elements.

You will learn about characteristics of the hardware itself and special characteristics that computer systems need specified. Keep in mind, in some instances, you must specify minimum values (e.g., microprocessor), maximum values (e.g., weigh no more than 10 pounds), or a range of values (e.g., 20 to 120 degrees Centigrade). You will need to determine which case applies to your situation, as there are no specific rules, except use common sense. Of course, your subject-matter experts will help you, if you need it. Naturally, if you decide to do one characteristic over the other and people disagree, they will comment. Thus, there are checks and balances to help you.

Physical Hardware Characteristics

What physical characteristics should you consider for every piece of hardware? The following list is not exhaustive, but it includes some common candidate items:

- Overall weight
- Size
- Geometric shape
- Volume
- Density
- Center of gravity
- Human portable

G. Koelsch, *Requirements Writing for System Engineering*,
DOI 10.1007/978-1-4842-2099-3_8

- Safety features
- Physical storage
- Packaging and integration constraints
- Power consumption
- Physical robustness
- Material
- Surface coefficient of friction
- Reliability
- Throughput

Again, this list is not exhaustive. These are the most likely characteristics you should consider, but there is no way to anticipate every unique aspect of every piece of equipment or physical item you will work on during your career. Here you will learn how to get to the 90 percent solution, and this should give you a foundation. Now examine each one in more detail. Some requirements that relate to these characteristics you may see elsewhere in this book. It demonstrates just how interrelated the characteristics of a system are.

Overall Weight

Think about a radiation sensor you want to install on a manned mission to Mars. The launch function must not only boost every gram of weight into orbit but also send it on its way to another planet. Weight is absolutely critical in these situations. You will encounter other situations as well elsewhere, such as one that you have already considered. Think of the individual dosimeter. You want it worn by individual soldiers, so it should be comparable to the weight of a wristwatch, something you are already accustomed to doing now. So, remember this requirement:

> 8-1 (5-8) The BOSS Individual Radiation Dosimeter shall weigh no more than 4 ounces.

Size

You need to address the height, width, and thickness of the devices, or the radius if spherical or cylindrical, elliptical, or any other geometric shape that is required. For example, if you have a unit dosimeter, it may need to be installed in several different vehicles, like an MRAP (Mine-Resistant Ambush Protected—don't you just love the convoluted way the military names things?) vehicle, M-1 tank, deuce-and-a-half truck, and AH-1 helicopters (AH = Attack Helicopter), for example. Naturally, you would need to list all the vehicles that need to house these unit radiation dose rate meters. Here we will talk about the dimension requirements:

> 8-2 The BOSS Unit Radiation Dose Rate meter shall be 10 inches high.
>
> 8-3 The BOSS Unit Radiation Dose Rate meter shall be 4 inches wide.
>
> 8-4 The BOSS Unit Radiation Dose Rate meter shall be 6 inches thick.

Other elements inside the device may drive the size of the device. Back in the old days, before light-emitting diode (LED) and liquid crystal display (LCD) monitors, tubes were necessary for TV and computer monitors and that constrained their minimum thickness. Radiation sensors have some similar restrictions in their minimum size.

Geometric Shape

What if the device will not be a standard box shape (i.e., nonrectangular)? Then you need to specify what shape it should be. It may even be nonplanar, spherical or cylindrical, elliptical, or any other geometric shape that is required. Think a jet's wing. How would you specify that? (Yes, very carefully.) You might need some graphics to represent it, as words may be insufficient. You will get to that a bit more when you are exposed to modeling and graphical representations later in the book.

For now, consider the radiation sensor on the manned mission to Mars. You have learned that all you are allowed is a particular spot on a spherical surface area, with the sensor allowed to be no more than 2 inches thick. You should consider something like the following:

> 8-5 The BOSS Mars Radiation Dose Rate meter shall project a square with an inner radius of 10 inches and an outer radius of 12 inches onto the spherical surface with an angle of 30 degrees on the x- and y-axes.

Granted, that is a little involved, but a picture will help to represent it (see Figure 8-1).

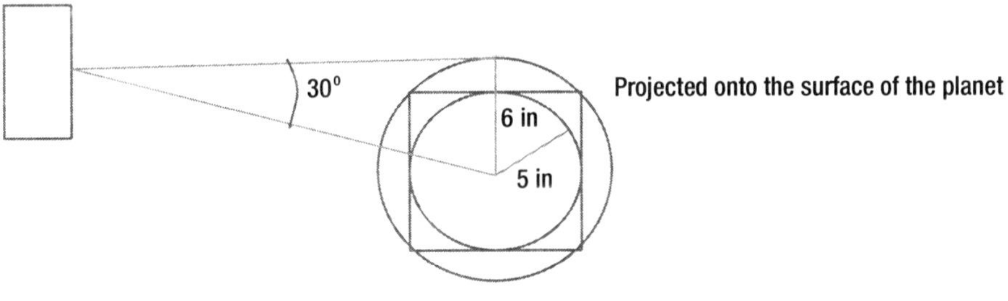

Figure 8-1. *Sensing area on the surface of Mars*

Volume

You may have situations where the three dimensions may not be as important as the total volume. In that case, you might have something like the following:

> 8-6 The BOSS Unit Radiation Dose Rate meter shall be no larger than 30 cubic inches.

The various constraints placed on your particular piece of hardware drive the volume requirement.

Density

Do you notice how these several values, dimensions, weight, volume, density, and center of gravity are related? Of course, they are interdependent. Thus, you will need to consider all of them, potentially.

In certain cases, the density affects things like ability to float in a liquid. Think of getting a rock to float. Yes, they exist (e.g., pumice). In this case, the density needs to be less than 1 gram per cubic centimeter.

Assume you have a requirement for the individual dosimeter to float if it is separated from the soldier.

> 8-7 The BOSS Individual Radiation Dosimeter shall have a density of less than 0.95 g/cm^3.

Center of Gravity

For those of you who do not remember, or know, what the center of gravity is, this is the point of the object where the weight can be concentrated for representing it in calculations. You might think it is in the center point of all the dimensions. That may be true if the density of the object is constant. What if it is not? Think of a rod. Assume the density of this rod is 2 Kg/M^3 on the left half and 4 Kg/M^3 on the right half. If you spun it around the middle point, it would wobble oddly because it is not spinning around the center of gravity. Take two eggs. Hard boil one and let it cool. Now spin each one. Do they spin the same? No. One has the yolk move to from one spot to another so it wobbles, while the hard-boiled one spins more evenly. Why? The hard-boiled one has a pretty uniform density, whereas the raw egg does not.

How does density affect the device? That depends on if it has to move in certain ways. Think of the jet mentioned earlier. Would you want the center of gravity on one of the wings? No, this would cause disastrous effects on the aircraft. Therefore, you should have something like this:

> 8-8 The XF-36 jet fighter shall have its center of gravity along the centerline of the fuselage.

This will not be the only requirement related to this, but this is just to illustrate one example here.

Human Portable

Is this device something that a person will need to carry? If so, that limits the size and weight of a device.

■ **Real-World Note** I worked with someone who was more than 250 pounds and 6 foot 4 inches tall. He developed a prototype of what he thought was man-portable. His device was 70 pounds. He neglected to take into account that some of the people who may carry this device themselves might be barely over 100 pounds. His prototype was impractical.

Guidance for carrying equipment for extended periods of time (like backpacking) is to have no more than a third of your weight. Therefore, if you weigh 150 pounds, you should carry only 50 pounds total. The military does not always follow that guidance, sometimes because of mission necessity.

Assume the following:

> 8-9 DRAFT The BOSS Unit Radiation Dosimeter shall weigh no more than forty pounds.

This is much higher than it should be, but it means that an individual of 120 pounds could carry it. It also assumes that they would carry nothing else. If however, their mission profile required them to carry 20 pounds of personal gear, food, and water, then the requirement will be as follows:

> 8-10 The BOSS Unit Radiation Dosimeter shall weigh no more than 20 pounds.

This device is still too large, coupled with the need for the military to carry more than 20 pounds of gear routinely. The weight they must carry now includes the armor they wear to protect against both firepower and explosives.

Safety Features

What particular items should you consider? Maybe you do not want any sharp edges that could hurt someone or could catch on items in its environment.

■ **Real-World Note** I remember when I was a teenager, a group of us went on canoe trips. One trip, I carried a cast iron Dutch oven packed incorrectly. I had the legs of the oven pressed against my back, causing some discomfort until I repacked it. Had I fallen on it, those legs would have certainly injured me—bruising me at a minimum or even puncturing me; it might even have broken my bones. I should have unpacked and repacked it so I was not exposed to potential injury, or I should have added significant padding to significantly reduce the risk of injury.

You must consider any aspect that poses a risk to safety, such as bruising, puncture, bone breakage, electrical discharge, blinding, deafening, or any other damage to life, limb, or even property. Think of mounting a machine gun on the fuselage of a biplane that shot through the propeller. If the gun fired at the wrong time, it would damage the propeller. What about radiation in space such that the satellite in orbit around Earth that must be exposed to that radiation? Also, what about the heat and cold extremes that same satellite would experience traveling in sunlight or during darkness. What particular items should you consider? All factors that could damage anything need to be considered.

Here is the safety features example:

> 8-11 The BOSS Unit Radiation Dosimeter shall not cause any electrical discharge to the outside of the device to prevent someone holding the device from being shocked.

Storage

Does your device need any special storage when waiting for shipment? An article was written about the new main battle tanks developed during the 1970s that were left out in the elements of Detroit with no protection from the northern winters. Some of the pieces may not have survived as well as originally anticipated, based on local news media reports.

> 8-12 The BOSS Unit Radiation Dosimeter shall be stored inside a warehouse so that it is not exposed to inclement weather.

Inclement weather may be imprecise. For this exercise, you should assume that a definition was provided earlier in the set of requirements or a glossary that defined what this is. Ideally, it is not raining or snowing inside. As an aside, the building that housed the space shuttle before launch actually had clouds form inside of it.

Packaging, Cooling, Heating, and Integration Constraints

Think of what you might have to do for digital, analog, and power circuits. Think of a satellite, how it is heated when exposed to the sun, and how it is cooled to near absolute zero when in the dark. What kind of insulation is required? How is it heated in the dark and cooled in the sunlight?

These are very specialized requirements, so here you see a modified a statement found in the NASA-GSFC Nano-Satellite Technology Development, SSC98-VI-5, document:

> 8-13 Since the top and bottom of the BOSS spacecraft are insulated, the inside of the cylindrical solar array shall not be insulated allowing internal heat transfer between the internal equipment and the solar array.

Again, this is an example of a specialized situation. While you may not be fully experienced in this technology, as you will be in some cases, you get the gist of the process. (GSFC means Goddard Space Flight Center.) However, if you are developing equipment that operates wherever the U.S. Army might operate from the heat of the desert to the colds of Alaska, hot and cold are environments that must be considered. Thus, while the satellite requirement is more severe, it is really only a wider range, so the requirement may not be so specialized after all.

Power Consumption

What is the power consumption for your hardware? Think of a trip to the Kuiper belt, about 2.8 to 5.1 billion miles away. Even assuming near escape velocity from the solar system, a spacecraft would travel for four to seven years at almost 94,000 miles an hour. Think of the power consumption you must have for that long of a trip (assuming the system achieves the necessary velocity). You need to have the ability to send messages on a periodic basis. What power do you need to transmit from there? That will drive how much power consumption you must have.

Next, consider simpler systems. You might have several subsystems within your entire system, you will need to consider the power consumption of each, and you will need to consider whether they work in different modes, where they may consume different amounts for the various modes. You will need a good mission profile to estimate the frequency of each mode.

For this example, consider one system only.

> 8-14 The BOSS Individual Radiation Dosimeter shall consume 0.01 watts per exposure.

The reason for this type of requirement might be driven by the small battery that might have to last 60 days without recharging or replacement, or some other constraint that the mission places on this. This also indicates that requirements can have some interdependency—in this case, power consumption versus the life of the energy source.

Material

Your environment may put certain constraints on the materials. You might need to specify whether it is plastic, metal, ceramic, or some special material depending on your situation. What if it needs to operate in the containment dome of a nuclear power plant? What kinds of material would you need for nuclear hardening? Think of a satellite in orbit that is exposed to significant changes in temperatures, micro-meteors, and solar flares, to name a few. There are only certain materials built to survive that.

For this example, you should consider something a little less severe.

> 8-15 The BOSS Individual Radiation Dosimeter material shall cause no reaction when exposed to human skin.

If, however, the specific compound causes most soldiers to break out in a rash, the soldiers would be inclined not to wear it and possibly forget it or lose it, defeating the purpose of having it.

Surface Coefficient of Friction

If you are going to have something in motion, you will want to define what the friction is to minimize the impact to the speed, unless you are in outer space, where there is no air to worry about. (Of course, you have other problems, like micro-meteors.)

Of course, there are some instances where you want surface friction. What if your tires have the tread worn off and you are driving in a heavy rainstorm? You will have a hard time gripping the road. Therefore, the amount of surface coefficient of friction is important.

> 8-16 The XF-36 jet fighter tires on its landing gear shall have surface coefficient of friction of 0.7 on dry pavement.

Of course, you would have to define the other coefficients for other conditions, such as wet, rainy, snow, and ice.

Physical Robustness

Physical robustness includes the steps taken to protect your system. Think of the plastic protector you place over the screen of your phone so it doesn't get scratched. If you wear eyeglasses, do you put a coating on it to protect it from scratching, or even to protect against intense light? Is the watch you wear needed for diving? Then you need it to be waterproof. Or depending on the depth you will dive, you may need it strengthened against certain pressure. What kinds of things must you protect it against? Then identify those elements and write requirements to address them.

If you do need them, find the resident expert to help you craft good requirements as the requirements are very environment dependent.

Reliability

This was talked about in Chapter 5, so we will not discuss it here. You learned about what makes a system reliable, hardware and software, and the learning measurements of reliability. This will not be repeated here; just remember that it does relate to physical characteristics.

Throughput

You will see this in the "Throughput Characteristics" section in this chapter, not here. The reason for this is because of the importance of throughput.

Do these physical characteristics apply to computer systems? If you are talking about the "box" that contains the computer components, then yes. However, software and operating systems have additional characteristics that you need to consider. This will be presented next.

Physical Computer Characteristics

Remember when every time you picked up a box that contained a software program, you saw somewhere on the box a list of minimum requirements describing what your computer needed to have in order to run the application? Here is a list of physical characteristics that you may need to specify. You should consider some or all of the following characteristics:

- On what microprocessor or microprocessors can the software run?
- How much physical memory (RAM—in this case, random access memory) must you have at a minimum for it to work?
- How much disk storage capacity must you have at a minimum for it to work?
- What devices can it run on? Laptops, desktops, phones, tablets?
- Is it designed to run on a stand-alone machine, or must it work attached to a server or even connected to the Internet (think of World of Warcraft)?
- Must this run on a network? If yes, then:
    - What kinds are supported?
    - LAN?
    - WAN?
    - Storage area network (SAN)?
    - Metropolitan area network (MAN)?
    - Wireless or wired?
- If this is client-server, what is on the client versus what is on the server?

For a commercial application you could find on your desk, you might find something like this requirement for the sample application:

> 8-17 The BOSS Application shall require the following parameters to run on a system:
>
> - 500 MHz or faster processer
> - 256 MB of RAM, with 512 MB recommended
> - 3.0 GB available disk space
> - 1024 by 576 resolution monitor or higher
> - Window 7 or Windows Server 2008 or higher

Of course, your requirements will vary, but you get the idea. Plus this gets very dated quickly, as it is just an example for a snapshot in time. Do not criticize how antiquated it may be. The original requirement could be written some years before. However, it does say higher, so it allows for updated requirements.

Throughput Characteristics

In this section, we'll look at the concepts of *throughput* and *latency*.

Throughput

Margaret Rouse, in her "throughput" definition on Tech Target's Search Networking, defines throughput as the amount of work that a computer can do in a given time period, in computer technology. In data transmission, throughput is the amount of data moved successfully from one place to another in a given time period. When discussing throughput, delays in the passing of such information are important and need to be addressed. This is called *latency* and is present as a subsection.

The Open Process Framework (OPF) web site's "Throughput Requirements" article gives some of the following examples of throughput requirements:

- "The application shall be able to successfully process a minimum of 150,000 customer orders per day including credit card authorizations under average loads."
- "The missile avionics system shall update the position of the ailerons 20 times a second."
- "At least 98% of the time, the application shall be able to successfully display the results of a keyword search in no more than 4 seconds."

Remember the discussion of performance in Chapter 4; you saw some examples, like this:

> 8-18 (4-32) The FBI BOSS Records Management Search Function shall return the results within 4 seconds, 80% of the time.
>
> 8-19 (4-41) The FBI BOSS Records Management Search Function shall return the results within 10 seconds, 80% of the time when there are 100 searches initiated within 10 minutes.

These examples show how a given computer can perform; the latter talks about specific transactions. Also, notice that you were provided these examples in different functional areas or topics elsewhere in your requirements areas. This demonstrates that the distinction between boundaries is blurry. It also helps to reiterate that there is no one way to organize the data. Do whatever way works best for you, unless your organization has a specific structure or has it mandated to you by a governing organization like the DoD.

Back to throughput: you will have more requirements besides the areas talked about previously. You will need to address data transmission. This has been done as well with the following example from earlier:

> 8-20 (5-50) The BOSS Unit Radiation Dosimeter shall have the ability to download up to 1000 transactions to the BOSS Dosimetry Archive Laptop in 5 minutes.

IBM, on its Transaction Processing Facility (TPF) Product Information Center web site, has an article, "System throughput (messages per second)," that defines the number of messages processed over a given interval of time as system throughput. It goes on to say that a business enterprise must identify its projected peak message rate in order to assess whether the system is an appropriate solution. This definition matches the definition in this text and is an important approach to take when defining throughput.

You need to emphasize system throughput for networks. This is an important aspect of WAN and LAN needs. Think of a regional company that does many transactions on a daily basis. Now look at a tool reseller. The corporate headquarters (HQ) buys the tools wholesale from the manufacturers, and each remote location sells the tools to their local customers.

You need to know the size of each record that is affected with each transaction. Assume that 1,000 bytes are captured with each buy and sell. It is possible that large wholesale record sizes are different from selling one tool or a small purchase. You will have to determine that for your situation. However, for simplicity of the example, you will use 1,000 for each.

In this tool example, assume you have 2,400 different tools in stock. On a daily basis, your company restocks 20 tools. Each of 50 sites averages 250 sales a day.

That works out that each LAN at the regional office has 250 sales by 1,000 bytes per sale, or 250,000 bytes sent in.

To get frequency, you need the time aspect also. If each transaction is when the sale is made, then, through the course of nine hours, that is 9 hours by 60 minutes by 60 seconds, or 32,400 seconds. Divide that into 250,000 bytes. That works out to 7.72 bytes per second. Not a very strenuous need.

Now you need to see how much is coming to the BOSS headquarters, the central point of the WAN; 50 times that 7.72 bytes per second is 385.80 bytes per second.

However, what if all the work is sent at 4 p.m. over the course of one hour? The same calculation gives 69.44 bytes per second per office and 3,472.22 bytes per second at HQ. Still that is not a significant value.

What if they were all sent within one minute at 4 p.m.? That gives 4,166.67 bytes per second for each office and 208,333.33 bytes per second. Now you are getting some throughput. What if this was in Southern Africa and you had only 64 Kbps lines? Would that be practical? You say yes, because each line going from the office is less than 64 Kbps. That is true, but you have only one 64 Kbps line coming into the central server. Therefore, it does not work. Now you see where the issue might come in.

This also indicates that you need to see what peak throughput needs are. If HQ mandates the 4 p.m. load, then you must consider that approach. Alternatively, think of an eBay or Amazon amount of throughput. Then you have to figure out what times are peak times. Are they weekday normal working hours? Are they after work? How much does the average transactions go up?

So, what do you write for the requirements? For your situation, you should consider the following:

> 8-21 The BOSS Tools Transaction Function at each regional office shall transmit 250 sales by 1,000 bytes per transaction daily throughout the day when the transaction occurs.
>
> 8-22 The BOSS Tools Transaction Function at the central office shall receive all regional office sales throughout the day when the transaction are transmitted.

You could have instead presented this as the actual transmission rates. However, if the sales force doubles or triples the number of tools or through changes in the sales workforce quadruples the number of sales per day by each regional office, it is much easier to update your values rather than recalculating the transmission rates each time. In addition, the values are not necessarily clear to everyone reviewing it to determine whether it is correct just by looking at the following requirement:

> 8-23 DRAFT The BOSS Tools Transaction Function at each regional office shall transmit 69.44 bytes per second per office per day.

While the information may be correct, how would a person know that by looking at it? This reiterates the artistry of requirements definition. There are multiple ways to craft a statement, but not all of them are the best way. Judgment comes into play.

To emphasize how important throughput is, we expanded on the topic here because of its importance. One lesson to remember is that one of the most challenging areas in development of systems is the connection between systems. The throughput necessary to support those connections is instrumental in the successfully communications between them.

Latency

As was introduced in this throughput section, you need to address the delays inherent in the movement of this data. It is important to define whether there are stakeholder restrictions to latency.

Andrew Heim defines latency as the amount of time it takes to complete an operation, according to his white paper "Make it Faster: More Throughput or Less Latency?" You must decide what units of measure time are most useful: milliseconds, microseconds, or nanoseconds.

You saw earlier when you examined search results, where latency was addressed, even though it was not represented in requirements there. Here you should have something like the following:

> 8-18 The FBI BOSS Records Management Search Function shall return the results within 4 seconds, 80% of the time.
>
> 8-19 The FBI BOSS Records Management Search Function shall return the results within 10 seconds, 80% of the time when there are 100 searches initiated within 10 minutes.

Latency may not be an issue for most cases. Experience on a particular system where, because of the data modeling of the system and an extra commercial off-the-shelf (COTS) package that added a layer between the user interface and the database, the system's query results could take up to 15 minutes to be returned. If this was a rare occasion, once a month for one or two users, that might be acceptable. However, it happened almost daily for the majority of the users. That latency was unacceptable. Therefore, latency was important in the design of the next system.

Also, think about a nuclear power plant. If an error condition occurred, would you want the response to the operator delayed by seconds or even minutes? No, you want the latency to be almost nonexistent in the situation.

Therefore, determine the latency drivers in your system. The web site article referenced for the previous definition spends some time discussing the comparison and contrast between throughput and latency. If you are going to work on measurement and control systems, you might want to read it.

References

Panneta, Peter V. "NASA-GSFC Nano-Satellite Technology Development, SSC98-VI-5." *12th Annual AIAA/USU Conference on Small Satellites*. Feb 2015, `http://digitalcommons.usu.edu/cgi/viewcontent.cgi?article=2235&context=smallsat`

Rouse, Margaret. "throughput" (definition). Tech Target: Search Networking. Feb. 2015, `http://searchnetworking.techtarget.com/definition/throughput`

"Throughput Requirements." 27 June 2005. Open Process Framework (OPF) `www.opfro.org/index.html?Components/WorkProducts/RequirementsSet/Requirements/ThroughputRequirements.html~Contents`

"System throughput (messages per second)." IBM TPF Product Information Center. Feb. 2015, www-01.ibm.com/support/knowledgecenter/SSB23S_1.1.0.9/com.ibm.ztpf-ztpfdf.doc_put.09/gtpc3/c3thru.html?cp=SSB23S_1.1.0.9%2F0-1-0-0-6-2

Heim, Andrew. "Make it Faster: More Throughput or Less Latency?" Feb 25, 2014. National Instruments. Feb. 2015, `www.ni.com/white-paper/14990/en/`

Exercises

Exercise 1

Drawing on the "Physical Hardware Characteristics" section of this chapter, write a good mission profile to describe a medic assigned to a unit during a field exercise who needs to carry the BOSS Unit Radiation Dosimeter.

Exercise 2

Look at the performance requirements 4-119 through 4-139 in Chapter 4. How many of those 21 meet the definitions in A) and B) here?

A. Throughput is the amount of work that a computer can do in a given time period, in computer technology.

B. In data transmission, throughput is the amount of data moved successfully from one place to another in a given time period.

PART III

Cradle to Grave Requirements

CHAPTER 9

How to Collect Requirements

The last eight chapters have spent extensive time defining what requirements to collect. In this chapter, you will learn how to collect them. The amount of time devoted to this approach does not diminish the importance of collecting all the requirements for a system. This chapter will spend a good deal on how best to do this. The simple answer says perform whatever works. Ah, there's the rub—finding out what way works. Dissertations have been written on this. At its foundation, you have to ask the stakeholders.

How you do this is affected by your organizational structure. Is it a larger organization that has a process established and you are one of several requirements engineers? If so, you are lucky. Not only do you not need to help define good processes, but also you are fortunate that you will have experienced REs to help you.

Alternatively, are you in a small team where you are the only RE and you do not have defined processes? This is the other end of the spectrum. You will be challenged to not only help set up the requirements team but run it as well. This book may not provide everything you need, but it should be a good start.

You are likely to be somewhere between the two ends of the spectrum.

More importantly is where you are in the requirements process. Are you at the very beginning of the project, where you are just beginning the requirements process? If so, you will be picking up someone else's work. In that case, you will not be able to influence or improve the process much as they are likely established and sometimes difficult to change—people can resist change at many levels. On the other hand, coming into a project that is underway, you do not have to try to set requirements processes in place, so that actually can make your job easier. You just need to follow what they currently perform.

Note Usually, in my career, I have come in during the definition process, and sometimes even in the operations and maintenance phase. It is likely you will experience similar exposure during your career.

I will introduce the concept of eliciting or collecting requirements. Specifically, I will talk about techniques to collect these requirements from questionnaires, group meetings, interviewing, following people, doing document analysis, prototyping, use cases, doing the work yourself, and reverse engineering. Finally, I will talk about analyzing the problems with elicitation.

G. Koelsch, *Requirements Writing for System Engineering*,
DOI 10.1007/978-1-4842-2099-3_9

Elicitation

What does elicitation/collecting mean in the requirements context?

Merriam-Webster's Collegiate Dictionary defines *elicit* as follows (for requirements engineering particular purposes): "to call forth or draw out (as information or a response)."[1] Elicitation is the noun of the verb *elicit*; it is the act of eliciting, or drawing forth the information from your stakeholders.

Merriam-Webster defines *collect* as follows: "to get (things) from different places and bring them together."

There is some discussion in the requirements engineering industry regarding the use of the word *collection* versus *elicitation*. Some say that you cannot *collect* requirements like you can collect seashells on the beach, just by wandering around and picking them up when you see them. They will go on about how much harder requirements are than seashells to find. They may have a point, emphasizing the drawing forth of the requirements.

■ **Note** In most of my career, however, I have heard (and used) the word *collect* rather than *elicit*.

Purists would insist on using *elicitation* over *collection*. The word choice is left to you; just know that you may have to be flexible should your audience (management, stakeholders, or users) prefer one definition over the other. Just a minor point, but it reinforces use of jargon discussed earlier.

Some sources recommend you use the term *gathering* instead of either of the other two. Merriam-Webster's Collegiate Dictionary defines *gather* as follows: "to choose and collect (things)" and "to get or take (things) from different people or places and bring them together."[2]

This last one seems to be closer to the collecting definition, but it is another one you can use. The objection by certain purists is that the collect and gather definitions do not transform the user statements into true requirements, which a good RE must do. The reality of this is that in most cases, you are not massaging the statements into requirements in the initial meeting but just gathering or collecting the users' statements. You perform the analysis later. After that transformation, then you get back with the users to validate what they said is captured correctly. The use of gather or collect is valid in the initial meeting phase.

What is key here is the communications of the process to the stakeholders. If they understand gathering or collecting better than eliciting, then use their word. Whatever terminology you employ, you should avoid giving the impression that the stakeholders are reluctant to give it to you. The truth is, it may be hard to get it from them, but you don't tell them that. You are trying to gain their trust and respect. Hinting at difficulty from them does not ingratiate you with them. Keep that in mind in the next section

---

[1]By permission. From *Merriam-Webster's Collegiate® Dictionary*, 11th Edition ©2016 by Merriam-Webster, Inc. (`www.merriam-webster.com/`)

[2]By permission. From *Merriam-Webster's Collegiate® Dictionary*, 11th Edition ©2016 by Merriam-Webster, Inc. (`www.merriam-webster.com/`)

when you learn ways to extract requirements from the various sources. (REs do not define *extract* as have other people, as that hints at something like pulling teeth without painkillers—an analogy you do not want to make.)

The next section of this chapter will spend a significant amount of time addressing the various techniques to collect/elicit/gather requirements.

Techniques of Elicitation

Which one is the best? The best way to answer that is—*it depends*. On what? It depends on your situation, your environment, your experience, your stakeholders' experience, your judgment, your management commitment, and your timeline to capture all the requirements. The correct answer is whatever techniques allow you to capture of them—vis-à-vis a combination of the techniques. It will likely change with time, different projects, different organization, and everyone's needs. It is difficult to answer because you must apply judgment to each project. The net result will likely be that you may not collect them all, with only a few techniques, hence the combination.

Elicitation Basics

Knowing you may be likely to miss some requirements, through no fault of you or the stakeholders, recall from Chapters 4 and 5 that the function and nonfunctional lists give you clues to topics you should ask about and investigate. When a user or stakeholder says that they do not need a particular aspect that is useful information too, as you have now bounded the problem. Remember, the boundary of a project is important so you know what to include and what to exclude.

Before you look at specific techniques, you need to consider a good categorization of the requirement sources.

Requirements Sources

Before you look at the techniques in the upcoming table, you need to consider a good categorization. You should do so with the following requirement sources. Think of them as people, paper, and projects (as a simple way to remember them); documents may be soft copy, so to keep the alliteration alive, use *pixels* then.

- Stakeholders
- Documents
- System in operation

These three sources come from the book *Requirements Engineering Fundamentals* (Rocky Nook Computing 2011), by Klaus Pohl and Chris Rupp.

Stakeholders

These are the people and organizations that directly or indirectly affect the system requirements. You will spend the most time collecting requirements with them. In some cases, you may collect more candidate requirements in documents, but that will take less time to do so. That will become clear when you examine each technique.

■ **Note** Just because one or more techniques takes more time does not diminish the importance or goodness of these requirements. Some techniques take longer by their nature.

Documents

These documents contain information important to the system that can contain requirements. Legacy system requirements documents, concepts of operations, policy documents, architecture documents, or anything that influences the system in question are important.

System in Operation

This could be the legacy systems (not always fully automated), predecessor system, or even competing systems; these all could influence what requirements apply to the system in question.

Next, we will introduce the technique overview mentioned earlier.

An Overview of Elicitation Techniques

During my career, I have used a wide range of techniques. Table 9-1 lists the types of techniques for elicitation I have used. Different REs and organizations approach this differently. To illustrate the different approaches, I have aggregated the recommended techniques from several reputable resources in Table 9-1: articles by Tom Mochal, Tyner Blain, and from the Eclipse Process Framework (EPF) requirements guidelines. All three of these resources provide reinforcement to my list. The indented techniques are the specific values specified in four sources, grouped in the numbered technique, to show the commonality. For example, under group meetings, the six different approaches qualify for this technique, but each is a variant that will be discussed. (See the "References" section later in the chapter for the complete citations.)

Table 9-1. *Elicitation Techniques by Requirement Sources*

Requirement Sources and Elicitation techniques	Mochal	Blain	EPF
Stakeholders			
1. Questionnaires/surveys	Yes	Yes	Yes
2. Group meetings			
Facilitated sessions	Yes		
Conduct workshops			Yes
Focus group		Yes	
Brainstorming	Yes	Yes	Yes
Requirements workshop		Yes	
Joint application development (JAD)	Yes		
3. Interviewing			
Interviewing		Yes	
Interview users		Yes	
Group interviews	Yes		
One-on-one interviews	Yes		
Study improvements made by users			Yes
Look at unintended uses			Yes
Talk to support teams			Yes
4. Following people around/observation	Yes	Yes	
5. Models			
Modeling			
Modeling in the agile methodology			
Storyboards			
State transition diagrams			
6. Use cases/scenarios/user stories	Yes		
Documents			
7. Document analysis			
Document analysis		Yes	
Interface analysis		Yes	
Study analogous systems			Yes
Examine suggestions, RFCs, and problem reports			Yes
8. RFPs	Yes		
System in Operation/Miscellaneous			

(*continued*)

Table 9-1. (*continued*)

Requirement Sources and Elicitation techniques	Mochal	Blain	EPF
9. Prototyping	Yes	Yes	Yes
10. Work in the target environment			Yes
11. Reverse engineering		Yes	
12. Tools			

Now that we have introduced the elicitation techniques in Table 9-1, you will learn about each technique. While this chapter tries to be exhaustive, some of the techniques you are likely to experience may be more eclectic and targeted to specific organizations. When such more narrowly focused techniques are presented, that will be highlighted to you.

Now we'll examine each of the 12 techniques, and I will include advantages and disadvantages where appropriate.

Questionnaires/Surveys

Questionnaires and surveys are designed for large user populations ranging from dozens to thousands, where meeting with all of them or interviewing them would be difficult to impossible. You can use these two basic formats. With a series of questions that have true/false or multiple-choice questions, you will get only the information you ask for. As part of the multiple-choice questions, they could include ratings such as "strongly agree," "somewhat agree," "neither agree nor disagree," "somewhat disagree," or "strongly disagree." You should ask how often certain tasks occur and provide selections to choose. This will help you decide which tasks are higher priority based on usage. You will also need to find out what drives the need. Ask if it is legal or policy driven, or the only way to gather the information the user needs.

This means you will get no deviation from the question, where other requirements may be lurking. Without the ability to probe for more information, you may miss some requirements. In addition, you must garner a significant amount of information about the system in question already before you can develop the questions.

Clearly, this option is necessary for the larger end of the spectrum of total users and/ or with users in remote locations. If instead you opt for the open-ended question, where you get more information, you ideally capture those outlying requirements you might otherwise miss. However, if you have only open-ended questions like the following, you will not be able to categorize and group answers easily:

> What works well with the current Search function?
>
> What does not work well with the current Search function?

If you have hundreds or thousands of users, how long would it take to analyze these results, especially if you have dozens to hundreds question? It would probably take a very prohibitively large amount of time.

In many cases, you may combine the two techniques, where most questions would be true or false and multiple choices, with a small (manageable) number of open-ended questions to increase the chances of catching those outlying requirements. Also, perhaps the preliminary information gathering can help you focus some open-ended questions such that they are very specific and thus not unmanageably open. The larger the population, the fewer open-ended questions.

One aspect you could ask at the end is if the user would be willing to answer a few additional questions one on one (face to face, e-mail, phone) to refine some answers. This is more likely with the open-ended requirements.

This works well for large populations of users spread over a large geographic region, and the system is quite consistent. It will not work if the system has a broad set of functionality that is not consistent everywhere.

Given the preparation time for this technique, you should probably use it in conjunction with other elicitation prior to the preparation of the questionnaire/survey.

Group Meetings

The meetings discussed in this section are different from interviews, which will be discussed in more detail in the next section. Group meetings have a slightly different structure than the open-ended questions of an interview. They are as follows:

- Facilitated sessions
- Workshops
- Focus groups
- Brainstorming sessions
- Requirements workshops
- Joint application development (JAD)

Who is invited to group meetings? Database administrators (DBAs) are different from normal users and different from report specialists, research specialists, system managers, access control, HR, payroll, and so on. Since you may be working with a variety of different people and roles, you may not include everyone in every meeting and have some meetings that are more specific to particular groups. This way you get requirements that affect specific users that do not affect others significantly. Part of the reason for this is because most people who are not part of a particular group will not participate in the discussion of those specific roles, and they usually wind up sitting there doing nothing. By having specialized meetings, you optimize everyone's time.

Group sessions work well when you need to address more people, and having multiple people helps encourage discussions and clarifications.

Facilitated Session

TechRepublic defines a facilitated session as a group (five or more) for a common purpose. This approach is faster than if you were to interview each user separately. By this definition, it could belong in the interview section. It is presented here because of the source's definition.

Focus Group

A Guide to the Business Analysis Book of Knowledge (Third Edition, IIBA 2015), also called the BABOK Guide, defines a focus group as a gathering of people who are representative of the users or customers of a product to get feedback. You can gather feedback about needs, opportunities, and problems to identify requirements, or you can gather feedback to validate and refine already elicited requirements. This type of meeting happens quite often especially if you cannot easily call together a larger group of users given the size or amount of time that can be devoted to the effort.

Joint Application Development/Requirements Workshop

A JAD, sometime called a *requirements workshop*, is a meeting to collect business requirements many times associated with a prototyping development methodology. JADs usually meet until the session objectives are completed, sometimes taking two to five days. For a requirements JAD session, the participants stay in session until you document a complete set of requirements and the stakeholders agree. Sometimes, you may create domain-model artifacts (like static diagrams and activity diagrams) to facilitate this process. You will examine these models in Chapter 12, not here.

For some meetings, you may want someone who runs the meeting and another who captures the data provided (aka *scribe*). The reason for this is that the facilitator can concentrate on running the meeting and keeping it under control. You will find that it is difficult to both run the meeting and capture all the notes from the discussion.

The biggest challenge, even though JADs/workshops can be very effective, is getting people to commit to this approach. Asking many people to stop doing their day-to-day job for days is asking a great deal. It may be one of the fewest used elicitation techniques because of this. It is strongly recommend that you do this away from the normal office and do not allow outside phones to interrupt the workshop. Some crisis may arise that may cause someone to stop participating. However, if people cannot get onto the network or check their voice mail at every break, you can have breaks end on time. Some people recommend that you have a workshop at an offsite location where people do not go home at night in order to encourage additional discussion among the group and so people are less likely to get distracted. This happens even less often than the workshops themselves, again from both a cost and time investment. This is something you need to consider.

For any type of elicitation meeting, not just JADs, you need to keep people on task, especially if the schedule is tight. Some groups may wander a bit on the topic and that may be OK, but it is a judgment call as to how long and how often it happens. However, maintaining focus is critical to accomplishing the goals and not losing participant focus. It is frustrating to devote time to this sort of effort and watch the conversation wander all over the place.

Support Teams

EPF recommends talking to support teams. This is not a new kind of meeting, but you want to meet with these types of people to talk separately from your general system users. You will have to decide whether this meeting is just an interview session (which will be presented shortly) or whether it is one of the other meetings that have been discussed in this section. The help desk, the system monitoring, system auditors, trainers, and even DBAs and those who deploy the system can be candidates for these meetings. Remember when these types were talked about at the beginning of this section?

One reason to meet with these people separately is that the other users may not care about one group's needs. For example, someone who audits the system for security reasons does not care about what the help desk needs, and people monitoring the system will not have the same needs as those who deploy the system. In fact, if some of these groups meet together, they may argue that other people's needs are wrong because they are not theirs. Hypothetically, auditors say that people monitoring the system for availability takes away from the audit function that collects data on who accesses the system and therefore system monitoring should be eliminated. You want to avoid such discussions. While they may not always happen, they can occur, and you want to mitigate the likelihood of them.

While the types of people and their associated needs may be unique to their responsibilities, the approaches to gather them are virtually identical to any user, such as interviewing them for their needs. Many times, their needs have been consistent over time, and they make an excellent start point by describing them. Additionally, look for the things they would like to have but do not. The next section discusses a good technique to support these user types.

Brainstorming

Last among the group meeting types is *brainstorming*. This is one of the more free-form and, frankly, fun approaches for eliciting requirements—well, at least for the ideas. The requirements come later.

The purpose of the session is to come up with areas that people may not have considered-. Here are steps to consider for the brainstorming session:

1. For each session, define the particular topic to explore.
2. Let the people identify as many ideas as possible.
3. Do not be limited by known technology, budget constraints, security restrictions, policies, and so on.
4. Do not criticize the goodness of ideas or debate whether they are practical.
5. Once all the ideas are captured, then refine and combine them (that's your job) to get joint agreement.

Real-World Note During a machine learning session, I also did a gap analysis where I researched topics on the Internet and came up with additional ideas that the users did not consider. I presented my suggestions (which we reviewed jointly), refined them, and included them with a final set of requirements.

This brainstorming process can be a precursor to *prototyping*. Prototyping is trying various approaches, especially dealing with how something may look on the screen for software. This way, you can experiment with some of the ideas generated from brainstorming. You may want to prioritize the ideas collected, so you may better understand which may be the most important to consider. If the users say that something really works badly, that is something to look at first potentially.

Even though brainstorming is designed to stretch thinking outside normal silos or constraints, sometimes it doesn't capture everything. This reinforces that you should do the preliminary research as described previously. Also, to help fill any gaps, you might want to consider other techniques to find all their needs, as in this next section.

Interviewing

This is the most important and most common method for eliciting requirements. It is the most important because you are getting the information directly from those who use the system on a regular basis. They will know it better than almost everyone else will. Besides being the most employed technique because of its importance, it is also the most time intensive. You will get some of the best information as you hear the needs directly from the users, and you have the best opportunity for delving into details as needed. It can also take more time, so depending on your timeline, you may have to target which users need interviewing.

The following are things to consider for running an interview:

- The number of people to interview
- The format of the interview (in-person, telephone, videoconference, or online)
- Segregating by user role
- Conducting the interview
- Items that enhance the interview

Size of Interviews Vary

You can interview users either one on one or in small groups. Several factors drive you to one or the other. The number of users may be very small, so only one may be available (e.g., a database administrator). If there are only two or three, you may get the chance to talk with only one of them. Alternatively, management may give up only one person from an organization to talk with you because the manager cannot afford to give up more time. Other times, you have the ability to talk with more than one person in a particular part of an office.

What is the ideal number for a group interview? Two to four is very good because you do not have too many people talking at once, and the people probably have similar responsibilities. However, as mentioned, you rarely have the choice. If you have five or six, that is workable. As you get larger, people can sometimes feel like they are wasting time. Why? With only one person talking at a time, that means everyone else is sitting there essentially doing nothing. If you have 12 people, up to 10 people may not be engaged. Also, in larger groups, some folks will tend to be reticent and contributions can be lost. Therefore, the number of people is a balancing act. Of course, you have this issue with any meeting (as mentioned in the previous section). If a chief of an organization wants an entire team there, you can offer two sessions, but if the chief insists, it is their call to make.

In-Person, Telephone, Videoconference, and Online Interviews

Here are the typical formats for performing interviews:

- In-person
- Telephone
- Videoconference
- Online

Many interviews performed face to face also called *in-person*. This works when you are more geographically localized so that you can meet with the people. This has the distinct advantage of seeing the people more directly, so you can pick up on nonverbal clues easier. Also, you may have a bit more flexibility to run over if need be, which telephone and videoconference may not have.

There is also the phone, but it happens without the benefit of nonverbal cues. These cues can help to reinforce points, like how unsatisfied someone is, or when someone has a confused look on their face, you may need to either rephrase your question or ask some probing questions to see why they don't like something. Phone interviews are more difficult but may be necessary when users are remote.

If you have the ability to video teleconference, you essentially come back to having a meeting but with the added need to watch the screen for nonvisual clues. Having more than one site on a screen may preclude you from getting good nonverbal clues, so pay attention. Depending on the reliability and throughput availability, you may have some limitations on resolution. However, as technology and bandwidth improves, these impacts continue to lessen. The size of the room and how good the sound capture is can impact how well you hear, so be aware of that. With an in-person interview with a larger group, more than one conversation may be a minor irritant, but with videoconferencing it is even more important to maintain good speaking discipline or you may miss important information.

Doing an online interview is more like a questionnaire than an interview, and you learned about that earlier. Also, you could have a much smaller group of people and send more open-ended questions.

Segregate by User Roles

When you do have groups, it is highly recommended that people with common needs be together. By that, if you have organizations with different focuses for the system, they may say that each other is wrong about the needs, when in fact their missions are different and hence have separate needs. Database administrators focus on maintaining the database, whereas the HR representatives are querying the personnel data regularly. Each type of person has different tasks, and you should talk to them separately. In addition, the DBA will likely be bored when HR is talking about their issues, since the DBAs are much more technical than the HR user. In addition, the HR users will likely be confused by the technical aspects that the DBAs discuss.

Running an Interview

How do you run an interview? Whether it is one or a few more people, there is not a significant difference. You basically ask questions about what the user does. In this respect, it is like the open-ended questionnaire. Ask them questions that will give them freedom to discuss a topic. What questions should you ask? As you would expect, the answer is that it depends. What kind of system is it? Is it a software application like the FBI Record Management System or a collection system like the BOSS Radiation Dosimeter System?

Ask what they do and then why they do what they have said, not how they do it, but why, so you understand if it is still necessary. A different design might obviate some of the steps user do. For example, having a concept search that can take name variations like Bob instead of Robert or accounting for different spellings of Mohammed will mean that users do not have to spend hours designing the right Boolean search to capture the information they need.

Ask the user how often they perform an operation. Get ideas for how long certain operations take (say, research results within the database.) What works well, what does not, and why? Have them give examples of their typical operations, explaining deviations and why. Ask questions as you go along. If you need them to slow down so you can write down everything, do so. At the end of the interview, ask if it is OK to ask follow-up questions. These follow-ups do not have to be in person. It could be on the phone or in e-mail. It is recommend you use e-mail because then you have their description in writing, you can save time capturing the requirements, and you are less likely to hear it incorrectly.

When you have a lot of ground to cover on a system, sometimes it is useful to break the discussions into topic areas so that you do not try to cover everything in one sitting. It is easier to do four two-hour interviews than an eight-hour day continuously. It is hard for you to concentrate for that long, and it is even harder to get users to give up an entire day. Spread over several days, or once a month if you are doing different functional areas, this works out better.

As was mentioned, interviews work better when everyone present is at the same level or has the same role. This is part of your preparation to ensure whenever practical that this is the case. If the people are managers and their subordinates, the subordinates are less likely to disagree with the manager who may speak the company line or talk about the ideal system when they do not have to use it every day. That can be as important as preparing your list of questions you want to ask.

■ **Warning** You may get people who disagree and say the other person is wrong. You have to listen and determine whether that is the case or the person has different needs. Generally, it is the case that different parts of the organization have different emphasis. For example, the person who is responsible for maintaining the security of a system is more inclined to want to lock data down, whereas the HR person may want to have access to more data. Neither is wrong; it is just that they may have different and potentially conflicting needs. You job is to capture both and allow for a balancing act.

Remember when Chapter 1 talked about the attributes of a good requirements engineering being communications, including listening with emphasis on active listening? It is during interviews (and any meeting for that matter) when you need to do that. Listen with your eyes and ears. Look for the nonverbal clues that give away some emotion. Do you see people reacting negatively to statements? Follow up on that. Honestly, that is where you can find some of the most critical aspects, because that alluded to the items that most bothered the users.

Your level of formality may even vary with the users. For example, if you are talking with managers, especially high-level managers, you may be more formal than you might with users who do not interact with these people as much. Sometimes you may have a more structured set of questions because the topic is broader than others are. For example, with searching, it might be more free-form, whereas when asking about all the known reports, you will have one or more questions for each of several dozen reports.

When you have looked at employee suggestions (later in the "Document Analysis" section of this chapter), which reinforces the interconnectedness of these topics, now is your opportunity to ask why they were added. This shows that you cannot go into these interviews cold. In other words, you cannot do this on your first day. You need to know something about the current system, the terminology, the user employee, and what their general goals are. One of the best sources for this foundation is discussed in the "Document Analysis" section coming shortly.

People often use things for purposes for which they were not designed. You can learn a lot from this.

Real-World Note Earlier in my career, I was using Microsoft Project. Microsoft originally designed as an application for, say, defining all the steps for building a house. I was tasked with preparing a schedule that rolled up all the development projects with the office's several dozen automation group applications. In later versions, it became better at scheduling.

Because many people in many different organizations in the United States, and probably the world, did this, Microsoft worked the application to support this kind of effort. You may be able to find such "workarounds" that people have done. They have the gem of an idea, because something doesn't work the way they want, or they have an idea no one else thought of. Ask if they have any suggestions like this.

Things That Enhance the Interview

Chapter 1 emphasized the importance of good communications. Interviewing is probably the biggest manifestation of that skill. Remember, no matter how long you have worked on a project, there are people who know more about the project, at least some aspect of it. Therefore, a know-it-all trying to get information from a user will fail—miserably. You need to establish trust and a rapport with the users. If a user says the radiation dosimeter takes too long, don't tell them they are wrong. Ask them why it takes too long. It may be that the performance requirement before said that the result should return in 10 seconds. To most users that is way too long. Maybe you are unaware of that requirement, or it may be that the device they have is not even meeting that requirement. Maybe when the battery gets low, it takes a minute to get the result. Never reject a person's statement. If it does not make sense, ask more questions to understand. Usually, you should go back to the people responsible for the system and find out what is happening. Occasionally, developers were unaware of issues you discover. In many cases, you can find out there was something wrong, and you can get it fixed.

Go in with an open mind. Think of the users as the teachers and you as the student. There is a reason why they have information you need, so try to learn from them. Be a human being; admit that you do not know everything and that the users can teach you. After all, your reason for collecting their needs is to help the users get a better system in the future.

Listening

In real estate, the cliché is location, location, location. For requirements engineering, it is listen, listen, listen. This is the most important aspect of communication. You may have been in meetings with one person who was not talking but just waiting for another opportunity to talk, but not listening. That is *not* communication. In my case, this was a rather high-ranking HR person. So, do not be like that. Look for the signs that someone is not listening well or is dominating the conversation as this can inhibit the interview process.

Things Change Over Time

As was stated earlier, requirements can change 1 to 4 percent per month. You have to deal with that. People resist change, and REs are no exception to that. How you will elicit requirements when they can change during a project? Be prepared for that. The same thing can happen to the users. Alternatively, the users have worked with change, and the new person or people may not agree with previous work. This especially happens when you have multiple meetings with the same group, especially as not everyone will make all the meetings. You will have to adapt.

Glossaries

Having your glossary of terms is useful when you are having these meetings. If terms are used that you do not understand (maybe you have not learned all of them yet), check your list. If it does not exist, get the term defined and then add it to your list.

Note Taking

This becomes as important as listening. If you hear something but do not write it down, it can be lost. In some cases, you may have recording equipment and can use that to supplement your notes but not completely replace it. Some people are hard to hear and may not pick up well on the recorder. Taking notes is an important skill that comes with practice, just like note taking in college. When practical, if you miss something, ask for clarifications or for someone to repeat something you may have missed. Believe it or not, this usually is well received by users as this tells them that what they are saying is important to you as you want to capture it—which you do! While taking notes, you also can jot down questions to follow up on, note discrepancies with other accounts, or anything else that may help with your requirements collection.

Follow-Up Questions

You should always use follow-up questions when you need them. From listening carefully, you will notice potential requirements that other people in the room may gloss over. There usually are nuggets there. This is a standard interviewing technique, as are most of the points here. As an example, say there's a user who monitors the system maintainability and needs to know the entire time it takes from the time the system breaks until it is fixed. You ask the question if he also needs to know when someone actually started working on the fix. The user asks why he would want that. You explain, as you learned in Chapter 5 in the maintainability section, that you need a value so he or she can determine the wait time associated with the fix, as the wait time may be the major issue, not the actual repair time. You will have demonstrated how to provide better information for the users.

Remember, Chapter 1 talked about the challenge of understanding users who are not sure what they need. When your users/stakeholders do not know what they need, that is going to put you at risk. In some cases, you may not be talking with the right people, so the correct fix is to find the right stakeholders. That may not always be easy, but make a point of determining whether there are others who can provide the information you need.

Failing that, you need to help the users find out what they need. Chapter 1 talked about how you need to be a translator from what they say they need to what they really need. You also sometimes need to guide them to help them to find what they need. This is where you careful questions and follow-up questions can make a difference.

■ **Real-World Note** When I was a graduate student, running labs to supplement the lectures, the students would come to me asking questions about how to find an answer. Rather than just give them the answer, I generally asked a series of guided questions that led them to find the answer themselves, so they would understand how to find answers in the future. This kind of careful questioning also works well when helping users to identify and clarify their needs.

If you said, "You understand their process is X, Y, and Z. Is that right?" They would have an answer. Maybe yes, maybe no, but it would not be enlightening for them and provide little value added to you. Instead, follow the approach presented here and guide them with questions that start at the general level and work down to more detailed questions, engaging them in the process. For example, you ask a user, "You understand how the system uses patronymic Russian names?" They answer with a yes. That doesn't tell you anything, as you expected them to explain it to you. Thus, you need to follow up with, "Could you please explain it to me, as this is a new concept to me?" This should get the conversation started.

Missing Knowledge

This is always information that people may not know. The challenge is that they may not know that they don't. This is why follow-up questions can be important to uncover some of this. You have to listen to what the user says that may hint at missing knowledge.

When you discover missing pieces, it can have a secondary relationship benefit. Nothing establishes trust more than an interviewer who offers an immediate solution to a user problem.

Real-World Note For example, during a query function interview, some users did not understand that there was a NEAR function when two terms might be more than one word apart. Say you are looking for the person named George Koelsch. However, references to the person could include his middle name, and a Boolean search of *George Koelsch* might not pick up George Anthony Koelsch or George A. Koelsch because the middle term separates the two parts of the name. By using the NEAR function, you can search for *(George, Koelsch) NEAR 2*, which means George should be within two words of Koelsch. It would even pick up Koelsch, George, which searching for *George, Koelsch* would not do.

Cultural/Language Differences

You may have to collect requirements either overseas or with foreign visitors visiting you. While culture and language influences can hinder the collection process, there actually is one serendipitous benefit to doing this. You will have translators. When the translators are talking, you will have the opportunity to catch up on your note taking and formulate your next questions.

Of course, the culture and languages difference do offer challenges. Just as organizations can have different cultures, different countries have them as well. How you treat people or say things may not translate very well. What might be humorous in the United States may not be in Mexico or Asia. So, you will need to research the culture or talk to people who know so you can avoid words or phrases that might have the wrong meaning there. Also, when people have a different language, not every word, especially in specialized fields, may translate well. Pay attention to the body language to see whether your counterparts look confused or may be reacting negatively to something. Try rewording to see whether that helps. If you have an interpreter, ideally they can help. Fortunately, in my overseas work, I have never really had an issue, but preparing may have helped mitigate issues.

Following People Around/Observation

As an industrial engineer, you can spend many a day doing this to learn what people do. First, it is very labor intensive, and depending on what the person is doing, you may not see everything. Think of someone watching you work on a spreadsheet. The observer would probably need to stop you and ask many questions. Second, many jobs are very repetitive, so you would see the same operations time after time. Third, how long can you observe someone—an hour, a full day, a couple of days? What happens if there are tasks that happen once a week, once a month, or once a year? Odds are you will not see all of those. Again, you cannot do this in isolation or you will miss requirements. Some advantages to this technique are that you can identify work or process flows, identify what things bother the user, notice any awkward steps they encounter, and identify any room for improvement. You can observe by watching only or by watching and asking questions. It depends on the nature of the work and how much information you need to collect. If a person must concentrate, say, performing detailed work, asking questions is impractical. However, if you cannot see all the steps or they happen too quickly, you may need to ask question. There may be utility if certain operations are repeated many times and saving even one or two steps could make a significant amount of time. Think of an assembly line where a task is done 1,000 times in eight hours. If you trimmed one second from that time, you would gain 36 more items per shift, or a 3.6 percent improvement. It will be up to the environment, the user, and you as to when you can safely ask questions.

Models

Models and modeling are techniques for representing requirements in a more precise manner than just straight text, which we recognize has the potential for imprecision. As a result, Chapter 12 will be devoted to various modeling techniques and has a brief examination of their advantages and disadvantages.

Document Analysis

In this approach, you read through existing project documentation to glean requirements for the future system. Document analysis does not require interaction with users. You can do it on your own. That said, users and stakeholders could provide some of these project documents, so do not rule them out. When you first start on a project, this is also an excellent way to rise up the steep learning curve.

What are documents that can help you understand your project? Here is a good starting point. Your project may have others or may have name variations from these. Nevertheless, this is a list to get you started.

- Business process description
- Concept of operations
- Existing requirements documents
- Existing interface documents
- Design documents
- User manuals
- Operations manuals
- Training manuals
- User suggestions
- RFCs
- Discrepancy and problem reports
- Competing or analogous systems

Document analysis is a start to eliciting requirements as part of gaining domain knowledge only. It does not end there. It only identifies what the system does not. It does not address what the system should do except maybe for what was implemented. It does not address the shortcomings of the system. Nor does it address what things it does incorrectly. Keep that in mind.

Now, look at each document type and examine how it can help you.

Business Process

If you have one or more business process analysts on your project, then you have someone who has or is doing a business process analysis of the system or area for which you are going to capture the requirements. This is excellent. If you do not, you should definitely consider creating one.

Why do you need this business process description? First, you need it so you understand what your current system is trying to do. As mentioned earlier, if you are new to the system, then this is an excellent method to learn about the system. Certainly, it will not give you everything, but it is a significant start. In addition, when you look at the existing requirements, you need to find where things have changed and learn what the gaps are. Sometimes, all that exists are diagrams that describe the system at a high level or PowerPoint slides that talk briefly about the current system. Remember, no information is bad if it provides a starting point.

As was said, you can even use the business process description document to generate the user stories for a system. More information will be presented about user stories in Chapter 13.

A business process description document can also be called a *concept of operations*. Many times a CONOPS, as it is shortened to, is written before the requirements phase begins. If so, that is good as you have the start of your work. In addition, the advantage will be that the CONOPS is written for the future system, whereas many business process descriptions may focus on the current system. A word of caution: while most CONOPS are written near the beginning of the lifecycle development phase, some are written near the end. Is this because the project is behind in doing their documentation? That's possible, but more than likely there is another cause. In most instances, the project is doing the CONOPS with the emphasis on the concept. By that, they are looking at the functions the system should do and be talked about at a higher level. In the later phase of the lifecycle, you may see where the emphasis in the CONOPS is on the operations. What you have here is an operations manual. While this is a useful tool, that is not the focus of this paragraph's discussion.

Notice that some elements of the CONOPS may have proposed implementation that you should discount. In addition, it will not be detailed enough to fully capture requirements, so you will have considerably more information to complete your requirements.

Existing Requirements

First, look for requirements for the existing system. This will likely provide a significant amount of information about what you should consider. Remember, however, they were crafted in a different time, with different technology, and, most importantly, with different expectations. You do not have any context with these requirements unless there is significant textual information added to the *shall* statements. You do not get a significant sense of how the requirements must fit together, or *flow*. You will need to gather that elsewhere.

Most importantly, you will need to ensure that all the requirements are still valid. Given the scope or size of the project, that may prove to be daunting. Nevertheless, it needs to be done. For those items you have changed, modify the requirement set. Modify the existing statements for those that have changed somewhat. For those no longer done, delete them (but confirm with stakeholders that it is true), and add what is new.

Existing Interface Documents

This is essentially the same kind of documents as the requirements documents, just between two systems. There is one important aspect to consider with interfaces—the boundaries may change with the new system. By that, some items that exist in other systems may come under your system's umbrella, and vice versa. So, do not take everything as gospel without the same validation as was talked about in the previous subsection. Make certain the boundary of your new system is well defined.

Design Documents

Design documents, when they exist, do not provide nearly the same information as a requirements document, in part because they focus on the implementation, which requirements engineers are not supposed to capture. That said, there still is useful information embedded in them. For example, you might learn what data elements are being stored and manipulated, what data is audited, and so on, basically topics that may not be defined or only partially defined elsewhere, like the existing requirements. There is a lot of chaff to weed through to get the wheat but that is still worth examining.

Manuals: User, Operations, Training, and Help

These manuals can prove to be very useful, with qualifiers. They are designed to describe how the system should be used, and they are very detailed. When gap analysis is talked about later, these documents may suggest areas that have not been fully explored.

The qualifiers deal with the following:

- These are details about the exact steps to take when using the system. However, it may not explain why you would do these steps.
- These are the current implementation and may not be appropriate for the future.
- In addition, they are implementation, so again you need to determine what functions should be retained.

Identified Problems and Changes

Another source for requirements for the system can come from user suggestions, RFCs, change requests (CRs), discrepancy reports (DRs), and problem reports (PRs). These documents (whether hard-copy documents or online) are likely the items that have changed since the original system was implemented. Many if not most may be specific changes to the implementation rather than just user needs, so examine them carefully. For example, someone who asks for the status of a current operation moved from the bottom of the screen to the top is not a need but more a user preference. However, it may indicate that the users need the capabilities to customize the user interface, or at the very least allow them to specify some preferences.

Sources may come from the configuration management process your organization has implemented, called the following:

- Request for changes
- Change requests
- Discrepancy reports
- Problem reports

DRs and PRs may be the same thing, just defined differently for various projects or organizations. In addition, RFCs and CRs may be the same thing just using the terminology of the office.

■ **Warning** Some organizations may use one term for both an RFC and DR. Just be aware of that.

Most people define an RFC or CR to be the documentation of changing a requirement, adding or deleting a requirement, or modifying an existing requirement. A DR or PR is when an existing requirement is not working correctly.

Also, check the Help documentation or service desk. Even if the item never causes something in the application to change, it may indicate items that seem to cause problems for the users, showing you places to improve in the future. This can also be a source of user suggestions that has not yet made it to the configuration management system.

Competing or Analogous Systems

If your project is to create the best report generator ever, wouldn't it be prudent to see what other report generators have done and done well to ensure you capture those capabilities at a minimum? It's not likely you will work on something that has been worked on for many years, but you get the idea. Look at other systems and determine what capabilities you might consider. They could be competitors or systems similar to yours.

■ **Real-World Note** Many times, I have looked on the Internet for capabilities that I need to capture in requirements. Of course, if it was something like a report generator, I had to do it only once and then reuse the requirements, but we've talked reuse before. This brings out another source of documents, those found on the Internet. When I was doing research on machine learning and its capabilities, I found a wealth of information on the Internet, so exploit that whenever practical.

You do not need to "reinvent the wheel" for each project. Do it once, by researching what is available, and then reuse. However, I emphasize that the Internet is an excellent source of capabilities.

Prototyping

Prototyping is a method of gathering requirements. In this case, you can gather preliminary requirements for an initial version of the solution, called a *prototype*. You show this to the users and stakeholders, and they can give you feedback, ideally generating more requirements.

■ **Warning** This approach tends to get into implementation, so be careful. Clearly, very detailed statements would be design specifications, so ensure you give implementation independent requirements, being more general in your statements. Otherwise, you will be doing the designers' work.

This can be useful in ensuring you are capturing the data elements the users need and how you need to group them. Those are valid requirements. You may need to iterate several times to get the information correct, so do not be surprised. In addition, you should not have to expect to do the prototype unless you have coding skills. Use developers for the prototype.

This technique has the advantage of helping with people who may not know exactly what they need, as was talked about in the "Missing Knowledge" section of this chapter. Prototypes do not need to be done on a computer. They could be drawn on paper as a sketch, PowerPoint slide or slides, even animation (think of a game), or a storyboard. The advantage to the users is that they get to see what could be presented. In addition, because you have engaged the users and stakeholders in the process, they feel much more engaged, and this helps tremendously with the successful introduction of the product. In fact, one of the hallmarks of the agile sprints is a demo at the end, with the associated advantages that have just been mentioned.

Remember, if you develop this on the computer, there is no code behind the options presented. This is just to get the look and feel, but most importantly the users' impressions to include confirmation of the data and how it is represented. One reason this technique can work is that people have difficulty trying to describe what they want on a blank page or screen. However, if you have something, even if it is not close to what the users need, they will be more than willing to comment on something. This helps to get the users started.

Prototyping can be built around use cases or scenarios if you have them. Alternatively, if not, the prototyping of various screen shots can help derive use cases and scenarios, not to mention user stories and requirements.

Use Cases/Scenarios/User Stories

Use cases are an important aspect that you need to understand; they're so important that an entire chapter will be devoted to uses cases and one chapter for user stories, Chapters 13 and 14, respectively. Know that it is an important aspect of requirements elicitation, one that has increased in importance with development methodologies other than the waterfall approach. The same applies to user stories as they have a vital importance with the agile development methodologies.

Working in the Target Environment

Another aspect of this technique is to do some of the work yourself. Whereas a seasoned user will go through the tasks possibly faster than you can observe, if you do it, you will need to do every step slowly to do it correctly. This way you are less likely to miss something. The biggest disadvantage to this is the time it takes to get proficient enough to experience. Clearly, doing this for something that has a steep learning curve makes this technique impractical. Think of learning a station at a nuclear power plant. It's not something you can learn quickly.

There are advantages. For starters, just working as the users do helps to build a rapport. In addition, you will have a better understanding of some of the problems that have pestered them. When you experience one of those challenges, they will go, "See, that's what happens to me ten times a day." You will gain a better understanding of the challenge and associated frustration.

When possible, take training that is offered for the current system. Not only does this give you a sense of how the system should operate, you will have the trainers as resources. They usually know some of workarounds to issues as well as the issues and challenges to the users. In addition, it gives you more experience on the system that you may not get just trying to do it yourself.

Request for Proposals

Governments and companies request potential vendors to submit a proposal. The submitted proposals are analysed, and then a vendor or contractor is chosen and awarded a contract to provide whatever service is requested. The RFP is the specification by the requestor defining they what. As a vender or contractor, the RFP you receive may dictate some requirements that you must meet. Also, as a contractor works for a customer organization (e.g., for federal or state government), you may have requirements levied on you. You analyze the RFP needs and respond with a proposal back with what you will do, stated in your requirements.

Usually the needs are too high a level to affect the requirements directly, more like goals than requirements. For example, if the RFP is a paragraph long and only says your organization needs to provide bicycles for employees to use to ride among the buildings on the campus, there is not much specificity there. However, if NASA has an RFP about a probe to go to Neptune and they list ten pages of needs related to the environments, speed of the craft, types of data that needs to be collected, and data transmission rates, then you have candidate requirements. Nevertheless, you must read this document to determine what affects your system and its associated requirements. Given the 30 years I spent as a contractor to the federal government, I used this occasionally.

Reverse Engineering

Reverse engineering is figuring out what the system does by taking it apart, if it is a piece of hardware, or deconstructing the code to figure out how it works. This is different from seeing what the system does; it's seeing how it does it. I used to work for a tire manufacturer. We had heard that a competitor would come out with almost an identical new tire some weeks after we did. The consensus was that the competitor bought the tires, deconstructed them, figured out our manufacturing process, and then duplicated it. This prevented them from having to spend all the time researching new tires. This is an example of reverse engineering.

I have never used this technique personally. That said, does that invalidate it as a source? Of course not. You will all experience limited exposure to situations and tools sets that you may use. This technique can be used when migrating from an existing system to a new system when insufficient documentation exists.

Note Reverse engineering can be abbreviated as RE. However, RE had been used to mean requirements engineering and requirements engineer. On a project, if this technique was used, you might end up with three versions of RE. Now you can see how jargon becomes important and how confusion can occur—not intentionally but with acronym creep.

Reverse engineering can help identify what the current system does. Think of an old mechanical watch that consisted of a wind-up spring and gears to move the hands of this analog watch. By opening up the case and examining the watch, you can deduce how it works. You can count the number of teeth on the gears to figure out how the movement of the gears work. This is a simple example of how reverse engineering can occur.

Reverse engineering neither identifies what the system *should* do nor identifies what the system does wrong. In the watch example, it only shows you what it does. You and your resident experts must figure out what the system should do and identify what the system does wrong.

Real-World Note I may have misrepresented this. I have done something closely akin to reverse engineering. When capturing requirements for a report generator, I found a manual that talked about all the capabilities that a particular application provided for report generating capabilities. I cherry-picked the functions that our particular project should have and wrote the *shall* statements for my report generator. In a sense, this is reverse engineering.

Tools

The TechTarget website lists some tools that might help with requirements gathering that will be presented later, such as the agile methodology (Chapter 13), requirements management (Chapter 11), and Unified Modeling Language (UML) (Chapter 12). In addition, TechTarget recommends some other useful resources such as books, articles, web sites, courses, and blogs for you to consider. There are many more if you want to research them. These are just a small sampling. You should not try to capture everything on the TechTarget web site or the hundreds of other sources. Just know they are there when you need them. Research them when the time is right.

Purpose of Elicitation

What is the purpose of requirements elicitation? You are going to collect/gather/elicit all the requirements for the program/project/system/system of systems in question. The steps you need to perform are the following:

1. Define the scope of the system.
2. Gain domain knowledge.
3. Decide on the elicitation techniques to use.
4. Elicit the requirements.
5. Perform gap analysis.
6. Complete the requirements.

Defining the Scope of the System

First, you must define the scope of the system. You need to know precisely where the system responsibility begins and ends. Ideally, you receive this at the start. Alas, the reality of it is that this does not always happen. So, you will need to help define these boundaries. Will they remain fixed? Not always. For example, if the new system will be follow an SOA, some small systems/applications that were stand-alone systems before may be services as part of your new system. In this case, the boundary of the new system has expanded beyond what may have initially been proposed. In such instances, the boundary definition may change because of what you uncover in your elicitation that others had not considered. This gets to how requirements change. Analysis forces people to make decisions they had not even known about initially. That is a good thing.

■ **Real-World Note** Back early in my career, one of my mentors told me that a good systems integrator (engineer/requirements engineer) is paid to ask the questions that have gone unasked. Take that to heart.

Gaining Domain Knowledge

Second, if you do not have full domain knowledge of the current and future systems, get it. Yes, that is easier said than done, but go back to the "Document Analysis" section and use that as a guide for starting that information gathering.

If you do not have a good BPD, then create one yourself. By virtue of you doing this, you will learn it better, and it can have additional benefits later in the requirement analysis process, as you will see.

What you will have when you are finished is basically a concept of operations but clearly focused from an implementation-independent view. Even if the users have some of the BPDs, you will need to go back and ask questions to fill in the gaps of knowledge. Odds are that if you do not understand the BPD, there is a gap in knowledge, or the business process has been changed and not properly documented.

Deciding On the Elicitation Techniques to Use

Once you have gained sufficient knowledge, you can begin. The reality of this is that, in many cases, management will determine when to start, and you try to gain as much knowledge as you can before the step starts.

An earlier subsection talked about using document analysis to start eliciting requirements as part of gaining domain knowledge, but it does not end with that, as was talked about before. Which technique do you use? The correct answer is more than one. Each has its advantages and disadvantages. To mitigate the disadvantages, you want to use as many as practical.

What factors should you consider in determining the techniques?

- Who are the stakeholders/users? (For example, if this is a commercial game, who represents the consumer, and how?)
- What is requirements engineering team domain knowledge?
- What is the availability of stakeholders/users?
- What is the location of stakeholders/users?
- What is the development team's domain knowledge?
- What is the stakeholders/users domain knowledge?
- What is management's commitment to eliciting the requirements?
- What is the schedule for eliciting the requirements?
- How big is the requirements engineering team?

Then you, and your team if you are part of or lead a team, must decide which techniques to use. Consider document analysis, interviews, and some group meetings. Use the others that have been discussed as you and your management team see fit. Trust me, management commitment here is absolutely essential or you will not have access to the people you need. If you have to get it, start with your management chain. If they cannot get agreement with your approach, you will have a hard road ahead of you, with less likelihood of success—to be quite honest.

Eliciting the Requirements

Now comes the challenging part, eliciting the requirements. Before you actually start, a bit more planning is in order. If you are likely to have more than 100 or 200 requirements, one session is unlikely to capture all the requirements. Your best bet is to take this larger program/system and break it into manageable chunks. You may need to apply most of the techniques to each functional area that you choose, or maybe by the team/organization that is affected by it. For example, the auditing team will work only on the audit function.

One additional suggestion is related to the functional area elicitation. The document analysis mentioned earlier can help establish many or most of these functional areas.

You will need to massage the information you collect. Remember, users do not speak requirementese. You do. You need to translate their input into good requirements, as has been discussed in all the previous chapters.

To define all the requirements, you need to understand what the users do right now. This is an important point to remember: it's not how they do it, just as good requirements do not define the how and only the what. Get them to tell you what they do.

You have to listen intently. However, know that they will skip over points. This is not intentional, but they know all what they do, and they do not include every little nuance. It is human nature. Part of that happens because they assume you know everything they do. Part of it is that they summarize. They are not accustomed to providing every step they do. Think of a user manual that describes how to do a new feature where the document describes every step, every keystroke, every click that the user must do. Most users do not think quite like that when they are talking. In fact, it is difficult for most people to do. If someone asked you to describe how you drive to work or school every day, would you give every street name, the distance, and the time associated with each step? More than likely you will say, "From my house I go two blocks north and turn left at the elementary school, through three traffic lights and turn right...." Many details are missing that MapQuest would provide. It is your job to learn the MapQuest "route" from the users rudimentary "directions."

If going from step 1 to step 2 does not make sense to you, chances are they have omitted something. Sometimes it is language or jargon that you do not know, and the missing information may be embedded in those words.

Think about signing into an application on a network. Someone is describing what they do when they first start their machine and get to this application. They say the following:

> First, I turn my machine on.
>
> I hit Ctrl-Alt-Del to log in.
>
> Then, I select the BOSS application.
>
> Finally, I run my audit report from the log of updates since yesterday.

That initially sounds like it is sufficient. However, the user did not give specific details about how they logged in. This is a system administrator, who has multiple networks to monitor. When they log in, they have to enter their user ID, password, and what domain they are examining. Because they did not give these specifics, you might miss that the login process requires the domain value. You need to ask them what they mean by logging in. Then ask what the domains are that they access. Can domains be added and deleted, or will they remain fixed? You get the idea.

Remember, Chapter 1 talked about the two different definitions of *recall*. The development group used the word to mean removing a bad record from the database. However, the people who would use the new system used the word to mean calling for a group of hard-copy documents from the archive. Think of what happens in a meeting the first time this comes up, and one group uses the recall with their meaning, but the other group of people hear that the use of it and cannot understand what was said because the meaning was "wrong" in their mind. This is going to happen. How do you know? This is where you have to observe. Sometimes people may challenge, but more often or not, people will just look confused. Not only do you have to listen, but also you have to watch, especially body language, facial expressions, and so on. Use anything that will give you an indication. In poker, this is called a *tell*—an indication that what the people are trying to indicate is not quite correct.

Reading requirements does not address how they flow or how they interact. The business process description shows that. If you understand that process better, you will have a better foundation for defining the requirements.

Then you need to show what you have captured with the users/stakeholders to confirm you translated it correctly. You will receive some pushback because they want their words exactly used sometimes. You have to explain the rationale for why you do it the way you do.

It may take more than one review to get concurrence. Remember this is a negotiation. You are not a dictator. Sometimes, managers will overrule some decisions, and you will have to live with some of those decisions if you cannot get your own management to stand up for it.

Performing a Gap Analysis

You are not done yet with collecting requirements. You have a challenging step to do. You have to find what everyone, including you, has missed. You might say, “If you have not captured it yet, how do you expect me to do it now?”

It is called *gap analysis*. There are some steps to take. Go back to the previous requirements document, or similar documents, like user manuals and so on, and then describe what people are doing. Find out the functions that are talked about that have not yet been documented in your requirements.

For example, you find that they have not done auditing of the changes to the database. Find out specifically what they need tracked. Is it every data element within the database or just key values? Do they need all adds, changes, deletes to user accounts (probably in almost all cases)? What about tracking all failed attempts to access an account? It could be just someone messing up his or her password or user ID once and then getting it right. What about trying six or seven times? Is someone trying to hack it?

Remember when we talked about all the different functional and nonfunctional requirements? One of the reasons these chapters discussed more topics than most sources examined was to give you suggested areas to consider for gap analysis. Go back, and look at each type to see whether it sparks any subject areas that you need to fill in some gaps.

Talk to experts on the system and ask what topics they think were missed. These are probably people on the development team, especially the operations and maintenance (O&M) team that has been dealing with the current system probably for years.

Once you have identified the areas, craft the requirements. You may need to interact with selected users/stakeholders to help them validate these new requirements.

Completing the Requirements

What constitutes being done with the elicitation phase? If you have done all the steps up to this point, are you finished? Chances are no, you are not. First, ensure that you have done all the steps to include actually writing proper requirements, vetting them with the affected stakeholders, and finalizing them so they are ready to be maintained. Has your management identified that you are not complete until you have a database fully populated with approved requirements? Or must you have a reviewed and approved requirements document? Or both?

The key here is the approval process. You will likely have to vet the complete set (in parts or as an entire whole) through one final review with senior stakeholders and/or management. Your organization mandates this. If you must capture a requirements document, look in the appendix for a format, if your organization has not directed a particular template. Likely, some part of it may require some business descriptions. If so, the BPD talked about earlier will serve you well.

There is one last aspect, albeit important, to keep in mind. Remember when earlier chapters mentioned the likely growth/change to requirements of 1 to 4 percent per month? You need to consider that. You must have a method to update your requirements to account for this change. Ideally your organization will have a change management, aka configuration management, process in place. If not, you need to establish one for your requirements. This is necessary to control and communicate changes to all affected parts.

■ **Note** The communications is as important, if not more important, than the control aspect—a problem that is missed far too often.

Problems with Elicitation

This chapter has alluded to some of the problems about to be discussed. First, you need to list what they are. A.J. McDermid gives the following three categories of these problems and ten specific problems:

1. Problems of scope
    - The boundary of the system is ill-defined.
    - Unnecessary design information may be given.
2. Problems of understanding
    - Users have incomplete understanding of their needs.
    - Users have a poor understanding of computer capabilities and limitations.
    - Analysts have poor knowledge of problem domain.
    - User and analyst speak different languages.
    - It's easy to omit "obvious" information.
    - Different users have different views.
    - Requirements are often vague and untestable, e.g., "user friendly" and "robust."
3. Problems of volatility
    - Requirements evolve over time.

Now, examine each problem and see how to address it.

Problems of Scope

Problems of scope deal with defining the boundary of the system broadly enough, but it should still ensure they are requirements and not design.

The Boundary of the System Is Ill-Defined

Not only was this talked about this earlier in this book, but also it was stated in the previous section that you must know the boundary of the system. This needs to be defined at the start of the project, and the major stakeholders must agree on the boundaries of where the system begins and ends. Not only will this include the major users, but people like the DBAs, architects, and other technical people should be included in this decision.

As was stated in the previous section, during elicitation you may find that the boundary may need to change. In this situation, get back to the same stakeholders who agreed upon the boundaries to begin with, and vet this proposed change with them. Once you have presented the suggested modification, then abide by their decision. You may have additional requirements to collect as a result of this change. If it includes adding significant new functionality, this may translate to extensive additional work.

Unnecessary Design Information May Be Given

It was reiterated from Chapter 1 and many times throughout the book that you must write your requirements independent of implementation. That said, there are some situations where architectural constraints will modify that edict. Thus, your only challenge will be in deciding when something is implementation or is a constraint. A clue is if a developer says, "How about if we try…"; then you know that is probably implementation. However, if the project architect says, "Our systems must all follow the SOA," then you have a constraint.

Problems of Understanding

Problems of understanding deal with poor communications between the users and the RE.

Users Have an Incomplete Understanding of Their Needs

Of course, users don't understand all their needs. Part of that is because they only see a portion of the system, that which they use. You can compensate by talking to a diverse set of users to ensure you get a broader perspective. In addition, there are certain key stakeholders/users that you must talk with to ensure you get complete coverage, such as the DBAs and system monitors.

Users Have Poor Understanding of Computer Capabilities and Limitations

It probably is not a great revelation that users may not know computer capabilities and limitations, nor should they. That is the job of the designers and developers to exploit. It is also your job to help clarify points to them when you can. For example, if a particular type of search causes the system to take considerable longer, if they know that, they may not default to that type of search. You can point that out when you are talking with them.

In addition, when the users are not familiar with newer technologies, like say machine learning, you can offer requirements that address more capabilities because of your gap analysis, with the requirements vetted through the users.

Analysts Have Poor Knowledge of Problem Domain

You were just transferred to a new program that you know nothing about, other than you initially hearing about it. Of course, you will not be an expert on the project's domain. There are techniques for gathering that knowledge, like doing documentation analysis, especially the business process description. If one does not exist or it is not a good one, write one yourself. Do whatever you can to get yourself up on the learning curve. Sometimes it takes months, and not just one or two, before you become knowledgeable enough to understand much of what people are saying. Ask many questions.

■ **Real-World Note** As the adage goes, the only stupid question is the one that goes unasked. I have promoted this idea since graduate school, and it has served me well throughout my career. Mostly that has been borne out.

User and Analyst Speak Different Languages

Most users are not computer programmers. They were not hired for that skill set. Therefore, you have to be aware of biases that some people have. Certain computer engineers and developers think all users must be very literate in computers, when they are not. There still are people who are almost functionally computer illiterates. They can do some things but get out of their comfort zone quickly and are extremely uneasy. Be aware of that.

■ **Real-World Note** I remember working with some network engineers who crafted a fix to a particular user problem. I pointed out that some of the steps were incomplete. The head engineer said that the users should know that stuff. He had the misconception that everyone thought as he did, when they do not.

The "Purpose of Elicitation" section in this chapter mentioned the *recall* example as one where the analysts and users had a different meaning for the same word. This happens all the time. That is why there is a chapter on jargon and language to help overcome this challenge. The best advice is to be cognizant of it and observe people when you are talking. Look for those clues when someone is confused, and follow up on it to see whether there is a language barrier.

Ease of Omitting "Obvious" Information

This is the trap that people assume a certain amount of information that everyone knows. That is one advantage to starting out as not being a full domain expert, as you will notice missing information and ask questions when you are confused.

Conflicting Views of Different Users

The previous section talked about this. Many times, this is because of different responsibilities, and you need to capture multiple points of view. In a few cases, you get wrong information from people. This is a bit more problematic. Here you have to find out which source is incorrect and eliminate it. It may be because the person does not know any better. You will have to decide whether you need to correct the person. The best way may be to involve the help desk to guide the person to the proper approach.

Requirements Are Often Vague and Untestable

Most everything focused on in this book has worked to eliminate the vague words from your requirements vocabulary. Trust me, when you get to a review of your requirements, someone will point out when you slip up. Just be vigilant when you craft your requirements, and after a break in time, review everything you have written and do a sanity check all of the good attributes against the requirements.

Problems of Volatility: Requirements Evolve

Problems of volatility deal with change. Chapter 2 and the previous section discussed this requirements growth of 1 to 4 percent a month. If you know this is going to happen (and it will), you can prepare for it.

Requirements Evolve Over Time

Having a change management process helps because it gives a process for vetting those potential changes and how they might affect what you have already. Also, soon you will learn about the agile approach for requirements definition, which helps to mitigate the growth issue by capturing requirements close to when the development will occur so that the growth is then taken into consideration at that time.

Process Improvement

As mentioned before, many times, you do not come into a project at the beginning. You may be partway into requirements collection or partway into the development, or you the system may be deployed and your project is in the O&M phase.

Sometimes the processes are not well defined or even well understood. You can help bring process improvement. You will have more success after you have experienced this more. Alas, you may not always have that option, so research more about your organization and what processes are in place to see how you can augment them. Only in rare cases should you throw out what processes are in place and start over.

■ **Real-World Note** I have seen a new program manager do this, with only a little knowledge. He did not rely on current expertise and made changes that were not for the better, just adding chaos and not mitigating it. (Think of Dilbert's pointy-hair boss.)

Ideally, you will find yourself somewhere in between the two ends of the spectrum (neither total chaos nor processes that are so rigid that you cannot make any improvements) that you can see what works and then decide what areas can be improved. You will also need to see who in management will sponsor your improvements. Without support or a champion who will help, you will not be able to succeed, no matter how good your proposed improvements. Keep in mind, this champion may not be one person, and it does not have to be a high-up person. It could be your team lead, your program manager, or even a more important stakeholder. If you find that person or people, establish a rapport with them, they you have started on the correct path.

Don't abuse that champion, as they have full-time jobs too. Use them at the critical points and sparingly. That will take some judgment on your part. However, you are smart, and you are trying to do the correct thing. Remember, you will not always succeed. That is not a reflection on you, and it doesn't necessarily indicate others are bad or made an incorrect decision. They may be aware of other factors that may preclude your approach ever or for a period of time.

Sometimes the ideas for process improvement can come from the stakeholders themselves. This can be seen in the following real-world experience.

■ **Real-World Note** A few years back, when I began introducing the process for eliciting requirements for a replacement system, one of the senior stakeholders asked if we were going to review all the requirements at once. The requester objected to sitting in the same room for two weeks straight when reviewing requirements for the current system. I had proposed breaking the tasks into function areas so we could accomplish the review in a few hours at a time spread with intervening breaks of days or weeks, which was much more manageable for everyone, especially from a resource commitment time. The stakeholders found this much more acceptable.

The point to be gained from the real-world note is that improvements can come from various sources, not always you.

Throughout, this book has preached that thinking is your most important skill. In this case, where you want to improve the requirements process, you need to not only convince yourself of all the alternatives and their associated advantages and disadvantages but also convince your champion and then ultimately your entire organization. So, spend some time on that. Do it correctly.

References

Mochal, Tom. "10 techniques for gathering requirements." January 2, 2008. TechRepublic U.S. Feb. 2015, www.techrepublic.com/blog/10-things/10-techniques-for-gathering-requirements/

Blain, Tyner "Ten Requirements Gathering Techniques." November 21, 2006 *Tyner Blain blog* Feb. 2015, http://tynerblain.com/blog/2006/11/21/ten-requirements-gathering-techniques/

"Guideline: Requirements Gathering Techniques" *Eclipse Process Framework (EPF).* Feb. 2015, http://epf.eclipse.org/wikis/openup/core.tech.common.extend_supp/guidances/guidelines/req_gathering_techniques_8CB8E44C.html

Pohl, Klaus and Rupp, Chris. *Requirements Engineering Fundamentals.* Rocky Nook Publishing, April 21, 2011, p3-1 to 3-2.

A Guide to the Business Analysis Body of Knowledge, 3rd Edition (IIBA 2015)

McDermid, J. A. Requirements Analysis: Problems and the STARTS Approach. In IEE Colloquium on 'Requirements Capture and Specification for Critical Systems' (Digest No. 138), 4/1-4/4. Institution of Electrical Engineers, November 1989 http://ieeexplore.ieee.org/xpl/login.jsp?tp=&arnumber=199038&url=http%3A%2F%2Fieeexplore.ieee.org%2Fiel3%2F1950%2F5163%2F00199038.pdf%3Farnumber%3D199038>

Merriam-Webster's Collegiate® Dictionary, 11th Edition ©2016 by Merriam-Webster, Inc. (www.merriam-webster.com/)

Exercises

Exercise 1

You have a small HR application for tracking the job positions used within the company of 369 people who manufacture smartphone cases. Describe what elicitation techniques you would use for collecting the requirements for this system and why.

Exercise 2

You have a larger help desk system for your nationwide corporation that is networked together with 1,138 users. Describe what elicitation techniques you would use for collecting the requirements for this system and why.

CHAPTER 10

User Interface Requirements

With the explosion of so much software that people use in their daily personal and professional lives, the user interface (UI) is absolutely critical to the successful use of that software. However, I must point out that it is also one of the more challenging areas to define requirements. You will see approaches to help overcome this. I will examine what areas to consider as part of UI requirements, consider using existing standards (which we will talk about more in this chapter), and look at how you need to address people with disabilities. First, let us examine what UI requirements are.

Introducing UI Requirements

On one project, the first exposure to helping define UI requirements started with a stakeholder saying the following statement:

> 10-1 DRAFT The system shall be user-friendly.

Is this a good requirement, based on what you have learned so far?

Absolutely not! In fact, how many of the attributes does this violate? Frankly, many if not most of them. Yet, you will run into users and stakeholders who will give you needs like this. Your job requires you to be a translator. You have to translate what a user says they need into what they really need.

A bit of philosophy here: people will tell you that SE and specifically requirements engineering (RE) is a science. Yes, requirements engineers apply many scientific principles to SE and RE. However, take the previous example. What scientific principles would you apply to convert that statement into real requirements? You cannot think of any? Absolutely correct.

This translation is an art form. If it were truly scientific, people would teach those principles and it would be much easier to accomplish. That is why translating the user statements into what they realistically need is harder than it looks (hence the title of this book is *Writing Requirements for System Engineering*). Yes, many needs are relatively easy to capture once you understand the principles that have been discussed. However, the reality of it is that it gets more difficult when you move beyond those easy aspects.

Nowhere is that more manifested than in the definition of user interface requirements. In part, a user interface is an implementation. Of course, what is good is clearly subjective, and requirements cannot capture subjectivity.

G. Koelsch, *Requirements Writing for System Engineering*,
DOI 10.1007/978-1-4842-2099-3_10

How can you capture user interface needs? One approach, and many projects take this, is to define user interface standards.

■ **Real-World Note** I worked with one recent application where one organization we worked with had defined a document with dozens of specifications of how a UI should work. What this did is save me from having to capture a potentially long list of requirements by referencing these standards.

If such a standard exists, write a requirement as follows:

> 10-2 All applications generated in (Our Office) shall follow the (Specific Project or Organization) User Interface Standard.

Here's an example:

> 10-3 All applications generated in BOSS shall follow the BOSS User Interface Standard.

There may be some UI standards on the Internet that you can use and reference. You, or someone, can define UI standards for your organization, and then you can reference that standard in the previous requirement. One example that we will mention again later is the U.S. Navy's Human Factors Analysis and Classification System (HFACS).

One caution about UI requirements: you need to worry about specifying implementation. For example, a standard might be the following:

> The dialog must be outlined in medium gray with rounded corners and have a background of color of blue gray.

That is a reasonable standard statement. However, if you specified that as a requirement, clearly you have moved into implementation. Why does this work as a standard? By itself, it does not, but an organization, in its development of the UI standard, had done research into color schemes and crafted a series of related standard statements that had chosen a particular color scheme and used it consistently in throughout the standard. By referencing the standard, you avoid that potential trap of defining implementation.

Another approach that is used extensively is prototyping. This is highly recommended. Here a candidate UI is built, with no real code behind it, to show the users how it looks, and users and stakeholders can view the various screenshots (maybe nothing more than print screens) and decide what they like and what needs improvement. Also important is to demonstrate the navigation paths. In other words, how does the user flow from one element to another? Then, when the UI is agreed upon, it is captured as a design specification.

Many times during agile sprints, user stories (more on these later in the book) can have small aspects of the UI shown as part of the demo at the completion of the sprint.

Failing that, what do you do? You will have to define some UI requirements yourself. That leads to the next section. It should be pointed out that these UI needs affect both the computer systems (for example, the FBI Records Management System) and the hardware systems (again, like the BOSS Radiation Dosimetry system). A device that reads information it has collected needs to present the data in a readable format just like a software application must do. It is just that not all software UI aspects may apply to a hardware device.

Improving the User Interface

The UI describes how the user interacts with the system. That sounds easy. However, it is not as you have already seen. This will continue to be examined throughout this chapter.

The user interface is the implementation of usability. Chapter 5 stated that usability is how effectively users can learn and use a system. This section will cover important topics to consider when you define requirements related to the UI, look at how to ensure error message provide useful information, examine how the sciences of human factors can improve the UI, and even look at an excellent resource the U.S. government provides to optimize the UI, which is next.

Government UI Improvements

The article "Improving the User Experience," from the Usability.gov web site, is captured in the following "Interface Guidelines from Usability.gov" sidebar. These guidelines provide a good list of items to consider when documenting UI requirements or UI standards.

INTERFACE GUIDELINES FROM USABILITY.GOV

This sidebar is an extract from the Usability.gov web site and is an excellent starting point for items that should be considered for UI requirements.

Choosing Interface Elements

Users have become familiar with interface elements acting in a certain way, so try to be consistent and predictable in your choices and their layout. Doing so will help with task completion, efficiency, and satisfaction.

Interface elements include but are not limited to the following:

- *Input Controls*: Buttons, text fields, check boxes, radio buttons, drop-down lists, list boxes, toggles, date field
- *Navigational Components*: Breadcrumb, slider, search field, pagination, slider, tags, icons
- *Informational Components*: Tooltips, icons, progress bar, notifications, message boxes, modal windows
- *Containers*: Accordion

There are times when multiple elements might be appropriate for displaying content. When this happens, it's important to consider the trade-offs. For example, sometimes elements that can help save you space put more of a burden on the user by mentally by forcing them to guess what is within the drop-down or what the element might be.

Best Practices for Designing an Interface

Everything stems from knowing your users, including understanding their goals, skills, preferences, and tendencies. Once you know about your user, make sure to consider the following when designing your interface:

- *Keep the interface simple*: The best interfaces are almost invisible to the user. They avoid unnecessary elements and are clear in the language they use on labels and in messaging.
- *Create consistency and use common UI elements*: By using common elements in your UI, users feel more comfortable and are able to get things done more quickly. It is also important to create patterns in language, layout, and design throughout the site to help facilitate efficiency. Once a user learns how to do something, they should be able to transfer that skill to other parts of the site.
- *Be purposeful in page layout*: Consider the spatial relationships between items on the page and structure the page based on importance. Careful placement of items can help draw attention to the most important pieces of information and can aid scanning and readability.
- *Strategically use color and texture*: You can direct attention toward or redirect attention away from items using color, light, contrast, and texture to your advantage.
- *Use typography to create hierarchy and clarity*: Carefully consider how you use typeface. Different sizes, fonts, and arrangement of the text to help increase scanability, legibility and readability.
- *Make sure that the system communicates what's happening*: Always inform your users of location, actions, changes in state, or errors. The use of various UI elements to communicate status and, if necessary, next steps can reduce frustration for your user.
- *Think about the defaults*: By carefully thinking about and anticipating the goals people bring to your site, you can create defaults that reduce the burden on the user. This becomes particularly important when it comes to form design where you might have an opportunity to have some fields pre-chosen or filled out.

Candidate UI Topics for Requirements

The "Standards" section in Chapter 5 talked about UI standards. To refresh your memory, standards are rules put in place within an organization or across organizations so operations work consistently. For this section, they are rules or directions for how to handle the user experience. Think of the menus within Microsoft Office and how the same commands are in the same place and the same steps activate it and shortcut keys. These are excellent examples of UI standards. You should consider the following requirement:

> 10-4 (5-30) The BOSS shall follow this company's Organizational User Interface Standard.

While a UI standard is not presented in this book, here is a list of topics for that could be used as a foundation a standard. Or if you cannot establish as standard, these are topics for you to use to craft UI requirements:

- *System feedback*: XXX?

  Drag and drop: How does the system indicate what you are dragging and where you put it?

  Response time: How does the system tell you it is working or when it is done?

  System message: What kind of information does the user receive when a message is provided? Does it tell them what to do, instead of just saying something cryptic like 404 error?

- *Desktop*: How is the screen presented to the user?

  Icons: What kinds of icons are used, and are they consistent throughout an application and across applications?

  Task bars: How do task bars work?

  Pop-up windows: How do they open and close, and what can they perform?

- *Navigation*: How can the user move around the screen?

  Toolbar: How is the main menu presented?

  Drop-down menus: How are drop-down menus presented and used?

  Trees: How does the user move around the application from screens and tabs?

  Tabs: How does a user move from one field to another?

  Grids: How is data laid out on the screen?

  Keyboard shortcuts: What are the keystrokes that are used in the system, like Ctrl+C for Cut, for all the operations of the applications?

- *Forms*: How data is entered to the system?

  Data entry fields: How are fields presented to the user ?

  Push buttons: How are buttons represented, 3D vs. 2D?
- *Color scheme*: What colors are used on the screen?
- *Fonts*: What fonts are used, and what sizes are allowed?
- *Help*: What help is provided to the user?

  Online help: How do people get help about the functions and operations within an application? Think of the ? in the upper-right corner of Microsoft Office applications.

  Context-sensitive help: How can some get information about items in the application?
- *Training*: How do people get guidance for training on an application?
- *Demos*: Is there guidance for users to see guided tours of the application, so they understand how to use it?

Notice that the previous list works well for a software program. Does this same list of topics apply to a hardware example, say the Radiation Dosimetry system? Oh, there are some aspects that do apply (such as data entry), but many, if not most, may not apply to a hardware project. However, for each system you must look at it and decide for each case, as there are no specific generalities that apply.

Obviously, the UI standard would be much more specific than the UI requirements would be. For example, you might have the following requirements for help:

> 10-5 The BOSS shall provide online help for all users describe all functions within the system.
>
> 10-6 The BOSS shall provide context sensitive help for all data entry values, screens, and forms within the system.

While it may not have many more requirements, the User Interface Standard could have more specific statements.

Error Conditions

Remember, Chapter 1 talked about translating what users say they need into what they really need. Here is an extract of that:

> A stakeholder says, "When this specific error happens <insert their error here>, I need a red flashing button up in the upper-right corner of the screen." They are telling you how to implement it. What they really mean is, "When an error condition happens, I need a message of what is wrong and how to proceed." For example, if you have operating system (OS) errors, you might need a different requirement.

As was said before, "But more on that later." Well, it is later now. Remember earlier in the "Candidate UI Topics for Requirements" section, you saw that a 404 error is not good. You want messages to provide information that is useful to the user, telling them how to continue past the error message, what steps they should take to fix the error, or whatever other rectification steps they should consider. You need to write requirements for error conditions like the following example:

> 10-7 For the BOSS Date Entry function generates an error condition, it shall present a message of what went wrong and how the user is to proceed.

OS errors were mentioned earlier. How should you handle these? As was said, these error messages can be very cryptic. Then you might need something like the following:

> 10-8 When the BOSS Date Entry function spawns an Operating System error condition, the system shall intercept the OS condition, translating the condition into a message of what went wrong and how the user is to proceed.

The goal would be a message designed and implemented like the following:

Your file cannot be printed at this time. Check to see if the printer is turned on, or connected to your device. If that does not work, check with your network engineer for assistance Click OK to continue. **OK**

Human Factors

There is one area that significantly affects user interfaces, and that is human factors. Ergonomics is also a synonym for human factors. The International Ergonomics Association explains them this way:

> *Ergonomics (or human factors) is the scientific discipline concerned with the understanding of interactions among humans and other elements of a system, and the profession that applies theory, principles, data and methods to design in order to optimize human well-being and overall system performance.*

You can see from this definition just how much human factors (HF) can affect UI. You may even hear expressions like HCI, which means human computer interface. HF helps to influence and/or direct HCI. Alternatively, you may hear about HFE, human factors engineering. They are all related. What are some of the topics that could be included in HF?

- Aesthetics
- Consistency in the user interface

- Online and context-sensitive help
- Wizards and agents
- User documentation
- Training materials

As you have read this chapter, you have seen some of these topics before. You will now see some additional items that show other elements, both from a positive and a negative perspective. So, look at the following sidebar.

ERGONOMICS EXPERIENCE: A BAD ONE

Some years ago, I worked for a government agency that had done some HF examination of their computer workstations. They had placed the keyboard for the desktops below the standard desk level, which was good. However, they did not have the mouse adjacent to the keyboard. No, they did not have it on the desktop either. They had a special mouse pad holder that was raised a few inches above the desktop. I was moving about 5 inches up and to the right to the mouse probably hundreds of times a day, rather than just moving my hand to the right (yes, I am right-handed). By the end of the day, my wrist hurt. That was a good example of bad ergonomics.

You need to ensure violations such as those in the sidebar do not happen on your project, through either good UI standards or requirements that prevent such an abuse.

Next, you can see some small refinements to the user experience, but they can have an important impact because they can ensure that the application does not either adversely affect the user's use of the system or dramatically irritate a user who has to wait too long before doing the next step.

As was presented in Chapter 8 on physical requirements, *throughput requirements* deal with how much data passes through a system or a portion of the system. An article called "Throughput Requirements" on the Open Process Framework (OPF) web site (`www.opfro.org`) points out that "Some throughput requirements are based on human psychological limits" and includes the following list:

- The average typist can type continuously if movements between fields are less than 0.2 seconds.
- The average typist takes approximately 1.35 seconds to switch gears mentally when moving from one set of typing to another (which usually occurs when data entry clerks move from one screen to the next).
- The average person will wait for no more than 20 seconds before looking for something else to do (and less, if you consider an Internet shopper).

What does this mean to you? Somehow either the UI standards help to prevent violations of these guidelines or you need to consider requirements that help to follow such guidelines. Here are some examples:

> 10-9 The BOSS data entry function shall allow the movement from one field to another to take no more than 0.2 seconds.
>
> 10-10 The BOSS data entry function shall allow the movement from one screen to another to take no more than 1 second.

These human factors influence what UI requirements you craft, or given specifications for the UI standard. However, it should not completely drive what you build, but like everything else, influence the design.

User interface topics can fill a book on their own (as many topics in this book), and that is outside the scope of this book. Fortunately, there are many great resources available when you work that particular area. Here are a few (complete references are in the "References" section):

> "Use Cases" from Usability.gov
>
> "Throughput Requirements" from the Open Process Framework (OPF)
>
> "Human Factors Analysis and Classification System (HFACS)" from the United States Navy

That said, there is one more important topic to discuss, Section 508 Compliance.

Section 508 Compliance

The federal government has mandated one aspect of usability to be implemented for most applications used by the U.S. government, especially those that the public accesses, to allow people with various diversity challenges to be able to use those applications and web pages. By "various diversity challenges," the government means people with some visual impairment to include color blindness, hearing impairment, or physical disabilities that restrict how someone could use a computer or any electronic service that the government provides.

The following excerpt from "Resources for understanding and implementing Section 508" on the government's `www.section508.gov` site indicates when it applies:

> *In 1998, Congress amended the Rehabilitation Act of 1973 to require Federal agencies to make their electronic and information technology (EIT) accessible to people with disabilities. Inaccessible technology interferes with an ability to obtain and use information quickly and easily. Section 508 was enacted to eliminate barriers in information technology, open new opportunities for people with disabilities, and encourage development of technologies that will help achieve these goals. The law applies to all Federal agencies when they develop, procure, maintain,*

or use electronic and information technology. Under Section 508 (29 U.S.C. '794 d), agencies must give disabled employees and members of the public access to information that is comparable to access available to others. It is recommended that you review the laws and regulations listed below to further your understanding about Section 508 and how you can support implementation.

Here are the instances where Section 508 does not apply:

- *In the event that a Federal department or agency determines that compliance with the standards issued by the Access Board relating to procurement imposes an undue burden, the documentation by the department or agency supporting the procurement shall explain why compliance creates an undue burden.*
- *This section shall not apply to national security systems, as that term is defined in section 5142 of the Clinger-Cohen Act of 1996.*

What does this mean to you? Obviously, if you fall under a federal agency, you must address 508 compliance. It is required. Do you need to identify each statement as a separate requirement? No. Point to those areas that apply to your project. For example, if there is no web site, that section of compliance does not need to be included as a requirement.

What if your organization does not fall under the jurisdiction of Section 508? Then, you are not required to address it. However, if your management has interest in including some aspects, maybe because of the size of the company or the need to support a diverse workforce, then you may include some aspects. Pick and choice was sections are appropriate based on your stakeholder input. There is no set prescription for what parts of 508 compliance should apply.

The official federal web site on Section 508 compliance is an excellent resource if you need to implement support for those who have disabilities to determine whether you should add requirements to support them. Even if it is not critical or required, it is useful to read about Section 508 requirements because they give some insights on how to support a very diverse user population. Relevant portions from Section 508 are included in Appendix C of this book.

References

International Ergonomics Association. "Definition and Domains of Ergonomics." `http://www.iea.cc/whats/`

U.S. government. "Use Cases." *usability.gov*. Feb. 2015, `www.usability.gov/how-to-and-tools/methods/use-cases.html`

"Throughput Requirements." 27 June 2005. Open Process Framework (OPF) Feb. 2015, `www.opfro.org/index.html?Components/WorkProducts/RequirementsSet/Requirements/ThroughputRequirements.html~Contents`

United States Government. *Resources for understanding and implementing Section 508*. Feb. 2015, `www.section508.gov/`

US Navy, "Human Factors Analysis and Classification System (HFACS)" Naval Safety Center web site, `http://www.public.navy.mil/navsafecen/Pages/aviation/aeromedical/HumanFactorsHFACS.aspx`

Exercises

Exercise 1

How many attributes of a good requirement in Chapter 2 does this following requirement violate? Which ones?

10-1 DRAFT The system shall be user friendly.

CHAPTER 11

Managing Requirements

In this chapter, you will learn why you need to manage your requirements, learn how requirements have been managed over time, learn what types of tools you can consider to control your requirements, and finally discover what data elements associated with your requirements you will need to capture with your *shall* statements.

Why Should You Manage Requirements?

Once you have begun collecting requirements, it is important to manage them, meaning the following:

- You need a way to track what happens to them.
- You must understand how they have changed over time.
- You have to allocate them to user stories and/or use cases.
- You have to assign requirements to various sprints within an agile release.
- You must identify which developers and test worked on the requirements.
- In addition, you will find with time and different projects many other questions that will come up during the project's life.
- If your project uses some configuration management or change management (CM) process (if it is run well, it should), you will also need a technique to integrate CM and requirements management (RM).

As you can see, you capture not only the requirement statement, and its unique identifier, but also what else in the project this specific requirement is linked with, such as the design specifications derived from the requirement and all the testing elements linked with the requirements. This will allow the project team to manage the requirements and everything they touch.

Next, you will get a sense of how RM has evolved over the years.

G. Koelsch, *Requirements Writing for System Engineering*,
DOI 10.1007/978-1-4842-2099-3_11

A Bit of a History Lesson

Now, look at what has happened in the past several decades. The typical process for capturing requirements involved recording them in a document of some kind. Decades ago, REs captured them on paper and wrote them up on typewriters. As technology evolved, the typewriter was replaced by computers and word processing software, which made the process more efficient. With the computer, everything was recorded digitally and managed as a unit. During this process, REs were required to make changes by updating individual pages, usually with a change request documented by the configuration manager. In addition, documents had a change page that listed all the changes to help manage them. For larger systems, the change pages started getting really numerous with all the changes and affected requirements and even maybe what the change was. Think how involved it would become when there might be thousands of requirements. Yes, this kind of management was done and, in some cases, still is. Looking back on it now, it was the best that was available at the time but seems so rudimentary by today's standards. Because some organizations are slow to change, you may see evidence of this method of managing requirements (probably in archives but I hope not still employed). I was doing it as late as 2011. You will see why this became cumbersome shortly.

This way of documenting requirements was a long involved process, and significant changes could take months to keep current. REs did not think this was a major problem, having a slow and methodical approach, when systems development took years to accomplish. However, as time when on, newer and more dynamic development methodologies were implemented, like RAD, XP, and agile. Requirements managers (RMs) needed to adapt as well. (Notice that RM can have two different meanings? Ah, this should be not shock to you after reading Chapter 3 on specialized language.) By this time, REs exploited the newer techniques available to us, recognizing a word processer was not as sophisticated at finding information. Yes, there is the Find function, but you had to search for them one at a time.

▪ **Note** Once newer word processing versions came out that listed all the search hits in a column at the left, that was a significant improvement in finding all occurrences of a word or phrase, but by then, most REs had moved onto more robust approaches, as you will see next.

As things like spreadsheets came out, REs used spreadsheet like a database for tracking requirements. Spreadsheets appeared in the late 70s and moved into significant business use in the 80s. While some nongovernment organizations may have started using spreadsheets for RM, some of the limited capabilities of the spreadsheets, with limited numbers of records and not yet robust database functionality, did not help engineers with requirements. By the time the third millennium started, the right functionality appeared, however, and REs migrated to spreadsheets. The Microsoft Excel Find All function allows you to use that search on just one spreadsheet or on the entire workbook. That speeds the process significantly. Granted, spreadsheets may not be as robust as certain database implementations, but a spreadsheet is usually available in the office without any additional cost.

There are now are more robust or specialized tools requirement management tools, and we'll see how the reliable standby spreadsheet compares with them in the next section.

While the move to spreadsheets was ongoing, some enterprising engineers used database programs that existed in-house and used them to track requirements. Eventually, software applications dedicated specifically to requirements management came to the market as requirements engineers, system engineers, and project managers saw the benefit of such applications. Applications like Requisite Pro and DOORS are currently available.

Tip Using the Find All feature in an entire workbook, you can count all the requirements by searching all *shall* statements—a nice little trick.

WORD PROCESSING LIMITATIONS

Before analyzing various tools for requirements management, look at why the word processing approach significantly limits our ability to maintain our requirements. Consider a project I worked on. I had developed more than 4,000 requirements to capture the requirements. Remember, having more than 1,000 requirements for a sophisticated project is not uncommon. Believe me, the days of dozens or a just more than 100 requirements are gone. I have worked on systems that had more than several hundred user stories to more than 1,000 user stories. However, I digress.

I want you back on those 4,000 requirements. If I created a requirements document, I averaged about 10 requirements a page. That works out to a 400-page document. However, I had another quandary on this particular project. It turns out there were 11 variations on the application that were very similar but not identical. I needed to allocate each requirement to the appropriate variation. Assume it averages out to seven applications mapped to each requirement. That leaves 2,800 requirements for each tool. If a requirements document was generated, that would be 280 pages for each project. Thus, that would be 11 documents that size, which translates to at least 3,080 pages to try to manage. You have generated a small encyclopedia set just of your requirements. Clearly, this is cumbersome. In addition, when I changed one of the requirements, I have to do it on average in seven different places. Trying to duplicate them accurately is hard and subject to errors. Clearly, this approach is impractical. I know. I found it so.

What Types of Tools Should You Consider?

As a teaching tool, this entire section will use an example analysis for comparing the requirements management tools by examining tools I have used during my career. This is not exhaustive, and it is not intended for you to think so. I am showing what was important, and analysis expresses only a relative comparison. You can do something like this to map to your specific needs and help determine what works for you. Thus, this is a starting point for you, as your needs will vary for your organization, and each project may have different needs. So, keep in mind that this analysis is specific to my experiences as an example for you.

Before the analysis of the effectiveness of each tool, you need to know some attributes that a good requirements management tool should have.

■ **Note** For your use, your mileage may vary. You may not have all the same needs I have had, so modify this list as you see fit. Regardless, you will at least have a foundation.

Attributes of Effective Requirement Management Tools

Here are the attributes considered in the analysis:

- Ability to capture all the requirements needed for the project.
- Update baseline requirements quickly when changes affecting the requirements are approved.
- Capture additional data besides requirements and numbers, like Requirements Verification Traceability Matrix (RVTM) methods, test procedures, dependencies to other requirements, standards, and so on.
- Visually represent all the information on an as-needed basis.
- Support various development methodologies: waterfall, spiral, RAD, XP, agile.
- Easily search various fields (such as finding a specified set of requirements and displaying all of them at once).
- Generate a hard copy of all or a subset of requirements.
- Ability to capture all the requirements that span multiple projects (variations of applications that are related).
- Tool is not too complex to use easily.
- Not limit the requirement engineer in his/her work.
- Good documentation.
- Flexible (most tools use Microsoft Excel to import and export; some use Microsoft Word but only for documentation generation, not requirements management).
- Ease of installation.
- Good online help.

The Tools

I have used the following candidate tools in my career:

- Typewriter (yes, I am that old)
- Word processing
- Spreadsheets
- Borland CaliberRM
- IBM Rational RequisitePro
- Smartbear ALMComplete
- IBM DOORS

There are many more tools than these, so this is not a comprehensive list—nor is it intended to be. This will show the relative comparison to each other, not perform an absolute quantitative analysis, in part since no absolute analysis can exist as your needs vary. The important point is to outline the key attributes, how I evaluate tools, and get you started with some that I find useful. Furthermore, technology changes all the time, so understanding how to evaluate tools is more important than a list of recommendations.

■ **Note** For more information about the full range of available tools, see the following articles:

"Requirements_Management_Tools," 6/12/2013. Ludwig Consulting Services, LLC
`www.jiludwig.com/Requirements_Management_Tools.html`

"List of Requirements Management Tools," Software.Process.Management 2016,
`-http://makingofsoftware.com/resources/list-of-rm-tools`

The evaluation also includes an estimate for cost impact. The typewriter includes a cost for the machine just for relative values but not for the time for data entry (nor with any of the other such tools). For Microsoft Word (word processing) and Microsoft Excel (spreadsheets), the analysis assumes $0 since everyone has access to this or a similar package. If you do not have a suite of productivity software like Office, consider free open source tools like OpenOffice or subscription suites such as Office 365 or Google Apps, which are affordable, and you always have the most current version. The dedicated requirements tools range from the high hundreds to thousands per seat, depending on licensing, and so on. Therefore, I chose a median cost of $2,000 for these dedicated applications.

Rating of the Tools

Table 11-1 uses a scale from 10 (ideal) down to 1 (worst implementation). These are not absolute values but how the tools compare with each other. Of course, I base this analysis on my experience and what I know of other professionals' preferences. Keep in mind, you might not choose the same value for each cell. Not everyone will choose the same values, but my analysis should be pretty close to that of most experienced REs.

Table 11-1. *Rating Requirement Management Tools*

Capability	Typewriter	Word	Excel	CaliberRM	ReqPro	ALMComplete	DOORS
Capture all the requirements	10	10	10	10	10	10	10
Update the baseline quickly	1	6	10	9	9	9	9
Capture additional data	1	4	8	9	9	9	10
Visually represent all information	1	5	9	8	9	6	10
Support development methodologies	1	2	4	8	8	9	10
Easily search various fields	1	4	8	8	10	9	10
Generate a hard copy	1	5	9	9	10	9	9
Span multiple projects	1	2	7	8	8	8	8
Not too complex	3	5	8	8	9	8	8
Not limit the engineer	1	4	9	8	8	6	10
Good documentation	1	3	9	7	9	3	9

(*continued*)

Table 11-1. *(continued)*

Capability	Typewriter	Word	Excel	CaliberRM	ReqPro	ALMComplete	DOORS
Flexible	1	4	8	6	8	5	10
Ease of installation	1	10	10	7	7	4	6
Good online help	1	10	10	8	8	1	10
Cost	7	10	10	3	2	2	1
Total	32	84	129	116	124	98	130
Total without cost	25	74	119	113	122	96	129

What does this chart tell us? With cost included, Excel is second only to the top application in the industry, DOORS, by a slight margin. If you remove cost, Excel is still second to DOOR but very comparable to all four of the dedicated requirements tools examined in this chapter. Yes, these are my estimates based on experience working requirements in my career. This gives you a first-blush comparison.

■ **Note** Each attribute was weighted equally. Depending on how you will use a tool, this might not be valid for you. This will be revisited this in the exercises at the end of this chapter.

Regardless, while Excel is not a dedicated requirements tool, it provides most functionality that a good requirements engineer demands without extra cost and other overhead that can be associated with a COTS purchase. Excel certainly does not provide every bell and whistle, yet it is still is very good tool to use for requirement engineering, at least as a starting point.

If you have the ability to consider a dedicated tool, do a great deal of research to find what capabilities it has above the ones discussed in this chapter. You will understand your needs better than anyone else. Vendors may specialize in support for agile development, RAD, waterfall methodology, or some specific focus. Find the ones that fit your situation. You know your computer environment, so take that into consideration. Find which tools support the appropriate configuration. Do you use client-server, stand-alone network, separate test environments that do not connect to the operational environment, web-based, or can you connect to the Internet? Find the candidate tools that fit your situation. Of course, try to find out the limitations of the application. Whenever possible, get a demo package and spend as much time examining it to see whether you can work with it.

Importing

If you have started out with a smaller project and it has grown or you just started out using Excel and the requirements management tool you ordered has arrived, there is one additional function you need to consider—import. You have several dozen or hundreds of requirements already collected, and you want to get them into the new database without having to either rekey everything (God forbid) or copy and paste every individual *shall* statement into one record at a time. You need a good import capability that captures the entire spreadsheet into the database.

■ **Real-World Note** I had a project that saddled me with significant policy updates planned every year. As a result, I needed to add dozens of requirements at a time, including sometimes eight to ten pages or more of requirements. Even after the initial standup of the database from my spreadsheet, I still used that importing capability. This is important.

Tip Find out if the import works for changes to existing requirements. This is not a showstopper. Nevertheless, it is important to know as not all of them do. The reason I mention this is my successors on a project ran afoul of this, saying the program's import did not work, even though I had thoroughly documented the process. It turns out, I was correct in my steps, when applied to new imports. It did not work for replacements. Therefore, for those they needed to go back to the traditional "cut and paste" approach.

What Requirement Values Should You Manage?

Requirement values are those data elements associated with a requirement to fully describe what it is, such as the *shall* statement, the number associated with it, and so on. We will examine this is detail shortly. Realistically, there is no one answer to what values should you manage. It depends. This is not a cop-out, but the reality is that every project, or every office, may have different needs or different ways of managing projects. Some want requirements integrated with testing. Some want requirements integrated with the agile management approach. Some may want both, or some may want requirements as a stand-alone approach.

First, you will consider general values for just the requirements stand-alone approach. Why? That is the foundation that the others will work from. Once you have that, then you can move on from there. Tables 11-2 through 11-4 will also explain the rationale for each field. Besides having a good background, you get the benefit of knowing the importance of each and when you can include them or when they are not as important. This gets back to the goal of teaching you to think, and customizing or tailoring your requirements management to your specific program.

Requirements Fields

As previously mentioned, the requirements fields are identified, and then the purposes of the fields and any format constraints are provided. The order is not set. That depends on how best you want to organize it. Some tools may dictate that for you, whereas others may allow you to move them around, within limits. This is also something for you to consider in your decision from the previous discussion. Now, examine Table 11-2, the requirements fields.

Table 11-2. *Requirements Fields*

Field	Purpose
Unique Identifier	This is a required field. This must be unique throughout the project. You will search on this. Notice this does not say number here, as you have flexibility for how you want to do this. You could just have a one-up number for every requirement you add. Remember, depending on how you group requirements or where you insert it, it may not always be sequential. Or you could do it by sections, say 1.2.4.5 and 3.5.99 as you go down in levels, yet not everyone has to be at the same level. You could do both. Or you could have an alphanumeric field like RPT-262 and SEC-359. Do what works for you. In addition, if you are using a dedicated application, you have to consider what your dedicated tool will allow. Ask about this. If you are not using a dedicated requirements management tool, you need a unique identifier for searching.
Date Created	This is so you know when the requirement/user story was created in your repository. This helps when you need to look at how requirements change with time, or count metrics, and other forms of analyzing requirements growth. Any standard date format, say, mm/dd/yyyy.
Requirement/ User Story	This required field is your *shall* statement. Other than the unique ID, this is the most important field. This is where your write the *shall* statement. Give yourself sufficient space here. 128 characters may not be sufficient. That is about 21 words. Look at your requirements and see how many times that would be not enough. 256 or even 512 characters might not be enough when you look at a list. There is a trap also with making it too large, where you cannot even show a view that has more than one requirement statement. One tool did not show requirements in a list; you had to look at it one requirement at a time or generate a report. Give yourself flexibility.
Title	This is not a required field. In some homegrown tools, you may not use this. However, you can use it for sections or an alternate numbering scheme. It depends how the tool uses it. Some RM tools have made this mandatory, and it had to be unique. Then you need to figure out how you want to populate it. Format, text field.
Version	This can be the version when the requirement was added to the project, or it can be the current version to help ensure everything is up to date. Format, text field.

(*continued*)

Table 11-2. *(continued)*

Field	Purpose
Author	Who wrote the requirement? You may not always stay on a project from cradle to grave (in fact, most times this may happen), so it is good to know who wrote it. This might help if you need to research something and you need to know who to talk with. On the other hand, you may notice trends of certain people don't have the benefit of this same training you get, and you might need to revisit some work. Format, text field.
Priority	Usually these are just categories like High, Medium, or Low. Maybe Critical is added. This gives an initial importance of the requirement. For example, transitioning the data from the old project to the new project is critical since it is needed before any work like searching can be performed. Format, text field, or a fixed picklist.
Rank	This is an optional field. This helps to identify within a priority the order that requirements/user stories should be completed. This is particularly important when dependencies are necessary. For example, you need to transform the metadata from the old structure to the new structure before ingesting data. Format, text field.
Status	This field is driven by what your project needs. Usually when you first create the requirement, this is New. Then you can have whatever you need here: accepted, deleted, deferred, completed, withdrawn, rejected, verified, implemented, approved. Format, text field, or a picklist, either fixed in some RM tools, or editable by an admin (preferable).
Source	(Optional) What drove the requirement/user story to be written? It could an HR policy, security needs, stakeholder mandates, and architecture constraints. Format, text field.
Risk	(Optional) Complexity, difficulty, technological challenge that could affect the completion of this requirement. If you need a particular concept search that your organization has not yet acquired, this could restrict the ability to implement this need.
Assigned to	(Optional) Which designer or implementer has the assignment to work? Format, text field.
Rationale	(Optional) Reason the requirement/user story was included or rejected. Format, text field.
Comments	(Optional) Additional information that might help to understand the requirement/user story or more information about other values in a particular field. Format, clearly a free text field.

(continued)

Table 11-2. *(continued)*

Field	Purpose
Verification Method	(Optional) This is a prelude to the verification work to be associated with a requirement/user story and a review of what was talked about regarding the verifiable attribute of good requirements. Methods are usually selected from the following values (you are not going to define how it's verified; just choose a method): • Test: A measurement to prove or show, usually with precision measurements or instrumentation, that the project/product complies with requirements. • Analysis: A quantitative evaluation of a complete system and/or subsystems by review/analysis of collected data. • Demonstration: To prove or show, usually without measurement or instrumentation, that the project/product complies with requirements by observation of results. • Inspection: To examine visually or use simple physical measurement techniques to verify conformance to specified requirements. • Simulation: Executing a model over time to simulate a portion of the system. Format, text field, or a picklist.
Stability	(Optional) Indicate whether the requirement is not fully defined. Some use TBD (To Be Determined) if no known value is captured or the value is uncertain. TBR (To Be Reviewed) is used if the value captured is closed but not exact. Format, text field.
Due Date	(Optional) The date the requirement/user story is (or should be) delivered. Date format says mm/dd/yyyy.
Product	(Optional) If the overall set of requirements applies to variations of a project and each requirement needs to be allocated to one, several, or all of the products. Think of a sophisticated macro applied to Microsoft Office applications used in your IT department of the company. Format, text field.
Subsystem	(Optional) If the project is large enough to have subsystems, this allocates the requirements to the appropriate subsystem or subsystems. Yes, some can apply to multiples. Think of the reliability requirement that is allocated with the same value to each subsystem. Format, text field.
Type	(Optional) This is the type of requirement that you may want to group requirements: functional, nonfunctional, architectural, structural, behavioral, performance, design, derived, allocated. You may use some, all, or none of these. Format, text field, or a combination box where you can choose one or more.

(continued)

Table 11-2. (*continued*)

Field	Purpose
Latest Update Date	(Optional) This helps with version of requirements. This is also useful when you want to look at the history of changes. Within some RM tools (except possibly spreadsheets), you may be able to see a given requirements history and see how it has changed over time. Date format say mm/dd/yyyy.
Parent/child	(Optional) This is useful when one higher- level requirement spawns subordinates that are related to but decomposed from the origin. You can show the linkage with this identification. Format, text field.
Dependencies	(Optional) If requirements need to be accomplished in a specific order, they should be indicated here. For example, a replaced value needs to be retained when the value is updated, before a history of changes can be generated. Format, text field.
User Story Identifier	(Optional) If you are using both user stories and requirements, you will map one or more requirements to a user story. Format, text field.
Use Case Identifier	(Optional) If you are using both use cases and requirements, you will map one or more requirements to a use case. Format, text field.
Model Identifier	(Optional) If you are using both a model and requirements (or user stories/use cases), you will map one or more to a portion of a model. (This will make more sense when approaches are presented in a later chapter.) Format, text field.
Attachments	(Optional) If documents need to be linked to this requirement/ user story to help reinforce the reason for it, include the linkage here. Maybe if a policy document is associated with a group of requirements, you could provide it here (usually for just one in the group of requirements). Linkage.

There may be more that you will think of or encounter in your career. Add, change, or delete from this list as you see fit. You will not use all of the fields on every project.

Note In some dedicated requirements management tools, the application generates a unique identifier for you. This is driven by how they implement your program. Given that you cannot change the value, as it may be just a one-up number based on when you enter the requirement, it may not suit all of your needs. You may still need to create your own unique identifier, based on section, functional area, or any other reason for grouping your requirements. Here, the RM application may drive your business process, rather than follow yours. You need to control your requirements the way you need to, not solely driven by someone else's application. Using a field like the Title field mentioned earlier might substitute for your unique identifier.

Requirements Associated with Testing Fields

Table 11-3 contains candidate fields that can be associated with testing.

Table 11-3. *Addition Requirements Fields Associated with Testing*

Field	Purpose
Unique Identifier	This is required only if a separate table from the requirements is used. If the following data is in the previous requirements table, this field is not required again. Format, alphanumeric.
Test Creation Date	Date the test was created. Date format, say, mm/dd/yyyy.
Test Case Identifier	The test case that the requirement was allocated to. Format, text field.
Requirement verified	This is not the status of the entire test case, but the verification of the requirement/user story/use case. Usually, the response is Yes or No. Sometimes, if there are multiple parts, not all are passed, just some. In that case, it is a partial. This gets to the need for atomic requirements. However, in the case of specific order, this cannot always be achieved. In the case of partial, the counting of successful requirements verification gets complicated. Format, text field.
Comments	Add any additional information that came out of testing this requirement, (e.g., maybe problems with testing, or deferring for some reason). You should relate these comments to the testing phase, not the requirements definition or management phase. Format, text field.
NOTE:	Not all test fields are duplicated here. This just tried to capture additional information that is specific to requirements and user stories.

Requirements Associated with Agile Fields

Table 11-4 includes candidate fields that can be associated with the agile methodology.

Table 11-4. *Addition Requirements Fields Associated with Agile*

Field	Purpose
Unique Identifier	This is required only if a separate table from the requirements is used. If the following data is in the previous requirements table, this field is not required again.
Sprint	Identify what sprint or sprints this requirement/user story is allocated to. Format, text field or a picklist.
Planned Release	Identify what release this requirement/user story is allocated to. Format, text field or a picklist.
Time to Accomplish	The time it will take to implement the requirement/user story. Text field using hours, days, weeks, whatever your project uses.
Actual Time to Accomplish	The time it took to implement the requirement/user story. Format, text field.
Comments	Add any additional information that came out of implementing this requirement/user story (e.g., maybe problems with designing, deferring for some reason, or possibly additional work was required to get the work to be accomplished due to unforeseen circumstances). These comments should be related to the implementing phase, not the requirements definition or management phase. Format, text field.

You may have more values for additional aspects of your project. You will have to decide which if any not included here need apply. No one can anticipate every variation within the world or how every unique project is managed.

References

"Requirements_Management_Tools," 6/12/2013. Ludwig Consulting Services, LLC <www.jiludwig.com/Requirements_Management_Tools.html

"List of Requirements Management Tools," Software.Process.Management 2016, http://makingofsoftware.com/resources/list-of-rm-tools

Exercises

Exercise 1

The requirements management tool comparison table did not include weighting of factors. Determine what the total will be with the following weights: cost 3.0, help 2.5, flexible 2.0, multiple project 2.0, additional data 3.0. What does this new total value mean?

Exercise 2

Assume all fields have 18 characters allocated to them, except the requirement/user story field and the comments fields, which have 500 characters. Also, assume you use only one database table, but all the fields are listed in the tables. Determine how much storage is needed if all the space is fixed for 100, 1000, and 10,000 requirements.

Exercise 3

For the individual dosimeter project talked about throughout this book, please identify what fields you think in the three tables in this chapter you should apply to this project and why.

PART IV

Alternatives to Shall Requirements

CHAPTER 12

Supplementing or Replacing Standard Requirements

The entire book up until this point was spent talking about requirements as purely *shall* statements. This concept of requirements was the foundation of the waterfall development methodology, starting with hardware and then translated to software. However, other types of requirements are referred to such as *user stories, use cases,* and *modeling.* Now you will be exposed to these types of requirements and how you can use them to supplement or replace *shall* statements. This and the next two chapters will discuss each topic so that you will be able to create them as needed, and why.

One of the significant drawbacks of the waterfall method for software development is that once you capture requirements, you freeze that baseline at that point. Given that, on average, requirements for a project change from 1 to 4 percent per month, the scope of the project may change significantly by the time it is delivered. The waterfall method is not agile enough in many cases. Thus, newer approaches were needed. With rapid application development (RAD), use cases came into being. With the advent of extreme programming and other agile methodologies, user stories came into being.

In addition, modeling techniques become important for programs to represent information to aid in the development of the hardware and software. This chapter will briefly introduce each subject and then examine the advantages and disadvantages of each.

One additional point to make about a collection of *shall* statement: it is not the easiest document for users and stakeholders to understand and then review and comment on. As a stakeholder whose primary purpose is to use a particular system to do their job, they are not necessarily well versed in requirements. If they are exposed to hundreds or even thousands of *shall* statement in a long list, with little paragraph descriptions to give context to them, they may not be able to get a comprehensive picture of the system. Thus, having another way to either replace *shall* statements or supplement them will obviously help these stakeholders comprehend the proposed system.

This chapter covers a variety of approaches and tools that can supplement or replace the traditional requirements techniques discussed thus far.

G. Koelsch, *Requirements Writing for System Engineering*,
DOI 10.1007/978-1-4842-2099-3_12

- User stories and use cases are exceptional cases because they are uniquely valuable for capturing certain kinds of requirements that traditional *shall* statements do not handle as well. They also are general approaches that are often especially useful with agile development. Therefore, they are introduced in this chapter but discussed in more depth in two dedicated chapters that follow this one.
- Modeling provides tools that are particularly useful for supplementing technical requirements, but only some modeling techniques work for ordinary user and stakeholder requirements. In this chapter, I will focus on a couple of techniques that are more generally useful for users and stakeholders (such as swim lanes) and then introduce techniques that have more specialized application for technical users. There are additional resources you will find useful if you have a need to write more specialized requirements, and I'll note those resources and include them in the "References" section.
- There are some additional tools that can serve as useful supplements in the requirements gathering process, and I will cover those briefly in the final section.

User Stories and Use Cases

If there are alternatives to writing *shall* statements, why was so much time spent focusing on them? Excellent question. First, as you will see in the "Supplement to Requirements" section in this chapter, *shall* statements are not going away. Second, understanding all the aspects of requirements is an excellent foundation to have to write user stories and use cases. Without that foundation, it would take you considerably longer to craft user stories and use cases, as you will see in the next two chapters, in which we look at these topics in more depth. In addition, when you see the advantages and disadvantages of the various alternatives, you will have a better basis for comparison.

User Stories

A user story follows this type of template:

> 12-1 "As a <role>, I want <function/feature> so that <benefit>."

Where the role is the type of user, the function or feature is what the user does or uses, and the benefit is why the user would want to use this function or feature. For example, a user story could be as follows:

> 12-2 As a cell phone user, I want to retain a list of selective phone numbers that I have received so that I can choose which numbers I want to reuse later.

Notice how easy it is to read? That is a significant benefit for users and stakeholders to understand them. This is a big advantage in that users can understand these even better than *shall* statements.

User stories work well with the agile methodology. The user story and subordinate acceptance criteria (which will be talked about in the next chapter) can be refined as the user story approaches the sprint in which the development team plans to work on it. This helps to negate the effect of requirements scope creep, unlike in the waterfall approach where you must create all the requirements up front.

Does this mean that user stories are the pinnacle of requirements technology? While it goes a long way to fix requirements problems, it still has some limitations. Because the development team intends to accomplish each user story in an individual sprint, some areas that you need to define do not fit well. Nonfunctional requirements, especially performance, are much harder to capture as a user story. Remember, in the "Availability" section in Chapter 5, you saw the following requirement:

> 12-3/5-54 The BOSS system shall be available 99.99% of the time.

How would it look as a user story?

> 12-4 DRAFT As a BOSS user, I want the system to be available 99.99% of the time so that the system provides the availability I need since it is a mission-critical function.

That sounds like a reasonable user story, and on the surface, it is. However, can the development team accomplish that in one sprint? Assume the development team has six user stories it is responsible for developing in a given sprint. Does availability apply to each user story? Technically, yes. Then, how do they verify that it is accomplished? What about all the work accomplished before the sprint in question. Does the availability user story apply to them? Yes. Now you start to see the conundrum—one availability user story may not address how it should be applied to an application development. In the next chapter, you will see this discussed a bit more to suggest how you might consider it.

Use Cases

Usability.gov provides some good information on use cases (as do other sources). They say that a use case is a written description of how users will perform tasks on your system.

What elements should be included in a use case? Depending on how in depth and complex you want or need to get, use cases describe a combination of the following elements:

- *Title*: This is an identifier or name of the use case.
- *Description*: This is a brief description of the purpose of the use case.
- *Actor*: This is anyone or anything (another system) that performs a behavior—who is using the system. This is not limited to one actor.
- *Preconditions*: This is what must be true or happen before the use case runs.
- *Postconditions*: This is what must be true or happen after the use case runs.

- *Triggers*: This is the event that causes the use case to be initiated.
- *Main success scenarios (aka basic flow)*: This is a use case in which nothing goes wrong.
- *Alternative paths (aka alternative flow)*: These paths are a variation on the main theme. These exceptions are what happen when things go wrong at the system level or an alternate condition causes a change to the basic flow.

Table 12-1 is an example of a use case (12-5).

Table 12-1. *A Use Case with Basic and Alternative Flows*

Title	Dial a Phone Number
Description	Use your cell phone to enter a phone number.
Actor	Phone users.
Preconditions	Actor has a cell phone.
Postconditions	The phone connects to the number called.
Triggers	A need to call someone.
Basic Flow	1. Turn on the cell phone. 2. Select the dial option/app. 3. Key in the number. 4. The phone rings.
Alternative Flow	1. Select from a list. 2. Select the dial option/app. 3. Choose the number from the list provided. 4. Tap the number desired. 5. The phone rings.

■ **Note** Dialing a wrong number or needing to redial the number if the phone was not answered would not be part of this use case as the goal is to dial a number. A different use case could cover the option for handling the answering of a call.

You can see that this is much more detailed than a user story and provides more data than *shall* statements. One significant advantage use cases have over *shall* statements is that the sequence of steps is addressed well.

Naturally, there are some challenges with this approach.

Use cases are not so good for system centric functions such as batch processing, data warehouses, and very computationally intensive functions. How would you represent a complex algorithm? Think of the software to control an interplanetary spacecraft, with significant mathematical calculations.

In addition, nonfunctional requirements, especially performance, are harder to capture and craft. They have no actors, and they do not have alternate flow readily apparent. Additionally, many users are not comfortable trying to understand this structure.

■ **Real-World Note** I have primarily used use cases when the "customers" were developers, not real users or stakeholders. This is because developers are generally more technically inclined than the general-population stakeholders. They can follow the structured format and sequence of steps.

Use cases may work better for the waterfall approach, as they are prepared up front, not necessarily as just-in-time development. Of course, you can create use cases this way, but there is potential for impact to other use cases—usually referred to as the *ripple effect* where a change ripples through other areas. For example, if you have four use cases dealing with using people's roles and responsibilities to determine what functions they can access, and if you change one use case, you will need to verify that one change does not affect any other use case.

You have learned to perform gap analysis during the *shall* statement analysis. That approach also applies here. How easy is it to ensure all aspects of every use case are captured? With *shall* statements, you have very detailed statements that address each point. There is much more detail in a use case, and with the overlap potential between use cases, there is the possibility of small gaps appearing adjacent to these use cases. You may be missing some alternative flows that are not obvious to you. Alternatively, they are just very miniscule use cases that are not obvious. This does not mean that you cannot find them, but it may be challenging. More time will be spent analyzing this in Chapter 14.

Supplementing Your Requirements

Supplementing requirements means that you can use user stories, use cases, or combinations of them, in conjunction with *shall* statements.

Because of the flow of steps in use cases, there is a benefit of preparing them. It may be you do not need to do it for everything within your system. However, it provides additional detail that a list of hundreds, or thousands, of *shall* statements does not provide.

User stories have the benefit of being much more understandable to users. On one project, the collection of *shall* statements was taking much longer than initially anticipated. The RE working with management decided to craft user stories with the users and stakeholders but add the *shall* statements for the development team. This worked out well, as both the stakeholders and developers received the level of detail that they needed respectively.

Replacements for Requirements

This section will address the possibility that user stories or use cases can work as a replacement for requirements. Each one of these approaches will be looked at individually. User stories are intended to act as stand-alone requirements. Seeing the success of methodologies that use them demonstrates that they do work as replacements. It is safe to conclude that user stories without *shall* statements can work.

■ **Real-World Note** The most recent example I have worked with where this occurred was a small development team of three people. The team lead had worked on this project for years and had an extensive understanding of the project. The requirements were documented only with user stories, without any *shall* statements. The team stated that they did not require the level of detail provided by *shall* statements, as the user stories provided what they needed. Not only did this team perform the coding but also the testing. I have observed other teams where there were separate coders and testers, and in most of these cases, the *shall* statements helped support the user stories. Nevertheless, there are cases where users stories can completely replace *shall* statements.

Use cases also are intended to act as stand-alone requirements. Seeing the success of methodologies that use them demonstrates that they do work as replacements. Thus, it is safe to conclude that use cases without *shall* statements can work.

■ **Real-World Note** I worked on a recent project that used the rapid application development methodology. Again, it worked because the development team had used use case definition without *shall* statements for years. I was the requirements team lead, and all of my team members had been coders before, so they knew the precise level of detail the developers needed, and they provided it. The structured use cases were provided to developers who understood what the users needed. Thus, use cases can be used instead of *shall* statements.

The gist of performing use cases and user stories with or without *shall* statements comes down to "It depends on the situation." What is the situation, and how will you use the information? The stakeholders and their level of understand and technical sophistication will drive much of the focus, as well as what your organization is comfortable with doing. As a junior requirements engineer, you may not have a lot of say on this. In addition, seeing different approaches over your career can help lend credence to your recommendations.

Now, onto our next topic.

Modeling

Chapter 9 talked about how good requirements gathering techniques may not successfully capture all requirements. Some things don't lend themselves to representation in natural language text, so we can look to examples of pictures that can capture things more effectively than words and mathematical precision that doesn't translate well into words. Modeling and other graphical representation techniques are attempts to provide that precision and leverage the strengths of visual imagery.

Modeling is an approach to represent a need in a more precise manner than can be achieved by just text only. Modeling uses more structured approaches to represent information that can be a varied combination of text and graphics. Modeling can vary from relatively simple graphical representations to very complex approaches that include multiple techniques.

Why is modeling useful for requirements? The natural language used to write text is not always as precise as REs would like it. Mathematics is precise, yet humans have not found a way to translate all words into equations. Modeling is an attempt to provide that precision.

That is not to say you should not use modeling techniques or graphics. If you do, make certain what you use is appropriate for your audience. Take into consideration the level of technical expertise of your users and stakeholders. Remember, the goal is to communicate effectively with them.

Back in the ancient history of chisels and stone programming days called Hollerith cards, programmers were supposed to write flow charts to plan out programs to prevent writing bugs into the code. Being undergraduates, programmers looked for shortcuts to get the programs written quickly and easily, so they ignored that advice, to their detriment. As programs grew more sophisticated, techniques improved beyond those rudimentary flow charts they should have used.

General Modeling

You will examine approaches that might use a graphic representation that might help enhance the message of the text you have written so that users can better understand, like swim lanes.

When you do use modeling and other graphical techniques, make certain what you use is appropriate for your audience. You will examine the technical level associated with each technique in its respective section. Take into consideration the level of technical expertise of your users and stakeholders. Remember, the goal is to communicate effectively with your target audience—stakeholders who will help you gather requirements.

In some cases, if your organization uses no modeling or graphic representation techniques, you may want to consider one or more to enhance communications. The more likely situation is that your organization already uses one or more models, so you need to be aware of them so you can then learn the technique.

There is one significant drawback to modeling—users/stakeholders may be model-illiterate. By that, they do not have the technology background to understand various models. You will be exposed to the use of swim lanes as one approach that might use a graphic representation that might help enhance the message of the text you have written so that users can better understand.

However, the more technical in nature of the model, the less likely a typical nontechnical user will glean information from it. Consider those when you evaluate ways to represent requirements.

If models do not effectively support the users, why would REs employ them? The primary purpose is to enhance the understanding of the requirements for the designers and developers and even requirements engineers. There are two subsections in the modeling section specifically targeted for user/stakeholders, "Models for Ordinary Requirements" and "Tools That Can Aid Requirements Gathering." Does that mean they can be used only for that audience? Of course not. It just means that these tools are much better when your audience is not so technically focused. The specialized modeling techniques work much better for technical audiences.

Models for Ordinary Requirements

Here I will present modeling techniques for capturing requirements in a graphic or model representation. Before looking at the swim lane or data flow diagram and trying to draw any conclusions on these techniques, here is some real-world experience that should prove enlightening.

I worked on two projects where a modeling technique was used in place of *shall* statements. The first project had DFDs created, and the other project just business rules created. For these two projects, because the developers had received the same training in the use of the modeling technique, they were able to understand the data. However, because stakeholders were accustomed to seeing *shall* statements, these people could not follow either approach well and still wanted *shall* statements.

The conclusion could be summarized as follows. When the users of modeling-related requirements understand the model, models can be used effectively. Experience shows that just a graphic or model representation will not always work well with stakeholders who do not have experience with said models.

Swim Lanes

Swim lanes are an easy method to depict what functions are performed, grouped by the different portions of an organization, and showing the sequencing of those functions. We are going to break them into either all the rows or all the columns (it makes no difference which way you break it) to represent the different organizations, teams, or processes—who is responsible for specific tasks. Using columns is preferred if you have a much smaller number of organizations than the various steps. Otherwise, you can use them organized by rows.

Lines show where that particular person or group of people (or maybe even a particular process) is affected or takes some action. Having lines on both sides justifies the name *swim lanes*, just like in a race in a swimming pool.

Then, the arrows show the sequence of events. You may have labels for the task sequence, if it makes sense.

Figure 12-1 is a swim lane example that presents how to access a BOSS system.

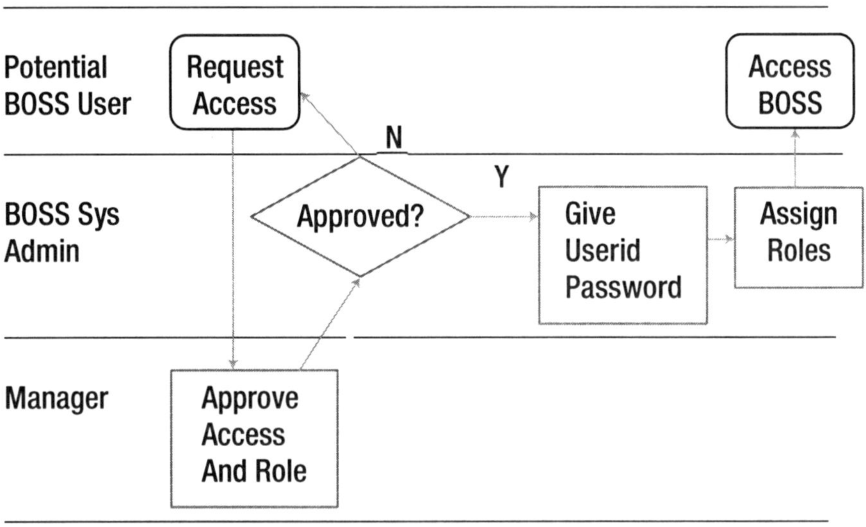

Figure 12-1. *Swim lanes*

This a simple example, but it illustrates how the different groups of users in this example have the information flows through the system, simple though it is. It starts with a potential user requesting access. Once the manager approves the request and assigns the roles, then the sequence goes through the various tasks to the natural end of the user accessing the system. Notice this example did not provide labels to the tasks as there was not a natural grouping of tasks.

This example has not shown what happens if the user forgets their password. That would be another swim lane chart.

You might ask why the manager would disapprove a request. It is possible the individual is not in the proper department to have access. Other things may happen outside this if the potential user needs to appeal the request. Alternatively, that could be some enhancements you might make to this chart.

What this technique may help with is inefficiencies. Are too many actions happening in one swim lane that is slowing down the process? This technique does not show how long it takes, but you can do some analysis. In this example, once the decision is made, there are only two steps to get the access to the user. However, what if after giving the access, the sys admin had to go back to the manager, or a supervisor to the user, and get the information and then get approval from HR? You see how additional steps cause the sequence to balloon out of control. It is the analysis of the swim lanes where its benefit arises, in addition to the graphical representation to help understand the process.

■ **Warning** This applies not only to this technique but also to virtually all graphical representations. Do not try to represent every task in a system on one swim lane diagram. This would be massive and hard to follow. Like you do in the agile methodology, break them into manageable chunks to aid readability and map more to smaller functions within a project.

You might hear swim lane flowcharts called Rummler-Brache diagrams. Most people take the simpler route and just call them swim lanes.

Since this technique was proposed in 1990, it has become one of the more popular techniques used to supplement requirements, including business analysts using them to depict business process even before requirements definition may begin.

Data Flow Diagrams (DFDs)

In the 1970s, the computer industry embraced Edward Yourdon's structured analysis. One significant technique to perform this approach to analysis was *data flow diagrams*. Data flow diagrams show the flow of data within a system in a graphical manner.

Understand that DFDs do not show timing of the flow, or any workflow information such as the sequence as performed in series or parallel.

DFDs start with what is called a level 0 DFD, called a *context diagram*. This defines the system and its interactions with the external entities, where these entities receive data from the system or send data to them. The only flows depicted on the context diagram are data flows.

Now look at an example of the BOSS Radiation Dosimetry System as was discussed in this book, as shown in Figure 12-2.

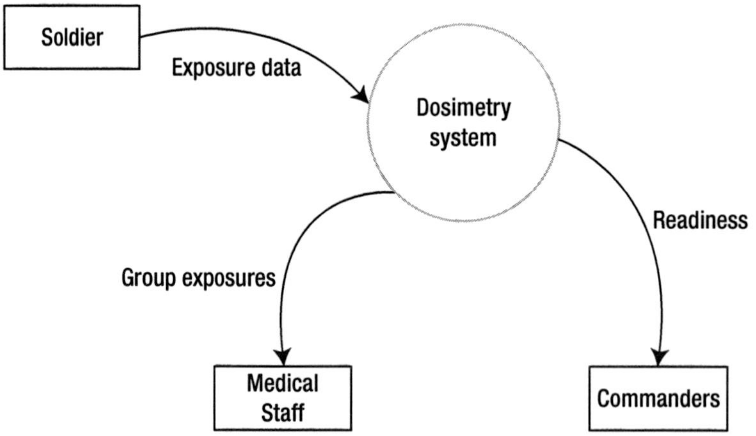

Figure 12-2. *Context diagram*

To understand the processes within the system, you must expand the system into multiple processes in level 1 (see Figure 12-3).

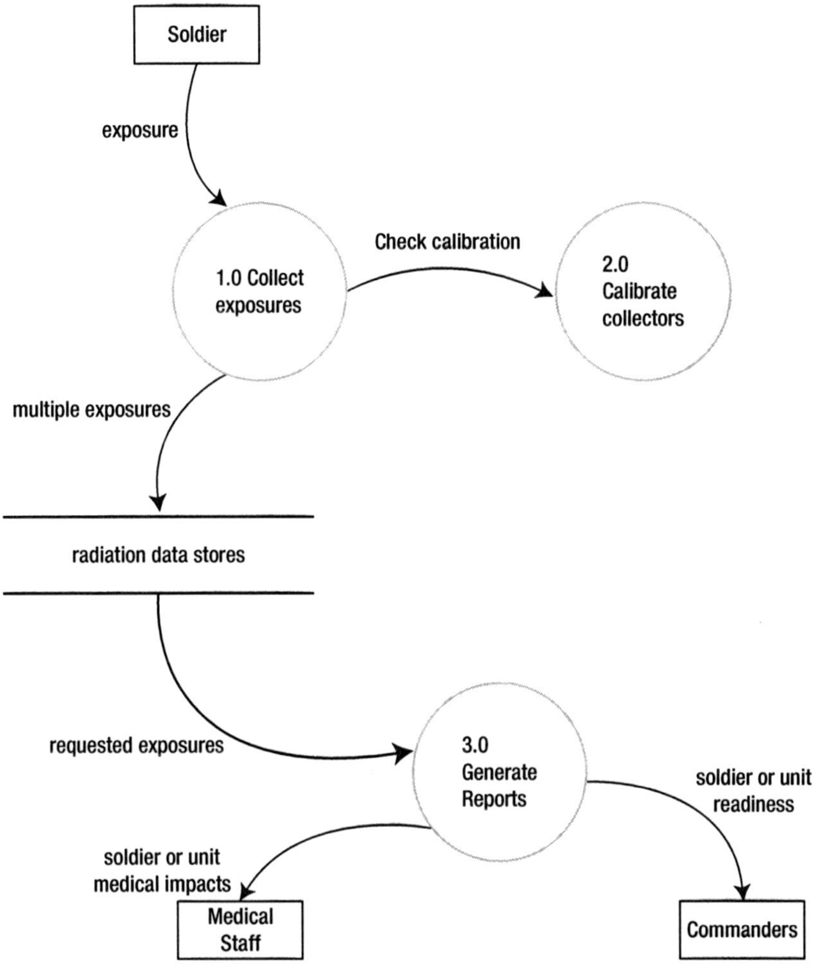

Figure 12-3. *Level 1 DFD*

You can see how the system is subdivided into processes (the circles), where each process addresses one or more data flows to or from external entities. It also has been identified any internal data stores for the system to perform its functions. Also, any data flows are shown between the internal processes.

First, you need to understand the notation used in the diagram. Accept that you are being exposed to one particular notation, whereas as you research this, if you will use it, there are many tools that use different variations in notations. The notations used here are as follows:

- Circles are processes.
- Curved lines are data flows.
- Rectangles are external entities.
- Parallel lines contain the internal data stores.

On the Agile Modeling web page, the "Data Flow Diagram (DFD)s: An Agile Introduction" article gives some excellent common modeling rules for creating DFDs that are highly recommended. These are those rules as presented in the article:

1. *All processes must have at least one data flow in and one data flow out.*
2. *All processes should modify the incoming data, producing new forms of outgoing data.*
3. *Each data store must be involved with at least one data flow.*
4. *Each external entity must be involved with at least one data flow.*
5. *A data flow must be attached to at least one process.*

Remember, the purpose of the sections in this chapter is to provide supplements to textual requirements that have been discussed up until this point in the book. While there may be some advocates who stipulate some of these techniques may replace textual requirements, this text is not advocating that.

■ **Real-World Note** I used DFDs in my career, in conjunction with a computer-aided system engineering (CASE) tool. (CASE tools are applications designed to help system engineers perform their functions, as you can see from what CASE stands for.) The team spent time creating DFDs after capturing a complete set of *shall* statements. When we completed this effort, the DFDs were provided to the development team, not to stakeholders.

How low a level you should decompose your DFDs to has not been addressed. The logical answer is as low as you need to go. That said, guidance in the industry is about the third or fourth level. Clearly, if you are down to eight or ten levels, you might want to rethink what you are doing. You are not trying to design a system, just provide information to assist in the development.

Does it seem like this is a good complement to textual requirements? It depends. If you will have significant data stores and manipulation of them, you might want to consider DFDs as a complement to your requirements. Notice that the diagrams are fairly bare of details. DFDs are very useful to depict how data flows within a system, particularly if the project has large, complex data flows. Clearly, a designer might use them, but you will have to decide whether the stakeholders will benefit by them.

Specialized Modeling

Some organizations apply specialized modeling techniques. In that case, you will likely be involved with using them. In some cases, you will prepare the results of your requirement work for the technical consumers using these techniques. Other times, you may be the reviewer of someone else who does the conversion of your requirements to ensure requirements are captured correctly. Or you may just be someone who reads the results of these techniques for informational purposes. In any of those cases, you will need to learn and understand the technique in question.

Also, remember in Chapter 9, we talked about some of the smaller groups within stakeholders such as database administrators, network engineers, system operators, and so on, who are technically savvy? If needed, some of these tools may be useful for them.

This text is only to make you aware of these specialized modeling techniques. There are extensive resources that exist that can aid you in learning about them. The following is a small list of some of the more popular techniques. This is not an endorsement of any of them, as each has their purposes. There are many more that provide the technical data in various formats, both text and graphic representations, to varying degrees of structure. The key takeaway is that some time is needed to use the techniques and understand the data resulting from its analysis.

This section introduces the techniques when you need to write more specialized requirements for the technical audiences:

Unified Modeling Language™ (UML): UML is a modeling language that is intended to analyze requirements to formulate a design, which is managed by Object Management Group (OMG), and now is an ISO standard.

Extensible Markup Language (XML): XML is a markup language to define a file format that is human-readable as well as machine-readable. The document or file does not do anything; it is just a method for representing the file or document.

Rational Unified Process (RUP): RUP is process that added a section specifically for requirements, which is UML based.

State transition diagrams: State transition diagrams show the actions that occur based on specific events, eventually showing all the states of that object. They work well for single objects but are not as effective as many objects are added to a system being analyzed.

System Modeling Language (SySML): SySML is a modeling language for system engineering designed to support all phases of the development lifecycle, including requirement specification. It too is a variation of UML.

This list is certainly not exhaustive but, again, it provides some representative tools that you might use. If they do not serve the needs of situations you encounter, there are other available tools and techniques you can research and employ.

See the reference section for sources that can provide additional information on these subjects.

Tools That Can Aid Requirements Gathering

Affinity diagrams and storyboarding are good tools to use with stakeholders when you are in the process of collecting requirements. In contrast, swim lanes and data flow diagrams are representation methods to use to document requirements after they have been collected to help with the precision of what you have captured. The following two techniques help to drive out the ideas and needs for the system the REs and stakeholders are discussing.

Affinity Diagrams

An *affinity diagram* is a sophisticated idea for organizing information. You solicit ideas on a particular subject area, whatever it is. You let the people write these ideas, all of them, no matter how outlandish or pie-in-the-sky they may sound. Once you have finished with the idea capture, you now want to bring some structure to them by providing some grouping. It could be one level of grouping or two—whatever works for the group. As a requirements engineer, you may come up with additional refinements to this as your experience tells you, but you should still vet it with the stakeholders.

Therefore, you start with something like Figure 12-4, which shows the results of the brainstorming by the stakeholders dealing with search ideas.

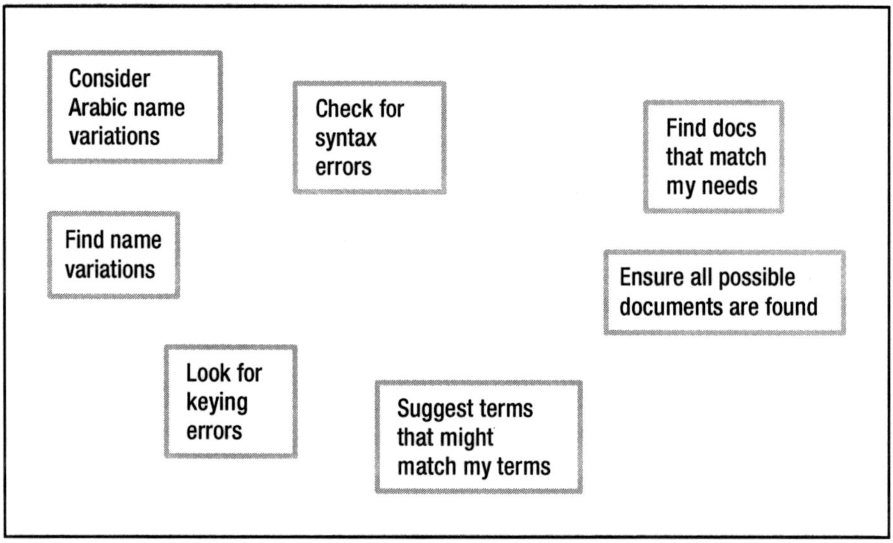

Figure 12-4. *Affinity diagram 1*

You can see there is no order. After applying some structure, you might have something like Figure 12-5.

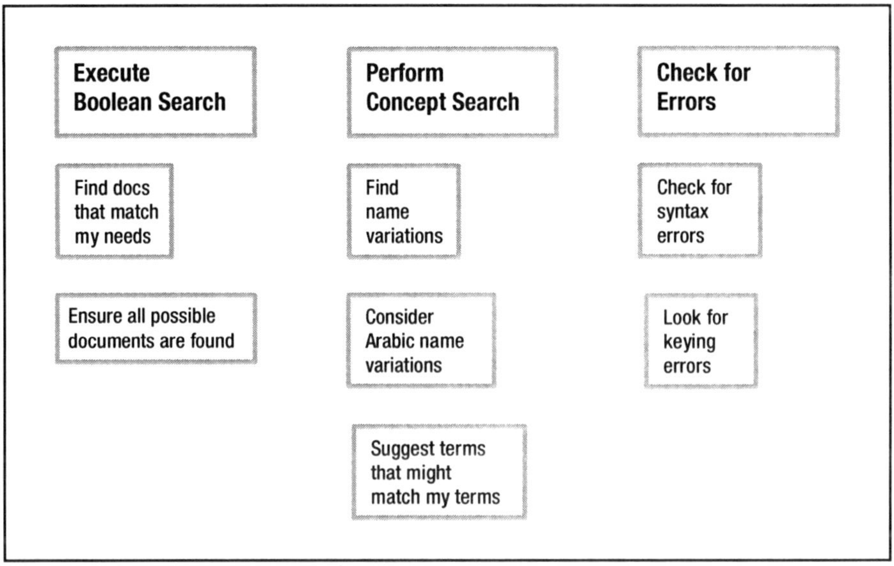

Figure 12-5. *Affinity diagram 2*

■ **Real-World Note** This is an excellent technique to use in conjunction with brainstorming as I have done on one of my projects. We used the sticky notes people filled out as the foundation for user stories for specific functional areas. We reviewed the results twice after the initial brainstorming to ensure we captured everything correctly.

Just so you know, if you run across the following names, an affinity diagram can also be called an *affinity chart* or *K-J method variation*.

Thus, affinity diagrams are an excellent technique to use in requirement elicitation.

Storyboarding

Storyboards are illustrations or images displayed in sequence so you can visualize a motion picture, animation, motion graphic, or interactive sequence. This can include how a human interacts with a computer. Believe it or not, but storyboarding was developed at Walt Disney Productions during the early 1930s. If it works for something as successful as full-length movies or *The Three Little Pigs* short by Disney, think of the benefit it can bring to system engineering. How can you use it to define requirements?

Before you get to the particular use, make certain you understand what it is.

One aspect of the word *storyboard* you want to consider is the word *story*. Just as you captured requirements in user stories, storyboards depict some aspect of the system by showing what some interaction is as a graphic. It could start out as what the user interface looks like, the menu options, whether on the top or bottom of the screen; it may be a snapshot or just hand-drawn on a piece of paper or white board. You can write on, erase, cross out, throw away, or whatever you need to do.

The point is that storyboarding is interactive between the engineers and stakeholders. This type of exchange is informal so that the small group of people feels comfortable enough to provide input. Having been involved with such exchanges, they can be fun. The point is to get the ideas flowing. This is a visual way of brainstorming.

Watch that some people do not dominate the conversation thereby inhibiting others from contributing. It may not be important to drill down all the details for a particular function but to get the general process. You can define the detail later. What is important, say, in a workflow aspect that you saw in a use case, is to show how it flows. It is one thing to read pages of description of what should be done. It is another to see even a crude, hand-drawn representation of it—like how or when the branching of alternatives or exceptions occurs.

You can achieve a consensus from the stakeholders even before a sprint or iteration demo occurs, thereby steering the developers to a more successful sprint. There will be creative and innovative ideas provided that no one may have considered without this specialized brainstorming. Let the ideas flow because you will not know what may come out. The nicest thing to hear is, "How about if we do...?" since this means that people are engaged. That is what you want. After all, your stakeholders will be representative of different types of users, who do not need all the same things or think the same way. You want to have those difference brought out to enhance the storyboards.

Here is a sample storyboard for a piece of software I have worked on. It is not important what this is, other than to see items on the screen.

Figure 12-6 is the first screen, with the main menu, and the crude avatar that will be the user's guide through the application.

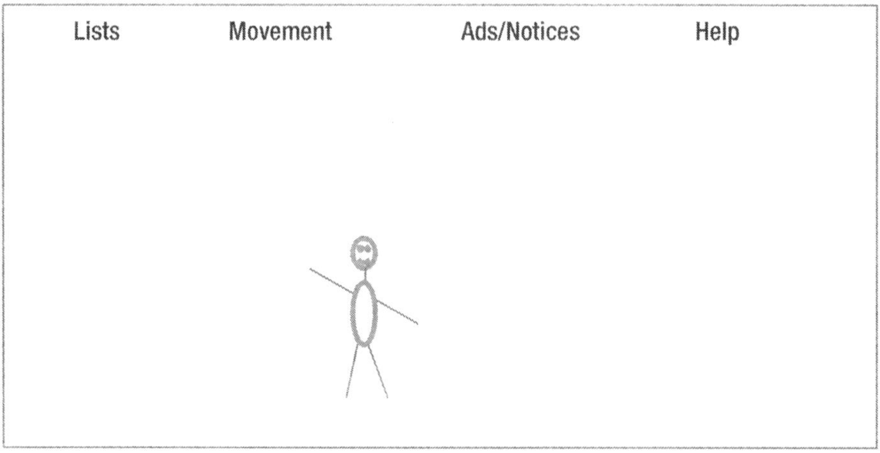

Figure 12-6. *Sample main menu screen*

Next, each of the four pull-down menus are portrayed as separate storyboards as if someone was sequencing through each of these menus. Figure 12-7 shows the Lists pull-down menu.

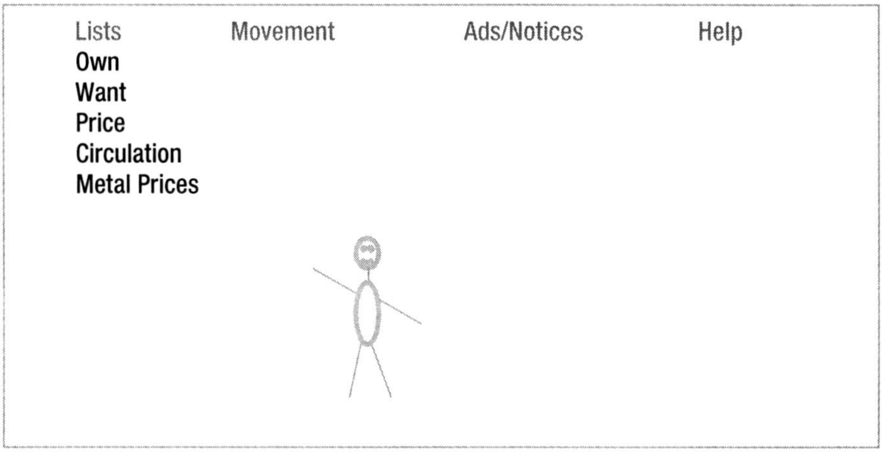

Figure 12-7. *Lists pull-down menu screen*

Figure 12-8 shows the Movement pull-down menu.

Figure 12-8. *Movement pull-down menu screen*

Figure 12-9 shows the Ads/Notices pull-down menu.

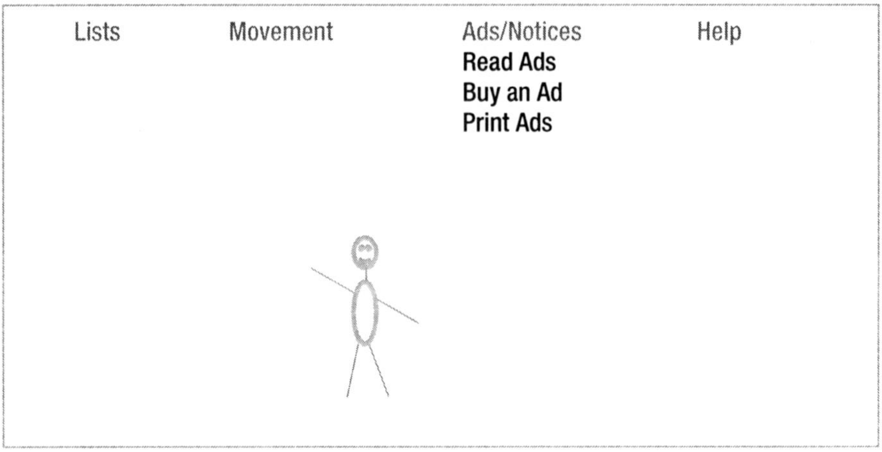

Figure 12-9. *Ads/Notices pull-down menu screen*

Figure 12-10 shows the Help pull-down menu.

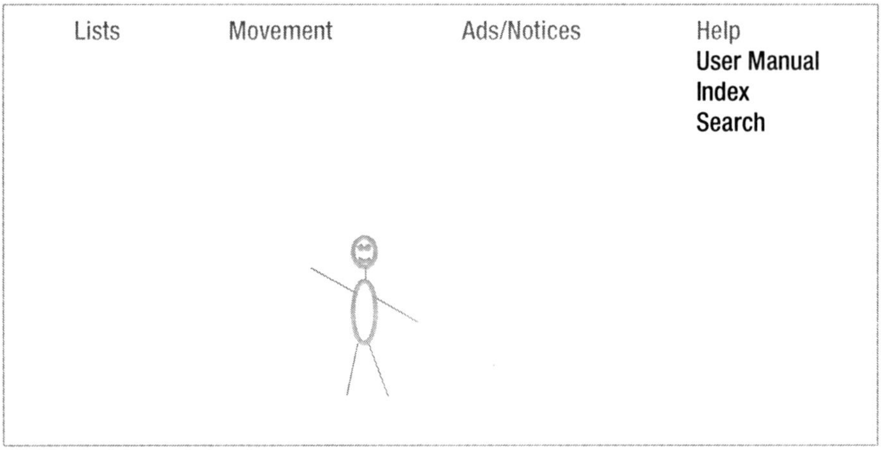

Figure 12-10. *Help pull-down menu screen*

What would happen is each of the storyboards is shown in the sequence, and the people evaluating them would look at each and discuss each one. They would agree on the sequence of the action, which is an important aspect of storyboarding—showing how the "story" evolves. These same people would then look at each screen and discuss everything that is presented and decide whether everything is in the correct place. Consider whether something needs to be deleted or added.

Once this is done, people could storyboard what happens for each item on these pull-down menus.

This is just one screenshot for the app. The figure in the screenshot is the avatar who guides the user through the application. The words on the top line are the titles of the pull-down menu. The words below are the pull-down menus themselves. Naturally, you cannot pull down all menu options at the same time. It is presented to demonstrate all the anticipated options. You might notice that typical items such as File, with Save, Save As, New, and Print, are not listed. That might be in the future, or it may not apply to this app.

Is this approach something that can aid requirements definition? At first blush, you could argue that this is for defining the design implementation. In addition, at the surface, yes, that is definitely a significant benefit of storyboarding. Nevertheless, you will learn things that people do not like or things that work well that do contribute to requirements. For example, if someone is talking about how hard the screen looks for doing a search, you realize that the challenge for the user is that the complexity of trying to find "squishy" subjects can be difficult with complex Boolean searches; you realize that concept searches might help. Alternatively, when they are talking that how hard it is to figure out all the nicknames based on proper names like Richard or James or to figure out all the spellings of Mohammed, again a different tool or series of tools besides Boolean may be in order.

Therefore, the answer is that, yes, storyboarding is useful for requirements definition. This is a very useful graphic representation to use. Also, it is fast. You can invest an hour or so but come up with a lot of useful information. It may be useful to have multiple sessions to let people come up with ideas a second or even a third time. When they have a chance to sleep on it, you will be surprised by what happens.

■ **Real-World Note** I write science fiction, and believe me, this storyboarding/brainstorming technique I have used extensively. Having a group of writers brainstorming gets lots of crazy ideas flowing. Most are not applicable, but there are gems that come from it. I have let the ideas, whether just verbally or graphically as in a storyboard, allow me to ferment my ideas to come up with even better ideas. Use the same techniques for software development.

■ **Note** Whereas storyboarding is the beginning of defining some subjects like the user interface, it evolves into prototyping, which was discussed in Chapter 9.

Where does storyboarding end and prototyping begin? Actually, that boundary is blurred. Once someone does some actual coding, even if there is no functionality behind it other than stubs, then you have gotten to the prototyping phase. In addition, prototypes actually can be working flows from one step to another by selecting items. Storyboards do not have that interactive nature. After all, they are just a few related pictures.

Then where does brainstorming end and storyboarding begin? Good question, and about the only distinction that can be made is that if you are gathering ideas with visuals rather than text, you are doing storyboarding.

In summary, yes, storyboarding is a useful tool for requirements definition.

■ **Note** Ambrose Little wrote an interesting article titled “Storyboarding in the Software Design Process” for *UX Magazine* that you may want to read to get more information about this subject. See the “References” section.

Other Supplements to Requirements Process

The topics in this section don’t directly supplement requirements themselves but provide additional insights into your requirements process. As with the modeling techniques talked about earlier, the intention is not to completely educate you on this topic, but introduce it, in the event that your organization exposes you to it and at least be aware of how it might affect your requirements collection and management.

The topics to be discussed are the following:

- Commercial off-the-shelf (COTS)/government off-the-shelf (GOTS)
- IEEE standards
- ISO 9001
- Capability Maturity Model (CMM)/Capability Maturity Model Integration (CMMI) levels of maturity
- International Council on Systems Engineering (INCOSE)

Off-the-Shelf Solutions

Off-the-shelf solutions do not directly affect how you create your requirements, but these packages affect how you track your requirements against their implementation. Commercial off-the-shelf software and hardware is just that—something you can run down to your local store or vendor and buy. The simplest example of COTS is Microsoft Office or any of the individual packages such as Microsoft Word. It can be installed on your system, and you can start using it. What does this mean to you as an RE? Now if you were considering installing Microsoft Office or Microsoft Project onto your computer or network, you might not need to specify requirements. However, if you were going to consider procuring a more specialized application for your organization, should you craft requirements for your use? Consider getting a benefits package for your HR department. Absolutely, you should define what your organization needs. Remember, you write requirements to be implementation independent. COTS could be one way to answer the requirements. What you do then is look at COTS packages to see how they compare to your requirements. There are even open source packages that may be zero cost.

Government off-the-shelf packages are produced by a government. Essentially it is a COTS but produced by a government. This means that if you support a government organization (i.e., the federal government, state governments, and even local governments) and if that government produces an application that has utility to other organizations, they have shared it with other government organizations. You would handle any requirements just as you would for a COTS package, craft the requirements, and then look to see whether a GOTS package exists that can be used. This difference may be that you may not need to pay for it.

Real-World Note For example, I supported an application that provided the ability to apply security classification to documents. This application was shared among more than two dozen portions of the federal government organizations but was developed only once and used by all the organizations. The application started out as a development effort for one agency but was recognized as the best implementation and then was shared with other organizations. Naturally, the requirements were captured once, and then the other organizations received the benefits of them without having to capture their own set, eliminating duplication of effort. I also used some GOTS packages. Again, requirements and development were done once and shared by many. This shows the advantage that requirements can be done once, central and shared with many organizations, and thus the development is also done centrally and implemented consistently.

Once a solution is developed in-house, by a company or governmental entity, other parts of the company or government shouldn't devote resources for creating something analogous. Additional, the federal government has broadened the use of GOTS for certain related fields. Once the government has paid for a system, other government organizations that perform a common function should not need to pay for the system again. This reduces cost for requirements definition and development, as well as providing consistent implementation, which for certain functions can be very important. This broader use of GOTS shows that governments can perform some things correctly by being innovative.

If you go about your requirements collection properly, when you are done, you can now use your list of requirements to compare various COTS programs to see which ones meet your requirements. Of course, it is likely that not each requirement will be met. You should consider how many are not met and decide what to do with your requirements. Can you live without the remainder? If not, do you want to see whether the vendor will add what you want, especially if you can justify that others might benefit from it? If you cannot live without some of the requirements, as dictated by your stakeholders, then you have to see about getting someone in-house to add it. Thus, you will need to ensure the program has the ability to add features easily, usually called *hooks*. If not, you might need to consider a different package that does have hooks but a few less of your required features.

Consider an example where you have 100 requirements for a particular application. You find only one COTS package that comes close to your needs. Eight-two requirements are met. What do you do with the remaining requirements? For this example, 16 requirements are specific report requirements that are needed. The application does not provide those reports. However, by examining the reports capability, the COTS package will work with your in-house reporting tool. By having the development team set up reports using the COTS package data, those 16 reports will be provided. That leaves two requirements that are not met. You and your stakeholders will need to decide whether you can live without those capabilities. If so, you are done. If you cannot, then some additional way needs to be found to have the two requirements met. You could ask the vendor to do it, if it is something the vendor believes other customers will use. Or you might have to pay the vendor to do it for you. If that is too costly, you will have to find some way to have them implemented in-house.

A CAUTION ABOUT COTS

The COTS package usually does not document all the inner workings to you, mostly for proprietary reasons. Some of your management team or stakeholders may not understand that. Here is a caution related to an incident that occurred to me some years ago. It deals with a mixture of modeling and COTS. A COTS package was selected to capture and manage employee benefits. It was part of a larger development effort to modernize the HR processes for the organization. We were partway through our customization, test, and transition into the production environment when a request came from one of the people working at the central office who managed the entire HR program.

The request was for our COTS team to provide DFDs for our application. I pointed out that as a COTS package we had no insight into the inner workings of the vendor's application, so generating DFDs was virtually impossible for us to create as the vendor would not supply the proprietary information that it would take to generate the DFDs. This did not seem to placate the requester.

Before I went any further, I asked why they wanted the information. The response was that they wanted to use our COTS package for the foundation of the entire umbrella project. To which I responded with the following analysis: "So, checking for understanding here, you want to base the entire HR umbrella program on one small COTS package that has maintenance releases every six months, and every 18 to 24 months they release a complete new release, which means every other application (more than a dozen) will need to rework their applications based on that schedule. Is that what you are asking for?"

There was a pause on the other end of the phone before the requester said that they would get back to me. I never did get a follow-up from that person. I thought that was the end of it. Wrong, six months later, a different requester asked the same question! I gave the same answer and got essentially the same response.

The caution is that COTS does not give you the insight into the inner workings of the application. This may not be obvious to everyone, so you may need to educate those people.

IEEE Standards

Remember, Chapter 2 referred to IEEE standard 830-1998. IEEE is the Institute of Electrical and Electronics Engineers, a professional organization of more than 400,000 technical professionals. If your organization follows their standards, then it behooves you to become knowledgeable about these standards and determine how that will affect your efforts. Alternatively, if your organization does not have any standards that it follows, the IEEE may be a source of standards that help improve your organizational processes.

ISO 9001:2008

ISO is the abbreviation used for the International Organization for Standardization. (To have an abbreviation that was consistent for all languages, the organization chose ISO from the Greek *isos*, which means "equal.") The point is that ISO is an international organization for standardization, and ISO 9001:2008, "Quality Management Systems - Requirements certificates," is the standard they have for requirements. If your company uses this as standard, again it behooves you to become knowledgeable of their standards and determine how that will affect your efforts. If your organization does not have a standard, this could be one to consider, especially if you have international dealings. That said, there are some companies that feel the ISO 9001 standard is cumbersome, so be careful. That is not to say do not use it, but look at it carefully. This will fit better with a more traditional waterfall development methodology. With agile, it might inhibit the agile nature of that methodology.

■ **Note** The ISO document does not have a requirements definition and maintenance section; they embedded the requirements discussion throughout the document. Thus, it will take more effort for you as an RE to ensure you are following their guidance for creating and maintaining your requirements.

CMM/CMMI Levels of Maturity

The capability maturity model (CMM) was developed to assess government contractors' processes to perform on a contracted software project. While it was intended for software development, it can be used for general business process like it has in many government and commercial industries worldwide.

The maturity model is a set of structured levels that describe how well the behaviors, practices, and processes of an organization can reliably and sustainably produce required outcomes.

The CMM model's application proved to be a challenge. Applying multiple models that are not integrated across the organization can be costly in training, appraisals, and improvement activities.[1] The Capability Maturity Model Integration (CMMI) project[2] fixed this problem so that the CMMI model has superseded the CMM model.

The model examines five aspects of your business.

- Maturity levels
- Key process areas

[1]"Capability Maturity Model," Wikipedia (see the "Reference" section)
[2]"Capability Maturity Model Integration," Wikipedia (see the "Reference" section)

- Goals
- Common features
- Key practices

The maturity model is a set of five structured levels that describe how well the behaviors, practices, and processes of an organization can reliably and sustainably produce required outcomes. The Wikipedia article "Capability Maturity Model" describes them like this:

1. **Initial** (chaotic, ad hoc, individual heroics): The starting point for use of a new or undocumented repeat process. If this is what you have, you do not want to stay here—this is problematic.
2. **Repeatable**: The process is documented sufficiently so that repeating the same steps may be attempted.
3. **Defined**: The process is defined/confirmed as a standard business process.
4. **Managed**: The process is quantitatively managed in accordance with agreed-upon metrics.
5. **Optimizing**: Process management includes deliberate process optimization/improvement.

What you will need to know if your organization, or someone you are interviewing with, is CMM level 3 is that means they follow the capability maturity model and you will need to follow it. Do understand that regardless of what level an organization is, it means that the processes work well. The higher the level, the greater chance that the processes do work well, but there is no guarantee. It is not a statement categorically that the product is excellent. It may increase the chances of a better product, but again, it is no guarantee.

The CMMI Institute states that there are three CMMI models. Part of each model shares practices with the other models since these practices apply to any business. Naturally, each model has practices that are unique because each model has a different focus. The three models are

- CMMI for Acquisition
- CMMI for Development
- CMMI for Services

The one most of interest here is the CMMI for Development model, since they designed it for businesses that focus on developing products and services. The process areas that comprise CMMI for Development are Product Integration, Requirements Development, Technical Solution, Validation, and Verification. So, naturally, REs are interest in the Requirements Development process, which will delve into detail about converting customer requirements into requirements used by developers. Thus, if your organization uses CMMI, you will need to follow their processes, so research it well.

Understand that this model fits the waterfall methodology better than the agile methodologies.

INCOSE

INCOSE is the International Council on Systems Engineering, which is not a standards organization but an organization that can be helpful for you in your career and one you should consider joining not only as an excellent resource but also as a good networking source.

On their website, they state, "The International Council on Systems Engineering (INCOSE) is a not-for-profit membership organization founded in 1990. Our mission is to share, promote and advance the best of systems engineering from across the globe for the benefit of humanity and the planet."

Their vision is to be the world's authority on systems engineering, and their goals are the following:

- To provide a focal point for dissemination of systems engineering knowledge
- To promote international collaboration in systems engineering practice, education, and research
- To assure the establishment of competitive, scalable professional standards in the practice of systems engineering
- To improve the professional status of all persons engaged in the practice of systems engineering
- To encourage governmental and industrial support for research and educational programs that will improve the systems engineering process and its practice

They also have student memberships. Here is what it takes to qualify for student membership.

Members qualify for a Student category if they are an undergraduate or master's or graduate student and if their course load is at least three-fourths of full-time in an engineering or related field. (For example, if the full-time student course load is four per semester, then the student must be enrolled in three or more courses in order to qualify for the student membership rate.)

You may want to consider joining.

References

US Government. "Use Cases". *usability.gov*. Feb. 2015, `www.usability.gov/how-to-and-tools/methods/use-cases.html`

IEEE-SA Standards Board. *IEEE Std 830-1998, IEEE Recommended Practice for Software Requirements Specifications*. Sponsor: Software Engineering Standards Committee of the IEEE Computer Society, Approved 25 June 1998.

International Organization for Standardization (ISO). *ISO 9001:2008 - Quality Management Systems—Requirements*. 2008

Phillips, Mike and Shrum, Sandy. "Which CMMI Model Is for You". August 2011.*The CMMI Institute*. Feb 2015, `http://whatis.cmmiinstitute.com/sites/default/files/documents/Which_CMMI_Model_Is_for_You_2014.pdf`

Wikipedia. *Capability Maturity Model.* Feb. 2015. http://en.wikipedia.org/wiki/Capability_Maturity_Model

INCOSE. Feb 2015, www.incose.org/

Following are sources to consider for additional information on modeling techniques.

"Data Flow Diagram (DFD)s: An Agile Introduction". Agile Modeling webpage. Feb. 2015, http://agilemodeling.com/artifacts/dataFlowDiagram.htm

"Swim Lane Diagrams, Mapping and Improving the Processes in Your Organization". *Mind Tools.* Feb. 2015, www.mindtools.com/pages/article/newTMC_89.htm

"Introduction to OMG's Specifications: UML". *Object Management Group (OMG).* Feb. 2015, www.omg.org/gettingstarted/specintro.htm#UML

"Introduction To OMG's Unified Modeling Language™ (UML®)". *Object Management Group (OMG).* Feb. 2015, www.omg.org/gettingstarted/what_is_uml.htm

Beal, Vangie. "XML, a tweet". *Webopedia.* Feb. 2015, www.webopedia.com/TERM/X/XML.html

Mullaney, Jennette. "Modeling selection". *SearchSoftwareQuality TechTarget.* Feb. 2015, http://searchsoftwarequality.techtarget.com/tutorial/Software-requirements-gathering-techniques

Mullaney, Jennette. "Modeling in the agile methodology". *SearchSoftwareQuality TechTarget.* Feb. 2015, http://searchsoftwarequality.techtarget.com/tutorial/Software-requirements-gathering-techniques

Microsoft Development Network webpage, Modeling User Requirements, Visual Studio 2013 Feb. 2015,, http://msdn.microsoft.com/en-us/library/dd409376.aspx

Little, Ambrose. "Storyboarding in the software design process". *UX Magazine.* Feb. 2015, http://uxmag.com/articles/storyboarding-in-the-software-design-process

Kruchten, Philippe. "What Is the Rational Unified Process?". 2001. *IBM.* Feb. 2015, www.ibm.com/developerworks/rational/library/content/RationalEdge/jan01/WhatIstheRationalUnifiedProcessJan01.pdf

"RUP Fundamentals Presentation", *electronic Research Association (eRA) National Institute of Health.* Feb. 2015, http://era.nih.gov/docs/rup_fundamentals.htm

Bell, Donald. "UML basics Part II: The activity diagram", Sep. 2003. *IBM Global Services.* Feb. 2015, www.therationaledge.com/content/sep_03/f_umlbasics_db.jsp

"SysML Open Source Specification Project". *Systems Modeling Language (SysML).* Feb. 2015, http://sysml.org/

"What is a SysML Requirement diagram and how is it used?". *SysML Forum.* Feb. 2015, www.sysmlforum.com/sysml-faq/

CHAPTER 13

User Stories

Why do REs write user stories? That is an excellent question. The answer is that in some circumstances the scope of requirement elicitation is greater than the benefit of collecting and writing *shall* statement requirements, or a process can be captured in ways more accessible to the users who need to validate the requirements.

For example, I have seen cases in which a simple function was used by many users across many groups in an organization. Rather than spending countless hours interviewing different user types from various groups, it proved more effective and efficient to write stories about how the stakeholders used the function.

In such cases, we are able to craft statements that users would understand better and also employ a more flexible approach that fit better with an agile development methodology. User stories provide a more streamlined and flexible approach to requirements that enable teams to manage the development effort in a much more dynamic environment.

In this chapter, you will learn more about what user stories are, their benefits, and how you can use them to supplement or replace traditional requirements.

Anatomy of a User Story

First, you will examine the parts of a good user story. Then, you will learn the six attributes of a good user story and look at each of the attributes in detail.

Parts of a User Story

What does a user story consist of? The previous chapter presented that a user story follows this type of template:

> "As a <*role*>, I want <*function/feature*> so that <*benefit*>."

Or this type:

> "As a <*who*>, I want <*what*> so that <*why*>."

Simple, right? Well yes, and no. In theory, it sounds simple like most theories do. Of course, it is. In fact, that is the whole point of a good user story is to be simple. Naturally, the challenge occurs when you write them. Now, examine what the three parts of the story are.

G. Koelsch, *Requirements Writing for System Engineering*,
DOI 10.1007/978-1-4842-2099-3_13

The *<role>* is the person, the people, or even a system, application, or service that is doing or affected by this, also known as *<who>*. For example, "As a taxpayer submitting my taxes, ..."

Here are some examples:

> As a search user, ...
>
> As a system administrator, ...
>
> As an HR user, ...
>
> As a payroll user, ...
>
> As a report reader, ... (you do not need to say *user* every time, as in the earlier system administrator case)
>
> As a workstation user, ...
>
> As a radiation dosimetry user, ...

You want to be as specific as is practical. Break down the user to the particular role that they are doing. Do not just say, "As a user, ..." as that is not specific at all.

The *<function/feature>* is the action the *<role/who>* needs. Clearly, this is the most important aspect of the story of the three. This describes *<what>* is wanted. For example, "As a taxpayer submitting my taxes, I want the 1040 form instructions written to a fifth-grade reading level ..."

Here are some examples:

> ... I want to query records...
>
> ... I want to display query results...
>
> ... I want to sort query results...
>
> ... I want to filter query results...
>
> ... I want to print query results...
>
> ... I want to capture radiation exposure readings...
>
> ... I want to read radiation exposure readings...

Again, you want to define this down to the lowest level of the function as possible. You will see more about this shortly.

The *<benefit >* is the benefit the user will achieve with this *<function/feature>*. You want to know *<why>* the user wants this user story.

Here are some examples:

> ... so that I can access data.
>
> ... so that I can display data.
>
> ... so that I can print data.
>
> ... so that I can generate reports in the format I want.
>
> ... so that I gather the radiation exposure data of soldiers in the nuclear battlefield.

You can see this is one aspect that the *shall* statement did not provide, the reason why this user story should be done. This goes a long way in helping the users and stakeholders to understand the benefits of the current or new system.

Then, put all three parts together and you get this example:

> 13-1 As a taxpayer submitting my taxes, I want the form instructions written to a fifth-grade reading level so that 99% of the taxpayers will understand what they are filling out on the form.

While this type of user story is unlikely to happen soon (think of the run-up to April 15 every year), this is just an example. Think about this user story, whether it meets the criteria of a good user story, and you can examine it at the end of the chapter. Here is another one:

> 13-2 As a cell phone user, I want to retain a list of phone numbers selectively that I have received so that I can choose which numbers I want to reuse later.

Notice how easy it is to read? That is a significant benefit for users and stakeholders to understand them. This is an advantage to the user who can understand user stories even better than *shall* statements. User stories work well with the agile methodology. The user story and subordinate acceptance criteria can be refined as the user story approaches the sprint where the story will be implemented. This approach of writing user stories near the time they are implemented helps to negate the effect of requirements scope creep, unlike in the waterfall approach where you must create all the requirements (whether *shall* statements or user stories) up front.

Here are a few more examples to consider:

> 13-3 As a person logging onto BOSS, I want to have three tries to get my login ID and password correct before the system rejects my login attempts so that one or two mistakes do not punish me.
>
> 13-4 As a bike rider, I want the push on the hand brake so that when I need to stop, the bike will respond.

As you can see, you can write user stories for both hardware (bikes) and software (logins).

Attributes of a User Story

Just as there was a section defining what made a good requirement, there are attributes of a good user story. Bill Wake coined the acronym INVEST to describe those attributes. Here is what INVEST stands for:

- Independent
- Negotiable
- Valuable
- Estimable
- Small
- Testable

Now, consider each one of these attributes of a good user stories.

Independent

Independent means that a story can be developed, tested, and even delivered on its own. You want to write a story so that it can stand on its own. Here are some examples:

> 13-5 As s soldier in a nuclear battlefield, I want a way to collect radiation exposure levels so that my unit and I will know my exposure in order to manage my exposure levels both militarily and medically.
>
> 13-6 As an FBI Records Manager, I want to be able to view any record so that when I need to examine it, I can.

You might wonder whether each of these stands by themselves, making them truly independent. In these cases, and for many of the user stories you write, they may not be purely independent. So, what is a requirements engineer to do?

Not to worry. Almost every story you write should be able to have some independence. Think of the viewing the record story shown user story 13-6. You cannot view a record if it does not yet exist in some repository, and then if you query it, you need to be able to do so. You probably won't get just one record, but a listing of them. You may have many other functions such as printing, sorting, filtering, exporting, and so on, that you might want to do. That does not mean you cannot write it the way it was presented earlier. You just need to write each of those other functions as separate user stories. Therefore, you could have the following:

> 13-7 As an FBI Records Manager, I want to be able to view a listing of records I requested so that when I need to examine them, I can.
>
> 13-8 As an FBI Records Manager, I want to be able to print a listing of records I requested so that when I need to examine them, I can.
>
> 13-9 As an FBI Records Manager, I want to be able to sort a listing of records I requested so that I can organize them the way I want them.
>
> 13-10 As an FBI Records Manager, I want to be able to filter a listing of records I requested so that I can organize them the way I want them.
>
> 13-11 As an FBI Records Manager, I want to be able to export a listing of records I requested so that I use them outside the application.

You may need to have more functions, but you get the idea. Granted, you would not see all the search-related function at once. However, each user story here should allow the developers to produce something that they could demonstrate at the end of the sprint, which is the goal of the user story and the associated user stories for that sprint.

You need to consider the same process for the radiation dosimetry project where you might have the following:

> 13-12 As a soldier in a nuclear battlefield, I want a way to determine how much radiation exposure I have received so that my unit and I will capture my exposure.

You may think of more user stories also, like reporting of the entire unit, and so on.

One advantage to having the user stories independent of each other is that you can move them around, execute them in different sprints, or keep some on the backlog for a while. That flexibility is the primary purpose of user stories, and independence allows that to occur.

If two user stories seem very tightly coupled, that means they probably depend on each other and probably belong in one user story. Of course, you still need the story to be small, which will be talked about later in the chapter.

Remember in Chapter 2, the *I* meant implementation independent. Does it still mean that here too? Absolutely. Many sources may not say that, but it is still true here. Granted, it is a goal, but follow it just like you do in *shall* statements for the same reason, so you do not restrict the developers, allowing them to do what they are best at—develop.

Negotiable

Unlike in requirements development in the waterfall methodology, as you have seen earlier in the book, that remain fixed once they are captured, a group of user stories is not a contract etched in stone. You can discuss, develop, refine, update, and even reject a story as time passes. You negotiate a user story with stakeholders until all parties affected, including the development team, are satisfied with the definition.

Once a story goes on the backlog, this negotiation process can occur at any time while it resides there. This is because as the user story gets closer to being designed and developed, all parties have the ability to learn more about the story and define the needed details.

This provides one of the best advantages of the user stories—flexibility. Remember how the waterfall requirements collection "froze" the requirements until delivery? Remember how the biggest drawback of that is the one or more percent requirements changes per month? By negotiating the user stories as they become close to being developed, you help to eliminate that scope creep because you reevaluate each user story and update it as appropriate with what you know at that time, rather than waiting months or even years as in the waterfall method. Think of this as just-in-time requirements definition. By crafting user stories (or reviewing and revising previously written ones), you capture the need precisely when you need it, and your understanding of the requirements is current. That 1 to 4 percent requirements change per month is eliminated. This is a major success for this agile approach.

Thus, the negotiation can come at multiple times until just before the story is worked on during a sprint. For example, early on a user story may look like this initially as a placeholder:

> 13-13 As an FBI Records Manager, I want to be able to delete a temporary record from the repository so that records I am no longer required to retain can be deleted.

Six months later, the stakeholders and you revisit this story the month before the developers will work on the story during the upcoming sprint. You meet with the users and stakeholders (or use a technique or techniques discussed in Chapter 9), and after you presented the story and asked if this is still correct, the record manager stakeholders have clarified it as follows:

> 13-14 As an FBI Records Manager, I want to be able to delete a temporary record from the repository **in accordance with the records retention schedule prescribed by National Archives and Records Administration (NARA)** so that records I am no longer required to retain can be deleted.

■ **Note** The bold text is what was added. This points out the use of techniques to highlight changes. Microsoft Word has the Track Changes capability that can be useful. It is good to show what is added, deleted, and changed. If that is not practical, maybe you should show the before and after story. Sometimes if there are adds, deletes, and changes inside one story, with Track Changes turned on, it is difficult to read, so showing the before and after stories works better. That is a judgment call by you.

Also, consider that Microsoft Excel also provides Track Changes. You may not be aware of this as it is not in the same place on the menu as in Microsoft Word. Track Changes is useful when you are drafting statements. Once you finish them and want to maintain them in the future, you should consider versioning, which will be discussed at the end of this section.

You need to consider the same process for the radiation dosimetry project where you might have the following:

> 13-15 DRAFT As a soldier in a nuclear battlefield, I want a way to determine the radiation exposure so that I can see how it is affecting my ability to perform my military mission.

This user story may be as written because that was what someone initially asked for. However, the military leaders determined this not a valid factor to be considered by the individual soldier, so they revised the story as follows:

> 13-16 DRAFT **As a commander in a nuclear battlefield,** I want a way to determine the radiation exposure so that I can see how it is affecting **my unit's** ability to perform **its** military mission **at the squad, platoon, and company levels.**

Then, the medical staff renegotiated it as follows to be within their policy:

> 13-17 As a commander in a nuclear battlefield, I want a way to determine the radiation exposure **in accordance with the Radiation Exposure Medical Policy** so that I can see how it is affecting my unit's ability to perform my military mission, at the squad, platoon, and company levels.

Again, the bold is the text that was added to the previous version of the user story. FYI, the title Radiation Exposure Medical Policy was just fabricated to illustrate what someone may identify.

There is no limit to the number of times that you may renegotiate a user story. You may get it correct the first time. Alternatively, you may refine it just before the sprint, or any number of times in between the first time you crafted it and the developers worked on it in the sprint. There is no right or wrong number of times. The correct number is whatever number of times is necessary to get it correct.

The main point here is to get everyone to understand what the user story means. Once the stakeholders are satisfied with the text (with your help, of course), then the developers will examine it and may ask for some additional information or clarification. If you as the RE cannot provide the information, you will need to take the story back to the stakeholders.

One additional aspect you may want to consider is that you may need to track the changes from the first version to the final version. (This is where a good database tool helps with this.) The reason may be that the original stakeholder who asked for user story 13-15 sees the final user story (13-17) and says that his user story was deleted. With the tracked history, you can point out the evolution of the user story into the final one. If the stakeholder says they want 13-15 added back in, you can point out the decision that turned their version into 13-16 overrode their initial request. Now you see what the negotiation is. This reinforces the point made earlier in this book: requirements definition is an art form, and this negotiation process is a primary reason for it. Note, having a good comments field helps to explain why revisions were made and to clarify decisions that affected the wording of the version.

Another form to track history is in documents that track different versions. Microsoft SharePoint allows you to track different versions of documents. Some dedicated requirements tools provide versioning of requirements in whatever form you capture them (e.g., *shall* statements, user stories, use cases). There are also dedicated configuration control/management packages that may allow versioning at the element level (e.g., *shall* statements, user stories, use cases) rather than at the document level. You want the version down to that element level.

Valuable

The user story must provide value to the end user. While this seems obvious, it is not always clear to all parties. Here's an example:

> 13-18 As a machine learning user, I want the function to present the mathematical representation to me so that I understand why some entities are chosen over others.

A developer might think a particular function is fun and needed, whereas the real users think it is of no use to them. In fact, how many of the stakeholders would even understand what this would mean? Yet, if the application was a tool for machine learning developers, this may be a valuable tool. On the other hand, if this user story was asked for when there is no such need, it may be a user story you can eliminate.

Bear in mind that not all end users see the value of everything. Here's an example:

> 13-19 As a system administrator, I want the ability to add, change, or delete any record in the repository so that I can fix any errors made by other users of the system.

Administrators who know the need to audit database transaction to protect the integrity of the data know its value. On the other hand, a person who just queries the same database might not see the value of auditing for their use, although many if not most people would recognize its value to the technical people. In those instances, you need to ensure that the technical need is captured. Therefore, it is important to consider that value is relative. This is why it is important to have representative stakeholders to ensure all aspects are affected, not just people who query the data or update it, but system monitors, system admins, and people who perform access control, to name a few.

Of course, the resources necessary to achieve the value comes into play in determining if it truly is valuable. For example, everyone could see many and varied needs and uses for the transporter of *Star Trek*. However, not only is the physics not well understood for it, but also the engineering necessary to achieve it certainly is nowhere near the capabilities of today. Much more importantly, the cost to achieve it is, well, unknown. For all intents and purposes, since you do not know how to accomplish it, effectively the cost is infinite.

As an aside, supposedly, there was a call (allegedly by Congress, in its infinite wisdom) to produce antigravity back in the 1940s and 1950s, in spite of the fact that general relativity said it was not possible. Well, there is no evidence of this antigravity unit to date. Therefore, it is of no value as a user story at this point.

So, you understand the point—when determining the value of a user story, it is important to include the practicality of achieving it, besides determining the desire by the end users. That is also one of the reasons you identify what role finds this function or feature useful and why, so that the user story supports that user. That should help you identify the appropriate user or stakeholder to talk to about this. By saying, "As a system administrators, ..." you know this functions supports them, and they would be able to provide the business reason why this function is important.

■ **Note** Do not try to figure these business reasons out by yourself. Whenever you can, get the stakeholder to do that for you. In many cases, you will know the reason why, and you should capture it, if the stakeholders have not provided it. Then, when you vet the user stories with the stakeholders, make certain you ask if the reason is correct. Otherwise, ask during the elicitation process what the reason is.

For the radiation dosimetry project, you might have the following:

> 13-20 As a tank commander in a nuclear battlefield, I want a way to determine the radiation exposure inside the tank so that I can determine what my team's exposure is and hence their fighting capability.

Estimable

A story to be of value must be estimable. By that, someone, maybe not who crafts the story, needs to be able to make an estimate of the complexity of the story and thereby determine the time it will take to develop and test it. Odds are, if someone cannot estimate it, then it is too complex and needs to be broken into simpler or smaller stories that can be estimable. You will learn about smaller in the next subsection.

As you get closer to the sprint where specific user stories will be considered for movement from the backlog to be worked in a sprint, the people who will estimate how long a story will take must examine the story to ensure they can estimate it. This is first a sanity check that the story is defined as well as it can be (see the "Negotiable" section earlier in this chapter). If there are any assumptions or clarifications the developers need, this will be the time to help drive those points out. Sometimes the first indication you have that a story is too big is when the developer or tester says that it is too big—that they cannot do it in one sprint. Then, as the RE, it is your job to break it down into multiple parts.

For example, you may have the following:

> 13-21 DRAFT As someone who searches my permanent records database, I want a concept search capability so that I will not miss important records that are related to what I want the search to find.

When the developers examine this user story, they say it is too large. So they suggest breaking it into the following:

> 13-22 As some who searches my permanent records database, I want a function that decides what terms are similar to the user-specified search terms so that the user will find search terms that capture the true intent of the search.

> 13-23 As someone who searches my permanent records database, I want a function that executes the concept term search so that I can retrieve the search terms.

> 13-24 As someone who searches my permanent records database, I want a function that displays the results of the concept term search so that the user can determine what terms best meet their needs.

It is possible that there are more user stories than this, but this illustrates breaking the stories into lower levels that are more manageable for developers. Also, this is a reflection of something you will learn about in the "Small" section in this chapter about themes, epics, and stories.

For the radiation dosimetry project, you might have the following:

> 13-25 DRAFT As a commander in a nuclear battlefield, I want a way to determine the radiation dose rate that my vehicles are exposed to so that I can collect raw radiation data for the battlefield.

In this case, what vehicles must have this? So, start with the following:

> 13-26 As a commander in a nuclear battlefield, I want a way to determine the radiation dose rate that my M-1 tanks are exposed to so that I can collect raw radiation data for the battlefield.

> 13-27 As a commander in a nuclear battlefield, I want a way to determine the radiation dose rate that my deuce-and-a-half trucks are exposed to so that I can collect raw radiation data for the battlefield.

> 13-28 As a commander in a nuclear battlefield, I want a way to determine the radiation dose rate that my attack helicopters are exposed to so that I can collect raw radiation data for the battlefield.

There would be a much longer list of vehicles than this, but you understand the idea.

The key point here is that the developers and testers will be doing the estimates, so it is their judgment that determines whether the story meets this attribute.

Small

A story needs to small enough so that it can be developed in hours or days or one or more weeks, depending on the size of your sprints. They should be small enough to be accomplished during just one sprint. As you have now seen, you now know how these attributes can be interrelated. If it is small enough, odds are it is estimable, and there's a greater chance that the story will have value to the users.

What criteria should you use to determine whether the story is small enough? If the story is vague, it may be because you have too much in it. Remove the vagueness by giving more detail to the story. If the developers and testers cannot estimate the story, chances are that the story is too big. Again, provide more detail and see whether you can break it down. In addition, if there are conjunctions in the story, it may be too large. Here's an example:

> 13-29 DRAFT As an FBI records manager, I want to add, change, and delete records from my repository so that I can manipulate the records as necessary.

It would be better to break this user story into three as follows:

> 13-30 As an FBI records manager, I want to add records from my repository so that I can manipulate the records as necessary.

> 13-31 As an FBI records manager, I want to change records from my repository so that I can manipulate the records as necessary.

> 13-32 As an FBI records manager, I want to delete records from my repository so that I can manipulate the records as necessary.

There is a general "stories" hierarchy in which one level is called *stories*. This hierarchy is called TES, which comes from theme, epics, and stories. The theme is the largest of the three, which is a collection of epics or many stories. It usually relates to a major function within a system. Here's an example:

> 13-33 The system will provide controlled access to the BOSS.

Clearly this does not follow the full user story format, and it is way too big to estimate and could not be done in one sprint/iteration.

The next level down is the epic, which is one large user story that needs to be broken down or already a group of related user stories. In the access function mentioned in the previous theme, consider the following:

> 13-34 As a BOSS system administrator, I want to add to person to the BOSS system so that I control who gets authorization to use the system.
>
> 13-35 As a BOSS system administrator, I want to define all BOSS system roles and responsibilities so that I control what functions specific groups of people can perform.

Roles and responsibilities refer to the different accesses a user could have such as a user who reads data, adds data, updates data, deletes data, or any combination of these roles. Of course, there may be more specialized roles like an administrator who also needs access.

> 13-36 As a BOSS system administrator, I want to assign BOSS system roles and responsibilities to a person so that I control what functions specific groups of people can perform.
>
> 13-37 As a BOSS system user, I want to log in to the BOSS system so that I am allowed to access the BOSS functions I need to perform my job.
>
> 13-38 As a BOSS system administrator, I want to audit all access so that I know who has performed all access adds, changes, and deletes. (This could be an admin, a manager, an auditor, and so on, depending on your project.)

Epics are useful early in the definition phase when you may not have a lot of information about the needs of the system. This allows you more time to focus on the high priorities on the backlog.

Finally, back to the user story level that was being developed, here is one example for the login epic:

> 13-39 As a BOSS system administrator, I want the login to the BOSS system to require a user ID and password so that unauthorized users cannot easily break into the system.
>
> 13-40 As a BOSS system administrator, I want no more than three login tries of password and user ID combination errors before the user ID is locked out of BOSS so that unauthorized users cannot easily break into the system.

How does the user ID get unlocked? Excellent question. The answer is that it depends. It could be one of the three following user stories (or some variation of it) based on what your management and senior stakeholders want:

> 13-41 As a BOSS system administrator, I want the lockout of a user ID to be unlocked after 30 minutes so that the user can try again without requiring the sys admin to unlock it.

■ **Note** User story 13-41 may make it easier for hackers, just FYI.

> 13-42 As a BOSS system administrator, I want the lockout of a user ID to be unlocked after 24 hours so that the user can try again without requiring the sys admin to unlock it.
>
> 13-43 As a BOSS system administrator, I want the system admin to unlock the lockout of a user ID so that I control who can access the system.

Consider either one of the first two, but always allow the third user story to be available also, especially if the user must wait 24 hours for it to reset; you might not want people waiting a day to retry, without being able to do their job.

Notice there is a relationship between the estimate and small attributes. If a user story is small enough, chances are good developers can estimate the time necessary to implement the story.

Now, examine the radiation dosimetry example from the "Estimable" section in this chapter:

> 13-44 DRAFT As a commander in a nuclear battlefield, I want a way to determine the radiation dose rate that my MRAPs are exposed to so that I can collect raw radiation data for the battlefield.

On further examination, a stakeholder states that all vehicles must use the same dose rate meter. That means you have to break user story 13-44 into the following:

> 13-45 As a commander in a nuclear battlefield, I want my MRAPs to use the standard dose rate meter so that I do not need to develop a meter unique to every vehicle.
>
> 13-46 As a commander in a nuclear battlefield, I want the standard dose rate meter to have an MRAP-specific mounting bracket so that I do not need to have a universal mounting bracket for every vehicle.
>
> 13-47 As a commander in a nuclear battlefield, I want the standard dose rate meter mounted on the outside of the MRAP so that it collects the raw data not influenced by the shielding offered by the MRAP.

It is ironic that this subsection called "Small" is the longest of the six sections on the attributes of a good user story. This is in no small way (pun fully intended) because of the difficulty in getting the user story to the correct level. You will need to work at it.

Testable

Lastly, the story must be verifiable (as you learned with requirements) but is called testable to allow the acronym INVEST to work (INVESV does not seem to cut it). A story is not completed until is it is *successfully* tested. If it does not pass testing, it is not complete. Thus, in the estimate process, people need not only to include time to code and test the code but also include time to rework errors and then retest. Just as one attribute of a good requirement is that it can be verified, the same is true for all user stories. Some demonstrations of a user story show that values in XML have changed, rather than showing changes in a user interface. The purpose is to demonstrate the user story works, not have a UI for every story.

On some projects, to ensure that the application worked properly, the entire last sprint in a release was dedicated to regression testing. The teams wanted to ensure that no story adversely affected anything in this application (i.e., the ripple effect) that supported hundreds of thousands of users. While most projects do not follow this approach, the number of issues caused once this application was deployed was very, very small. That is the ultimate goal.

Some reasons for untestable stories are the wording. Here's an example:

> 13-48 DRAFT As a user, I want an easy-to-use user interface so that I do not have difficulty learning and using the system.

This makes sense to a user or stakeholder, but how would you test or verify "easy"? Any such vague words need to be modified as follows (just as you learned when crafting *shall* statements):

> 13-49 As a user, I want the user interface to follow the BOSS User Interface Standard so that I do not have difficulty learning and using the system.

This is something that is testable or verifiable. Granted, if the UI standard is more than a few statements, this user story may not be small enough, but at least from a test standpoint you are moving in the correct direction.

Thus, just like with *shall* statements, you need to eliminate the vague words. That may be an issue when dealing with the users and stakeholders, but just as you were trained for those *shall* statements, you will be able to do it here.

Look at examples for the radiation project.

> 13-50 As a commander in a nuclear battlefield, I want the standard dose rate meter to be installed on the MRAP within 15 minutes by a soldier who requires no special training or tools so that the dose rate meter can be installed quickly and easily by any soldier.

> 13-51 As a commander in a nuclear battlefield, I want the MRAP-specific mounting bracket for the standard dose rate meter to be installed within one by the lowest ordinance unit that requires no special training or tools so that MRAP-specific mounting bracket can be installed quickly and easily by any soldier.

One other important aspect associated with testing is *acceptance criteria*. Given its importance to support the testable attribute, you will spend the next section learning about it.

Acceptance Criteria

Acceptance criteria, also known as completion criteria, is to help define when a user story is done (or complete—hence, you say the story is complete). At the end of the sprint, the demonstration is to show that the criteria are complete.

What makes good acceptance criteria? Walter Jackson said the following in his online article "What Characteristics Make Good Agile Acceptance Criteria?":

- There should be a clear pass/fail result (no partial results).
- They can be both functional and nonfunctional requirements.
- They can define boundaries of a user story.
- They can define parameters of a user story.
- They must be clear and without ambiguity.
- They should be implementation independent.

Do you notice how many of these criteria are the same as those related to *shall* requirements as you have seen in this book? That is in part that many of existing requirements can help to define acceptance criteria. In addition, data elements were not talked about before with respect to user stories. That is because the theory states you should not provide them in the story. So, where else should you place them but in the acceptance criteria?

Now, look at some examples. For instance, here is user story 13-27 with acceptance criteria added:

> 13-52 (13-27) As a BOSS system administrator, I want the login to the BOSS system to require a user ID and password so that unauthorized users cannot easily break into the system.

Acceptance criteria:

1. The user ID will be unique within the system with a minimum of six alphanumeric characters.
2. The password will be a minimum of eight alphanumeric characters, with a mix of uppercase and lowercase characters, one or more numeric characters, and one special character from !@#$%^&*().

   Now reconsider user story 13-40 with acceptance criteria:

   13-53 (13-40) As a BOSS system administrator, I want no more than three login tries with password and user ID combination errors before the user ID is locked out of BOSS so that unauthorized users cannot easily break into the system.

Acceptance criteria:

1. The error can be an incorrect user ID but a correct password.
2. The error can be a correct user ID but an incorrect password.
3. The error can be an incorrect user ID and an incorrect password.

   Now you should also reconsider 13-39:

   13-54 (13-39) As a BOSS HR administrator, I want to be able to add a new employee to the HR system so that we track all of our active employees.

Acceptance criteria:

1. I want a User record to contain: a. Name, b. Work e-mail address, c. Work phone number d. Home mailing address, e. Home e-mail address, f. Home phone number, g. Cell phone number.

Keep in mind that acceptance criteria are useful as a foundation for the testers to craft their tests for a user story. Do realize that acceptance criteria are not required for a user story. Provide them when they help. This may seem counterintuitive. If you want to know when the user story is complete, then you need acceptance criteria. As an exercise, go back and look at all the user stories from the beginning of this chapter. Is there anywhere you do not feel acceptance criteria are needed? Is it only one or two? A dozen? More than half? Most of them? Chances are more than half do not need them. With experience, you will learn. During the discussion with the stakeholders, there statements associated with a user story will help to indicate if completion criteria are need.

Consider the following for the radiation dosimetry project:

> 13-55 As a commander in a nuclear battlefield, I want the standard dose rate meter to display the exposure rate by the soldier activating the meter so that soldier can capture the reading at the location allowing a radiation overlay to the map.

Acceptance criteria:

1. I want radiation exposure, date, time, and location information.
2. I want the ability to refine the scale, such that the detail can be tenths of Rads, single-digit Rads, tens of Rads, hundreds of Rads.

■ **Note** You have to be careful. Acceptance criteria #2 assumes a certain implementation. In this case, it assumes an analog display, whereas the development may be digital, allowing all the data to be display on one screen. The criteria in question were provided just to illustrate the types of information you might capture in an acceptance criteria.

From Anantha Narayanan's online article "User Story Acceptance Criteria: The Art of Satisficing and Bounded Rationality," we can consider certain aspects of acceptance criteria. First, acceptance criteria do not need to be an exhaustive list, just something that keeps communications moving forward. Just like the user story, the acceptance criteria can change with time. They can even be refined during the sprint.

Size of stories

Just as the concept of user stories came from XP, XP introduced the concept of what they call a *spike*.

Note Not everyone even uses this term. I was introduced to it while researching this book even though I had used it. We just called the first user story the research user story and the second story the implementation user story. The titles are different, but the concepts are the same.

There are some instances where the definition of the user story is insufficient—not that the story is wrong or not small enough, just that the developers do not have sufficient understanding to correctly estimate what it will take to fully implement it.

Experience shows that the first user story can be done in one sprint and then the second in a later sprint. It was not always immediately after the first sprint, as the team may need specific tools that they did not have and needed to acquire them, which took additional time.

It could be the team does not understand all the technical challenges associated with a story, so they need to do some research or maybe some exploration. They may need to prototype multiple options and see which the stakeholders like at the demo at the end of the sprint. Believe it or not, this type of refinement goes a long way in keeping the stakeholders invested in the system by them helping with such decision making. What if it is to see whether a new technology brings benefit? It could be a particular programming technique or an automated test tool. Determinations of this type usually occur when the development team, including the testers, examines the user stories. They will determine whether a particular user story is a spike.

Assume they get to the following user story:

> 13-56 As a soldier on the nuclear battlefield, I need a device to capture gamma ray exposure between 200KeV and 1.00 MeV radiation exposures so that I know what I have been exposed to.

In this case, the developers do not know the precision of four candidate detection mechanism, so they want to test what they get.

Therefore, they might craft a new user story to test the exposure collection spectrum of each against their known radiation source. Once they complete it, they will determine which one meets their needs and then write an implementation user story against the decided device.

The two stories could look like this:

> 13-57 As the radiation dosimeter developer, I will test Devices A, B, C, and D against gamma ray exposure between 200KeV and 1.00 MeV energies against our simulated tactical nuclear radiation device so that I can determine the accuracy of each device. (Reference user story 13-56.)
>
> 13-58 As the radiation dosimeter developer, I will integrate the chosen device (from story 13-57) into the BOSS Unit Radiation Dosimeter device so that I implement the optimum collection device. (Reference user story 13-56.)

It is always useful to reference to the original user story and the two spike users stories to keep traceability.

You could have the following for the FBI Records Management project:

> 13-59 As an FBI records manager, I want the BOSS Records Management System to suggest record categories consistent with the NARA General Records Schedule so that I can save time by accepting good suggestions.

When the developers first examine this user story, they need time to investigate the best approach. They may suggest the following two stories:

> 13-60 As an FBI records manager developer, I want to examine the three candidate machine learning approaches to suggest record categories consistent with the NARA General Records Schedule of the BOSS Records Management System so that I can choose the best approach. (Reference user story 13-59.)
>
> 13-61 As the FBI records manager developer, I will implement the chosen approach (from story 13-60) into the BOSS Records Management System so that I implement the optimum machine learning approach to suggest record categories consistent with the NARA General Records Schedule. (Reference user story 13-59.)

Another reason to consider a spike is that the story may be too big to be estimated appropriately. The developers may use the spike to analyze the behavior in order to split the story into estimable pieces.

In addition, this spike approach should be used sparingly. If it seems to be happening a lot, it would indicate other potential problems, like under-trained developers, the user stories are not well-defined, or stakeholders are not providing good insights into their needs. Monitor it, and if they happen 1 or 2 percent of the time, you are OK, but if it is 10 or more percent, you are in the problem area.

Complement vs. Supplement to Requirements

In this and the next section, you are going to learn about whether you need to write *shall* statement requirements with user stories or not. This section will talk about how *shall* statements can complement user stories, so in this section, the answer is yes to *shall* statement with user stories.

Complement to Requirements

Actually, this discussion of whether or not to capture *shall* statements reverberates in the industry. The position here is that generally *shall* statements provide added value when used in concert with user stories. The "Acceptance Criteria" section talked about using requirements as candidate acceptance criteria. Obviously, that is one candidate area to exploit requirements within a project.

■ **Real-World Note** Go back to the discussion about my troubled requirements collection for that one project where we collected user stories with the stakeholders instead. You may not remember it as it was way back in Chapter 1, so here it is again:

> On a recent project, I had begun capturing the requirements the traditional way. In six to eight months, I had managed to capture the requirements for only the search function of the system. We had about a dozen major functional areas like this. The program manager was extremely frustrated by the lack of cooperation from the stakeholders, which was epitomized when she said, "It's going to take us five years at this rate!" Thus, a new approach was needed.

■ That new approach taken was to capture user stories, and it worked well. It took a year and a half to capture all the user stories for this large and complex system. Did the project use or write requirements? Of course. The project needed those detailed requirements to pass to the designers, developers, and testers. They did not need to be vetted with the stakeholders. Well, that was not entirely true; the project had special stakeholders involved like DBAs, system admins, and even developers and testers to ensure they were represented well, and the project allowed everyone to comment on and improve the *shall* statements.

You have heard all the reasons for writing the acceptance criteria. They are valid. The requirements that are allocated to a story are the respective acceptance criteria for the user story. No doubt this position on user stories will spawn discussion or even argument on the Web. Remember, purists are doing it to substantiate their theories. The reality of it is—if it works, do it.

Note For the successful agile developments I have worked, we did use both user stories and *shall* statement, and not always because of me. As for theory versus reality, see my discussion on availability calculations in the "What Can Go Wrong with Writing User Stories?" section of this chapter.

Replacement for Requirements

The previous section said *shall* statements complement user stories. This section will talk about how user stories replace *shall* statements. There are experts who advocate that well-crafted user stories do not require *shall* statements because if the stories are captured correctly, you do not need to capture *shall* statements.

I have given my preference in the previous section. It is my philosophy that more detail is better. Given the level of detail provided by user stories, they give a significant amount of detail. One big improvement of user stories, as stated earlier in this chapter, is that user stories explain why the need is important, which *shall* statements do not. If acceptance criteria are provided with the user story, much of the lower level of detail a *shall* statement would provide can be addressed by these criteria. Thus, user stories can and do replace *shall* statements.

That said, I have worked with user stories without *shall* statements because if the stories are captured correctly, you do not need to capture *shall* as well.

On one of the smaller systems, a development team of only three people, the team did not use *shall* statements. In this particular case, I was not actually responsible for crafting user stories, but I just provided oversight and suggestions, as another branch was responsible for the user stories. The approach worked because the development team knew the system very well and did all the testing, and adding *shall* statements would not have provided a significant value-added. More importantly, the system was not nearly as complex as most other applications that it interacted with. Therefore, a point to consider is the size of the development team, their knowledge base of the system, and the size and complexity of the system.

Which way you go for your organization is your call—unless your organization has made the call for you. That said, if there are issues with the requirements process, you might want to consider a change that would improve it.

In the case that user stories have been used in place of requirements, you need to provide more detail in the acceptance criteria, which you know from the previous section that this is essentially *shall* statement requirements, even if they do not have the word *shall* in them.

User Stories Traceability

In situations where you have *shall* statements with user stories, there is one important function you should always do. After you have all the user stories and requirements done, map every requirement to a user story. Sometimes it may be two or more user stories to a requirement. Purists might insist that it should be one user story to one or more requirements. While that is an admirable goal, it is not an absolute. Otherwise, for some unique situation, you might not be able to make it work.

For example, you have the following requirement:

> 13-1(RQMT) The system shall allow a locked user ID to be unlocked.

Looking back to the previous user stories, here's another example:

> 13-62 (13-41) As a BOSS system administrator, I want the lockout of a user ID to be unlocked after 30 minutes so that the user can try again without requiring sys admin to unlock it.

■ **Note** Requirement 13-62 (13-41) may make it easier for hackers, just FYI.

> 13-63 (13-42) As a BOSS system administrator, I want the lockout of a user ID to be unlocked after 24 hours so that the user can try again without requiring the sys admin to unlock it.

> 13-64 (13-43) As a BOSS system administrator, I want the system admin to unlock the lockout of a user ID so that I control who can access the system.

You should trace the requirement to all three user stories.

Experience shows that you should not be constrained to map one requirement to only one user story. It is a goal, but not a hard-and-fast rule based on experience. Just make certain the requirements are atomic as was taught to you in Chapter 2; then you will probably not go wrong.

For the radiation dosimeter project, you have the following requirement:

> 13-2(RQMT) The BOSS radiation system shall be painted with standard U.S. Army camouflage paint to match the soldier's uniform.

You might have the following user stories:

> 13-65 As a soldier operating in the desert, I need a radiation dosimeter that will blend with the desert environment so that the dosimeter does not stand out and give away my position.

> 13-66 As a soldier operating in the woodlands, I need a radiation dosimeter that will blend with the woodlands environment so that the dosimeter does not stand out and give away my position.

> 13-67 As a soldier operating in the arctic, I need a radiation dosimeter that will blend with the arctic environment so that the dosimeter does not stand out and give away my position.

At first blush, as in the previous "locked user ID" example, you might think you could just map requirement 13-2 to user stories 13-65, 13-66, and 13-67. However, that is incorrect. Requirement 13-2 clearly is not atomic. It should be rewritten as follows:

> 13-3(RQMT) The BOSS radiation system shall be painted with standard U.S. Army desert camouflage paint to match the soldier's uniform.
>
> 13-4(RQMT) The BOSS radiation system shall be painted with standard U.S. Army woodlands camouflage paint to match the soldier's uniform.
>
> 13-5(RQMT) The BOSS radiation system shall be painted with standard U.S. Army arctic camouflage paint to match the soldier's uniform.

You have used the user stories as a sanity check for the correctness of the requirements. This is something you need to examine during your mapping between requirements and user stories.

Once you have mapped everything, you might find some requirements that do not have user stories. Sometimes these processes do not fit within user stories. This is getting to some of the limitations of user stories. How do you write a user story for reliability for a system or query performance? This gets harder. However, more on that shortly. Then look for all the user stories that do not have any requirements associated with them. That means you are missing some requirements. Write them.

What you are doing is the gap analysis for both the user stories and the requirements. This is an excellent time to check your user stories and requirements against the checklist of functional and nonfunctional requirements to ensure that you cover everything, even if the users and stakeholders do not think of it.

■ **Real-World Note** A good way to compare and contrast user stories and requirements is to perform the following steps. First, I load all the user stories into Microsoft Word or Microsoft Excel. Second, I load all requirements in a spreadsheet. Third, I map all requirements to user stories. Fourth, I map all user stories to requirements. Finally, I look for that cells in the table that are empty, and these are the areas where there are gaps. New requirements and new user stories are required.

Even if you do user stories first and then the requirements, you should still do this step as a quality check on your work. You may be surprised how much you still missed. First, you need to find out whether there are requirements that have no user stories. If so, write the appropriate user stories. Of course, if there are user stories that have no requirements, add the requirements. This is a good check and balance.

There is one other source to help with gap analysis. You can use the Business Process Description to craft the user stories. This is usually an excellent way to do it. It also provides sources that you may have forgotten in the user stories and/or requirements. All the information is in one spot, and it is relatively easy to do them. Granted, for a large system, it could be hundreds of user stories. Even for smaller systems, several dozen user stories are needed to cover a small application to include the hardware on which it will reside. Do not ever forget that.

Maintain User Stories

One other aspect regarding the previous system was the work initially was in the operations and maintenance phase. Some new development was added, but that is not the point here. This is an important facet of this phase that you need to be aware of. When maintaining an existing system, user requests will come in that are specific to the user interface. For example, you might get something like the following:

> 13-68 As an FBI BOSS Audit Screen, I want the person who performed the action listed on one line and what action they took displayed on the line below so that I see the information without having to scan around the screen.

Immediately, your "implementation-specific" alarms should be going off (if you have learned well). You are not supposed do this kind of user story, just like you are not supposed to do implementation in *shall* statements. Some renegotiation is needed for user story 13-68 to get it closer to what the users want and the developers and testers need.

Here's another example that you may see:

> 13-69 As a Form Requester user, I need the form selection tab to include a list of the HR forms in one column, the Payroll forms in the second column, and the Procurement forms in a third column so that I can find the forms more quickly.

If you follow the INVEST approach, this story might need to be rewritten. However, would you want to? The user is asking for a specific change to the user interface that needs to be improved. These are not bad stories, as the users need improvements to the existing implementation. This is not the same situation when there is no design, where you do not want to constrain the designers. Here, the user is asking for a specific change. Rather than set up an entirely different process, go ahead and keep the paradigm of user stories if that suits your projects.

Another request may come in for the radiation dosimeter project where someone says the following:

> 13-70 As a soldier operating in the multiple areas of the world, I need the ability to repaint the radiation dosimeter from either desert, arctic, or woodland camouflage color to one of the other environments so that I do not need three or more different dosimeters.

Clearly this is a valid need, and it is implementation specific. Should you leave this one this way? Possibly not. What if the developers can create a technique for automatically changing the color without repainting it? Maybe it is like the original Kindle that had a black side and a white side to each minute ball that created each pixel, where they have three (or more) "faces" for the pixels on the outside of the dosimeter. Therefore, you might want to change it to read as follows:

> 13-71 As a soldier operating in the multiple areas of the world, I need a the ability to **change** the radiation dosimeter from either desert, arctic, or woodland camouflage color to one of the other environments so that I do not need three or more different dosimeters.

Notice that only one word changed from user story 13-70 to user story 13-71. Yes, sometimes it is as simple as modifying only one word. Clearly, user story 13-71 is better than 13-70, as you have learned.

In addition, you are going to find many, if not most, maintenance-type user stories might be written like user stories 13-68 and 13-69.

> This is not a bad thing.

Why? The major reason is that when you capture user stories for a development effort, you are supposed to give the developers free reign since there is no existing system that they are basing the effort on (even if there is a legacy system, that does not have bearing). Therefore, people will want tweaks and adjustments to the current implementation. Unlike *shall* statements where there is the potential of design specifications created by the developers, user stories do not necessarily have the equivalent. Thus, user stories are the only venue for communicating this information. Therefore, during O&M, it is acceptable to create implementation user stories. Again, certain theorists may argue this point. Remember the philosophy—if it works, do it.

What Can Go Wrong with Writing User Stories?

Remember how Chapter 1 talked about how agile and waterfall compared? Here it is again to refresh your memory.

Agile	42% successful, 49% challenged, 9% failure
Waterfall	14% successful, 57% challenged, 29% failure

As before, this is a significant improvement over the waterfall approach. Again, one of the significant factors is that the work is subdivided down to a very manageable level.

That said, agile had a 9 percent failure rate. Is the agile methodology responsible for that? Experience shows that the answer is no because there are so many other factors that were talked that could cause any approach to fail such as bad management, lack of resources, too short of schedule, and so on. Ideally, what you have learned has mitigated the requirements/user story definition phase issues.

Does this mean that user stories are the pinnacle of requirements technology? While they go a long way to fix requirements problems, they still have some limitations. Because each user story is intended to be accomplished in an individual sprint, some areas that you need to define do not fit well. Nonfunctional requirements, especially performance, are much harder to capture as a user story. Remember, the "Administrative Functions" section in Chapter 5 stated the following requirement:

> 5-54 (RQMT) The BOSS system shall be available 99.99% of the time.

How would it look as a user story?

> 13-72 As a BOSS user, I want the system to be available 99.9% of the time so that the system provides the availability I need since it is a mission-critical function.

That sounds like a reasonable user story, and on the surface, it is. However, can that be accomplished in one sprint? Assume the development team has six user stories it is responsible for developing in a given sprint. Does this apply to each user story? Technically, yes. So, how does the tester verify that it is accomplished? What about all the work that has been accomplished before the sprint in question? Does the availability user story apply to them? Yes. Now you start to see the conundrum.

Clearly, that user story is not something that can be done in one sprint. In fact, every service in the system, and even every functional area, must contribute to that. How do you overcome this?

For this example, assume you have ten functions within BOSS for this example. Then, write a user story for each function like the following:

> 13-73 As a BOSS user, I need the BOSS Function1 availability to be 99.99% so that I can perform my work on that function.

Notice, the focus has been on the function level, where a given function can be worked at the sprint level. Also, notice that the availability changed from 99.9% for the system to 99.99% to accommodate that you have ten pieces.

In this example, the original BOSS availability is a theme rather than an individual user story, and the ten functional availabilities are the user stories you will allocate to sprints.

Then there is the issue of how to verify this user story. That is something you should always consider when writing a user story. It can be done, albeit it is a challenge. Defining "how" is for the testers to accomplish, and that is why they get paid the big bucks. At least you should be able to conceive of a reasonable test. If you can, you have done your due diligence. The key word was "reasonable." If the verification required places a device on the dark side of the moon, that probably is not reasonable.

The Rally Help web page article titled “Write a Great User Story” talks about the top mistakes that people make. The potential areas are as follows:

- *Too formal or too much detail*: Stakeholders and users may write extremely detailed user stories. One fix to this is to include that information in the acceptance criteria. That way the good information is not lost, but it does not complicate the user story. Otherwise, if developers and testers see a very detailed story during the sprint planning, they might see all the details are present and may skip the detailed conversation. Communication is the central point of the user story, so do not do anything that will limit or restrict it.
- *Technical tasks masquerading as stories*: The success of agile largely comes from having a working piece of software at the end of a sprint. If some stories are just technical tasks, you may not end up with working code at the end of the sprint. This may be fixed by making it a spike as was talked about in the “Size of Stories” section in this chapter.
- *Skipping the conversation*: Stories may be vague before iteration planning. If you skip the acceptance criteria conversation, you can move in the wrong direction, miss boundary cases, overlook customer needs, and. most importantly, miss important communications—the hallmark of the agile process.

Summary

User stories with acceptance criteria are some of the best techniques you have as a requirements engineer. Take advantage of them. You have seen advantages, of which there are many, and disadvantages, which usually you can overcome. The point is to decide what approach you will use and stick with it. User stories are a sound approach to use. Decide whether you will include *shall* statements, but do what is necessary to capture the stakeholders’ needs.

References

Wake, Bill. “Invest in Good Stories and Smart Tasks.” August 17, 2003. *xp123 Exploring Extreme Programming*. Feb. 2015, `http://xp123.com/articles/invest-in-good-stories-and-smart-tasks/`

“What Characteristics Make Good Agile Acceptance Criteria?” March 25, 2013. Segue Technologies Inc. `www.seguetech.com/blog/2013/03/25/characteristics-good-agile-acceptance-criteria`

Narayanan, Anantha. “User Story Acceptance Criteria: The Art of Satisficing and Bounded Rationality,” 20 January 2012, *Scrum Alliance*. Feb. 2015, `https://www.scrumalliance.org/community/articles/2012/january/user-story-acceptance-criteria-the-art-of-satisfic`

Roth, Ronica. "Write a Great User Story." *Rally Help*. Feb. 2015, `https://help.rallydev.com/writing-great-user-story`

Exercises

Exercise 1

Look at this user story from the beginning of the chapter:

> 13-1 As a taxpayer submitting my taxes, I want the form instructions written to a fifth-grade reading level so that 99% of the taxpayers will understand what they are filling out on the form.

Does this user story meet the criteria discussed in this chapter? Why or why not?

Exercise 2

Write a user story (or stories) where the user needs to enter a user ID, password, and domain name. A domain name means that there is more than one particular location that a person could access the system. It is not important what these are, just that a person needs to enter a valid one. Include any appropriate acceptance criteria.

Exercise 3

In the individual dosimeter project you have been examining throughout this book, please identify user stories for this project. Rather than use an interview with stakeholders, use the requirements you have collected during the course of this book. (Yes, this isn't the ideal way to do it. The world is not always ideal, so this helps train you to use whatever you may have on hand.) Then, map all those requirements to the user stories. Have you found any gaps? Are they gaps in the user stories or requirements?

Exercise 4

Write user stories for your cell phone—not all the apps, just the basic needs of the phone portion.

Exercise 5

Will ten functions with an availability of 99.99 percent combine to be 99.9 percent for the entire system? Why or why not?

Exercise 6

Write some user stories to describe what the Radiation Dose Rate Mapping Laptop should do based on the description of this segment of the system described in the "Radiation Dosimetry Project" section in Chapter 1.

CHAPTER 14

Use Cases

Remember, Chapter 12 talked about how Usability.gov provides some good information on use cases. They say that a use case is "a written description of how users will perform tasks on your" system. You are going to spend some more time examining use cases so you can become familiar with them and learn when it is a good time to use them.

Part of the reason for use cases is that usually people do not capture these types of ordered requirements when writing *shall* statements. Use cases help to fix this.

Also, as you have seen in Chapter 12, use cases are written in plain English, albeit they are more structured than user stories, so it may take users and stakeholders a bit more time to understand them than user stories, but certainly they are much easier to comprehend than, say, 1,000 *shall* statements.

Note The goal is not to make you an expert in use cases. That said, you will receive sufficient information to be able to begin crafting use cases when you have the opportunity. However, most importantly, you should be able to read use cases and understand their benefits and disadvantages.

Writing Use Cases

In this section, you will learn the elements that make up a use case and the details that go into those elements and why you do it. Remember, use cases are excellent at capturing the sequencing of steps, which *shall* statements and user stories are not as good at. Use cases show all the branches, like a scenario, which has excellent use for testing as well as for understanding all the aspects of a particular need.

Use Case Sequence

Chapter 6 introduced ordering steps with the following sequence:

G. Koelsch, *Requirements Writing for System Engineering*,
DOI 10.1007/978-1-4842-2099-3_14

> Think of what you do when you sit down at your computer for the time in the morning, with it turned off. For example, in my case, I...turn it on. Wait, maybe I plug it in (when I am traveling). Then I turn it on and wait for the desktop to come up. I call up my applications I want open. I do my e-mail app first to check e-mail and have available for research. Then I open the word processor so I can write my books. I call up the file manager so I can open various files that may not be in my recent list in the word processor. (I break books into chapters for drafting them, but that is my peculiarity.) What you do may be different, but you get the idea.

Now you will learn how to capture what is described in free text in a more structure approach. Chapter 12 introduced the elements you should include in a use case, based on what Usability.gov provided for us.

- *Unique Identifier*: Any identifying system, alpha and/or numeric.
- *Title*: An identifier or name of the use case. It's highly recommended that it consists of a verb and noun at the very minimum.
- *Description*: A brief description of the purpose of the use case.
- *Actor*: Anyone or anything (another system, such as an application or device) that performs a behavior: basically who or what is using the system. This is not limited to one actor.
- *Preconditions*: What must be true or happen before the use case runs.
- *Postconditions*: What must be true or happen after the use case runs.
- *Triggers*: This is the event that causes the use case to be initiated.
- *Main success scenarios (aka basic flow)*: Use case in which nothing goes wrong. (This is also known as Normal Flow/Scenario, Primary Flow/Scenario.)
- *Alternative paths (aka alternative flow)*: These paths are a variation on the main theme. These exceptions are what happen when things go wrong at the system level or an alternate condition causes a change to the basic flow. (This is also known as *extensions*.)

There are optional fields you might consider:

- *Exception flows*: Error conditions that happen. This will be discussed more shortly as a variation of alternative flows. Not all use cases may have this.
- *Business rules*: Rules that influence or affect the use case. Not all use cases may have this (specific examples of these won't be provided because they do not always happen).

- *Special requirements and assumptions*: Additional factors that affect the use case. Not all use cases may have this (specific examples of these won't be provided because they do not always happen).

Here is that earlier example of a use case:

Unique Identifier	14-1.
Title	Dial a phone number.
Description	Use your cell phone to enter a phone number.
Actor	Phone users.
Preconditions	Actor has a cell phone.
Postconditions	The phone connects to the number called.
Triggers	A need to call someone.
Basic Flow	1. Turn on the cell phone. 2. Select the dial option/app. 3. Key in the number. 4. The phone rings.
Alternative Flow	2. Select from a list. 3. Select the dial option/app. 4. Choose the number from the list provide. 5. Tap the number desired. 6. The phone rings.

This use case fills in all the data elements of a use case. Additionally, you see the how low level a use case should be. Nothing should be skipped. A developer and a tester would be able to work from this. More importantly, a user and a stakeholder should be able to understand it and either agree with it or correct it. Now you will look at another use case.

Login Use Case

However, look at some other examples. Remember when Chapter 13, in the "Attributes of a User Story" section, talked about the access control? The following is a use case for logging onto the system. You may want to look back at the user stories to see what they cover.

Unique Identifier	14-2.
Title	Log in to the BOSS System.
Description	Gain entry into the BOSS System.
Actor	BOSS system users.
Preconditions	Actor has been enrolled in the BOSS system.

Post conditions	The actor gains access to the BOSS system.
Triggers	A need to use the BOSS system.
Basic Flow	1. Activate the BOSS system. 2. Move into user ID designated area. 3. Enter your user ID. 4. Move into password-designated area. 5. Enter your password. 6. Activate the user ID/password validation.
Alternative Flow	

The alternative flow was left blank since what alternate flows exist yet have not been examined. First, consider a "cancel" option because you might inadvertently activate the wrong option.

■ **Note** It happens. As experienced as I am, I am not perfect. Just ask my wife.

You will write "cancel" as an alternate flow for the 14-2 use case by writing the specific steps associated with this alternate flow. Choose the "cancel" option first before entering the user ID as an alternative flow. Remember, you may allow cancelation at any point before step 6 in the basic flow, but that also is left to you as an exercise. Therefore, you want to quit the login process, so you have the following alternative flow:

Unique Identifier	14-2a.
Alternative Flow	Alternate to step 2. 2. Activate the Cancel option

---

■ **Note** The unique identifier here is to show the variation of the original use case without repeating all the data that does not change. Follow this approach in this subsection and the next. What this will show is information added to use case 14-2, so think of this as a progression as you write the complete use case.

What about having the option to select a previous value user ID entered so you do not have to enter the value every time?

■ **Note** Of course, the same approach of a pull-down menu could be done for the password, but that is a question you need to validate with your system administrators or security personnel to determine whether they want to allow you to do this.

Unique Identifier	14-2b.
Alternative Flow	Alternate to step 2. 2. Activate the Cancel option. Alternate to step 2. 2. When a drop-down appears with previous user IDs, select the one you want.

What about when someone enters an incorrect user ID or password into the login process? Say you enter the wrong user ID and/or password, such as transposing two letters. You can handle these situations in one of two ways. The first method is to present them as just alternative flows. Alternatively, some sources recommend a separate box titled "Exception Flow." Now, look at both methods of presenting them.

Unique Identifier	14-2c1.
Alternative Flow	Alternate to step 2. 2. Activate the Cancel option. Alternate to step 2. 2. When a drop-down appears with previous user IDs, select the one you want. Alternate added after step 6. User access is denied since user ID or password does not match what is in the system. Repeat steps 2 through 6.
Unique Identifier	14-2c2.
Alternative Flow	Alternate to step 2. 2. Activate the Cancel option. Alternate to step 2. 2. When a drop-down appears with previous user IDs, select the one you want.
Exception Flow	Added after step 6. 7. User access is denied since user ID or password does not match what is in the system. 8. Repeat steps 2 through 6.

Now you have one failure to enter a proper user ID-password combination. You need to see how it looks for a second failure.

Unique Identifier	14-2d1.
Alternative Flow	Alternate to step 2. 2. Activate the Cancel option. Alternate to step 2. 2. When a drop-down appears with previous user IDs, select the one you want Alternate added after step 6. 7. User access is denied since user ID or password does not match what is in the system. 8. Repeat steps 2 through 6. 9. User access is denied since user ID or password does not match what is in the system. 10. Repeat steps 2 through 6.
Unique Identifier	14-2cd2.
Alternative Flow	Alternate to step 2. 2. Activate the Cancel option. Alternate to step 2. 2. When a drop-down appears with previous user IDs, select the one you want.
Exception Flow	Added after step 6. 7. User access is denied since user ID or password does not match what is in the system. 8. Repeat steps 2 through 6. 9. User access is denied since user ID or password does not match what is in the system. 10. Repeat steps 2 through 6.

Now you have two failures to enter a proper user ID-password combination. You need to examine how it looks for the third and final failure.

Unique Identifier	14-2e1.
Alternative Flow	Alternate to step 2. 2. Activate the Cancel option. Alternate to step 2. 2. When a drop-down appears with previous user IDs, select the one you want. Alternate added after step 6. 7. User access is denied since user ID or password does not match what is in the system. 8. Repeat steps 2 through 6. 9. User access is denied since user ID or password does not match what is in the system. 10. Repeat steps 2 through 6. 11. User access is denied since user ID or password does not match what is in the system. 12. Repeat steps 2 through 6. 13. User access is denied since user ID or password does not match what is in the system and the login process is stopped and the user ID is locked.

Unique Identifier	14-2e2.
Alternative Flow	Alternate to step 2. 2. Activate the Cancel option. Alternate to step 2. 2. When a drop-down appears with previous user IDs, select the one you want.
Exception Flow	Added after step 6. 7. User access is denied since user ID or password does not match what is in the system. 8. Repeat steps 2 through 6. 9. User access is denied since user ID or password does not match what is in the system. 10. Repeat steps 2 through 6. 11. User access is denied since user ID or password does not match what is in the system. 12. Repeat steps 2 through 6. 13. User access is denied since user ID or password does not match what is in the system and the login process is stopped and the user ID is locked.

Back to alternative path versus exception path: some sources will say that this is an exception path and requires a separate box from alternates. This is not required. That is for you and your organization to decide if you want to include them together or have them separate. Flow will be used in this text for consistency; just know that path will work also. It is a preference only.

■ **Real-World Note** One source I read stated that access control is not a valid use case since this process does not provide value added to the user. I would disagree that giving someone access to a system provides a tool to the user. In addition, knowing that only authorized users access the system provides control to stakeholders of the system. I also believe that this particular use case provides an excellent example of the various aspects that comprise a use case.

Next, put the complete use case together after you have completed writing it.

Unique Identifier	14-2 (finished).
Title	Log in to the BOSS system.
Description	Gain entry into the BOSS system.
Actor	BOSS system users.
Preconditions	Actor has been enrolled in the BOSS system.
Post conditions	The actor gains access to the BOSS system.
Triggers	A need to use the BOSS system.
Basic Flow	Activate the BOSS system. Move into user ID designated area. Enter your user ID. Move into password-designated area. Enter your password. Activate the user ID/password validation.

Alternative Flow	Alternate to step 2. 2. Activate the Cancel option. Alternate to step 2. 2. When a drop-down appears with previous user IDs, select the one you want. Alternate added after step 6. 7. User access is denied since user ID or password does not match what is in the system. 8. Repeat steps 2 through 6. 9. User access is denied since user ID or password does not match what is in the system. 10. Repeat steps 2 through 6. 11. User access is denied since user ID or password does not match what is in the system. 12. Repeat steps 2 through 6. 13. User access is denied since user ID or password does not match what is in the system and the login process is stopped and the user ID is locked.

Next is the complete use case with all alternate flows and exception flows.

Unique Identifier	14-2 (finished).
Title	Log in to the BOSS system.
Description	Gain entry into the BOSS system.
Actor	BOSS system users.
Preconditions	Actor has been enrolled in the BOSS system.
Post conditions	The actor gains access to the BOSS system.
Triggers	A need to use the BOSS system.
Basic Flow	Activate the BOSS system. Move into user ID designated area. Enter your user ID. Move into password-designated area. Enter your password. Activate the user ID/password validation.

Alternative Flow	Alternate to step 2. 2. Activate the Cancel option. Alternate to step 2. 2. When a drop-down appears with previous user IDs, select the one you want.
Exception Flow	Added after step 6. 7. User access is denied since user ID or password does not match what is in the system. 8. Repeat steps 2 through 6. 9. User access is denied since user ID or password does not match what is in the system. 10. Repeat steps 2 through 6. 11. User access is denied since user ID or password does not match what is in the system. 12. Repeat steps 2 through 6. 13. User access is denied since user ID or password does not match what is in the system and the login process is stopped and the user ID is locked.

As with user stories and *shall* statements, clarity is important. The structure of a use case does not mean that it instantaneously becomes clear and understandable. You, as the RE, must provide that clarity. Certainly, the structure helps by providing a template, but it still ultimately falls to you.

As a final point, look at that box that has the Basic Flow, Alternate Flow, and Exception Flow fields. That is very good information for helping with the development of test cases and procedures. Look specifically at Exception Flow, specifically the three strikes rule for accessing the system. Where does it indicate what can be wrong? It says a user ID-password combination that is wrong. A tester would need to test all possible combinations. They would need to try three wrong user IDs, three wrong passwords, two wrong user IDs and one wrong password, and one wrong user ID and two wrong passwords. Thus, a use case does not provide every single detail of both the developer and tester needs, but it is better than a user story.

Unit Dosimetry Report Use Case

Now, look at another use case. In this case, go back to the radiation dosimetry example project, for the Dosimeter Archive Laptop introduced in Chapter 1 and discussed Chapters 2, 4, 5, and 8. Specific requirements related to the project include

- *Chapter 2*: Requirements 2-21 to 2-32
- *Chapter 4*: Requirements 4-38, 4-71, 4-72, and 4-74
- *Chapter 5*: Requirements 5-5, 5-8, 5-13, 5-14, 5-23, and 5-42
- *Chapter 8*: Requirements 8-9, 8-14, and 8-15

In this case, after data has been collected from a unit after leaving a nuclear fallout area, the medical officer needs a report on the medical readiness of the unit. Therefore, you might have the following use case:

Unique Identifier	14-3.
Title	Run the BOSS Unit Dosimetry Report.
Description	Call up the BOSS Unit Dosimetry canned report.
Actor	Users of the Unit Dosimetry Report: Medical officer, unit commander.
Preconditions	The unit has been exposed to nuclear radiation, the soldiers wear individual radiation detectors, and the user has access to the BOSS dosimetry system.
Post conditions	The report is provided either in hard copy or soft copy.
Triggers	A user has a need for the Unit Dosimetry Report.
Basic Flow	1. Activate the BOSS Dosimetry reporting capability. 2. Select the Unit Dosimetry Report. 3. Select the unit that has been affected. 4. Identify the start date that indicates when the first exposures should be considered. 5. Identify the end date that indicates when the first exposures should be considered. 6. Indicate if the report will be hard copy or soft copy. 7. Activate the report execution.
Alternative Flow	Alternate to step 2. 2. Enter in a new unit designation since it is not on the list. Insert a new step 7. 7. Turn on printer. 8. Activate the report execution.

It is possible that additional alternative flows exist depending on if this report defaults to just a listing of each soldier and the exposure each has. For example, there may be options in the report for some summary values such as average exposure (totals mean nothing), people who exceed specific levels, highest exposure, *x* number of highest exposures, which the user may have available to them, and so on. In that case, you might expand the alternate flows as follows:

Unique Identifier	14-3a.
Alternative Flow	Alternate to step 2. 2. Enter a new unit designation since it is not on the list. Insert a new step 7. 7. Turn on printer . 8. Activate the report execution. Insert a new step 7. 7. Select average exposure. 8. Activate the report execution. Insert a new step 7. 7. Select display of the highest exposure. 8. Activate the report execution. Insert a new step 7. 7. Select display of the highest n-values exposures, where the n value is entered in. 8. Activate the report execution.

Look at those last three alternatives. What happens if the user wants more than one or any combination of the three? Can you rewrite it to be more flexible? Of course. See the following alternative flows.

Unique Identifier	14-3b.
Alternative Flows	Alternate to step 2. 2. Enter in a new unit designation since it is not on the list. Insert a new step 7. 7. Turn on printer. 8. Activate the report execution. Insert a new step 7. 7. Select average exposure or not. 8. Select display of the highest exposure or not. 9. Select display of the highest n-values exposures, where the n value is entered in or not. 10. Activate the report execution.

As before, now look at the complete use case for this radiation dosimetry project.

Unique Identifier	14-3.
Title	Run the BOSS Unit Dosimetry Report.
Description	Call up the BOSS Unit Dosimetry canned report.
Actor	Users of the Unit Dosimetry Report: Medical officer, unit commander.

Preconditions	The unit has been exposed to nuclear radiation, the soldiers wear individual radiation detectors, and the user has access to the BOSS dosimetry system.
Post conditions	The report is provided either in hard copy or soft copy.
Triggers	A user has a need for the Unit Dosimetry Report.
Basic Flow	1. Activate the BOSS Dosimetry reporting capability. 2. Select the Unit Dosimetry Report. 3. Select the unit that has been affected. 4. Identify the start date that indicates when the first exposures should be considered. 5. Identify the end date that indicates when the first exposures should be considered. 6. Indicate if the report will be hard copy or soft copy. 7. Activate the report execution.
Alternative Flows	Alternate to step 2. 2. Enter in a new unit designation since it is not on the list. Insert a new step 7. 7. Turn on printer. 8. Activate the report execution. Insert a new step 7. 7. Select average exposure or not. 8. Select display of the highest exposure or not. 9. Select display of the highest n-values exposures, where the n value is entered in or not. 10. Activate the report execution.

You can see that a use case is much more detailed than a user story and provides more data than *shall* statements. One significant advantage use cases have over *shall* statements is that sequence of steps is addressed well.

In an agile environment, you could do roughed-out use cases and spend more effort completing the detail as the use cases are coming up on the backlog for implementation. Thus, you can use cases with agile.

While you have seen a template to invoke when crafting use cases, there is no industry standard. Therefore, this may be organizationally specific. Do not be surprised in your career that you find them implemented somewhat differently in various organizations. Keep in mind that even within the same company, you might find different implementations. Experience shows that groups, divisions, and offices have different cultures, which can influence how they apply processes, so do not be alarmed about differences. Learn what they do, and if you can learn why they do it, you will understand, and you may be able to influence refinements that might improve processes in the future.

Gap Analysis

How will you know when you have all the use cases you need? That is the same challenge you had with *shall* statements and user stories. Apply the same techniques. Remember in Chapter 9 when you learned about writing a Business Process Description (BPD) document? Now is one of those times when a BPD will become useful. In fact, if you wrote the BPD document properly, it should go a long way to defining use cases, in that you should write in a logical, process flow manner, just like the users of the system would experience.

In the *shall* statement analysis, you had to perform gap analysis. That also applies here. How easy is it to ensure that all aspects of every use case are captured? With *shall* statements, you have detailed statements that address each point. With use cases, there is much more detail, and with the overlap potential between use cases, there is the possibility of small gaps appearing adjacent to these use cases. It may be that you are missing some alternative flows that are not obvious to you. Alternatively, they are just miniscule but separate use cases that are not obvious. It does not mean that you cannot find them, but it may be challenging.

When you are planning to craft your use cases, it is advisable to make a list of all your actors for your system. For example, for your BOSS HR system, you might have the following:

- *HR personnel user*: Someone who handles all the information about a person in your organization
- *HR payroll user*: Someone who handles all the payroll information about a person in your organization
- *HR retirement user*: Someone who handles all the retirement information about a person in your organization
- *Employee*: Someone who accesses the BOSS HR system to view the information about them
- *HR system administrator*: Someone who handles all the maintenance of the BOSS HR system

There may be more, but that is dependent on what is included in the system. Also, examine the actors for the BOSS dosimetry system, where you might have the following:

- *Soldier*: Soldier in the nuclear battlefield who wears a radiation detector
- *Radiation data collector*: Person who reads the individual radiation detectors
- *Medical officer*: User who needs to know the immediate and long-term implications of radiation exposure
- *Commanders*: Unit commander or higher who needs to know the status of his or her soldiers
- *Dosimetry equipment maintainer*: User who must maintain all the hardware and software for the entire system

You may notice overlap where two apparent different actors perform the same use case or use cases. In this case, you may want to redefine the actors such that the overlap is a new type of actor. The medical officer and commanders both have a need to know the immediate status of soldiers. Only the medical officers need the long-term effect—long-term means years out—say for Veterans Administration purposes, after the soldier leaves service. Therefore, maybe you consider the following redefinement to these two actors:

1. *People who need immediate status*: Commanders and medical officers who need to know the immediate status of the soldiers
2. *People who need long-term status*: Medical officers who need to know the long-term effects to the soldiers

Once you have listed each actor, list the potential use cases for each actor, as in Table 14-1 for the HR system and Table 14-2 for the radiation dosimetry system. These tables include likely use cases but may not be exhaustive. Of course, the use cases for your organization will likely be different.

Table 14-1. *BOSS HR System Actors and Use Cases*

Actor	Use Case Name
HR Personnel user	• Add new employee • Update employee information • Terminate employee
HR Payroll user	• Add new payroll information • Update payroll information
HR Retirement user	• Add retirement information
Employee	• View employee information • Update employee information (not everything) • Request change to employee information
HR System Administrator	• Monitor system • Give access to system • Update access to system • Correct corrupted data • Generate new reports • Update reports • Delete outdated reports • Perform maintenance on system

Table 14-2. BOSS Radiation Dosimetry System

Actor	Use Case Name
Soldier	• Receive individual dosimeter • Submit individual dosimeter for reading • Submit individual dosimeter for calibration • Turn in individual dosimeter when leaving the unit
Radiation Data Collector	• Collect data from individual dosimeter
Medical Officer	• Determine the immediate military operational status of a soldier from a medical perspective • Determine the immediate military operational status of a unit from a medical perspective • Determine the long-term medical impacts of a soldier
Commanders	• Determine the immediate military operational status of a soldier from a military perspective • Determine the immediate military operational status of a unit from a military perspective
Dosimetry Equipment Maintainer	• Calibrate individual dosimeters • Maintain calibration source • Maintain individual dosimeter reader • Maintain computer that receives data from readers • Maintain computer software

The next step would be to craft the use cases listed. This would follow the normal elicitation techniques you have already learned. It is just that you organize the data somewhat differently from user stories and *shall* statements. Remember, the biggest benefit to use cases is the stepwise sequencing of steps that *shall* statements are not as good at capturing. Also, you capture the alternate and exception flows. All this together provides complete interaction that *shall* statements do not by themselves without significant textual description associated with them.

One other aspect to consider for gap analysis, similar to what you do for user stories, is that you should map existing *shall* statements to use cases. Not only will this indicate potential *shall* statements you may have missed, but also, just like in user stories, you may find orphaned requirements that may need use cases.

Next, you will examine the advantages and disadvantages of use cases.

Advantages and Disadvantages of Use Cases

Just as you examined user stories for advantages and disadvantages, you will not look at each for use cases.

Advantages

A collection of easy-to-read use cases can be much easier to work with than, say, a list of 1,000 *shall* statements. They also capture the flow that *shall* statements generally do not. Chapter 6 made a serious attempt to capture this for *shall* statements. That said, it does not capture the same level of detail as a use case, especially when you consider alternative flows and exceptions that are difficult to capture. Even user stories do not capture these as well.

The use case approach does provide a benefit that user story definition also provides. Not only is it more readable than the *shall* statements, but it creates and maintains engagement of the users and stakeholders. This is because they have a say in what gets built as well as having a presentation of the requirements in a more understandable format.

The article "Use Cases" on Usability.gov says that this about the benefits of use cases:

> *Use cases add value because they help explain how the system should behave and in the process, they also help brainstorm what could go wrong. They provide a list of goals and you can use this list to establish the cost and complexity of the system. Project teams can then negotiate which functions become requirements and are built.*

Clearly understanding how a system should work is absolutely important. Additionally, knowing what aspects might deviate from the norm or go awry is nearly as important. Actually, the alternate flows and exceptions/error conditions are aspects that are not captured well by *shall* statements and certainly not by user stories. Alternate flows and exceptions are not always well understood when capturing requirements. In fact, it could be alternate flow and exception conditions needs are not traditionally explored well in business process analysis, requirements definition, and even design. People may spend time considering "what-if" during analysis (something science-fiction writers have been doing for more than 100 years). However, "what-if... else..." has not always been examined. These use cases give the ability to examine every aspect of a potential system, thereby helping in the gap analysis. This use case approach provides more context to the requirements than do user stories and *shall* statements.

The last two sentences in the Usability.gov benefits statement are not unique to use cases, as they are similar to user stories. If you understand that the "list of goals" is essentially the titles of each use case, you see that it is the same as the names of all the user stories. Alas, *shall* statements do not have the same type of "goal." Yes, *shall* statements can have section headings, but that does not necessarily have the same granularity and scope as either a use case or a user story.

Use cases have a good structure, shown in the "Writing Use Cases" section in this chapter in great detail. This will help not only you to craft a good use case, but also assist the stakeholders in reading and comprehending the use case. Use it and be consistent with it. Don't change the structure around within a project. Define your structure and stick with it. Of course, if it becomes apparent in a project that changes need to be made, then do it to all use cases for consistency. Otherwise, you will confuse the people who read it.

■ **Real-World Note** For the several different projects that used the agile methodology during my career, I have written use cases only once. It should be interesting to note that on that project the use cases were not presented to users and stakeholders—only internally to the development team. Does this mean you should not present them to stakeholders? No, that is not the intent at all. This was a management decision made before I came to the project. During my tenure on the project, there was no need to change that. In fact, with only a little guidance from you, you can present use cases to stakeholders. I just had not experienced it myself.

The "Gap Analysis" subsection discussed how the use case approach assists significantly in identifying gaps as you craft use cases. Not only does the listing of actors and their associated use case titles help with this, but also the alternate and exceptions flows help to mitigate many if not most of the potential gaps in the requirements analysis.

The "Login Use Case" subsection talked about the significant advantage the detail provided in the use case gives the testers. While user stories have acceptance criteria, use cases have much more detail to help in crafting test cases and test procedures. It provides more detail, just not all the detail, as you will see in the next subsection.

Another advantage use cases have over user stories and *shall* statements is that use cases provide more information that can be used for documentation, such as user manuals and design documents. Just as with the test documentation, use cases provide a foundation upon which to build from, just not all the detail that is needed for these documents.

Disadvantages

As was said before, use cases often are not quite as well understood by users and stakeholders as user stories. You have to decide if educating your user base on the exploitation of use cases is worth the investment in time. Given the advantages discussed, it might be. That said, there are some challenges with using them.

Use cases are not so good for system-centric functions like batch processing, data warehouses, and computationally intensive functions. How would you represent a complex algorithm? Think of the software to control an interplanetary spacecraft, with significant mathematical calculations. Who are the actors—gravity that affects every object in space? The spacecraft itself? Or the controllers back at NASA? What about the equations that represent celestial mechanics or orbital mechanics? They are complex when you talk about sending a spacecraft from the Earth to, say, Mars. How do you show every step of an equation?

In addition, nonfunctional requirements, especially performance, are harder to capture. They have no actors, and they do not have alternate flow readily apparent. Additionally, many users are not comfortable trying to understand this structure.

Wikipedia's "Use Case" article states that "there is a misconception that a use case is not agile." That is true if all use cases must be completely written at one time. This use case approach may work better for the waterfall approach, as the use cases are prepared up front, not necessarily just-in-time development. Of course, use cases can be created this way, but there is potential for impact to other use cases. For example, if you have four use cases dealing with using people's roles and responsibilities to determine what functions they can access and you change one use case, you will need to verify that each use case is not affected by that one change. Again, you have encountered the ripple effect, where one change could ripple through other potentially unsuspecting areas. Thus, the Wikipedia article is correct—use cases are agile.

You should be aware, because of the size of many use cases; they may not be small enough to work in an agile environment. If you need to craft use cases for agile developments, consider breaking the use cases into smaller, more manageable chunks so that they can be accomplished in two- to six-week sprints (organizationally dependent).

Again, the Wikipedia "Use Case" article says, "Use case developers often find it difficult to determine the level of UI dependency to incorporate in a use case." This is not a statement everyone necessarily agrees with. The statement is that the difficulty of determining the UI dependency is hard. That can be true. From what you have learned, you not should try to capture the UI in the use case. Remember, the tenant of "implementation independence" was emphasized for both *shall* statements and user stories. Well, it applies to requirement use cases as well. Thus, this challenge goes away for you as an RE. However, that is not to stop developers from writing "design use cases" in which case they may have this challenge of UI dependency. However, this limitation was avoided for you.

The next section will examine using use cases with or without *shall* statements. Especially in the "without" situation it will be addressed that over-reliance on use cases. You have seen where some aspects of requirements are not captured well by use cases. Keep that in mind.

While use cases provide excellent information for crafting test cases and test procedures, as was talked about in the three strikes rule in the login use case, the use case does not provide *all* the detail needed for testing, so do not rely on it for that. It is an excellent start point—but it's the foundation, not everything that is needed.

Earlier we talked about complexity such as algorithms, but there is another aspect to consider—data elements, especially if there are a lot of them. How do you handle, say, several dozen elements? Are you going to write one use case for a form that has all of them? While that might sound good at first blush, consider alternate flows and exceptions. Many items such as country may spawn different fields for Canada versus the Unites States. In the United States, we use states versus provinces and territories in Canada. Do that for two dozen elements and you will have a very large and difficult-to-read use case. It is recommended that you break the data elements into categories with manageable numbers of data elements to make the use case readable and less complex. What is manageable? That is difficult to determine without looking at the elements and the alternate and exception flows.

Time-driven events are not handled well by use cases. Who is the actor here? The passage of time? That does not work well. You might argue that the system itself is the trigger, but it is a combination of the system driven by the passage of time. This gets to the aspect mentioned earlier about forcing everything into a use case, when the methodology does not support it well.

Real-time systems are also not handled well. Think of a nuclear power plant. You have the humans running software that controls the reaction, but you have the nuclear pile itself doing its radioactive decay and nuclear interactions following the laws of quantum mechanics. How would you capture all the parts of this in use cases? If you want a lesson when these things broke down, read up on the meltdown in Three Mile Island in the 1970s. Alarms were blaring and lights were flashing that made it difficult for the operators who were trying to figure out what was going on, yet the operators could not shut off the alarms and lights so they could think.

While it will be mentioned again in the "Replacement for Requirements" section, it is stated here—use cases cannot capture every aspect of a system. This should be evident from the disadvantages in this subsection. To reiterate this, Karl Wiegers said the following in his book *More About Software Requirements: Thorny Issues and Practical Advice*:

> *Unfortunately, despite thousands of students I've taught in requirements seminars over the years, I have yet to meet a single person who has found this pure use case approach to work!*

This could not have been said any better, and this adds a wealth of additional experiences to reinforce the point. So, keep this in mind—use cases cannot satisfactorily address every aspect of a system.

In the next section, you will look at use cases complementing and replacing *shall* statements and then finish by looking at using use cases, user stories, and *shall* statements together.

Complement vs. Replacement to Requirements

Just as was done with user stories, in this section you are going to learn the following:

- Whether you need to write use cases with *shall* statements
- Whether you need to write use cases instead of *shall* statements
- Whether you can use cases, user stories, and *shall* statements as a complete set

Complement to Requirements

In this section, you will see how *shall* statements can complement use cases, so in this section, the answer is yes to *shall* statement with use cases.

Absolutely. The previous subsection discussed some of the disadvantages of use cases, such as the inability to capture nonfunctional requirements effectively, similar to the challenge that user stories have. Well, having use cases complementing *shall* statements will mitigate that problem. In addition, *shall* statements are not effective for capturing the full gamut of a set of ordered steps with branches, whereas use cases do this effectively and in fact much better than user stories.

The flip side is that use cases do not capture nonfunctional statements, algorithms, complex manipulations, batch processing, and other topics discussed in the "Disadvantages" section in this chapter, whereas the *shall* statements do. For example, how would you capture that a system should be available 99 percent of the time as a use case. It would not work as a step, nor any of the other attributes.

Thus, you should capture it as follows:

> 14-1 (4-6) (RQMT) The BOSS system shall be available 99.99% of the time.

You could then have a use case that determines what the value is for a system as follows:

Unique Identifier	14-4.
Title	Calculate system availability.
Description	Determines the system availability report.
Actor	User who requests the availability report.
Preconditions	The system has been running for a period and collecting operating parameters.
Postconditions	None.
Triggers	User who requests the availability report.
Basic Flow	1. Determine the total time since the last report. 2. Determine the total time the system was operating since the last report. 3. Divide the value in step 1 by the value in step 2 and multiply by 100%. 4. Provide the result to the requestor.

You could add a step that compares the value in step 4 to the value identified in requirement 14-1. Wait, you say, could you not specify the value of 99% in the step? Yes, you could. However, that step does not specify the force that the requirement has as a minimum acceptable value of 99%.

Thus, these two complement each other well.

Replacement for Requirements

Just as was said in the previous section that *shall* statements complement use cases, this section will talk about how use cases replace *shall* statements. There are experts who advocate that well-crafted use cases do not require *shall* statements, because if the stories are captured correctly, you do not need to capture *shall* statements.

Use cases are written with the user in mind (called *user facing* by some), which is true that use cases do capture well what the user may need. That said, use cases may never completely replace *shall* statements. Just as was discussed in the "Advantages and Disadvantages of Use Cases" section in this chapter, use cases do not capture items such as nonfunctional statements, algorithms, and batch processing. Being forced to capture these kinds of requirements purely as use cases will make the complex and difficult to read at best and totally incomprehensible at worst.

Look at the following *shall* statement:

14-2 (RQMT) The BOSS system shall use the following equation to represent gravity generated on an object by the earth:

$$g = GM/R^2$$

where g is gravity, G is the gravitational constant, M is the mass of the earth, and R is the distance between the object and the center of the earth.

Capturing that equation and the associated value in a use case would be difficult. For example, what is the actor? Defining the steps is difficult as gravity works all the time. Thus, you cannot easily write a use case for this type of need.

Therefore, it is not recommend that you capture requirements only with use cases.

All Three Together

Can *shall* statements, user stories, and use cases work together? Unquestionably. This way you take advantage of the benefits of each and help to diminish the disadvantages of them as well. Will you always get the opportunity to do all three? Unlikely. We have seen where use cases are excellent at providing a sequence of steps. If you have situations in your project where you have such sequences, use cases are your best bet. User stories are excellent at providing detail and, most importantly, descriptions of why a certain need is important—none of the others do that. Finally, they can cover what user stories and use cases cannot. For example, nonfunctional requirements do not work well with user stories and use cases, whereas *shall* statements capture these needs very well.

■ **Note** Combining methods is sometimes not well-received, especially from a junior RE.

References

U.S. government. "Use Cases." *usability.gov*. Feb. 2015, `http://www.usability.gov/how-to-and-tools/methods/use-cases.html`

Wikipedia. *Use case*. Feb. 2015, `http://en.wikipedia.org/wiki/Use_case`

Karl Wiegers, *More About Software Requirements: Thorny Issues and Practical Advice,* Microsoft Press, 2010, p11-4.

Exercises

Exercise 1

Write all the possible alternate flows for canceling the login process for all possible spots in the basic flow.

Exercise 2

Write an example of a use case for signing in with a user ID, password, and domain name. Three strikes and you're out.

CHAPTER 15

Revisiting Requirement Problems and Their Solutions

Remember, Chapter 1 talked about problems caused by requirements. Now, you will examine what things were taught to you that can eliminate, or at least significantly mitigate, these problems from happening.

Here is that previous list:

1. Insufficient requirements
2. Requirements creep
3. Volatility
4. Stove-piped requirements
5. Scope—boundaries can be ill-defined
6. Understanding users are not sure what they need
7. May not satisfy user needs
8. Misinterpretation—cause disagreements
9. Cannot verify the requirements
10. Wasted time and resources building the wrong functions

Now you will consider each point and analyze what you can do.

Insufficient Requirements

Reiterating the point, Chapter 1 stated that insufficient requirements means there are gaps in the full description of the system.

Now, look at what was discussed in this book to counter insufficiency.

G. Koelsch, *Requirements Writing for System Engineering*,
DOI 10.1007/978-1-4842-2099-3_15

Techniques were presented in Chapter 9 for how to collect all the possible requirements. It is strongly recommend that you use more than one technique to elicit requirements. Each has its benefits and costs in resources to achieve a good set of requirements.

Chapters 4 and 5 on functional and nonfunctional requirements listed dozens of topics for you to consider as part of a checklist for you to examine as candidate areas.

Multiple representations of requirement statements were presented: *shall* statements, user stories, and use cases to ensure the best representation of requirements.

Chapter 12's graphic representations and possible modeling were recommended to examine all aspects of requirements.

Do not rule out reviews of requirements by stakeholders, other people on the development team, and subject-matter experts in requirements engineering to help capture all requirements.

Time was spent in the book suggesting how to perform gap analysis to help find those missing requirements, such as reading system documentation and even creating business process descriptions to assist in finding those gaps.

Remember, the later in the development lifecycle that you take to find requirements, the more costly it is to implement them. Find them as early as you can.

Resist the urge of people to shortcut the proper capture of requirements. This is the most important aspect of developing the system. Do it right the first time.

Requirements Creep

Requirements change anywhere from 1 to 4 percent per month. Thus, to prevent the system from getting out of date, continue to capture them during the development phase. Agile-type methodologies where you refine requirements (whether *shall* statements, user stories, and/or use cases) as you get close to the sprint or iteration where the work will be performed significantly mitigates the scope creep.

Do not define all the requirements up front and freeze them for the entire development process. That begs for requirements scope creep. Note that in Chapter 13, we talked about writing user stories for agile developments but also discussed how *shall* statements and user stories can complement each other, especially since users stories are not as good at capturing nonfunctional needs.

Volatility

Chapter 1 defined volatility as a different kind of scope creep, which adds requirements. Volatility means that already existing requirements change. Basically, the same cure for requirements creep fixes volatility—define requirements as close to the implementation of the system, and you can avoid or mitigate volatility significantly. Again, in Chapter 13, where user stories are examined especially with the agile methodology where work is done in sprints with regular releases, even for projects that last for years. Doing more just-in-time requirements definitions (whether user stories, *shall* statements, or use cases), can help to overcome the volatility problem.

Stove-Piped Requirements

Actually, the text did an excellent job of explaining how to avoid this problem in Chapter 1, by not having your organization do it in the first place. If you have one part of your company or organization that does all the development, then the odds of this happening are significantly reduced. That is because you do all the work in your office. It should not be difficult to work with other teams and REs who are doing work. You should be able to share information and not "reinvent the wheel" each time.

If you have multiple development shops that are not resident in the same part of the company, then you might have more of a challenge, if there is not good communications or any communications among these shops. The onus will be on you to reach out to see what requirements others have done to see what you can reuse.

Honestly, this will be harder in the early part of your career to affect what could be a culture change. You should not try this in a vacuum but try to find an advocate who will champion your cause.

Real-World Note The times I have successfully accomplished culture change, I had such a champion. In one case, I was the one who documented common requirements, as they did not yet exist. This champion shared my requirements with others.

Do not ever underestimate the power of a champion.

The biggest area where you are likely to succeed is for the common functions such as a report generator, printing, access control, or searching capabilities.

You might want to set up working groups for REs to share work, seminars, or informal lunches to exchange information. Not only will this help to break down barriers within an organization, but also this helps to develop and grow your network. Not only may they help you when you have questions or challenges, but also they may be sources of career enhancements like better positions in the future.

Scope: Boundaries Can Be Ill-Defined

Chapter 1 said that ill-defined boundaries can be one of the main problems contributing to requirements gathering in general.

At the beginning of a project, get the major players together and get them to agree on what the scope of the project is, including very distinctly, where it ends and other systems/applications begin. Not only is this necessary to define the boundary of the new development but also to define what interfaces you need to capture.

Will it end there? Absolutely not. As you go through the elicitation phase, you may think that the boundary is moving. Then repeat the validation of that boundary. Determine what has changed; either you will have more or less functionality than was originally defined, maybe you have to redefine what is passing across the interfaces, or possibly both have occurred.

Just as requirements can change with time (in this chapter's reference to scope creep), the boundaries can too with time. So be on the alert for it. When you suspect it, ask. It is always easier to get an answer that says there is no change than to not ask and have significant ramifications further down the development process. Remember, those later changes are more costly, so identify them early and often.

You might ask if requirements can change without affecting boundaries. Yes, requirements can change without affecting boundaries, as we have mentioned with scope creep, but the knowledge of a particular function could become more detailed without affecting boundaries. Thus, the short answer to the question is requirements changes could affect the boundary, or it might not, depending on the breadth and depth of change.

Chapter 1 said that you can have challenges when you have to work across groups. This could be different departments within your company, or it could be across different companies, as I have experienced, when I have had to work across multiple organizations within the federal government. These different groups may have competing needs, and the boundaries may be interesting to define. One example, sometimes the management chain may need to be involved as other parts of the company become involved, or maybe different organizations altogether. A subset of this challenge is to be wary of people's egos getting in the way. Tread lightly until you are comfortable dealing with such situations. In fact, experience may not always prepare you for this regardless of your years or even decades of proficiency.

Understanding Users Are Not Sure What They Need

Chapter 9 was devoted to how to collect requirements. All of those techniques assist with overcoming this potential problem. Sometimes it is just a matter of having questions to ask to get them started talking.

Ask questions. That is the biggest tool in your tool chest. Of course, the key is knowing what questions to ask. Significant time was spent in Chapter 9 on this. Review it. Maybe it is something as simple as, "So, that means you think the system (insert your project name in here) is perfect." If that does not get them to disagree, then there is no hope. You want to get them talking. Once they start, listen to what they say, and start probing on the points they start to raise.

This does not mean most people will fall into this category of being reluctant with information. Take guidance in looking for the minority of people. You never know what gems they may have. In addition, if you get them engaged, they may be some of the best advocates for the new system when it comes along, because you were so helpful to them by wanting their input.

Experience shows that, in work sessions, when people start having fun, then the ideas and comments start flowing better. Does this work for everyone? No, of course not. Again, this demonstrates why this is an art, not science—people cannot be fully categorized and manipulated.

If people reluctant to participate, sometimes the best avenue is to focus on those who are more cooperative. On the other hand, maybe it is best to contact the reluctant person for a one-on-one discussion or via phone or e-mail because they may be reluctant to talk with other people around. For example, some introverts do not handle group environments as well as others, and providing them a better venue for their ideas may allow them to contribute. As was talked about in Chapter 9 using techniques of leading questions, such as "What is wrong with the current system?" or "If you could have anything you wanted for the system, what would you want?" can help start the conversation. Examining the various elicitation techniques in Chapter 9 may also help spark ideas to overcome reluctant people.

There is one small category that can be the most challenging to handle. If the users are openly hostile, it is best not to use them at all, as they will only disrupt the process. Of course, if they are the only one with particular knowledge, then you have to work with your management and possibly the management of the person in question. Do not go it alone. Ask for help and/or advice.

May Not Satisfy User Needs

With the listing of the types of functional and nonfunctional requirement types along with the elicitation techniques you have been taught, you should not miss groups of requirements that can be potentially missed (maybe not all types of requirements apply to every project, but it is a good start point). If you get to deployment and certain functions do not meet the users' needs, then there is some requirements that are missing. Also, if some requirements are not accurate, then it is possible that some needs may be missed. Vetting requirements with stakeholders can help to mitigate inaccuracies.

One additional way to prevent this is with the agile development. Because you get demonstrations at the end of each sprint/iteration, you get feedback from the stakeholders. You will learn quickly if something does not meet their needs before it goes too far. Corrections can be made quickly and deliver functions that are responsive to the needs.

In addition, because agile requires review of requirements just before the beginning of a sprint/iteration, you will get insights that alert you to gaps. Remember, just-in-time requirements keep the requirements current and focused on the topics of interest, and stakeholders will ensure proper requirements for that timeframe as well.

By vetting requirements through stakeholders, you establish the rapport that will help capture the right requirements. Because you listen to them, they will want to work with you and ensure they receive the right system.

Misinterpretation: Cause Disagreements

If the language used in the requirements is incorrect or not understood by everyone, then someone may not interpret it (and design it) such that it is not what the stakeholders and ultimately the users may want. Chapter 3 talked how you need to understand each word as well.

You worked through many example requirements to help you understand how to write precisely. Looking at the project's existing requirements can help. With the techniques presented throughout this book, you learned what is precisely written and what is not precise. In addition, you may start to see where other REs may not have followed the principles you now know. Learn from that.

■ **Note** Writers have used a technique called *workshopping* a story. By that, they submit stories to a group of writers who read it and critique it. Not only can they receive very valuable criticism but also by examining other peoples' works, they learn how to critique their own. Use the same technique for requirements.

Clarity is important. Precision deals more with the specific details being correct. Clarity has to do with the message you are trying to convey being clear to the reader. You have been provided three techniques within writing text to provide clarity: *shall* statements, user stories, and use cases. You were shown how each technique provides for enhancing the limitations of free text. Unfortunately, the burden still falls to you as the requirements engineer to write as clearly as possible. You have been provided tools, but ultimately it is your responsibility. Someone cannot write them for you; only you can write. Take advantage of others to review your work, especially as you start out your career. Experience helps. That said, even more than 30 years' experience does not guarantee that you will achieve perfection every time. Practice helps considerably, as well as insights from others, such as requirements engineers, stakeholders, and others on the development team. Each project is a team effort. Be open to their input and accept them willingly. Arrogance, at any point in your career, will not be an asset but a liability.

In addition, you have been provided with an overview of graphical techniques and modeling to assist in providing additional clarity. Keep in mind who your audience is and use these techniques and modeling with them in mind. Other than swim-lane-type graphics, most models will overwhelm most stakeholders. Some may be just whelmed. Keep that in mind.

Cannot Verify the Requirements

Obviously, verifying requirements is one of the attributes of a good requirement. If you can conceive of a method to verify a requirement, the testers charged with crafting and executing tests will be able to do so.

One technique to ensure you have achieved this is to have testers review the requirements. If they like the statement, then you have fixed this problem.

In addition, the other attributes of a good requirement support requirements that are testable. If it is atomic, you have decomposed it down to a reasonable level. For example, if the requirements are too high a level, then you probably cannot think of a good technique to verify it. You would probably need to come up with multiple tests, which would indicate the requirement needs to be decomposed. There may be other reasons for why a particular requirement might not be verifiable, as was discussed in Chapter 2. Your take-away is if you cannot verify a statement, it is not a good requirement.

Chapter 2 will not be repeated here. If you succeed in writing a good requirement, it will be verifiable. The final check for you is when you as an RE identify which of the five verification methodologies for each requirement will be used. If you can identify a reasonable method to verify the requirement, that statement should be verifiable.

Wasted Time and Resources Building the Wrong Functions

One of the traps of capturing requirements it that without priorities, every requirement takes on the same level of importance. That is not the case. A group of requirements that are performed dozens of times a day usually will have more importance than one that is performed once a year. One important element may overshadow this: if a legal or policy requires something, then frequency may not be a driver (but these legal/policy requirements are special cases).

Thus, assigning priorities based on frequency can help. Of course, there are policies and legal reasons that may dictate some requirements have higher priority than their frequency of occurrence may indicate.

In addition, with the agile methodology, with the stakeholders defining which requirements to work on, this will go a long way to eliminate functions that are not of interest to the users.

Chapter 1 mentioned a problem that can arise when the developers' interpretation of what is important can deviate from the needs, users, or priorities of the organization. Well, again, with agile if they try this, they will not get very far (a few weeks' worth of work at the most) before the stakeholders say they are going in the wrong direction. This will help to mitigate this problem significantly.

By fixing some of the other requirement problems discussed in this chapter, you may also help avoid this problem from occurring. For example, if you had the wrong boundary definition, you might waste time redoing what another system already accomplishes. So, by fixing the boundary definition (the scope—boundaries can be the ill-defined section in this chapter), you help to prevent the occurrence of wasted development time.

By proper requirements elicitation, you will help to prevent this also, as was reiterated earlier. Standards will help focus development in the proper implementation.

Summary

In summary, you learned information that has gone a long way to eliminating or mitigating these problems with requirements. Does that mean there are not other problems to address? You will no doubt encounter others, but these are the most often common and frequently cited problems. If you follow the processes and approaches herein outlined, you should do a good job of crafting and maintaining requirements throughout the lifecycle development.

Will you make mistakes? Absolutely. Everyone does. If it were easy, they would not need you to do it. The problem is that not everyone can do it. If you strive for perfection, while you will not achieve it, you will achieve excellence in the process. Achieve that excellence, and you will have a good career.

Remember, while you have learned many techniques, requirements engineering still is an art form. Be proud of your art. Translating what people think they need into what they really do need is not easy and certainly is not for the faint of heart. Embrace this and build from it—I am not talking about actually building the system here, but build your experience and confidence. You are going to experience some interesting projects that you might never have anticipated working on. Let this be a group of tools to help you do that.

Even if you do not write requirements, you know what to expect from people who do. Use this book and the enlightenment within as a guide to know what people who work for you need to do, even if you never have to do it yourself. Clarity has been brought to the process and helps software and hardware developments now and in the future.

Requirements engineering was not stagnant in the past, nor will it remain stagnant in the future. It will change. Embrace that evolution as it occurs. Ideally, you have gained insight to analyze these new methodologies and see what works best and what still needs improvement. Indications are provided where existing requirement techniques still need improvements. Use that as start point to see whether they have addressed those deficiencies. You have a leg up because you know what to look for, what to analyze, and what to critique. Knowledge is the commodity of the future, and this text should have helped you gain some. Use it, and have fun doing it.

Exercises

In chapter 1, you did two exercises. Now that you have completed the book, redo exercises 1 and 2 without looking at your original answers. Then, in exercise 3, you will come you new answers with those from chapter 1, and see how things have changed. Does it give you an idea how your perceptions have changed based on your new knowledge?

Exercise 1:

Examine the problems that can happen as described in the 'Challenges for Writing Effective Requirements ' section in this chapter and rank which ones you think are the most critical to fix and why.

Exercise 2:

Examine the problems that can happen as described in the 'Challenges for Writing Effective Requirements' section in this chapter and rank which ones you think occur most frequently and why.

Exercise 3:

Compare the results from exercise one and two from this chapter, and compare them to what you had written in chapter one. How has your assessment changed?

PART V

Appendixes

APPENDIX A

Acronyms and Abbreviations

This appendix lists the acronyms and abbreviations used in the book, for handy reference. Remember when Chapter 5 talked about including this reference? Well, this appendix follows the directives presented in that chapter. Remember, an *acronym* is defined as a word formed from the initials or other parts of several words, such as NATO, from the initial letters of North Atlantic Treaty Organization. An *abbreviation* is defined as a shortened or contracted form of a word or phrase used in place of the whole. FYI, many people use the term *acronym* for both.

Acronym/Abbreviation	Meaning
AH	Attack Helicopter
AKA	Also Known As
ARS	Audit Reporting Service
ASAP	As Soon As Possible
BLOB	Binary Large Object
BOSS	Big Organization's Suite of Services
BPD	Business Process Description
BPDD	Business Process Description Document
CASE	Computer-Aided System Engineering
CCNA	Cisco Certified Network Associate
CENTCOM	Central Command (DoD; includes Iraq and Afghanistan)
CM	Change Management
CM	Change Manager
CM	Configuration Management
CM	Configuration Manager
CMM	Capability Maturity Model
CMMI	Capability Maturity Model Integration
CONOPS	Concept of Operations

(*continued*)

G. Koelsch, *Requirements Writing for System Engineering*,
DOI 10.1007/978-1-4842-2099-3_16

Acronym/Abbreviation	Meaning
COPE	Common Operating Platform Environment
COTS	Commercial Off the Shelf
CR	Change Request
CRUD	Change, Read, Update, Delete
DBA	Database Administrator
DFD	Data Flow Diagram
DoD	Department of Defense
DOS	Denial of Service
DPI	Dots Per Inch
DR	Discrepancy Report
DSP	Defense Standardization Program
DTV	Digital Television
DVD	Digital Video Disc or Digital Versatile Disc
EIT	Electronic and Information Technology
EMP	Electromagnetic Pulse
EPF	Eclipse Process Framework
ERD	Entity Relationship Diagram
ESB	Enterprise Service Bus
FBI	Federal Bureau of Investigation
FRD	Functional Requirements Document
FYI	For Your Information
GOTS	Government Off the Shelf
GSFC	Goddard Space Flight Center
HCI	Human Computer Interface
HF	Human Factors
HFE	Human Factors Engineering
HIPAA	Health Insurance Portability and Accountability Act
HQ	Headquarters
HR	Human Resources
HTML	HyperText Markup Language
HUD	Housing and Urban Development
ICD	Interface Control Document
IED	Improvised Explosive Device

(*continued*)

Acronym/Abbreviation	Meaning
IEEE	Institute of Electrical and Electronics Engineers
INCOSE	International Council on Systems Engineering
INVEST	Independent, Negotiable, Valuable, Estimable, Small, Testable
IRS	Internal Revenue System
ISO	International Organization for Standardization
IT	Information Technology
JAD	Joint Application Development
KeV	Kilo-electron Volts
KISS	Keep It Simple, Stupid
LAN	Local Area Network
LCD	Liquid Crystal Display
LED	Light Emitting Diode
LSI	Latent Semantic Indexing
MAN	Metropolitan Area Network
MeV	Mega-electron Volts
MIL-STD	Military Standard
MRAP	Mine-Resistant Ambush Protected
MS	Microsoft
MTBF	Mean Time Between Failures
MTBM	Mean Time Between Maintenance
MTTM	Mean Time to Maintain
MTTR	Mean Time to Repair
NARA	National Archives and Records Administration
NASA	National Aeronautics and Space Administration
NBC	Nuclear, Biological, Chemical
NIH	National Institute of Health
NLP	Natural Language Processing
O&M	Operations and Maintenance
OMG	Object Management Group (not Oh My God)
OOP	Object-Oriented Programming
OPF	Open Process Framework
OS	Operating System

(*continued*)

Acronym/Abbreviation	Meaning
OSI	Open System Interconnection
PR	Problem Report
RAD	Rapid Application Development
RAM	Random Access Memory
RAM	Reliability, Availability, Maintainability
RE	Requirements Engineering
RE	Reverse Engineering
REM	Roentgen Equivalent in Man
REST	Representational State Transfer
RFC	Requests for Change
RFP	Request for Proposals
RM	Requirements Management
RM	Requirements Manager
RMA	Records Management Application
RMA	Reliability, Maintainability, Availability
RUP	Rational Unified Process
RVTM	Requirements Verification Traceability Matrix
SA	System Administrator
SAN	Storage Area Network
SDM	System Development Methodology
SE	Systems Engineer
SE	Systems Engineering
SME	Subject-Matter Expert
SO	Security Officer
SOA	Service Oriented Architecture
SQL	Structured Query Language
SRD	Software Requirements Document
SRD	System Requirements Document
SRS	System Requirements Specifications
SSN	Social Security Number
SysML	Systems Modeling Language
TBD	To Be Determined
TBR	To Be Reviewed

(*continued*)

Acronym/Abbreviation	Meaning
TES	Theme, Epics, Stories
TPF	Transaction Processing Facility
TTY	Teletypewriter
UI	User Interface
UML®	Unified Modeling Language™
USB	Universal Serial Bus
User ID	User Identification
User ID	User Identifier
WAN	Wide Area Network
XLC	eXpedited Life Cycle
XML	Extensible Markup Language
XP	eXtreme Programming

APPENDIX B

Requirements Documents

These are potential requirement document formats you might consider if you need to generate a document. Obviously, if your organization requires one, they may have a template already defined. If so, use it. If you need to craft one but do not have a format, consider the following templates. Some work better for hardware-focused systems, and others are more for software systems. Choose the one that best fits your needs. One will not be recommended here.

A good starting point is the IEEE formats, as many other organizations start with one or more of these templates.

This appendix will not invest much detail in each format; it will just give the headings so you can research what might work best for you. As was stated earlier in the book, with requirements databases, you may not need to craft one of these documents, so we will not invest much of your time in reading these, other than to point to candidates that are mostly not much more than a table of contents.

DoD FRD Template

This is one example of what is called a functional requirements document template. Given the size of the Department of Defense, this is established as a standard template that should be used by anyone within the DoD to follow. Even if you are not supporting the DoD, it might have merit if you need a requirements document format. What you see for the title is the actual document as specified in the following source:

Source: Johnson, James A. Functional Requirements Document (FRD) for Department of Defense (DoD) <Project Name> Activity Address Directory/File (DODAAD/DODAAF) Reengineering Effort Requirements Statement. Defense Logistics Management Standards Officc, October 2003.

G. Koelsch, *Requirements Writing for System Engineering*,
DOI 10.1007/978-1-4842-2099-3_17

FUNCTIONAL REQUIREMENTS DOCUMENT (FRD) FOR DEPARTMENT OF DEFENSE (DOD) <PROJECT NAME>

Table of Contents

f. Other Logistics and Facilities Considerations

g. Transportation and Basing

h. Geospatial Information and Services

i. Natural Environmental Support

7. Force Structure

8. Schedule

Appendix A: Schedule

Appendix B: New or Expanded Data Element Requirements

Appendix C: Abbreviations and Acronyms

Appendix D: Drop Down Menu Choices for Data Entry

Comments on This DoD FRD

This is a more fixed format used by the Department of Defense. Clearly, with sections like "Threat" and "Geospatial Information," these are areas you may not be familiar with unless you work in this organization.

IEEE Document Formats

In the IEEE documentation, IEEE provides very useful document formats. IEEE is an excellent resource to use as you build your documents. Included here are four different documents:

- Software Requirements Specification
- Functional Requirements Document
- Data Requirements Document
- Requirements Definitions

Final Comments on Requirements Document Formats

If you look at all of these candidate formats, you will notice that many of the section and subsection names repeat. Frankly, that is not surprising as they are trying to address system requirements. The point is to consider which organization you want or to make your own hybrid. Like much of what was have discussed, there is no right or wrong way to do it. Whatever works best for you and your organization is right. Again, this emphasizes the art form that you now know as requirements analysis.

References

IEEE-SA Standards Board. *IEEE Std 830-1998, IEEE Recommended Practice for Software Requirements Specifications*. Sponsor: Software Engineering Standards Committee of the IEEE Computer Society, Approved 25 June 1998, p21 to 27.

Johnson, James A. *Functional Requirements Document (FRD) for Department of Defense (DoD) <Project Name> Activity Address Directory/File (DODAAD/DODAAF) Reengineering Effort Requirements Statement*. Defense Logistics Management Standards Office, October 2003.

APPENDIX C

Section 508 Compliance

Section 508 of the Rehabilitation Act of 1973 was introduced in Chapter 10. This appendix reproduces some key excerpts from Section 508 that provide background for the requirements, define when you must comply with Section 508 of the Rehabilitation Act of 1973, and provide general guidance on Section 508. The source for the information in this appendix comes from "Guidelines and Standards" on the United States Access Board web site:

`www.access-board.gov/guidelines-and-standards`

The excerpts in this appendix are exactly as they appear on the web site, as of August 2016, including section heading and subsection heading numbers. Not every portion of the web site is duplicated here, just select information that I deemed especially pertinent.

The Background for Section 508

This first section provides an excerpt about the background for the Section 508 Accessibility Program:

`https://www.access-board.gov/guidelines-and-standards/communications-and-it/about-the-section-508-standards/background`

Background

Section 508 Law and Related Laws and Policies

In 1998, Congress amended the Rehabilitation Act and strengthened provisions covering access to information in the federal sector. As amended, section 508 of the Rehabilitation Act requires access to the federal government's electronic and information technology. It applies to all federal agencies when they develop, procure, maintain, or use such technology. Federal agencies must ensure that this technology is accessible to employees and the public to the extent it does not pose an "undue burden." The law directs the Access Board to develop access standards for this technology for incorporation into federal procurement regulations...

G. Koelsch, *Requirements Writing for System Engineering*,
DOI 10.1007/978-1-4842-2099-3_18

Exemptions to Section 508

This section is an excerpt about instances in which Section 508 does not apply:

`https://www.access-board.gov/guidelines-and-standards/communications-and-it/about-the-section-508-standards/section-508-standards/preamble`

Section 1194.3 General Exceptions

This section provides general exceptions from the standards. Paragraph (a) provides an exception for telecommunications or information systems operated by agencies, the function, operation, or use of which involves intelligence activities, cryptologic activities related to national security, command and control of military forces, equipment that is an integral part of a weapon or weapons system, or systems which are critical to the direct fulfillment of military or intelligence missions. This exception is statutory under section 508 and is consistent with a similar exception in section 5142 of the Clinger-Cohen Act of 1996...

Section 508 Technical Standards

This section is an excerpt from Section 508 Subpart B regarding technical standards:

`https://www.access-board.gov/guidelines-and-standards/communications-and-it/about-the-section-508-standards/section-508-standards#subpart_b`

Subpart B – Technical Standards

§ 1194.21 Software Applications and Operating Systems

(a) When software is designed to run on a system that has a keyboard, product functions shall be executable from a keyboard where the function itself or the result of performing a function can be discerned textually.

(b) Applications shall not disrupt or disable activated features of other products that are identified as accessibility features, where those features are developed and documented according to industry standards. Applications also shall not disrupt or disable activated features of any operating system that are identified as accessibility features where the application programming interface for those accessibility features has been documented by the manufacturer of the operating system and is available to the product developer.

(c) A well-defined on-screen indication of the current focus shall be provided that moves among interactive interface elements as the input focus changes. The focus shall be programmatically exposed so that assistive technology can track focus and focus changes.

(d) Sufficient information about a user interface element including the identity, operation and state of the element shall be available to assistive technology. When an image represents a program element, the information conveyed by the image must also be available in text.

(e) When bitmap images are used to identify controls, status indicators, or other programmatic elements, the meaning assigned to those images shall be consistent throughout an application's performance.

(f) Textual information shall be provided through operating system functions for displaying text. The minimum information that shall be made available is text content, text input caret location, and text attributes.

(g) Applications shall not override user selected contrast and color selections and other individual display attributes.

(h) When animation is displayed, the information shall be displayable in at least one non-animated presentation mode at the option of the user.

(i) Color coding shall not be used as the only means of conveying information, indicating an action, prompting a response, or distinguishing a visual element.

(j) When a product permits a user to adjust color and contrast settings, a variety of color selections capable of producing a range of contrast levels shall be provided.

(k) Software shall not use flashing or blinking text, objects, or other elements having a flash or blink frequency greater than 2 Hz and lower than 55 Hz.

(l) When electronic forms are used, the form shall allow people using assistive technology to access the information, field elements, and functionality required for completion and submission of the form, including all directions and cues.

§ 1194.22 Web-based Intranet and Internet Information and Applications

(a) A text equivalent for every non-text element shall be provided (e.g., via "alt", "longdesc", or in element content).

(b) Equivalent alternatives for any multimedia presentation shall be synchronized with the presentation.

(c) Web pages shall be designed so that all information conveyed with color is also available without color, for example from context or markup.

(d) Documents shall be organized so they are readable without requiring an associated style sheet.

(e) Redundant text links shall be provided for each active region of a server-side image map.

(f) Client-side image maps shall be provided instead of server-side image maps except where the regions cannot be defined with an available geometric shape.

(g) Row and column headers shall be identified for data tables.

(h) Markup shall be used to associate data cells and header cells for data tables that have two or more logical levels of row or column headers.

(i) Frames shall be titled with text that facilitates frame identification and navigation.

(j) Pages shall be designed to avoid causing the screen to flicker with a frequency greater than 2 Hz and lower than 55 Hz.

(k) A text-only page, with equivalent information or functionality, shall be provided to make a web site comply with the provisions of this part, when compliance cannot be accomplished in any other way. The content of the text-only page shall be updated whenever the primary page changes.

(l) When pages utilize scripting languages to display content, or to create interface elements, the information provided by the script shall be identified with functional text that can be read by assistive technology.

(m) When a web page requires that an applet, plug-in or other application be present on the client system to interpret page content, the page must provide a link to a plug-in or applet that complies with §1194.21(a) through (l).

(n) When electronic forms are designed to be completed on-line, the form shall allow people using assistive technology to access the information, field elements, and functionality required for completion and submission of the form, including all directions and cues.

(o) A method shall be provided that permits users to skip repetitive navigation links.

(p) When a timed response is required, the user shall be alerted and given sufficient time to indicate more time is required.

§ 1194.23 Telecommunications Products

(a) Telecommunications products or systems which provide a function allowing voice communication and which do not themselves provide a TTY functionality shall provide a standard non-acoustic connection point for TTYs. Microphones shall be capable of being turned on and off to allow the user to intermix speech with TTY use.

(b) Telecommunications products which include voice communication functionality shall support all commonly used cross-manufacturer non-proprietary standard TTY signal protocols.

(c) Voice mail, auto-attendant, and interactive voice response telecommunications systems shall be usable by TTY users with their TTYs.

(d) Voice mail, messaging, auto-attendant, and interactive voice response telecommunications systems that require a response from a user within a time interval, shall give an alert when the time interval is about to run out, and shall provide sufficient time for the user to indicate more time is required.

(e) Where provided, caller identification and similar telecommunications functions shall also be available for users of TTYs, and for users who cannot see displays.

(f) For transmitted voice signals, telecommunications products shall provide a gain adjustable up to a minimum of 20 dB. For incremental volume control, at least one intermediate step of 12 dB of gain shall be provided.

(g) If the telecommunications product allows a user to adjust the receive volume, a function shall be provided to automatically reset the volume to the default level after every use.

(h) Where a telecommunications product delivers output by an audio transducer which is normally held up to the ear, a means for effective magnetic wireless coupling to hearing technologies shall be provided.

(i) Interference to hearing technologies (including hearing aids, cochlear implants, and assistive listening devices) shall be reduced to the lowest possible level that allows a user of hearing technologies to utilize the telecommunications product.

(j) Products that transmit or conduct information or communication, shall pass through cross-manufacturer, non-proprietary, industry-standard codes, translation protocols, formats or other information necessary to provide the information or communication in a usable format. Technologies which use encoding, signal compression, format transformation, or similar techniques shall not remove information needed for access or shall restore it upon delivery.

(k) Products which have mechanically operated controls or keys, shall comply with the following:

   (1) Controls and keys shall be tactilely discernible without activating the controls or keys.

   (2) Controls and keys shall be operable with one hand and shall not require tight grasping, pinching, or twisting of the wrist. The force required to activate controls and keys shall be 5 lbs. (22.2 N) maximum.

   (3) If key repeat is supported, the delay before repeat shall be adjustable to at least 2 seconds. Key repeat rate shall be adjustable to 2 seconds per character.

   (4) The status of all locking or toggle controls or keys shall be visually discernible, and discernible either through touch or sound.

§ 1194.24 Video and Multimedia Products

(a) All analog television displays 13 inches and larger, and computer equipment that includes analog television receiver or display circuitry, shall be equipped with caption decoder circuitry which appropriately receives, decodes, and displays closed captions from broadcast, cable, videotape, and DVD (Digital Video Disc or Digital Versatile Disc) signals. As soon as practicable, but not later than July 1, 2002, widescreen digital television (DTV) displays measuring at least 7.8 inches vertically, DTV sets with conventional displays measuring at least 13 inches vertically, and stand-alone DTV tuners, whether or not they are marketed with display screens, and computer equipment that includes DTV receiver or display circuitry, shall be equipped with caption decoder circuitry which appropriately receives, decodes, and displays closed captions from broadcast, cable, videotape, and DVD signals.

(b) Television tuners, including tuner cards for use in computers, shall be equipped with secondary audio program playback circuitry.

(c) All training and informational video and multimedia productions which support the agency's mission, regardless of format, that contain speech or other audio information necessary for the comprehension of the content, shall be open or closed captioned.

(d) All training and informational video and multimedia productions which support the agency's mission, regardless of format, that contain visual information necessary for the comprehension of the content, shall be audio described.

(e) Display or presentation of alternate text presentation or audio descriptions shall be user-selectable unless permanent.

§ 1194.25 Self-contained, Closed Products

(a) Self-contained products shall be usable by people with disabilities without requiring an end-user to attach assistive technology to the product. Personal headsets for private listening are not assistive technology.

(b) When a timed response is required, the user shall be alerted and given sufficient time to indicate more time is required.

(c) Where a product utilizes touch screens or contact-sensitive controls, an input method shall be provided that complies with §1194.23 (k) (1) through (4).

(d) When biometric forms of user identification or control are used, an alternative form of identification or activation, which does not require the user to possess particular biological characteristics, shall also be provided.

(e) When products provide auditory output, the audio signal shall be provided at a standard signal level through an industry standard connector that will allow for private listening. The product must provide the ability to interrupt, pause, and restart the audio at any time.

(f) When products deliver voice output in a public area, incremental volume control shall be provided with output amplification up to a level of at least 65 dB. Where the ambient noise level of the environment is above 45 dB, a volume gain of at least 20 dB above the ambient level shall be user selectable. A function shall be provided to reset the volume automatically to the default level after every use.

(g) Color coding shall not be used as the only means of conveying information, indicating an action, prompting a response, or distinguishing a visual element.

(h) When a product permits a user to adjust color and contrast settings, a range of color selections capable of producing a variety of contrast levels shall be provided.

(i) Products shall be designed to avoid causing the screen to flicker with a frequency greater than 2 Hz and lower than 55 Hz.

(j) Products which are freestanding, non-portable, and intended to be used in one location and which have operable controls shall comply with the following:

  (1) The position of any operable control shall be determined with respect to a vertical plane, which is 48 inches in length, centered on the operable control, and at the maximum protrusion of the product within the 48 inch length (see Figure 1 of this part - not provided in this text, check on the website).

  (2) Where any operable control is 10 inches or less behind the reference plane, the height shall be 54 inches maximum and 15 inches minimum above the floor.

  (3) Where any operable control is more than 10 inches and not more than 24 inches behind the reference plane, the height shall be 46 inches maximum and 15 inches minimum above the floor.

  (4) Operable controls shall not be more than 24 inches behind the reference plane (see Figure 2 of this part - not provided in this text, check on the website).

§ 1194.26 Desktop and Portable Computers

(a) All mechanically operated controls and keys shall comply with §1194.23 (k) (1) through (4).

(b) If a product utilizes touch screens or touch-operated controls, an input method shall be provided that complies with §1194.23 (k) (1) through (4).

(c) When biometric forms of user identification or control are used, an alternative form of identification or activation, which does not require the user to possess particular biological characteristics, shall also be provided.

(d) Where provided, at least one of each type of expansion slots, ports and connectors shall comply with publicly available industry standards.

Section 508 Functional Performance Criteria

This section is an excerpt from Section 508 Subpart C regarding functional performance criteria:

https://www.access-board.gov/guidelines-and-standards/communications-and-it/about-the-section-508-standards/section-508-standards#subpart_c

Subpart C – Functional Performance Criteria

§ 1194.31 Functional Performance Criteria

(a) At least one mode of operation and information retrieval that does not require user vision shall be provided, or support for assistive technology used by people who are blind or visually impaired shall be provided.

(b) At least one mode of operation and information retrieval that does not require visual acuity greater than 20/70 shall be provided in audio and enlarged print output working together or independently, or support for assistive technology used by people who are visually impaired shall be provided.

(c) At least one mode of operation and information retrieval that does not require user hearing shall be provided, or support for assistive technology used by people who are deaf or hard of hearing shall be provided.

(d) Where audio information is important for the use of a product, at least one mode of operation and information retrieval shall be provided in an enhanced auditory fashion, or support for assistive hearing devices shall be provided.

(e) At least one mode of operation and information retrieval that does not require user speech shall be provided, or support for assistive technology used by people with disabilities shall be provided.

(f) At least one mode of operation and information retrieval that does not require fine motor control or simultaneous actions and that is operable with limited reach and strength shall be provided.

Section 508 Information, Documentation, and Support

This section is an excerpt from Section 508 Subpart D regarding information, documentation, and support:

https://www.access-board.gov/guidelines-and-standards/communications-and-it/about-the-section-508-standards/section-508-standards#subpart_d

Subpart D - Information, Documentation, and Support

§ 1194.41 Information, Documentation, and Support

(a) Product support documentation provided to end-users shall be made available in alternate formats upon request, at no additional charge.

(b) End-users shall have access to a description of the accessibility and compatibility features of products in alternate formats or alternate methods upon request, at no additional charge.

(c) Support services for products shall accommodate the communication needs of end-users with disabilities.

Glossary

These are terms that are introduced in this book for your handy reference. Again, this is something worthwhile to include with your documents, and even in requirements databases.

Acceptance Criteria or Completion Criteria

Define when a user story is done or complete. (See also *User Story*.)

Access Control

Specify how users can access the system.

Accessibility

The degree to which a product, device, service, or environment is available to as many people as possible.

Accurate Requirement or Correct Requirement

A precise statement of the system's capability, its inputs, its outputs, its interfaces, and how it interacts with its environment.

Actor

Anyone or anything (another system, such as an application or device) that performs a behavior. This is not limited to one actor. (See also *Use Case*.)

Administrative Function

Maintain the system as a whole, usually by a systems administrator.

Affinity Diagram

An approach for organizing information. Ideas are solicited in a particular subject area. Then, bring some structure to them by providing some grouping.

Algorithm

Formulas or specific manipulations of data elements that need to occur.

Alternate Path or Alternate Flow

Paths that are a variation on the main or basic path theme. These exceptions are what happen when things go wrong at the system level, or an alternate condition causes a change to the basic flow. This is also known as extensions. (See also *Use Case*.)

Analysis

A quantitative evaluation of a complete system and/or subsystems by review/analysis of collected data. This is one of the verification methods.

Application

A program (e.g., a word processor or a spreadsheet) that performs one of the major tasks for which a computer is used.

G. Koelsch, *Requirements Writing for System Engineering*,
DOI 10.1007/978-1-4842-2099-3_19

Architectural Requirements

Standards based on architecture your organization mandates that your system in question must follow.

Archiving Requirements

When data within the system grows beyond the storage capacity, data must be moved to an archive, usually separate from the original data storage.

Atomic

Define each requirement to its lowest practical level.

Audit

Track data and what happens to it (e.g., added, deleted, changed, archived, deactivated, changed roles that can perform CRUD).

Authentication

A mechanism to validate that the person or system is authorized to interact with the system.

Authorization

This defines the varying access of data, who (or what system) may change, read, update or delete, deactivate, or reactivate the data.

Availability

How much of the time the system is operational.

Backup

A partial/increment and/or full copy of data, and possibly software, to prevent loss of information should a system crash occur. A complement to recovery.

Basic Flow, Basic Path, Main Flow, or Main Path

The main success scenarios (basic flow) use case in which nothing goes wrong. This is also known as normal flow/scenario, primary flow/scenario.) (See also *Use Case.*)

Business Process Description

A documentation of what the stakeholders describe they need to do, from daily repetitive tasks to daily, weekly, monthly, or any periodicity. This is a description of what they do, not how. This is not specific to a particular system or application but the steps they need to take and why.

Business Rule

Statements that define what the system needs to do or what features it needs. These are also used to define statements for use cases.

Capability

The phrase "the capability to" means the user has the option to invoke this function or not.

Capacity

The storage needed for the system.

Certification

The certifications that the organization or government requires for work done on your system.

Completeness of an Individual Requirement

When all the information necessary to define the function, the verb that describes what action the system should do, and the result of that action completes the description of the need.

Completeness of a Group of Requirements

When everything within the boundary is completely defined.

Completion Criteria or Acceptance Criteria

Define when a user story is done or complete. (See also *User Story.*)

Compliance

Whatever legal, regulatory, or policy need affecting the organization or type of project will have to follow whatever compliance is required of the system.

Concise

Requirements that are short and to the point.

Concurrency

The level of use on the system, e.g., how many users on the system and other capacity values. This is also called workload.

Connect to Other Systems

This not the interface specification. This addresses protection of the data that moves data to and from the systems.

CONOPS

A Concept of Operations, which can be a Business Process Description document or a shorter document emphasizing concepts, without some of the details a BPD provides.

Consistent

Requirements should not conflict with each other, should have consistent usage, and should use consistent terms.

Constraints

These statements are restrictions or limitations to what the system can do.

Correct

A precise statement of the system's capability, its inputs, its outputs, its interfaces, and how it interacts with its environment. (See also *Accurate Requirement.*)

Data Flow Diagram

A structured analysis technique that is a graphical representation of the "flow" of data through an information system.

Data Integrity

Maintains and assures the accuracy and consistency of data over its entire lifecycle.

Database

Define what data elements and formats to be used in the data that must be stored for the system.

Demonstration

To prove or show, usually without measurement or instrumentation, that the project/product complies with requirements by observing results. This is one of the verification methods.

Effectiveness

The ability to produce a result that is wanted or having an intended effect.

Efficiency

The ability to do something or produce something without wasting materials, time, or energy.

Elicitation

Drawing forth the information from your stakeholders.

Environmental

The external environments the system will need to operate in (e.g., temperature ranges, rain, wind, snow, humidity, dropped, jostled).

Epic

One large user story that needs to be broken down, or already a group of related user stories.

Estimable

Someone, maybe not who crafts the story, needs to be able to make an estimate of the complexity of the story and thereby determine the time it will take to develop and test it. (See also *User Story*.)

Exception Flow or Exception Path

An error condition that happens; a variation of alternative flows. (See also *Use Case*.)

Export

Moving data from the existing system to another destination.

Extensibility

Capable of being extended beyond the original.

Extensible Markup Language (XML)

XML is a markup language to define a file format that is human-readable as well as machine-readable. The document or file does not do anything; it is just a method for representing the file or document.

External Interfaces

A system, program, or application that is not part of the system, program, or application you are defining.

Facilitated Session

A group of people brought together for a common purpose, in this case to elicit/collect/gather requirements.

Fault Tolerance

Ability to operate in a degraded mode, where one or more components are not operating or only partially operating.

Focus Group

A gathering of people who represent the users or customers of a product to get information, in this case about needs/opportunities/problems to identify requirements, or you can gather it to validate and refine already elicited requirements.

Functional Requirement

Describes what functions a system should perform.

Gap Analysis

A technique to find those gaps in the requirement set that do not completely address all the needs.

Historical Data

In the case of requirements, this addresses the storage and growth of data, by examining legacy data, but also looking at changes from the legacy data to the new system data and projected growth.

Import

Moving data into the existing system from another destination.

Independent

The requirement attribute of being able to stand on its own and not require other requirements to define it.

Implementation Independent

A requirement should not contain any unnecessary design and implementation information.

Infrastructure

The kind of support services or items the system will need that will not be considered part of the system itself.

Inspection

To examine visually or use simple physical measurement techniques to verify conformance to specified requirements. This is one of the verification methods.

Interfaces

A system, program, or application that is not part of the system, program, or application you are defining.

Interoperability

The ability of a system (as a weapons system) to work with or use the parts or equipment of another system.

Interview

The most important and common method for eliciting requirements, by getting the information directly from those who use the system on a regular basis either one-on-one or in small groups by asking a series of preplanned and ad hoc questions that the users answer.

Joint Application Development

A JAD, aka a requirements workshop, usually meets until the session objectives are completed. For a requirements JAD session, the participants stay in session until you document a complete set of requirements and the stakeholders agree.

Jargon

The technical terminology or characteristic idiom of a special activity or group.

Maintainability

The measure of the ease and rapidity with which a system or equipment can be restored to operational status following a failure.

Manageability

The ability to manage the system to ensure the continued health of a system.

Mean Time Between Failures (MTBF)

This is the average operational time between failures.

Mean Time Between Maintenance (MTBM)

This is the average operational time between maintenance.

Mean Time to Maintain (MTTM)

This describes the average time the system is down for maintenance.

Mean Time to Repair (MTTR)

Describes the average time to repair a failure.

Modifiable

A document or a group of requirements can be modifiable by organization, such as by breaking groups of requirements that have functional similarity or by providing a document's table of contents or index, referencing other documents.

Model/Modeling

Models and modeling are techniques for representing requirements besides trying to use imprecise language, such as graphic representations.

Nonfunctional Requirement

Describes how the system should behave and defines what constraints are placed upon the system's behavior.

Performance

Metrics that define how much work a system performs, whether it is hardware or software.

Performance Profiles

Different performance needs based on variations of configurations driven by business needs, such as different sizes of offices and the associate numbers of people or significantly different performance attributes like throughput.

Physical Characteristics

Different hardware characteristics requirements, such as weight, dimension, shape, volume, density, center of gravity, storage, packaging, power, and material.

Platform

Where a piece of software is resident such as on computers, printers, scanner, servers, type of network, operating system, and any other peripherals for a computer system.

Postcondition

What must be true or happen after the use case runs. (See also *Use Case.*)

Power

Power the system needs, such as AC or DC; voltage like 5, 10, 12, 110, 120 volts; what cycles per second like 50 or 60.

Precondition

What must be true or happen before the use case runs. (See also *Use Case.*)

Prioritized

The priority that requirements need to be provided (i.e., critical, high, medium, low).

Privacy

The identity of a person or system or certain aspects of that system or person that needs to be protect, such as medical information, SSN, etc.

Process Improvement

When requirements process are not optimum, these are steps taken to mitigate requirements problems from surfacing that will adversely affect the development and ultimate implementation of the new system.

Rational Unified Process (RUP)

A development process that includes a process for requirements.

Recoverability

The ability to recover from some event, say the crash of a system. How quickly do you return to full operations?

Recovery

The complement to backup where when a system crash has occurred, this provides the information that was stored during the backup operation and restores it to the operational system so operations can begin again.

Regulatory

Whatever regulatory need affecting the organization or type of project will have to follow whatever compliance is required of the system.

Reliability

The quality or state of being reliable; it does not fail.

Requirement

Define a need, desire, or want to be satisfied by a product or service.

Requirements Engineer

Someone who collects, coordinates, advocates, and manages requirements.

Requirements Document

A document that captures all the requirements associated with a system, which can include additional boilerplate information about the system such as a business process description or concept of operation.

Resiliency

Defines what must be preserved when an outage of the system occurs.

Response Time

How quickly the system provides requested information.

Reuse

Using information multiple times, in this case, requirements, so that information is not created from scratch multiple times.

Reverse Engineer

A process of gleaning information from something made and/or programmed to understand what is does or how it does it.

Robustness

The system does not crash easily and is able to withstand changes that might weaken it.

Scalability

Capability of being easily expanded or upgraded on demand.

Security

Measures taken to guard against espionage or sabotage, crime, attack, or escape.

Simulation

Executing a model over time to simulate a portion of the system. This one of the verification methods.

Small

A user story that can be developed in hours or days or one or more weeks during just one sprint. (See also *User Story*.)

Spike

The definition of the user story is insufficient. (See also *User Story*.)

Stability

How long something would maintain its effectiveness.

Stakeholder

Someone who has a stake in an enterprise.

Standards

Rules that are levied on the project from legal, policy, or organizational sources.

State Transition Diagram

Show the actions that occur based on specific events, eventually showing all the states of that object. They work well for single objects but are not as effective as many objects are added to a system being analyzed.

Storyboards

Illustrations or images displayed in sequence to visualize a motion picture, animation, motion graphic, or interactive sequence, to include how a human interacts with a computer.

Structural Requirements

This refers to the structure of hardware systems and addresses how hardy the piece needs to be such as wind shear, any force applied to the system, or what it is exposed to such as lightening, rain, snow, hail, salt, seawater, freezing, heat, and oxidation.

Supportability

The inherent characteristics of design and installation that enable the effective and efficient maintenance and support of the system throughout the life cycle.

Swim Lanes

To quickly and easily plot and trace processes and, in particular, the interconnections between processes, departments, and teams, where they are broken into either into all the rows or columns to represent the different organizations, teams, or processes responsible for specific tasks.

Systems Modeling Language (SysML)

A modeling language for system engineering designed to support all phases of the development lifecycle, including requirement specification. It's a variation of UML.

System

A group of related parts that move or work together.

Test

A measurement to prove or show, usually with precision measurements or instrumentation, that the project/product complies with requirements. This is one of the verification methods.

Testability

How easily can something be tested.

Theme

A collection of epics or very large collection of user stories.

Throughput

How much of a given resource can move through a given point in a system, such as how much data goes through a line between systems.

Traceable

Traceability to an origin and to future development or enhancement documentation.

Transaction

Transactions, which include corrections, adjustments, and cancellations, address changing, deleting, deactivating/canceling, and error checking and handling records of data.

Trigger

The event that causes the use case to be initiated. (See also *Use Case.*)

Turnkey system

A complete system that provides not only software but also the hardware and everything in between (e.g., operating system, connectivity).

Unified Modeling Language (UML)

A modeling language that is intended to analyze requirements to formulate a design, which is managed by Object Management Group (OMG) and now is an ISO standard.

Unambiguous

A knowledgeable person interprets each requirement statement only one way.

Understandable

A reasonable user or stakeholder must be able to interpret that statement so that it matches their perception of the subject.

Unique

A requirement is different from all other requirements associated with a system

Usability

To be convenient and practicable for use; usability is how effectively users can learn and use a system.

Use Case

A written description of how users will perform tasks on your system, especially in a sequence of steps.

User Interface

Describes how the user interacts with the system.

User Story

A statement that defines a need a defined person has and a reason why they have the need.

Verifiable

A type of demonstration that a requirement performs what it is asked to accomplish.

Verifiability

How easily something can be verified.

Verification Method

This is type of verification to be associated with a requirement/user story.

Volatility

Already existing requirements change with time.

Wait Time

The time from the onset of the failure until the work begins on the failure.

Workload

The level of use on the system (e.g., how many users on the system, and other capacity values). This is also called concurrency.

eXtensible Markup Language (XML)

A markup language to define a file format that is human-readable as well as machine-readable. The document or file does not do anything; it is just a method for representing the file or document.

Bibliography

12th Annual AIAA/USU Conference on Small Satellites. Feb 2015, http://digitalcommons.usu.edu/cgi/viewcontent.cgi?article=2235&context=smallsat

Beal, Vangie. "XML, a tweet." Webopedia. Feb. 2015, www.webopedia.com/TERM/X/XML.html

Bell, Donald. "UML basics Part II: The activity diagram," Sep. 2003. IBM Global Services. Feb. 2015, www.therationaledge.com/content/sep_03/f_umlbasics_db.jsp

Blain, Tyner "Ten Requirements Gathering Techniques." November 21, 2006 Tyner Blain blog Feb. 2015, http://tynerblain.com/blog/2006/11/21/ten-requirements-gathering-techniques/

Boehm, B.W. Software Engineering Economics. Englewood Cliffs, NJ: Prentice-Hall, 1981.

Centers for Medicare & Medicaid Services CMS eXpedited Life Cycle (XLC) Interface Control Document Template. Feb. 2015, www.cms.gov/Research-Statistics-Data-and-Systems/CMS-Information-Technology/XLC/Artifacts.html

"Data Flow Diagram (DFD)s: An Agile Introduction." Agile Modeling webpage. Feb. 2015, http://agilemodeling.com/artifacts/dataFlowDiagram.htm

Davis, Alan M. Software requirements: Objects, Functions, and States. Prentice-Hall, Inc. Upper Saddle River, NJ, 1993

Department of Defense. DI-SDMP-81470 Department of Defense (DoD) Interface Standard Documents. Data Item Description, 1 August 2003

DoD MIL-STD 962D. 1 August 2003. Department of Defense Standard Practice: Defense Standards Format and Content. Feb 2015, http://everyspec.com/MIL-STD/MIL-STD-0900-1099/MIL_STD_962D_1179/

"Guideline: Requirements Gathering Techniques" Eclipse Process Framework (EPF). Feb. 2015, http://epf.eclipse.org/wikis/openup/core.tech.common.extend_supp/guidances/guidelines/req_gathering_techniques_8CB8E44C.html

Heim, Andrew. "Make it Faster: More Throughput or Less Latency?." Feb 25, 2014. National Instruments. Feb. 2015, www.ni.com/white-paper/14990/en/

Housing and Urban Development (HUD) System Development Methodology (SDM). January 2009. Release 6.06, U.S. Department of Housing and Urban Development. Feb. 2015, http://portal.hud.gov/hudportal/documents/huddoc?id=sdm.pdf

G. Koelsch, *Requirements Writing for System Engineering*,
DOI 10.1007/978-1-4842-2099-3_20

IEEE-SA Standards Board. IEEE Std 830-1998, IEEE Recommended Practice for Software Requirements Specifications. Sponsor: Software Engineering Standards Committee of the IEEE Computer Society, Approved 25 June 1998.

INCOSE. Feb 2015, www.incose.org/

International Organization for Standardization (ISO). ISO 9001:2008 - Quality Management Systems – Requirements. 2008

"Introduction to OMG's Specifications: UML." Object Management Group (OMG). Feb. 2015, www.omg.org/gettingstarted/specintro.htm#UML

"Introduction to OMG's Unified Modeling Language™ (UML®)." Object Management Group (OMG). Feb. 2015, www.omg.org/gettingstarted/what_is_uml.htm

"What Characteristics Make Good Agile Acceptance Criteria?." March 25, 2013. Segue Technologies Inc. www.seguetech.com/blog/2013/03/25/characteristics-good-agile-acceptance-criteria

Johnson, James A. Functional Requirements Document (FRD) for Department of Defense (DoD) <Project Name Activity Address Directory/File (DODAAD/DODAAF) Reengineering Effort Requirements Statement. Defense Logistics Management Standards Office, October 2003.

Jones, Capers. "Chronic requirements problems." November 26, 2012. The World of Software Development. Dr Dobb's. Feb. 2015, www.drdobbs.com/architecture-and-design/chronic-requirements-problems/240012797

Jones, Capers. Software Assessments, Benchmarks, and Best Practices. Addison-Wesley Professional, 2000

Karl Wiegers, More About Software Requirements: Thorny Issues and Practical Advice, Microsoft Press, 2010.

Kruchten, Philippe. "What Is the Rational Unified Process?." 2001. IBM. Feb. 2015, www.ibm.com/developerworks/rational/library/content/RationalEdge/jan01/WhatIstheRationalUnifiedProcessJan01.pdf

Lalli, Vincent R., Kastner, Robert E. and Hartt, Henry N. Training Manual for Elements of Interface Definition and Control, NASA Reference Publication 1370. January 1997.

Little, Ambrose. "Storyboarding in the software design process." UX Magazine. Feb. 2015, http://uxmag.com/articles/storyboarding-in-the-software-design-process

Lou Wheatcraft. October 9, 2012. "Using the correct terms – Shall Will Should." Requirement Experts. Feb. 2015, www.reqexperts.com/blog/2012/10/using-the-correct-terms-shall-will-should/

McDermid, J. A. Requirements Analysis: Problems and the STARTS Approach. In IEE Colloquium on 'Requirements Capture and Specification for Critical Systems' (Digest No. 138), 4/1-4/4. Institution of Electrical Engineers, November 1989

Meriam –Webster Online. An Encyclopedia Britannica Company. Feb. 2015. www.merriam-webster.com/

Microsoft Development Network webpage, Modeling User Requirements, Visual Studio 2013 Feb. 2015, http://msdn.microsoft.com/en-us/library/dd409376.aspx

Mochal, Tom. "10 techniques for gathering requirements." January 2, 2008. TechRepublic U.S. Feb. 2015, www.techrepublic.com/blog/10-things/10-techniques-for-gathering-requirements/

Mullaney, Jennette. "Modeling in the agile methodology." SearchSoftwareQuality TechTarget. Feb. 2015, http://searchsoftwarequality.techtarget.com/tutorial/Software-requirements-gathering-techniques

Mullaney, Jennette. "Modeling selection." SearchSoftwareQuality TechTarget. Feb. 2015, http://searchsoftwarequality.techtarget.com/tutorial/Software-requirements-gathering-techniques

Narayanan, Anantha. "User Story Acceptance Criteria: The Art of Satisficing and Bounded Rationality," 20 January 2012, Scrum Alliance. Feb. 2015, https://www.scrumalliance.org/community/articles/2012/january/user-story-acceptance-criteria-the-art-of-satisfic

Office of the Under Secretary of Defense (Acquisition, Technology, and Logistics). DoD 4120.24-M Defense Standardization Program (DSP) Policies and Procedures. March 2000.

Panneta, Peter V. "NASA-GSFC Nano-Satellite Technology Development, SSC98-VI-5."

Phillips, Mike and Shrum, Sandy. "Which CMMI Model Is for You." August 2011.The CMMI Institute. Feb 2015, http://whatis.cmmiinstitute.com/sites/default/files/documents/Which_CMMI_Model_Is_for_You_2014.pdf

Pohl, Klaus and Rupp, Chris. Requirements Engineering Fundamentals. Rocky Nook Publishing, April 21, 2011

Roth, Ronica. "Write a Great User Story." Rally Help. Feb. 2015, https://help.rallydev.com/writing-great-user-story

Rouse, Margaret. "throughput definition." Tech Target: Search Networking. Feb. 2015, http://searchnetworking.techtarget.com/definition/throughput

"RUP Fundamentals Presentation," electronic Research Association (eRA) National Institute of Health. Feb. 2015, http://era.nih.gov/docs/rup_fundamentals.htm

"Swim Lane Diagrams, Mapping and Improving the Processes in Your Organization." Mind Tools. Feb. 2015, www.mindtools.com/pages/article/newTMC_89.htm

"SysML Open Source Specification Project." Systems Modeling Language (SysML). Feb. 2015, http://sysml.org/

"System throughput (messages per second)." IBM TPF Product Information Center. Feb. 2015, www-01.ibm.com/support/knowledgecenter/SSB23S_1.1.0.9/com.ibm.ztpf-ztpfdf.doc_put.09/gtpc3/c3thru.html?cp=SSB23S_1.1.0.9%2F0-1-0-0-6-2

"Throughput Requirements." 27 June 2005. Open Process Framework (OPF). Feb. 2015, www.opfro.org/index.html?Components/WorkProducts/RequirementsSet/Requirements/ThroughputRequirements.html~Contents

United States Government. Resources for understanding and implementing Section 508. Feb. 2015, www.section508.gov/

US Government. "Use Cases." usability.gov. Feb. 2015, www.usability.gov/how-to-and-tools/methods/use-cases.html

Wake, Bill. "Invest in Good Stories and Smart Tasks." August 17, 2003. xp123 Exploring Extreme Programming. Feb. 2015, http://xp123.com/articles/invest-in-good-stories-and-smart-tasks/

Wiegers, Karl, and Joy Beatty. Software Requirements, Third Edition, Microsoft Press, 2013.

"What is a SysML Requirement diagram and how is it used?." SysML Forum. Feb. 2015, www.sysmlforum.com/sysml-faq/

"What is functional and non-functional requirement." Stack Overflow. Feb. 2015. http://stackoverflow.com/questions/16475979/what-is-functional-and-non-functional-requirement

Wikipedia. Capability Maturity Model. Feb. 2015. http://en.wikipedia.org/wiki/Capability_Maturity_Model

Wikipedia. Characteristics of good requirements section. Feb. 2015. http://en.wikipedia.org/wiki/Requirement

Wikipedia. Use case. Feb. 2015, http://en.wikipedia.org/wiki/Use_case

Zargar, Ali. "Supportability." Tech 101 class lecture from Department of Aviation and technology at San Jose State University. Feb. 2015. <www.engr.sjsu.edu/azargar/Tech-101/TECH%20101-Supportability.ppt

Index

G. Koelsch, *Requirements Writing for System Engineering*,
DOI 10.1007/978-1-4842-2099-3

E

F, G

H

I

J

K

L

M

N

O

P, Q

R

CPSIA information can be obtained
at www.ICGtesting.com
Printed in the USA
LVOW07s2009251016
510223LV00008B/66/P

9 781484 220986